E … y private
a … dge
U … University
of … Fellowship
an … vious
pu … e Royal
So…

Thames & Hudson world of art

This famous series provides the widest available range of illustrated books on art in all its aspects.

If you would like to receive a complete list of titles in print please write to:

THAMES & HUDSON
181A High Holborn
London WC1V 7QX

In the United States please write to:

THAMES & HUDSON INC.
500 Fifth Avenue
New York, New York 10110

Printed in Singapore

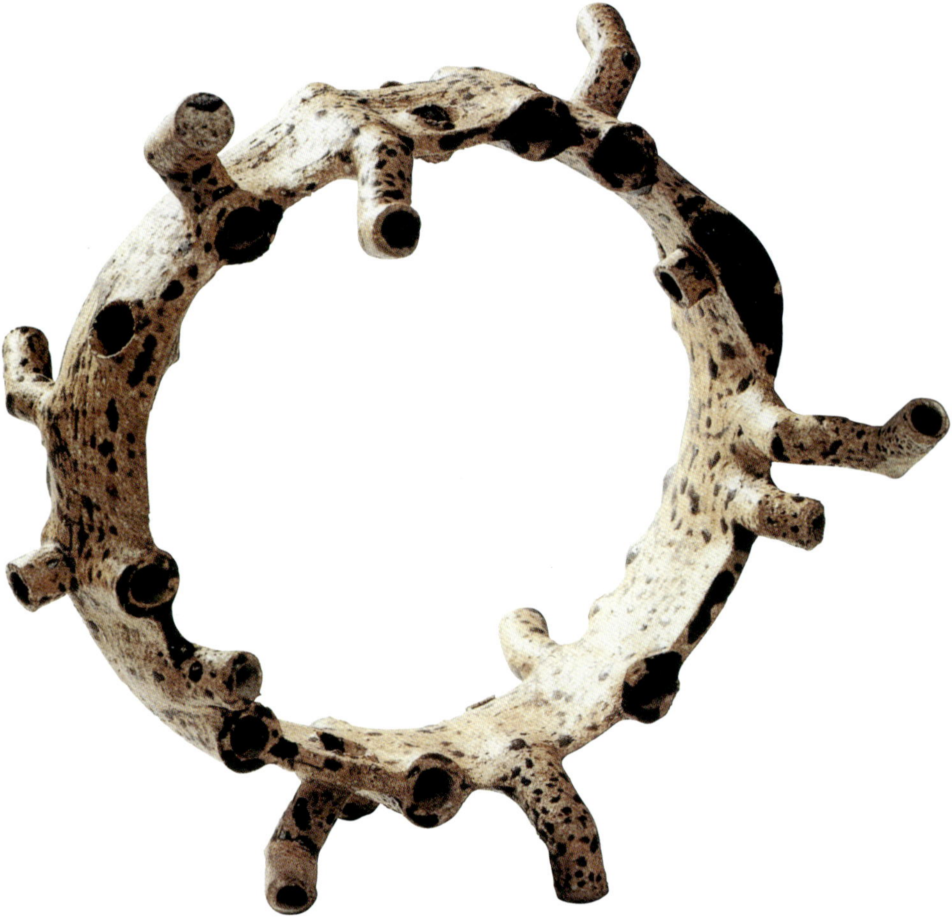

Edmund de Waal

20th century ceramics

178 illustrations, 77 in colour

Thames & Hudson world of art

For Sue

Acknowledgments
Much of the research for this book was made possible through a Leverhulme Special Research Fellowship held at the University of Westminster. I am grateful to both institutions for their generous support. For advice and stimulating conversation, I wish to thank colleagues including Chiaki Ajioka, Marjan Boot, Alison Britton, Christie Brown, Garth Clark, Emmanuel Cooper, Gabi Dewald, Terry Ellis, Rupert Faulkner, Sir Christopher Frayling, Mikako Goto, Alun Graves, Paul Greenhalgh, Tanya Harrod, Charlotte Horlyck, Yuko Kikuchi, Carla Koch, Keiko Kitamura, Bettina Koppe, Bodil Laursen, Frank Lloyd, Martina Margetts, David McFadden, Kevin Murray, Kimpei Nakamura, Simon Olding, Jennifer Hawkins Opie, Barley Roscoe, Shin Sang-ho, Adrian Sassoon, Julian Stair, Robert Teed and Jorunn Veiteberg. Laurie Britton, Helen Beard, Carina Ciscato, Ana Maria Henke, Susie Powell, Anna Maria Velardi, Hortense Suleyman and Victor de Waal helped with translation and research. Ellen Root helped greatly with picture research. I am particularly grateful for the boundless patience and clarity of my editor Philip Watson. Above all this book could not have happened without the imagination and support of my partner Susan Chandler, to whom it is dedicated.

Note
Japanese and Korean names are set out according to Western custom: the given name is followed by the family name.

(title page)
1 **Kazuo Yagi**, *Zamsa no sampo* (Walk of Samsa), 1954

First published in the United Kingdom in 2003 by Thames & Hudson Ltd, 181A High Holborn, London WC1V 7QX

www.thamesandhudson.com

British Library Cataloguing-in-Publication Data
A catalogue record for this book is available from the British Library

ISBN 0-500-20371-7

Designed by John Morgan
Printed and bound in Singapore by C.S. Graphics

Contents

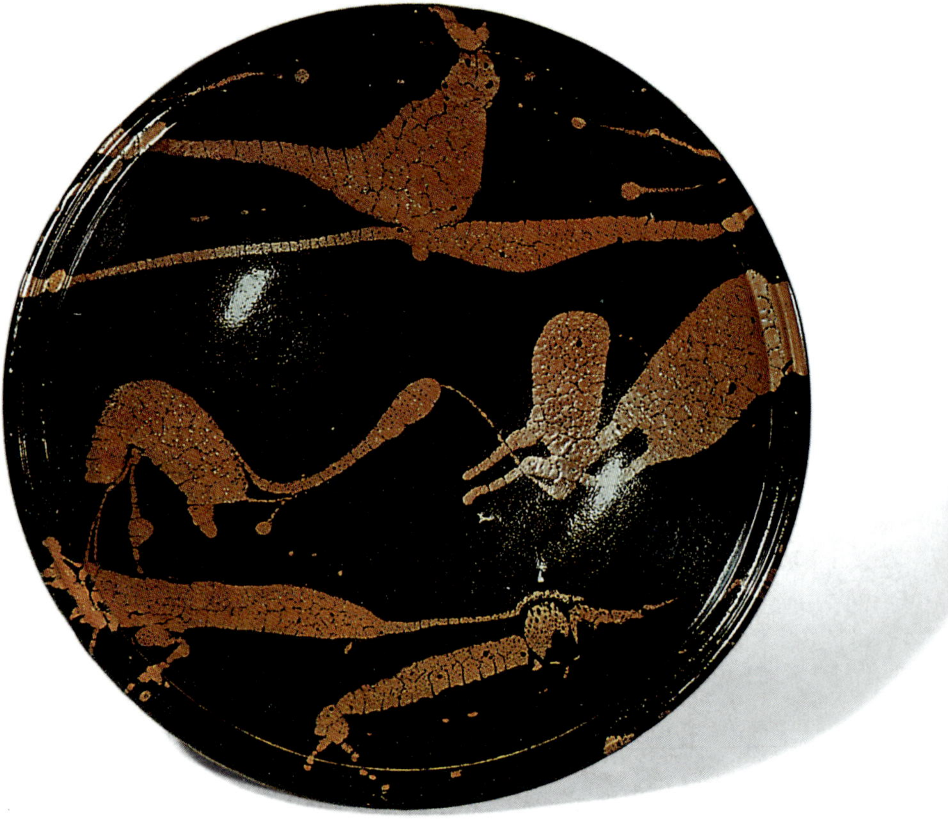

Introduction

This book attempts to map a century of ceramics, territory that is both complex and much fought over. The book is structured in four chronological chapters in each of which key thematic areas are discussed. Some of these themes are addressed in international terms, while some are treated as specific and local in nature. I hope that this approach will reveal unexpected correspondences and connections. Many of the surveys to date have discussed factories or potters or artists as if they were completely disassociated from the times in which they were living, and as if they were completely unaware of their contemporaries. Rather than producing a survey in which only a shooting gallery of iconic pots or famous artists are presented I have tried to reveal the contexts in which these ceramics were made and why they were made.

Who made what is a far from straightforward question in ceramics. The authorship of ceramics is rarely as simple as the stock image of the solitary (usually male and rural) potter throwing a utilitarian-looking vessel might suggest. Though some of the ceramics made in the twentieth century have been designed, made, glazed, decorated and fired by potters working alone these are the exceptions: the idea that one person should possess all the skills necessary to create ceramics emerges early in the twentieth century as a radical response to a perceived fragmentation of skill into smaller and smaller specialisms. The image of self-sufficiency, often involving reference to historic, or vernacular or more 'authentic' pottery traditions, was to prove such a potent one that the matrix of alternative ways of making ceramics has been obscured. For the reality is that ceramics of the twentieth century have often been the products of complex relationships. There have been collaborations between potters and industry, between architects and craft workshops, between artists and potters. There have been collaborations mediated by galleries, by the State, and by academic institutions, as well as those forged out of personal friendship. And these collaborations often reveal the implicit hierarchies of value attached to the different elements of design or decoration or actual manufacture of an object. Even within the workshop the relationship of a

2 **Shoji Hamada**, *Large Dish*, 1962, *kaki* (persimmon) glaze trailing over tenmoku glaze (d. 53.6 cm/21⅛ in).

potter to an apprentice, journeyman, technician, or the firer of a kiln, is far from simple. Where the 'authorship' of an artwork lies tells us a great deal about the nature of these relationships.

Ceramics in the twentieth century have been made for display in the vitrine, or collector's cabinet, for actual or intended domestic use, for the spaces of the museum and the art gallery, even for cladding the interior or exterior of a building. They have been used in performance and in installation art. Far from there being only one trajectory, bluntly that of the kitchen table to museum display, the history of the century is a complex and extended field of possibilities. Ceramics have been made as awards for revolutionary Soviet heroes, as the decoration for a Viennese nightclub, for the window of a 1930s New York department store. They have been made to shock the middle classes by English bohemians, and to placate the 'honest working classes' in Sweden. Ceramics were at the centre of the debates about national identity, used in the great National Expositions at the turn of the century to dramatize facets of essential style and character. At the turn of the twenty-first century in the new wave of Expositions they are provoking similar questions. Where ceramics sit in the picture plane, how near to them you were

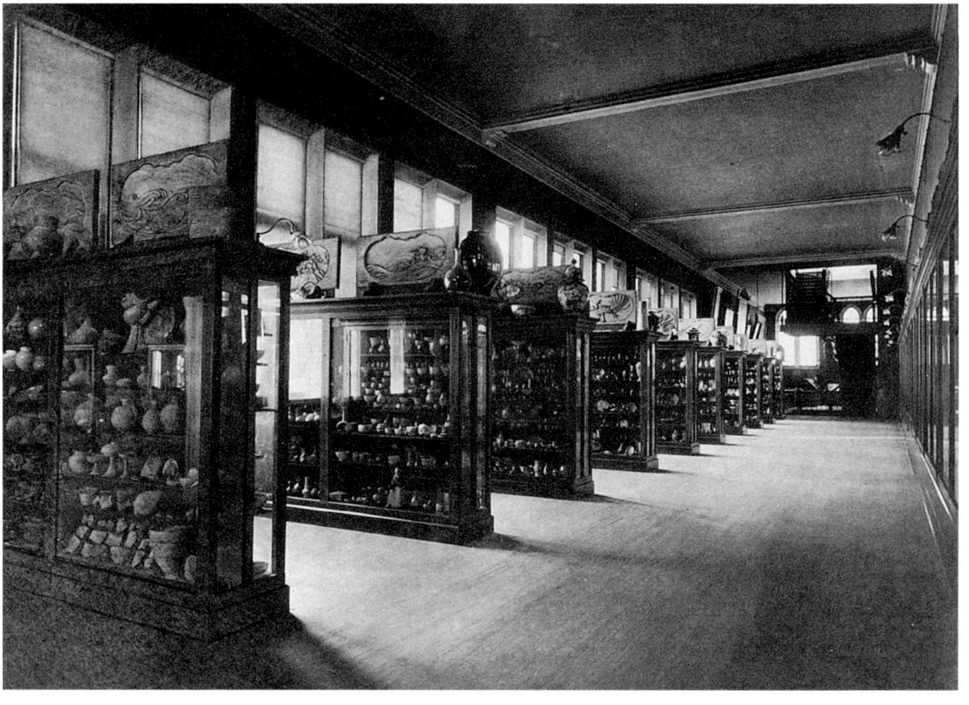

3 Cases of Japanese pottery in the Museum of Fine Arts, Boston, Massachusetts, *c.* 1900.
This collection of Japanese pottery, then the largest in the West, was assembled by the American collector Edward S. Morse, 'the result of twenty years continuous labour in which no pains have been spared to secure accuracy; yet with the last page I can only express regret that I cannot rewrite the whole work.' The vitrines were arranged by the locality of the kiln, with no differentiation between kinds of work. It gives a good sense of the density of display popular at the turn of the century. Many of Morse's ascriptions have been proved to be erroneous.

allowed or invited to come, has been posed often throughout the century. And as the identity of domestic space has changed so has the meaning of ceramics: the idea that meaning could lie in how they were handled or placed rather than in their decoration became significant. For some, the idea that you could pick up the object and take 'sensuous possession' of it became the endpoint for their art; for others it is an irrelevance.

Many of the themes are recurrent, many of the questions asked by artists from different generations seem to parallel each other. Indeed the question of whether ceramics can be said to be a single discipline, or a series of disciplines that use a similar material, has been rehearsed throughout the century in exhibitions and books. The construction of a canon of great ceramic works is made telling by what it leaves out, just as much as by what is included. The English potter Bernard Leach's *A Potter's Book* (1940) famously left out all figurative ceramics, most European decorative traditions and American ceramics in their entirety. Conversely his inclusion of particular kinds of Japanese ceramics authenticated their significance in the West. How the canon has developed reflects the anxieties about appropriate and inappropriate kinds of ceramic work.

A division can be made between the normative aspect of the discipline (repelling the less suitably qualified) and the sheer quantity of interesting 'outsiders' who have been drawn to use clay. Part of the scope of this book is to examine how these 'outsiders', whether artists like Pablo Picasso, Joan Miró or Cindy Sherman, sculptors like Tony Cragg, or architects like Thorvald Bindesbøll or Peter Behrens, 'belong' in ceramics. Fierce criticism of the work of these 'outsiders' has come from both within the ceramics world and from outside; critics from the art world have dismissed these artists' ceramic work as 'light relief'. Isamu Noguchi's substantial body of ceramic work was described as a playful excursion into a insignificant and essentially decorative area. The relationship between these artists and sculptors and their highly technically able ceramic collaborators has mostly been overlooked: even the most playful of Miró's ceramic assemblages needed the skill of an adept potter – in this case the Catalan potter Josep Lloréns Artigas – to be glazed and fired. However this book questions whether it is precisely this element of play, a liberation from expectation or technical knowledge, that has made their work so innovative.

The relationship between ceramics and sculpture in the twentieth century is a particularly complex one.

The contemporary question of whether 'ceramic sculpture' exists emerges out of the debates in the first twenty years of the twentieth century about the virtues of modelling in clay against carving in stone. The formlessness of clay and the speed with which you could work with it was held up in contrast to the resistance of stone: this was to imply that clay could been seen as a 'fallacious' material. Some sculptors, however, such as the German Expressionists Ernst Barlach or Paul Rudolf Henning, made claims for the primacy of clay as a sculptural material, arguing that sculptors had become 'blind to clay': although it was used for modelling, in the process of casting the original clay model was destroyed. They, on the other hand, argued that clay had particular characteristics, and that fired clay could preserve a spontaneity that was unique. Paul Gauguin asserted that ceramics was a 'central art' rather than a merely decorative appendage to other greater arts, offering a different way of pursuing sculptural concerns.

Yet while artists and sculptors (from Matisse to Lichtenstein) who have used ceramics across the century have often taken the ceramic vessel as their starting point, many have sought to distance themselves from the notion of the vessel itself. The vessel has been seen as 'demotic' and commonplace, contaminating the aspiration for their work to be seen as sculpture. At its simplest this is no more than a matter of status. Sculptors are seen to have a different order of possibilities for their work than ceramicists – more interesting galleries, more extensive criticism. It can be claimed that the extraordinary interest in installation that developed at the end of the twentieth century – how ceramics are presented in galleries – reflected the movements in sculpture to bring into the foreground issues of display. By making installations, whether a 'still life' grouping of objects or covering the floor of a museum with drying clay slip, ceramicists were gaining control of the framing of the artwork. A longer view of ceramics in the twentieth century shows that these issues were already keenly discussed in Vienna and Prague before the First World War.

The languages in which ceramics have been described, critical, art-historical, and aesthetic as well as technical, also constitute a crucial part of this history. For much of the century there have been polemics and manifestos alongside the handbooks and manuals. Though there has been much embattled and defensive attitudinizing around the reasons for making ceramics, the literature on ceramics is diverse and invigorating. It includes

Miró's journals, Lucio Fontana's reviews of Picasso's ceramics, Gauguin's reviews of ceramic exhibitions, Henry van de Velde on the horrors of Meissen porcelain, a Marinetti-inspired Manifesto of Futurist ceramics, the poet John Ashbery on Funk ceramics, the Danish potter Axel Salto on the power of transformation in ceramics, and the writings of art critics as diverse as Roger Fry and Clement Greenberg. As little of the extensive Japanese literature on ceramics has been translated, few in the West have been able to read the often combative writings of critics, novelists and poets as well as potters. There has been little published that falls outside the more quietist axis supplied by the Japanese *mingei* or folkcraft movement under their leader, the critic and collector Soetsu Yanagi. These *mingei* texts revolve around the positioning of the contemporary potter in relation to tradition. Much of the antagonism to this movement has simply gone unremarked: this has profoundly affected the understanding of Japanese ceramics in the West. Writing on ceramics has helped to create – and delimit – the spaces in which ceramics operates.

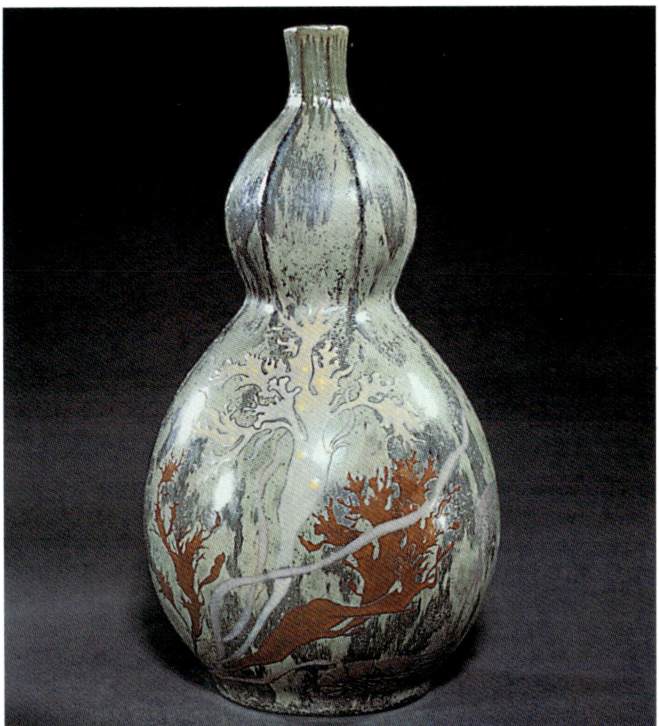

4 **Léon Rigolet** for Sèvres, *Aquatic Double-Gourd Vase*, 1900–11 (porcelain, h. 25.5cm/10 in). This was made at a time when Sèvres was the pre-eminent force in European ceramics. The vase's complex depiction of seaweed and shrimps involved the skills of many different people including the designer, thrower, modeller and painter. The hierarchies of skill are shown in that the underside of the vase has only the designer's monogram and the factory mark.

Many of the debates about the value of ceramics at the turn of the nineteenth into the twentieth century centred on the relationship of the elaborate techniques used in the great European and American ceramic factories to artistic expression. Most of the criticism was of exiguous technique, though sometimes there was criticism of excesses too: 'the chemist rather than the artist is directing the experiments... it is deplorable to see prints of village churches and the Grand Canal underlying a splendid sang-de-boeuf glaze,' as a review in the Burlington magazine in 1911 put it. The apogee of the art pot can be seen in works like these, with their laborious techniques and their 'splendid glazes': they project the image of the pot as the accomplishment of the artistic chemist. As the French potter Taxile Doat, one of the great innovators at Sèvres at the end of the nineteenth century, had pointed out, ceramics was indeed the art of the chemist: 'Whether a ceramicist is a painter or a sculptor, architect or simply a technician, to obtain a successful result he must also be a chemist.' The publication of Mendeleyev's Periodic Table of the Elements in 1871 had allowed potters to understand how materials could be substituted for each other and thus how glazes could be altered. Chemistry, though, could still be seen as the province of gentlemanly pursuit, rather than a profession in its own right. The transition sometimes went the other way. Alexandre Bigot, later famous for his pioneering architectural ceramics, left his Chemistry Professorship in Alsace to experiment with pottery after seeing the Oriental pots at the Paris Exhibition of 1889.

The evangelical concerns of the Arts and Crafts movement to educate the public by bringing good design before them led to the 'art pot'. These pots were not aimed at a popular market, however, but were often expensive objects that reflected a rarified panoply of influences from the Moorish to the Oriental. Art potteries flourished towards the end of the nineteenth century in America, Europe and Britain. The art pots were the products of many different hands. An art pot could be thrown by one person, trimmed by another, the glazes mixed and applied by others, decorations, gilt and ormolu mounts designed by yet more. This use of labour was well known.

For the last thirty years of the nineteenth century Sèvres was the centre of radical technical experimentation in ceramics. This focus led to the pioneering of the techniques of 'pâte sur pâte' (where layers of clay slip were applied to give depth) and the 'procès barbotine'. Barbotine, a way of mixing clay with metallic oxides, gave a sense of depth within a glaze, of patterns emerging from a haze of colour. As such it was compared, contentiously, with the work of the Impressionists, where the thickness of brushwork was apparent. Both these ceramic techniques were highly labour intensive. Indeed it seemed that their very purpose was to dramatize skill, to show just how much labour has been expended. The art pot could be said to constitute a theatre of skill.

In many of the ceramics created at Sèvres at the end of the nineteenth century, to identify a process of 'actual making' of the pot itself would be fruitless. The author of the pot was the designer, the conductor of the multitude of highly skilled workers at the factory: he was the one who might sign the base of the pot. Sèvres's preeminence at the end of the nineteenth century can be measured not only through the ways international rivals tried to surpass particular glazes or techniques, but also through the hostility that artists and potters working outside the factory felt towards it.

The language used to describe these ceramics was that of the arcane, of potters' secrets, of knowledge withheld. The familiar iconic image of the Chinese potter at the end of the nineteenth century was dramatized by the legendary Pousa, who threw himself into a kiln in order to achieve a particular and transcendent glaze, whose life became part of the glaze. The French potter Ernest Chaplet destroyed all his glaze notebooks before his death, as did the founder of the Ruskin Pottery, the English potter William Howson Taylor. Apart from some notable exceptions, particularly Taxile Doat's essays on high-fired glazes published in *L'Art et Décoration* in France and in translation in *Keramic Studio* in America, glazes were regarded as prized secrets. Some glazes were named after the potters who created them: 'Le Rouge Dalpayrat' or 'Grueby green', for instance. The nature of International Expositions helped to create this somewhat febrile atmosphere, with rival factories competing to introduce new glaze effects.

At the start of the twentieth century the particular and passionate focus for research was on how to recreate the *flamée* glazes, the rich *sang de boeuf* (ox blood) red copper glazes found on eighteenth-century Chinese court porcelains. These lapidary high-fired glazes epitomized the 'secrets' of Oriental ceramics. They fluxed into hybrid colours of iridescent greens and reds or streaked and crawled into broken patterns: they seemed to possess an innate 'natural' wilfulness beyond the control of the potter.

The tension between the purpose of the potter's hand and his

5 The Ruskin Stand at the Ideal Home Exhibition, 1908. Contemporary reviewers dwelt on the lavishness of glazes; William Howson Taylor's Ruskin Pottery boasted in 1904 of 'blues, greens, purples, clair-de-lune, pink, crushed strawberry, yellow, turquoise and combinations of these colours, also others which are more difficult to reproduce, such as a special blue, robin's egg blue, sang-de-boeuf, peach bloom, lustres, crystalline, shagreen.' Many potteries ascribed French or opaquely Orientalist names to their glazes to give them extra cachet.

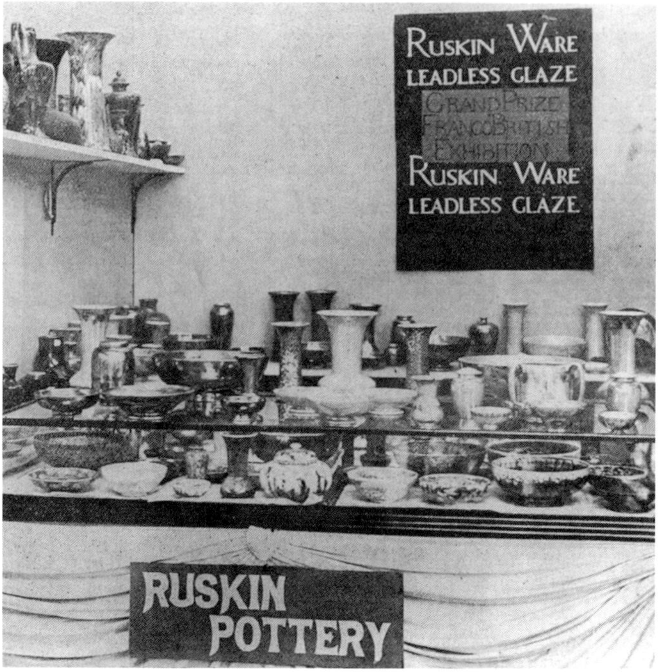

inability ever wholly to control the material at his command is suggested by Charles Binns's description of the first potter throwing the first pot:

The imagination readily pictures the scene. A hot Eastern sun. A few mud huts. Beside one of these a rude barbarian seated in front of the new wonder. The inhabitants gather round and watch as the potter presses his clay on to the top of the wheel. Murmurs of wonder arise as the shapeless mass is formed into a hollow vessel as though by supernatural power, and the successful man is elevated to the position of a magician, and eventually, by tradition, into that of a god.

The complete, almost kinaesthetic, involvement in the process of making projected onto the act of throwing implies a withdrawal away from the minutiae of the world into an act of original creation. This is the identification of potter with pot, of a loss of self through making art or becoming one with the work. Austrian poet Rainer Maria Rilke suggested in his essay on Rodin (1903) that modern art, in the process of becoming 'Dissociated from all big-sounding, pretentious and capricious phraseology, ...suddenly appears to take its place in the sober and inconsiderable life of everyday, among the crafts.' In a letter of 1907 he writes of the 'hours I was able to spend in Rome watching a rope-maker repeat in his craft one of the world's oldest gestures, just like that potter in the little village on the Nile – to stand by his wheel was so indescribably and mysteriously fruitful for me.'

For the many studio potters of the mid-century who embraced the philosophy of the English potter and writer Bernard Leach, the act of throwing was an act of recuperation. This was a highly morally inflected identification of pottery with the inner life, as if the centrifugal impulse of throwing mirrored a drawing of oneself into a continuity of tradition.

No technique is inert or ahistorical. Throwing a pot on a wheel comes with heady associations of creating form out of formlessness, of an almost hieratic power to create metamorphosis. It is only through an act of recuperation that the thrower of pots can hope to regain the ideal, where the worker would be an artist and the artist a worker. Throwing a pot has moved from being a diminished activity to one accorded almost spiritual resonance.

Conversely, in postwar Japan it was only by rejecting the preeminence given to the wheel as a signifier of continuity that the young potters of the Sodeisha movement could place themselves in the 'sordid world'. By cutting up and rearranging parts of thrown pots, by breaking down the central volume of a thrown pot, these potters provoked savage reactions. For the Sodeisha group in 1950s Japan it was Jomon pottery, the archaic figures disregarded by their parent's generation, that seemed to embody the possibility of making ceramics powerful, expressive, 'central'.

Throughout the century the canon of acceptable historical precedent is an area of shifting sand. The epitome of beauty for one generation becomes a decadent symbol of bourgeois taste for another. As soon as one tradition becomes collectable, it seems, it is seen to lose its potency. The porcelains made for the Chinese court in the eighteenth century, considered in Europe to be the highest and most aristocratic expression of ceramic art at the turn of the twentieth century, became regarded as 'decorative' and hence of little consequence. The changing fortunes in Europe of different styles of Chinese, Korean and Japanese ceramics reflect a general principle by which the earliest ceramics are invested with condensed significance, and later ceramics are regarded as a falling off from these primal forces. For Gauguin, making ceramics in the 1880s, it was pre-Columbian pottery that reminded him that 'Ceramics aren't a matter of mere futility [une futilité]. In the most distant of times, with the American Indians it was a central art.'

The acute interest in the pots of the Orient seemed to provide a lineage for the art pottery of the turn of the twentieth century. There was the cult of collecting oriental blue and white, the 'blue' of the Pre-Raphaelites and of Oscar Wilde's circle, centred on porcelains' rarity and exoticism. Porcelain was imbued with a diffuse sense of mystique, rich with indecipherable patterns. It belonged to what Swinburne called 'the fairyland of fans, the paradise of pipkins, the limbo of blue china, screens, pots, plates, jars, joss-houses, and all the fortuitous frippery of Fusiyama.' These exotic Oriental ceramics were seen by both British and French critics as 'perfectly and essentially aristocratic.' Philippe Burty wrote in a series of lectures to the Union Centrale des Arts Décoratifs on 'The Pottery and Porcelains of Japan' that patronage had created the link between refined objects and refined collectors.

Both Oriental ceramics and the new art pottery avoided any hint of utility, their function being to decorate drawing rooms rather than be used in kitchens. There were showrooms in Paris that specialized in the display of the new decorative arts, the Maison de l'Art Nouveau opened in 1895 by Siegfried Bing, and Meier-Graefe's La Maison Moderne, Liberty of London or Tiffany's Studios in New York. Here contemporary decorative arts were shown alongside these aristocratic arts of Japan or China. Buying conferred exclusivity, a handed-down sense of aristocratic patronage, to the purchaser.

6 This cartoon appeared in an album (no. II, *c.* 1936) compiled by the Very Reverend Milner White, Dean of York, a leading collector of studio ceramics in Britain in the 1920s and 30s, and patron of William Staite Murray, Bernard Leach, Shoji Hamada and Michael Cardew.

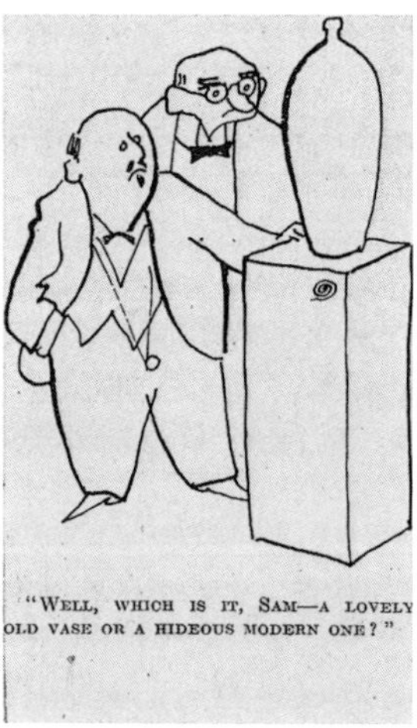

Not all Oriental ceramics were as refined as the court Chinese porcelains. There were also the new pots being exhibited from Japan. First shown at the Paris Exposition in 1878, these were the tea wares, pots that had emerged from the vernacular and rural traditions, and had been chosen by tea masters as expressions of vigour and freedom. Often warped or slumped, and mainly monochromatic, the emphasis was on gesture – either in the flow of glaze or in the marks of throwing. These new kinds of pots required a particular aesthetic, a late Victorian commentator acknowledging that 'a connoisseur must have been specially educated when he consents to pay ten or twenty guineas for a water holder that might be easily mistaken for a drainpipe, partially blackened by fire and ornamented by patches and streaks of brick colour.' Bafflement gave way to a grudging respect for what was described in 1901 as 'a world in which pottery was not ashamed of its earthy origin or the human fingers that fashioned

7 **Maurice Biais**, *La Maison Moderne*, *c.* 1900 (lithograph). La Maison Moderne, Meier-Graefe's gallery in Paris, showed decorative arts including ceramics in a fashionable and contemporary way. Here a modish lady scrutinizes Japanese-inspired pots in a display case designed by Henry van de Velde.

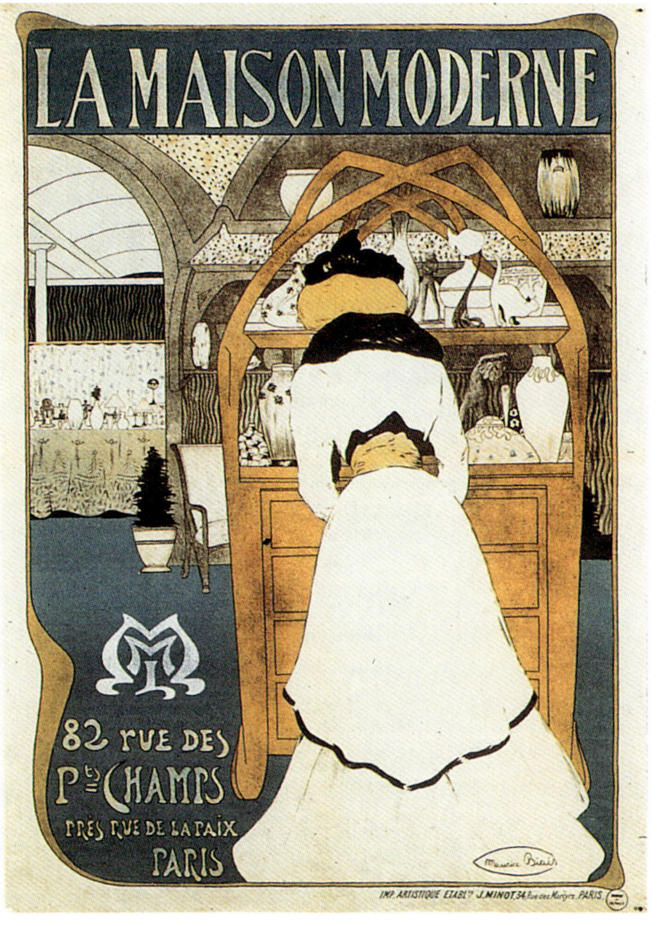

it, but was content in the satisfactory fulfilment of its mission.' The British designer Christopher Dresser wrote in his report on the Japanese pottery he had seen on his visit in 1871:

I have before me some specimens of Japanese earthen-ware, which are formed of a coarse dark-brown clay, and are to a great extent without the finish which most Europeans appear so much to value, yet these are artistic and beautiful. In the case of cheap goods we spend time in getting smoothness of surface, while the Japanese devote it to the production of art effect. We get finish without art, they prefer art without finish.

Certain traditions were often valued for the way they used a technique or a material. It was as if the modern potter, faced by the terrifying decision of how to create a style, looked enviously at those who seemed untroubled by such self-consciousness. Vernacular potters could be romanticized as living embodiments of a tradition, lacking individuality and unable to conceptualize their own position. The ways in which vernacular traditions have been framed – those of Native American ceramics and of Korean potters come to mind – are also part of the story of twentieth century ceramics. In the early years of the century it is possible to see the search for specific local qualities of materials as a symptomatic search for the irreducible national character. Traditions were mined for their 'essential' qualities. Before the First World War the potter Reginald Wells was using the English slipware tradition in this way, making decorative earthenware pots in emulation of medieval precursors. In France, at the same time, the French potter André Metthey was exploiting the faience tradition of white tin-glazed earthenware. Both were metropolitan potters: both emphasized their distance from contemporary taste through a bravura display of unimpeachably 'authentic' technique.

Particular materials also allowed new modes of expression. Stoneware, the quotidian clay of country potters, more refined than the coarse red earthenware of cooking utensils and flower pots, but not yet as precious as porcelain, was first used by Chaplet and other French ceramicists in the 1880s. As a material it was emblematic. It was a vernacular material, not associated with the great industrial manufacturers, and it therefore seemed to be closer to 'authentic' production. This notion of authenticity expressed an anxiety about the validity of art production. The idea of a 'truth to materials', of a direct response to perceived qualities of clay or fire, stands directly counter to the aesthetic of highly worked materials in subservience to an artist-master. Indeed, instead of the endless working of clay (normally porcelain) and then its clothing in slips and glazes and enamels, and even the subsequent use of bronze mounts to elevate still further its preciosity, there was the radical idea of showing the fired clay itself. What Binns had called 'dead ground', the expanse of unglazed fired clay at the base of the pot, was finally allowed to be seen.

The American theorist Thorstein Veblen wrote in his book *The Theory of the Leisure Class* (1899):

Of hand labour are certain imperfections and irregularities in the lines of the hand wrought article, showing where the workman has fallen short in the execution of the design. The ground of the superiority of hand-wrought goods, therefore, is a certain margin of crudeness... a matter of nice discrimination.

Rather than trimming a pot to achieve a clear, uninflected surface potters began to leave the marks made in throwing the pot. The spiralling concentric rings made by the pressure of the fingers into the wet clay became one of the 'honorific' marks of the authentic pot.

There was a search for other traditions that seemed to be more 'real', including authentic ways of working – prospecting for, digging and refining your own clay, building and then firing your own kilns with wood. This way of working crosses the century, from the Bauhaus in the early 1920s where the pottery students – the 'Dornburgers' – were encouraged to dig clay in the woods, to the explosion in popularity in the 1990s of wood-firing in a Japanese 'anagama' or climbing kiln. Many of the most heightened descriptions of the potter at work centre on this immersion in process. In 1910 the French critic Robert de la Sizeranne described Ernest Chaplet:

the potter talks about the fire, as a sailor talks of the sea. The reason is simple. The potter proposes, the fire disposes. The potter moulds, the fire paints. The potter can only give the fire colours, give it air or smother it... As the kiln is fired, the colours change, the colours break through, change, become and 'turn', lighten or darken, become other colours... The pale green becomes a bright green, then the green becomes blue, the blue becomes white. The pink becomes red, red becomes yellow, yellow becomes black.... In him is a scientist and a gambler. He moves around and around the frightening crucible wherein lies the mystery. He despairs, stops the firing, leaves... He swears that it won't be a success, that he doesn't care, that he won't open the kiln. So be it! He doesn't care! ...he alone has sought out chance, looked for the accidental, praised catastrophe. Nobody has more closely collaborated with Nature...his work even looks like nature, like stones or rocks...

Chaplet's art is, in the words of contemporary critic Roger Marx, 'un art de rêveur' (a dreamer's art): something that brings him a kind of transcendence. In contemporary descriptions there is this recurrent theme of reverie around firing: it reflects a new image of the Orientalist potter at one with the process – something that was far from the image of the art potters of Sèvres studiedly at work.

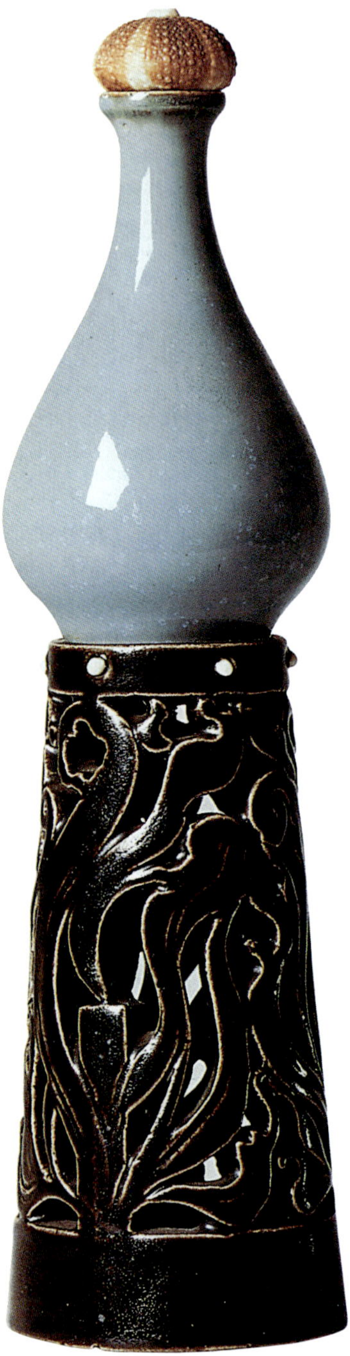

Chapter One 1900–20

The Theatre of Technique: Doat and Robineau

In 1909 the great French ceramicist Taxile Doat took up a position as the first Director at the School of Ceramic Art at the People's University in University City, a suburb of St Louis, Missouri, in the United States. Doat's appointment – the move from the preeminent state-funded ceramic factory in the world to a new Midwestern American college – reveals much of the complexity of the world of ceramics at that moment. It shows the fierceness of the internationalism of the time: the reach of such design magazines as *The Studio* and the round of International Expositions meant that factories were keenly aware of stylistic and technical change. New glazes were researched and marketed in the hopes of prizes and the increased prestige: the pressure for innovation and innovators was extreme. Doat's move from Sèvres to America shows the shifting balances of the time: a famous international potter had value beyond the confines of a factory. Even the state patronage of Sèvres, the factory that had coaxed many of the most remarkable technical accomplishments of the last thirty years, could be superseded by the muscle of a new kind of patronage – that of the art college.

Doat was famed internationally: he had been a key part of the success of Sèvres at the end of the nineteenth century and was the winner of numerous gold medals at International Expositions for his porcelain. His reputation lay in his mastery of the most sought after of techniques: the Oriental 'grand feu', or high-fired glazes that seemed to be in state of spectacular suspended flow. With their carefully modulated forms – often with complex piercing and carving – Doat's pots were essentially historicist. They pulled together into a single piece numerous references to other historic ceramics or to natural forms: each pot was a highly self-conscious calibration of precious glazing and forming. If the art pot could be described as a complex of technical and artistic collaborations subsumed into the genius of the one named, famous potter or designer, then these creations were the culmination of the art pot. Each piece was the product of many

8 **Taxile Doat**, vase, 1900 (porcelain, h. 20.8 cm/8 in). This ensemble brings together many of the preoccupations of turn-of-the-century art pottery. The central vase quotes from Chinese porcelains, the stopper is a painstaking emulation of a natural form while the use of a stand emphasized the rarified nature of the object.

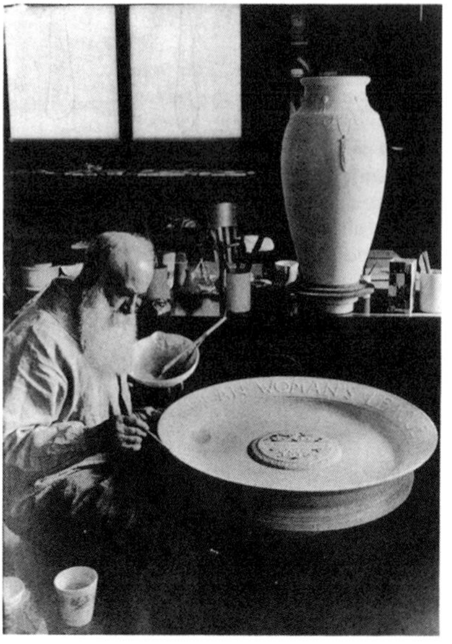

9 **Taxile Doat** working at the School of Ceramic Art, People's University, University City, St Louis, Missouri, *c.* 1910

different craftsmen and technicians, with Doat acting as the conductor of the whole exercise.

Doat's appointment followed an extended period of overtures. Between 1899 and 1909 Doat had published articles on his glazes and firing techniques in the pioneering American magazine *Keramic Studio* edited by the potter Adelaide Alsop Robineau (1865–1929) and her husband, Samuel. The founder of the American Women's League and the People's University, the newspaper and magazine publisher Edward G. Lewis persuaded Doat to have a 'conference with the League's architects in order that the erection of one of the most perfectly designed and equipped art potteries in the world might be immediately begun.' Lewis had a vision of a rich cultural centre in the Midwest and wanted the very best for his art pottery. The wave of philanthropic enthusiasm that brought this into being capitalized on the momentum of the china-painting movement, a movement whose huge popularity can be traced by the plethora of magazines and textbooks that catered to a predominately female readership. The movement was for some a hobby, a shared social activity whose outcome was characterized by Robineau as the china-painted 'stereotyped spray of flowers and the inevitable butterfly', while for others it was an economic necessity. But china-painting stood for Lewis as the epitome of amateurism, and something to be overthrown.

The experiment of Lewis's People's University reveals much of the contemporary attitudes towards the proper use of clay and the place of technique. The restraint of naturally wilful forces by the civilizing hand of the potter threw the emphasis in the finished object onto the successful accomplishment of technique. This was most forcefully and influentially expressed by the English potter Charles Fergus Binns (1857–1934) who moved to America in 1897 and became the first director of the New York College of Clayworking and Ceramics in 1900. He advocated strict control and application of technique. In order to remove any marks of the hand he would throw even very small forms in three sections before turning them on a lathe and reassembling them. His view was that 'Glazes must acknowledge the artistic restraint by which the whole work is controlled. Not an ear drop of molten glaze must pass the limit. At the bottom of every piece is a tiny rim of dead ground, a bisque line of demarcation. This far the glaze can come but not further'. It was as if there was an appropriate standard of propriety for both pot and potter.

The *Scarab Vase* of 1910 by Adelaide Alsop Robineau stands as the ultimate example of this foregrounding of technique and to the ways in which art pots of this period dramatized the amount of work that had gone into their construction. Subtitled the 'Apotheosis of the Toiler', it is a fearsomely complicated paean in pierced porcelain to the nature of 'toil'. The scarab, taken by Robineau as an exemplar of discipline and propriety, provides the motif for the vase. Its construction was recorded by the British-

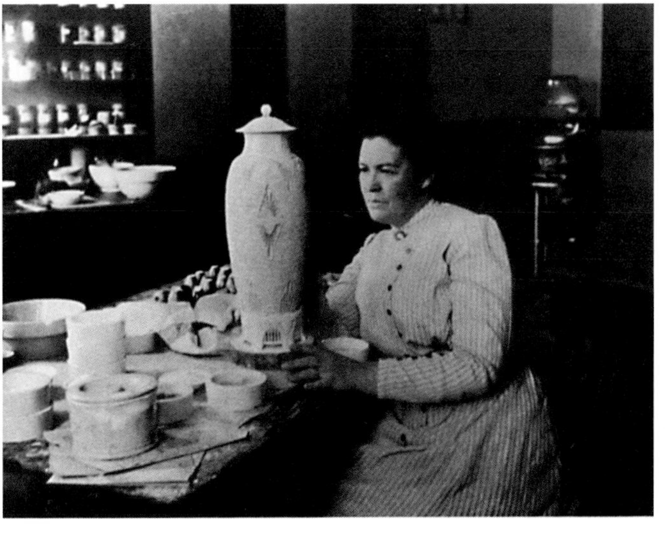

10 **Adelaide Alsop Robineau** with her *Apotheosis of the Toiler (Scarab Vase)*, People's University, St Louis, 1910.
Frederick Rhead, her contemporary, wrote, 'I have seen the Scarab vase in all its stages of construction. Many times Mrs Robineau would work all day, and on an otherwise clean floor there would be enough dry porcelain dust to cover a dollar piece and half an inch more carving on the vase.'

born potter and fellow member of the School of Ceramic Art, Frederick Rhead (1880–1942):

It is definite fact that carving or excising is the most risky process of all. The carving cannot be well done until the piece is dry, and it is impossible to cut with the freedom possible in wood and ivory. The material is so short and brittle that any undue pressure will chip the surface. A line or excised surface of any depth must be extremely carefully scraped away bit by bit, gradually going deeper. A slight difference in the pressure of the tool, and considerable work, if not an entire piece, can be ruined.

Like Binns's 'dead ground', this is a description of clay as an intractable rather than a plastic material, one to be treated scrupulously. Many of the art pots of this type were displayed raised on Oriental stands, emphasizing the preciosity of the object, and their relationship to an unchanging historical canon. Here, as with several other of Robineau's and Doat's works, a ceramic stand is even incorporated into the object. With some pieces (e.g. *Vase with Daisy Cover*, 1914) Robineau carved intricate lids in emulation of the porcelain lids made for some Japanese jars: clay is made to enact the properties of other materials.

It is interesting that this labour – the piece is said to have taken one thousand hours – should have been so public. Both Doat and Robineau were scrutinized, kiln openings were observed by a crowd:

About everyone except the chief of police and the president of the United States was invited to peep through the spy-holes while [the kiln] was under fire. Photographers were dragged in and everyone and everything was photographed... The opening of the kiln was a breathtaking affair. So many people were in the kiln room that it was hardly possible to open the kiln door. Doat in a cutaway coat was there in all his glory. It was most impressive.

This is the theatre of skill that characterizes art pottery and art potters in action. Robineau went on to achieve great success, winning the Grand Prix at Turin in 1911 for a group of fifty-five of her porcelains, demonstrating her throwing of porcelain at Sèvres to prove that her perfectly formed pots weren't cast. Her ceramics, though never again quite as intricate as the *Scarab Vase*, continued to uphold the values of flawless, minutely controlled techniques of carving, excising and modelling.

11 **Adelaide Alsop Robineau**, *Apotheosis of the Toiler (Scarab Vase)*, 1910 (porcelain, h. 42.2 cm/16⅝ in). Robineau worked painstakingly with a crochet needle to carve the vase's design. Its title reflects the sanctity of hard work, and the mystical reverence associated with the ancient Egyptians' depiction of the scarab beetle as a sacred charm.

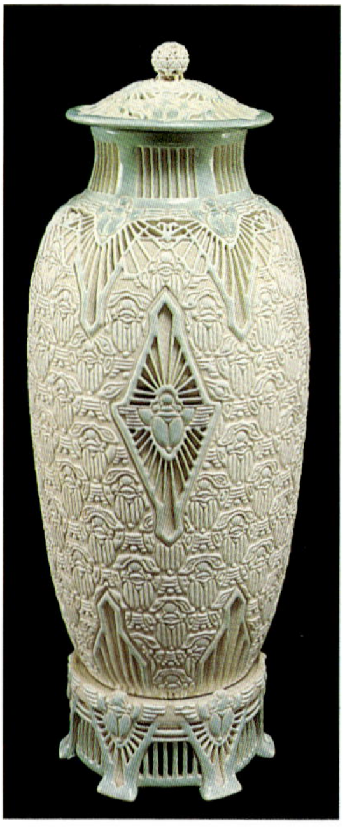

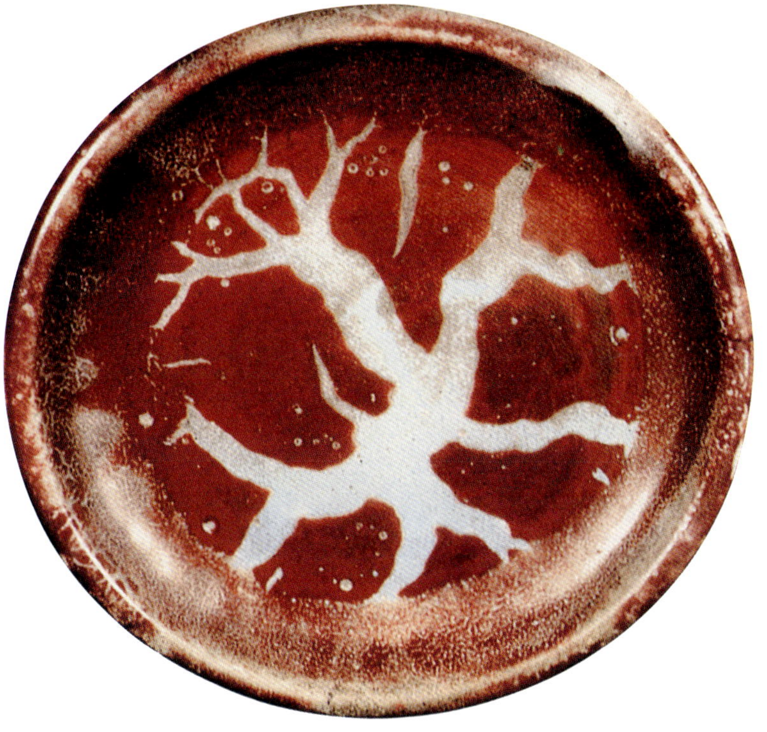

12 **Ernest Chaplet**, dish with copper red glaze, *c.* 1900 (porcelain).
Copper red glazes were held to be 'wilful' glazes, prone to dramatic effects as in this dish. These glazes seemed to epitomize the special drama between fire and glaze felt to be present in Oriental ceramics.

Orientalist styles: Chaplet to Bindesbøll

It is to the work of Ernest Chaplet (1835–1909) that many of the great changes that occurred in the early twentieth century can be traced. He was a pivotal figure in European ceramics, not only the master of iron-red *flamée* glazes and the acclaimed rediscoverer of *sang de boeuf*, but highly instrumental in establishing stoneware as a new medium and introducing it to, amongst others, Gauguin. He was born in Sèvres and had trained as a young man at the factory, becoming highly skilled in both making and glazing and closely involved with the introduction of the barbotine technique. After encountering the Japanese stoneware pots at the 1878 Paris exhibition he persuaded the Limoges manufacturers the Haviland Brothers to let him develop stoneware as a commercial enterprise. These strong and simple forms, often derived from the vernacular pottery he had seen in Beauvais, were then decorated with naturalistic scenes of country figures, flowers and animals, rich enamel colours contained within sharply delineated incised frames. The clarity of the images (very close in style to the pictures of the English childrens' book illustrator Kate Greenaway) and their framing within the austere demarcations of the pots show an attempt to make a new kind of pottery: they are a sort of artistic reverie on the possibilities of country pottery. Chaplet's success lay in aestheticizing the vernacular.

In 1887 Chaplet began to research both porcelain and *flamée* glazes, handing the workshop over to Auguste Delaherche, and choosing to work in his own studio. Unlike his collaborative efforts with the stoneware, Chaplet was to make, glaze and fire these pieces himself. The much recounted story of his attempts to find the 'secrets' of these rich glazes creates an almost mythic picture of struggle. It was compounded by the image of the potter alone in the studio without technicians or helpers, the drawing to himself of all those roles previously differentiated and given to others. This idea of a solitary relationship of struggle with material, rather than public Sèvres-like mastery of it, indicates the radical nature of Chaplet's project. As the influential founder and publisher of *The Studio*, Charles Holme was to write of Chaplet and the other leaders of the French stoneware movement: 'the true art of the potter... by the happy choice and manipulation of his clay and glazes, and his thorough understanding of the mysteries of firing, has rendered himself independent of the painter, or any other collaborator.' In this way these new

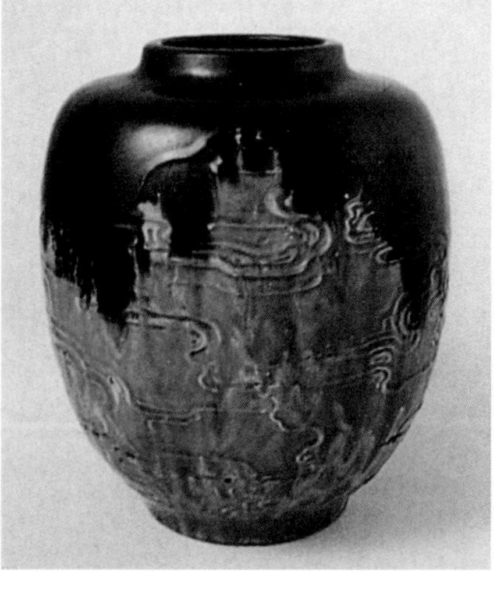

13 **Emile Decoeur**, vase, *c.* 1900–10 (stoneware). Pots inspired by Japanese ceramics often highlighted fluxing glazes and irregular forms. Decoeur even gave ivory lids to some of these Japoniste jars.

independent potters like Chaplet were close to Rilke's definition of the modern artist (see p. 14). In Chaplet's ceramics, with their softly thrown forms and their flowing glazes, this sense of a process of struggle is palpable. They are much smaller than many of the art pots of Sèvres, rarely over 12 inches (30 centimetres) tall, and based almost entirely on Chinese forms, baluster and bottle vases, dishes and bowls. Unlike Binns's reassembled forms they were thrown in one piece.

In the work of Auguste Delaherche (1857–1940) 'art without finish' comes to the fore. Like Chaplet, he used rich Oriental glazes, but instead of historicized Chinese forms he developed a new vocabulary of ribbed and faceted shapes over which the matt glazes break and run. These are forms that are close to gourds, with a distinctive organic feel that connects him to the Japonisme of the day. As a contemporary critic said: 'some modern specimens of Japanese pottery are curiously and intentionally deformed – crooked, twisted, or bulging like a sack of potatoes – and, nevertheless, in the most refined taste.' Several French ceramicists followed the Japanese style with almost slavish respect; Paul Jeanneney (1861–1920) had small ivory lids carved for his jars in emulation of Japanese tea wares. For those who did not know these pots' antecedents this work must have appeared mysterious. Emile Decoeur (1876–1953), exhibiting at the Paris Salon d'automne in 1907, showed work whose abstraction of mark-making baffled contemporary critics, one of whom

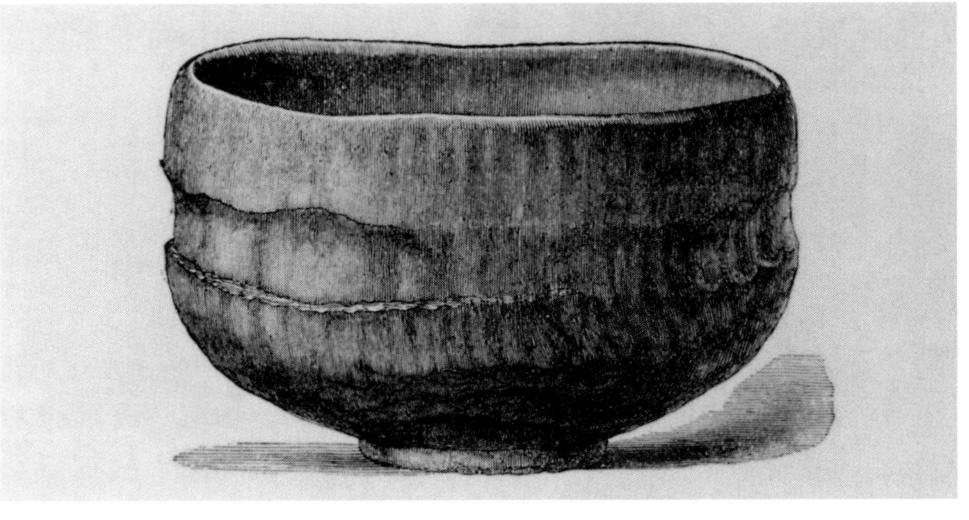

14 Tea bowl, raku ware, *c.* 1750. This illustration from *Japanese Pottery* by A. W. Franks, published in 1880, was one of the first books to show tea-ceremony wares. Franks describes this tea bowl as 'rudely made [with] broad scoring on the sides'.

grumbled: 'it is impossible to judge the work of the orientalists in the absence of any criteria.' The complaint marks the passing of the art pot: this kind of new orientalist pot seemed to demand a different kind of criticism.

For one artist these criteria – the framing of ceramics as an autonomous art – would be applied only after his death. In 1925 at the Exposition Internationale des Arts Décoratifs et Industriels Modernes in Paris, the Danish committee posthumously exhibited several of the ceramics of the Danish architect and designer Thorvald Bindesbøll (1846–1908). The modernity and contemporaneity of Bindesbøll's designs was seized on, and he was claimed as a pioneer by succeeding generations. Nikolaus Pevsner wrote that 'No radicalism of Bindesbøll's force can be found anywhere else.'

Bindesbøll first decorated pots in 1883 in the style of Italian maiolica. With artist friends he was briefly part of the Copenhagen 'Kunstnerkeramik' (artists' ceramics group), a group that involved itself deeply in the decoration of pots. In 1891 Bindesbøll started to use facilities of the Copenhagen Earthenware Factory in Valby where he worked for the last fourteen years of his life. He exhibited at the World Exposition in Paris in 1889, and again in 1900, showing twenty-five ceramic pieces. Ceramics were a vital part of his oeuvre: in 1900–1, in addition to his architectural work, and designs for silver and textiles, he produced sixty-five dishes and vases. He was committed to ceramics as a discipline, soon directing factory throwers into making complex compound forms, vases with deep rolled rims and pieces of considerable scale (up to 30 inches/80 centimetres in height). His forms are sturdy and unaccentuated – far from the swirling, etiolated handled forms of Art Nouveau. His very personal decorative repertoire (he eschewed glazes that took away from any sense of the form of the vessel) throws attention onto the drama of the play between image and abstraction. His debt to Japanese ceramics is evident: Bindesbøll was an exceptionally well informed artist in a milieu of highly cultivated collectors and intellectuals, where both Oriental pots and the ceramic work of Gauguin would have been well known. Chaplet had exhibited in Copenhagen, and Arnold Krog, the influential art director of the Royal Copenhagen Factory, had visited Paris and seen Bing's collection of Japanese ceramics. Bindesbøll's understanding of the possibilities in ceramics (using fragmentary patterns, working with the surface of the vessel) show that he had gone way beyond the Orientalism of his

15 **Thorvald Bindesbøll**, dish, 1901 (glazed earthenware, d. 44.5 cm/17½ in). Bindesbøll's designs are uncompromising, often no more than a monochromatic scattering of broken foliate elements across a large shallow dish; the sgraffito lines that break up the surface are deeply inscribed into the clay, the slip vigorously applied.

16 **Thorvald Bindesbøll**, vase, 1906 (glazed earthenware, h. 30.8 cm/12⅛ in). In a homage to Hokusai's famous picture, Bindesbøll's vase has a tumultuous breaking wave of blue brushstrokes below a deep black shoulder of fluxing glaze: the unglazed terracotta surface of the pot is left unhidden. There is a transparency of technique here that reveals a passionate engagement with how marks can be made in clay or how glaze fluxes in the kiln: this is 'direct working' in clay.

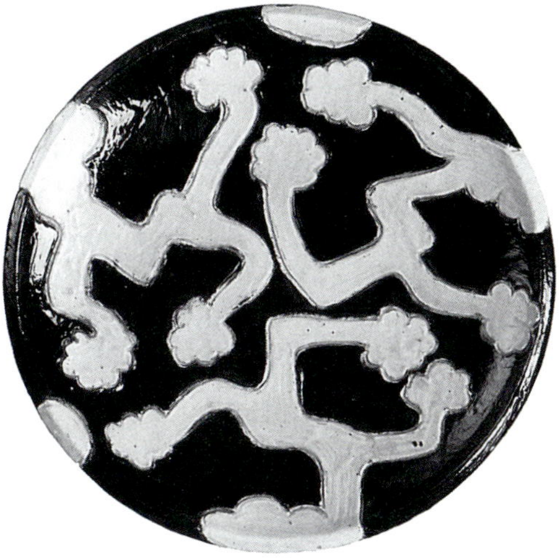

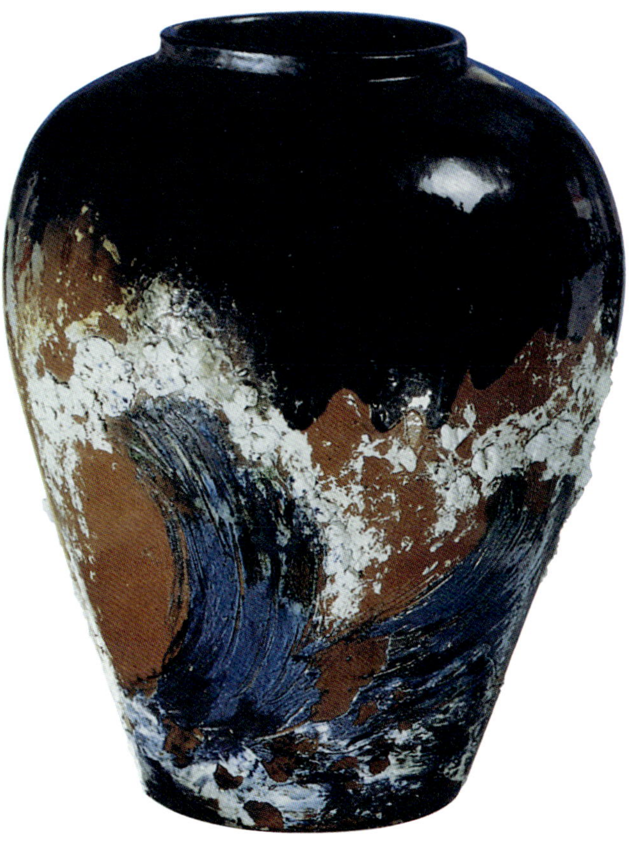

contemporaries towards an expressionism where the pot is treated as a three-dimensional canvas for mark-making rather than simply painting.

For some artist-potters of the period like Chaplet and Delaherche, ceramics were an 'art de rêveur' (dreamer's art) – symbolized by the image of the sailor in the storm, a giving over of control of effect to the process of making and firing. This set them apart from those like Robineau, for whom the art pot was an exercise in deliberation. What bound these disparate approaches together however was a sense of the place of the pot within the hierarchy of the arts. Whether through an abdication of skill, or a theatrical demonstration of skill, these artist-potters felt that the art pot was steadily achieving status and recognition against the mass of industrially produced ceramics. Though that status was to prove to be equivocal and their evident absence of utility was to be questioned by the succeeding generation of artist-potters, from this point the art of ceramics was inextricably linked to the idea of a singular, passionate engagement between one person and clay.

Art Nouveau

Much of the symbolism of Art Nouveau came from an intense projection of the artist's relationship with nature. Many of the ceramic works of the period reflect this with a heady distillation of organic forms and colours: forms reflect sensual moments of metamorphosis with unfolding buds and leaves, fish caught in currents of water, stretching figures or perching dragonflies. Alongside the imagery of a transient animate world came new glazes that shimmered and fluxed: surfaces were created to reflect the instability of the subject matter.

Some of this was intelligent commercial styling, as across Europe and Scandinavia major ceramics factories (including Rozenburg in Holland, Nymphenburg in Bavaria and Rörstrand in Sweden) responded to the 'modern style' of the Paris Exposition of 1900. Art Nouveau architecture and decorative arts had received intense attention, with sinuous curvilinear forms and a range of natural imagery that for some verged on the decadent. For others, organicism was more involved. At Rozenburg under the direction of J. Jurriaan Kok, the imagery of these Art Nouveau-inspired ceramics was startling: meticulously painted crab claws, antennae and dragonflies entwine with convolvulus across extravagantly thin porcelain. In Hungary, the Zsolnay factory gathered huge international attention at the International

Exhibitions at the start of the century, its vast fountain providing the centrepiece of the Hungarian Hall at the Esposizione Internazionale in Milan in 1906. Zsolnay was an ambitious company that brought in many leading artist-designers to work on their sinuous forms, but was principally renowned for 'Eozin', an iridescent lustred glaze which accentuated the intensely stylized forms with their highly modelled raised decorations. There is a deep sensuality in much of this work: vases are created as burgeoning, growing forms.

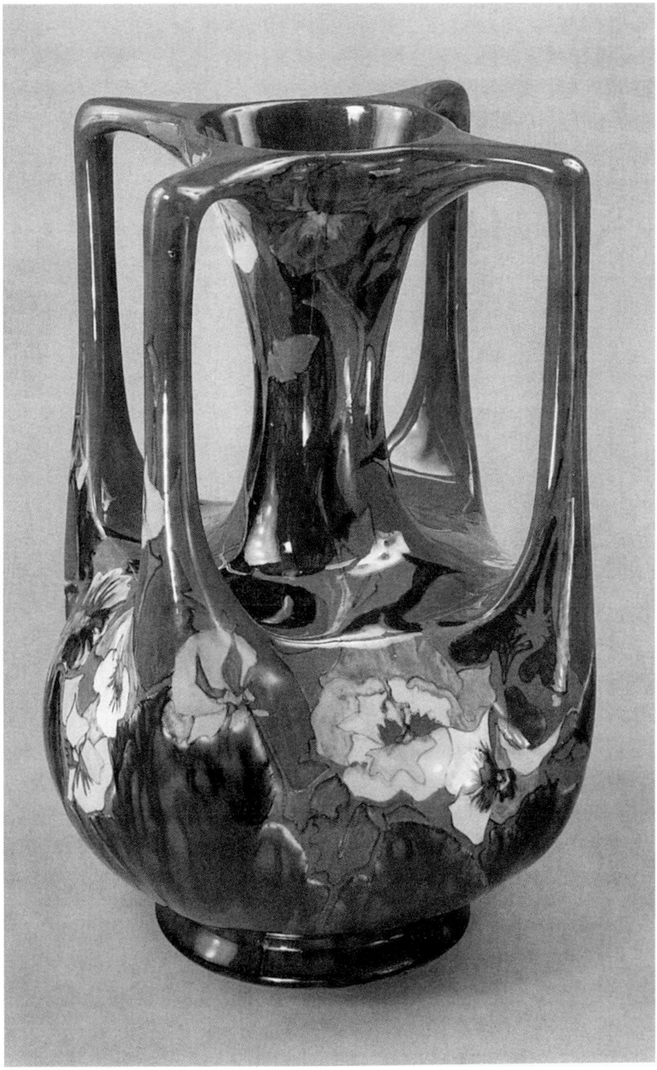

17 **Rozenburg** vase painted by W. P. Hartgring, 1903 (faience, h. 32cm/12⅝ in).
Rozenburg in The Hague became a leading factory under its art director, J.Juriaan Kok. It was known for both its eggshell porcelains and for its faience. The imagery was often heady, with burgeoning flowers or unruly tendrils, all painted with intense deep colour.

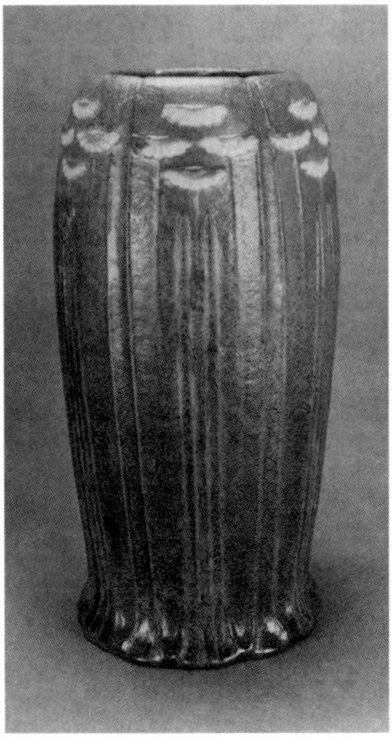

Less fervent were the watermelon green faience ceramics of the American William Grueby (1867–1925) with their gentle gourd forms and raised ribbed panels. Where Zsolnay was sinuous, Grueby's work possessed what has been described by the art historian Kirsten Keen as a 'structural naturalism'. Grueby, the owner of an architectural ceramics factory, was so struck by the work of Delaherche at the World's Columbian Exposition of 1893 in Chicago that he experimented until he had a glaze with similar matt qualities: 'Grueby green', his signature dense, light-absorbing glaze, pooling slightly in the declivities of the leaves modelled onto the vases. At the Paris Exposition of 1900 Grueby was sensationally awarded both a gold and a silver medal, and his international standing was further enhanced when Samuel Bing became his European agent.

The ceramics from Louis Comfort Tiffany's studio produced between 1904 and 1914 showed a different sensibility. Tiffany, a leading figure of the American decorative arts, was a dealer with a taste for the exotic and an outstanding designer of glass and jewelry. Immensely knowledgeable, he had exhibited Delaherche, Bigot and Taxile Doat in New York before deciding to design his own ceramics. His 'favrile' ceramics (a precious amendation of the Old English term 'fabrile', craftsmanship) were first shown in St Louis in 1904. Just as Grueby had re-interpreted Delaherche's forms in a more American idiom, so Tiffany designed ceramics that are often divided into almost rhythmic sections by grasses or plant stems.

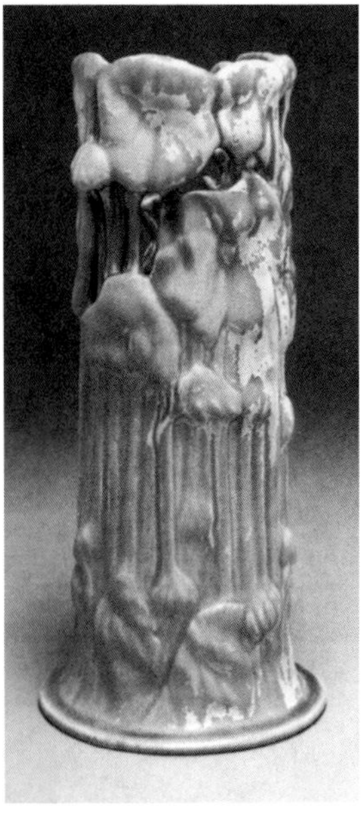

The work of the American potter Artus Van Briggle (1869–1904) shows how deeply the image of metamorphosis permeated the ceramics of the period. Van Briggle trained at the Cincinnati Art Academy before joining the premier American art pottery Rookwood in Cincinnati, Ohio. Rookwood had been started in 1880 by Maria Longworth Nichols as a club for women china painters, but had rapidly become a commercial success with its complex slip decoration and naturalistic imagery. In 1893 Rookwood sent Van Briggle to Paris for further study: here he was exposed to the burgeoning of Parisian Art Nouveau. On his return he developed a palette of subtle matt glazes that owed much to the trend for sensual tactility. In 1898 he started an independent studio in Colorado where he worked until his early death. From this 'frontier' country Van Briggle emphasized the specific local quality of his inspiration, decorating his pots with flowers indigenous to the area – aspen leaf and columbine, amongst other more conventional motifs. This was more than a convenient sales pitch for an American's ceramics exhibited in Paris: it is the projection of the artist at one with their locality, both grounded and inspired by nature. Van Briggle's projection of self or, more accurately, submission of self into nature, is vividly present in his use of the figure in his ceramics. In his *Despondency* vase of 1902, a slumped figure, head in hands, is wrapped around the opening of the vessel. The void of the pot seems to accentuate the depth of emptiness of the mood. As the art historian Christoph Asendorf has put it: 'The interlaced ornamentations of Jugendstil, in which things and people melt decoratively together, are made a poetic principle.'

18 **Ruth Erikson**, Grueby Pottery, Grueby Faience Company, Boston vase, *c.* 1900 (earthenware, h. 42.5 cm/16¾ in).
American potteries were noted for the number of leading women designers. It was also common for women to be employed as decorators. At the Grueby Pottery a man would throw the pot and then women decorators would apply thin coils of clay to the surface, modelling them into the stylized leaves and stems for which Grueby ware was known.

19 **Louis Comfort Tiffany**, vase with pansies, 1904–10 (stoneware, h. 25 cm/9¾ in).
The Pansy vase, pierced so that it metamorphoses from a container for flowers into a vessel seemingly made from flowers, reveals the ideas of a designer who was continually pushing towards an aesthetic where objects symbolically enact their function.

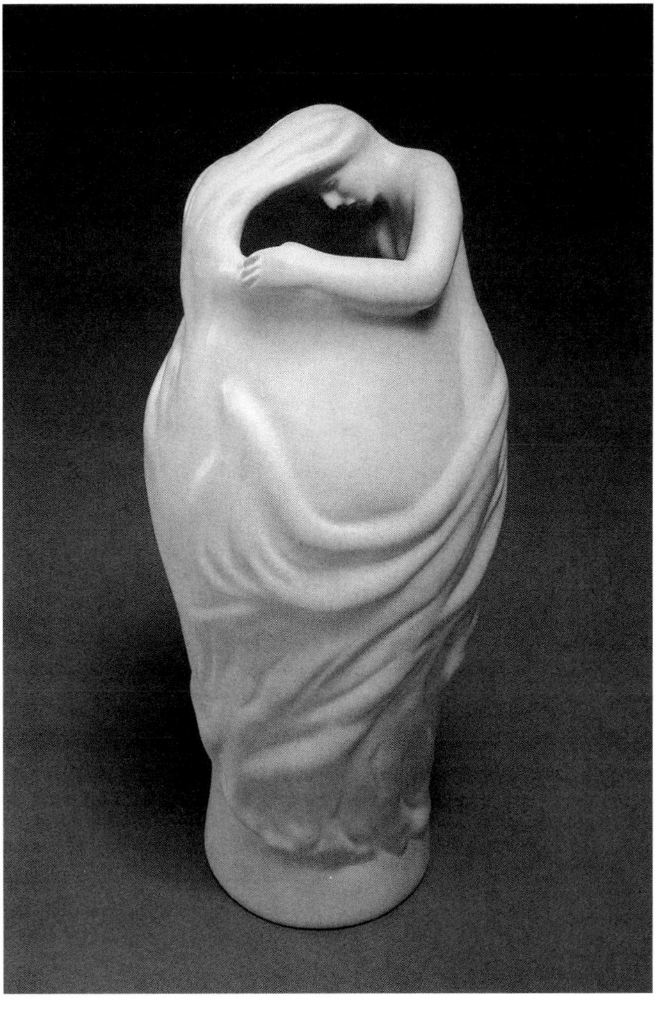

20 **Artus Van Briggle**, *Lorelei Vase*, 1901 (earthenware, h. 26.7 cm/10½ in).
The figure of the siren emerges from the body of the pot, her hair swirling like water around it. By a semantic shift the woman elides into a vessel. Van Briggle presents the drama of the intense aesthetic or sexual moment, a diffused congress with nature. Women, he suggests, are essentially susceptible to metamorphosis.

This novelty of approach, connecting the metamorphosis of a vessel with those natural forms, required a different way of thinking about decoration. Surface is no longer to be perceived as the ground for pattern, but as an extension of an internal process. This was noted by a critic in 1907 in the work of the Martin brothers, the four eccentric potters who worked in London from the 1870s until the 1910s (see caption, below left). The pots of theirs that are often called gourd vases resist easy description, seeming to belong to a middle world of objects between discarded natural forms (such as seed pods, or sloughed snake skins) and ceramic vessels. This bringing together of throwing, modelling and carving to create ambiguous forms that still seem to be in uneasy flux, is something particularly associated with the Martin brothers, some of whose forms are benign, while others brim with menace. Indeed it is in 'Martin ware' that the grotesque, the disquieting portrayal of animals or people taking shape in or out of vessels, finds its place.

The passage made by the Martin brothers towards this kind of vessel was lengthy. In the 1870s their pots show countless barely digested historicized sources, an eclecticism that included Celtic, medieval German, Persian and Attic pottery, but gradually their interest became focused on using the fashionable contemporary Japonisme for decoration on salt-glazed pots, in which fish swim amongst stylized weeds, or birds perch on jagged branches. These achieved a modicum of success, though more than once they apparently made gallon beer jars and the taps for acid jars to make ends meet. Wallace Martin also made peculiar bird sculptures,

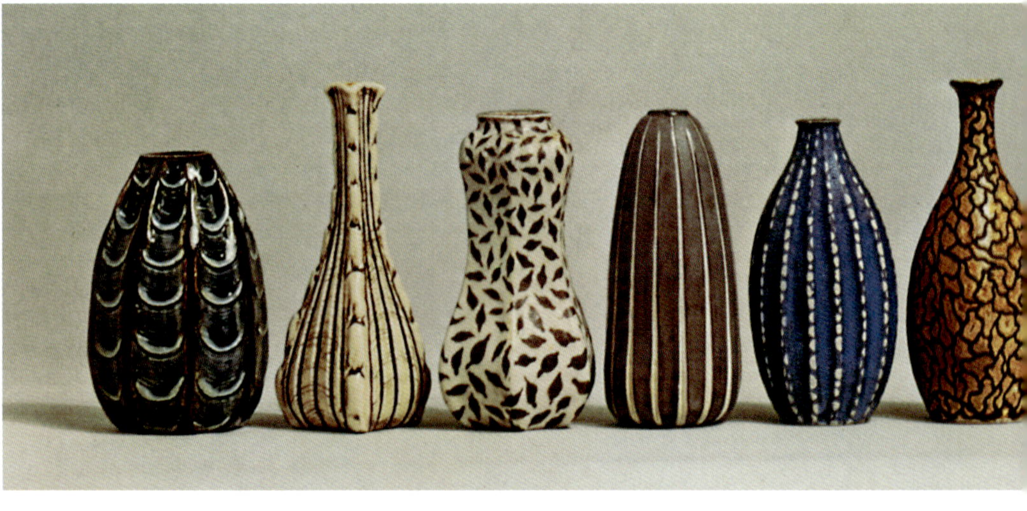

21 **The Martin brothers**, vases 1897–1914 (max. h. approx. 12 cm/5 in).
'The quaint and irregular shapes given to the various objects are uncommon without being bizarre. The decoration is, for the most part, intimately connected with the manufacture of the object, and not, as it were, an afterthought. When Nature decorates her own productions, such as an egg, a shell, a flower or a fruit, she does not reproduce the forms of other natural objects. She does not paint a lily on an egg... Each one of these objects has a particular type of decoration... the outcome of form and growth.' *The Studio*, 1907

22 **The Martin brothers**, 1912. Left to right: Walter, Wallace, Edwin. Charles is missing. Visible are a grotesque satirical jug with a smiling face (foreground centre), and 'Wally-birds' (centre and foreground right).

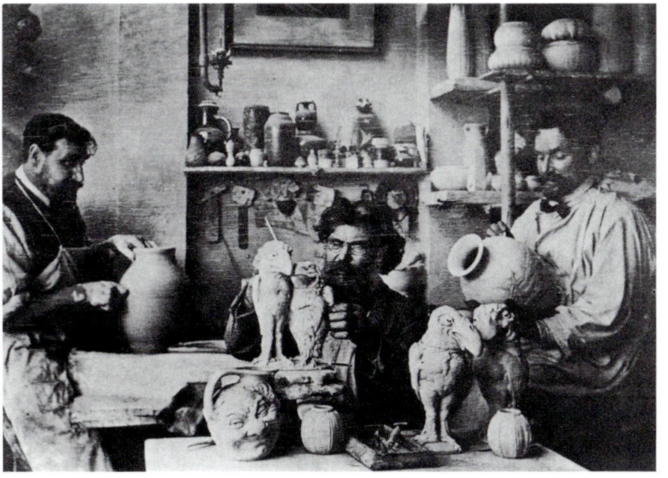

tobacco jars in name, in which his modelling abilities were allowed free reign. These 'Wally-birds', hugely beaked and with a piercing gaze, are loosely connected to the Victorian culture of savage anthropomorphic caricature. They are part of an oeuvre that included treatments of pikes, dead parakeets and satyrs alongside contemporary political figures.

Each of the brothers was noted for a particular skill: Robert Wallace was the modeller, Walter the thrower and glaze-chemist, and Edwin decorated, while Charles looked after the business side with haphazard energy. Their independence from exhibiting societies or the patronage of large factories meant a precarious existence that has led them to be credited as the first true studio potters. But their independence, though feted, disguised a more complex situation, a mixture of wilfulness ('the pots in their showroom are not arranged like the crockery in an ordinary shop, and there is no effusive display of antagonism towards dust', wrote a critic in 1910) and bad luck. The brothers frequently fell out, and also relied on outside help from another potter in the studio. Indeed the gourd vases, which can be seen as the most radical of the Martin ware, were the work of one brother alone – Edwin.

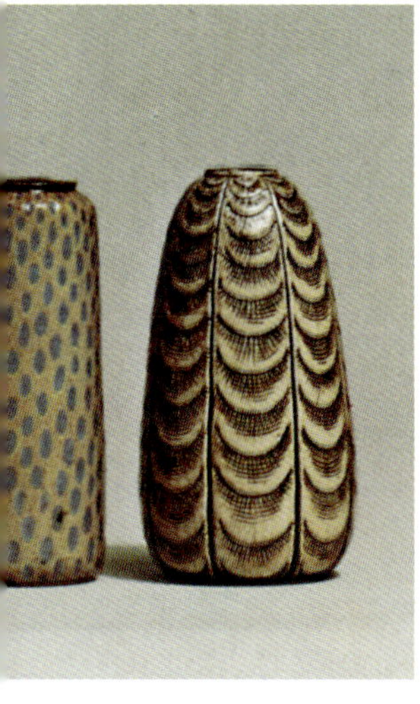

The almost kinaesthetic experience of making pots found its most extraordinary exponent in the work of the American potter George E. Ohr (1857–1918): 'When I found the potter's wheel I felt it all over like a wild duck in water'. In Ohr's pots there is the sense of an unfolding of spatial possibilities: forms are stretched, joined, collapsed, ruffled or dimpled in ways that are deeply sensual. This unfolding, the metamorphosis of one form into another, was something that as a natural showman he relished. When demonstrating at his workshop in Biloxi in Mississippi or at the national or country fairs, he was, in some ways, emphasizing the singular nature of creation. The corporeal qualities of these forms are more than exercises in technique.

Ohr's reluctance to part with what he described as his 'clay babies' (charging considerable sums for them, and demanding that many be kept together as a collection) was an indicator of his projection of himself into his art. His disparagement of his contemporaries was grounded in what he perceived as their coldness and lack of engagement with the process of creation, seen in the multiplicity of people who contributed to the making of a single pot: 'it Don't Take A Doz to Accomplish Art Pottery', as he fiercely put it. As a consequence few critics could sympathize with this alarmingly heterodox figure who, in Rhead's words, 'deliberately distorted every pot he made in order to be violently different from any other potter'. It was not until the rediscovery of Ohr's own collection of over 7000 pots at his old warehouse in 1968 that his work was reappraised. The Martin Brothers and Ohr can be regarded as maverick precursors of the studio pottery movement, both in attempting independence from others to achieve complete ownership of the finished piece, and in their own identification with the corporeal nature of pottery. Their work also echoes the concerns of Gauguin and the Expressionists as to the centrality of the mark of the hand in making ceramics.

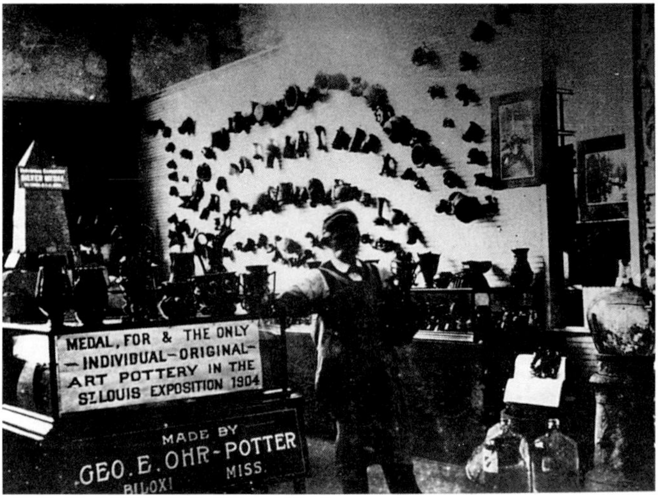

23 **George Ohr**, *c.* 1905.
'This is what I [can] do, with four pounds of clay on the wheel – blindfolded – turn a jug, put a corncob stopper in it, change the corncob into a funnell, have the funnell disappear, and have a jar, change the jar into an urn and half a dozen other shapes.'

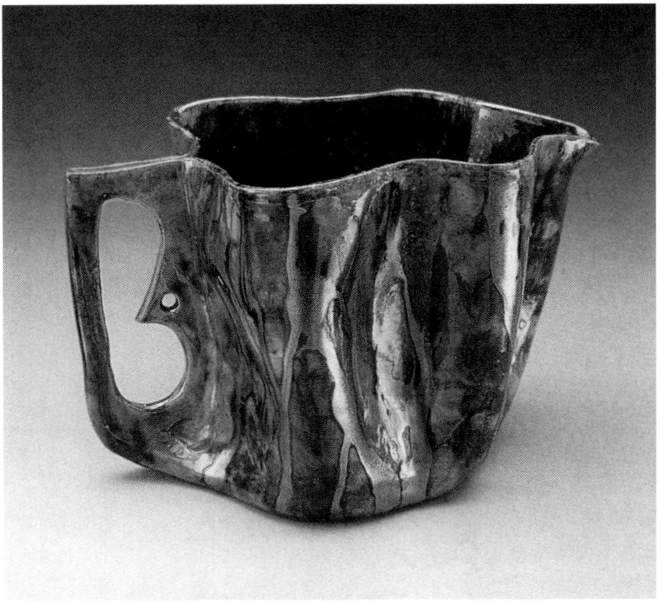

24 **George Ohr**, pitcher, *c.* 1895–1900 (earthenware, h. 12.7 cm/5 in).
'According to the Good Book, we are created from clay, and as Nature had it so destined that no two of us are alike, all couldn't be symmetrically formed, caused a variety to be wabble-jawed, hare-lipped, cross-eyed, all colors, bow-legged, knock-kneed, extra limbs... I make disfigured pottery – couldn't and wouldn't if I could make it any other way.'

Gauguin and Expressionism

The image of the peasant in the landscape, a traditional touchstone of French art, finds a different aspect in Gauguin's ceramics. At the start of his association with Chaplet in 1886 he had decorated vases and pitchers thrown for him in stoneware with scenes of peasant life: this early flat decoration showed the contemporary influence of Japanese woodcuts, but only meagre interest in form. This was something that changed totally when he started to handbuild his ceramics. He wished to 'replace the thrower of pots by intelligent hands that are able to powerfully communicate the life of a figure... to give to the art of ceramics a new *élan* for the making of new forms through hand building.' By setting the thrower of pots (capable of making many versions of the same form) in opposition to the 'intelligent' hand (making individual judgments about each piece) he was highlighting his distance from mechanical manufacture. In claiming that the idea of direct working in the material allowed for spontaneity Gauguin gave potency to the idea of working in an unmediated way with clay.

Over the next year Gauguin produced over seventy pieces. The forms of the vessels seem wanton, they overflow with an abundance of extraneous handles and lips, vessels with multiple openings. Some seem to connect with the archaic pre-Columbian ceramics that Gauguin undoubtedly knew from his childhood in

Peru, but their latent anthropomorphism is more complex still: these are ceramics whose orientation is alive to new possibilities. They were mostly unglazed so that the rich tonalities of Chaplet's brown stoneware lend them a vernacular disguise, their striking modernity playing with their apparent archaicism. Where glaze is used Chaplet's rich and bloody copper glazes add further incongruity and sensuality.

Gauguin's ceramics were exhibited by Chaplet at the Brussels Exposition of 1896, in Paris in 1900 and at the 1906 retrospective. Gauguin engaged with the possibility of ceramics as an art – not clay as a material for sculpture – with an alternative history that he could lay claim to and revitalize. 'Needless to say Sèvres has killed ceramics... with the American Indians it was a central art. God gave man a little bit of mud, with a little bit of mud he made metal, and precious stones, with a little bit of mud and with a little bit of genius.' That ceramics were a 'central art' with a mythic past connects the worlds of Ohr and Gauguin. Neither of them doubted their own significance, and they both took a robustly dismissive attitude to technique as an end in itself.

For the artists of Die Brücke (the Bridge), the German Expressionist movement, Gauguin was a key influence. Gauguin's self-identification as a 'savage from Peru' and his vision of direct working with materials was consonant with their emotionally charged handling of subject matter. The painter Emil Nolde's (1876–1956) evocation of primitive people creating without drawings 'with the raw material in the hand between the fingers' conveys this sense of passion and urgency. Nolde's ceramic works

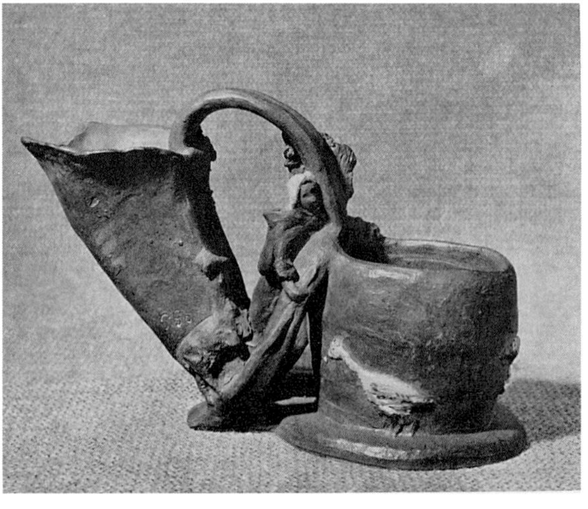

25 **Paul Gauguin**, *Double-vessel with Breton girl*, 1886–87 (stoneware, h. 13 cm/5⅛ in).
In Gauguin's pots, as in the archaic pre-Columbian pottery that he loved, figures emerge out of vessels or decline into them or become vessels themselves. Another of Gauguin's vessels is made up of two boys' heads with a handle formed by the neck of a swan.

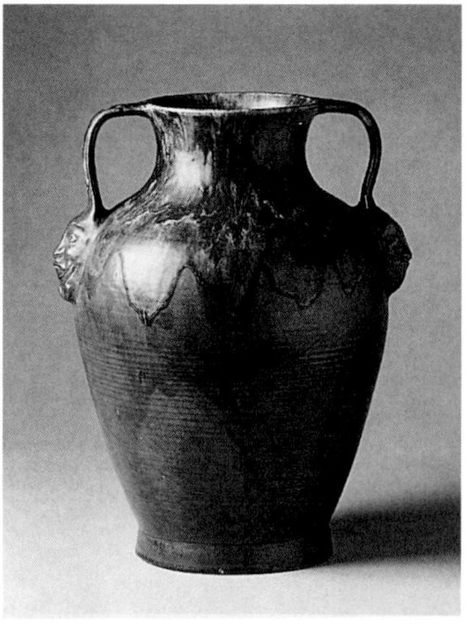

26 **Ernest Barlach**, double-handled vase, *c.* 1905 (stoneware, h. 42 cm/16½ in).
Barlach's work in ceramics expressed his 'mythic vision' of the role of sculpture. His figures in both stoneware and porcelain (the Blind beggar, the Russian peasant) crossed medievalism with contemporary social concern.

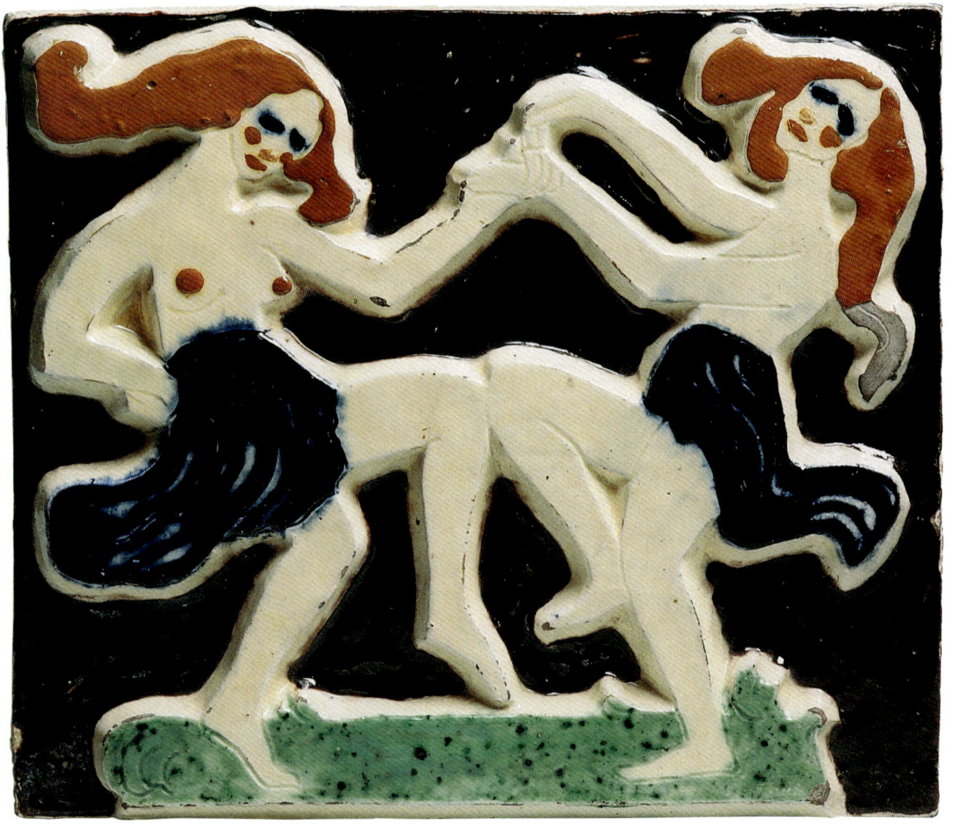

27 **Emil Nolde**, tile, 1913 (29 × 33 cm/11½ × 13 in). 'Our age has seen to it that a design on paper has to precede every clay pot, ornament, useful object, or piece of clothing. The products of primitive people are created with actual material in their hands, between their fingers. ...The primeval vitality, the intensive, often grotesque expression of energy and life in its most elemental form – that, perhaps is what makes these native works so enjoyable' (Emil Nolde).

– plates painted with masks, female dancers, and animals – were made in a pottery at Flensburg in Northern Germany. For Nolde, as for Gauguin before him, 'farm peasant wares' expressed the vitality that he sought.

For the sculptor Ernst Barlach (1870–1938) too, clay allowed for a direct working that he found so stimulating that he advocated its more widespread use in his book, *Keramik, Stoff und Form* (1908). Barlach's collaboration with the highly skilled potter Richard Mutz (1845–1931) – renowned for both his architectural ceramics and his Orientalist glazes – allowed him to make both glazed figures and vigorous gargoyle-like modelled heads applied to vases to create a grotesque and almost medieval impression.

Although the great majority of Expressionist sculpture was carved from wood – its particular association with African and Oceanic art was central to Die Brücke – clay was also used. Paul Rudolf Henning (b. 1886) wrote 'Ton – Ein Aufruf' (Clay –

a Manifesto) as part of a larger work on modern art published by the Kunsthaus Zurich in 1917. He argued passionately for clay, alleging that contemporary artists, 'in spite of their daily handling of clay, are completely removed from actually working with its specific qualities. They have lost all feeling for modelling clay according to its nature; ...the clay model's only purpose is to create and facilitate flexibility of creative composition within a different medium.' Henning suggested a different way of using clay, and invoked it with passion. 'Piercing', he wrote, is 'making the "hollow" visible, the shard audible! The expression of a work of art can be increased to vehement heights by means of this rhythmic piercing and by the inclusion of... *colour*.' In his own work he attempted to achieve these rhythms. His sculpture *The Dance of Charlotte Bara*, for instance, made in three parts from terracotta, with an echoing of similar shapes in each of three components, was an attempt to evoke the dancer's intensely symbolic dances. The ambition of Barlach and Henning's attempts to articulate a different rationale for the sculptural use of clay prefigured some of the most interesting figurative work by sculptors like Alexander Archipenko and Isamu Noguchi in the 1920s and 30s. Above all it claimed a central place for the symbolic use of clay in relation to the figure.

Ceramics and painting

The taxonomy of painting on ceramics was complex. The painters employed by the great ceramics centres of Sèvres or Limoges were mostly anonymous and would often only paint part of a pot, figures or foliage or border patterns. Towards the end of the nineteenth century an artist, if well enough known, might be allowed to leave his or her monogram on the base of a pot. But the idea of painters actually being able to choose their own subject matter was novel. The question of whether painting on ceramics was merely 'decorative', in some way either a diminution of the painter's art or the elevation of the ceramicist's, was to haunt ceramics throughout the twentieth century.

The debate was manifested by the collaboration between the potter André Metthey (1871–1920) and the Fauves (French for wild beasts), the group of artists associated with the collector and dealer Ambroise Vollard. Metthey was a painter and sculptor who was largely self-taught in ceramics, and he felt that his peers were amongst his painter friends rather than ceramicists. He asserted that faience (tin-glazed earthenware), though disparaged by Sèvres, offered an artist a huge field of possibilities; his researches

28 **André Metthey**, preparatory sketches, *c.* 1910–11.
Metthey's gouaches show his passion for Persian ceramics and his desire to relay traditional decorative forms into a modern idiom. They also demonstrate the painterly care with which he planned his work.

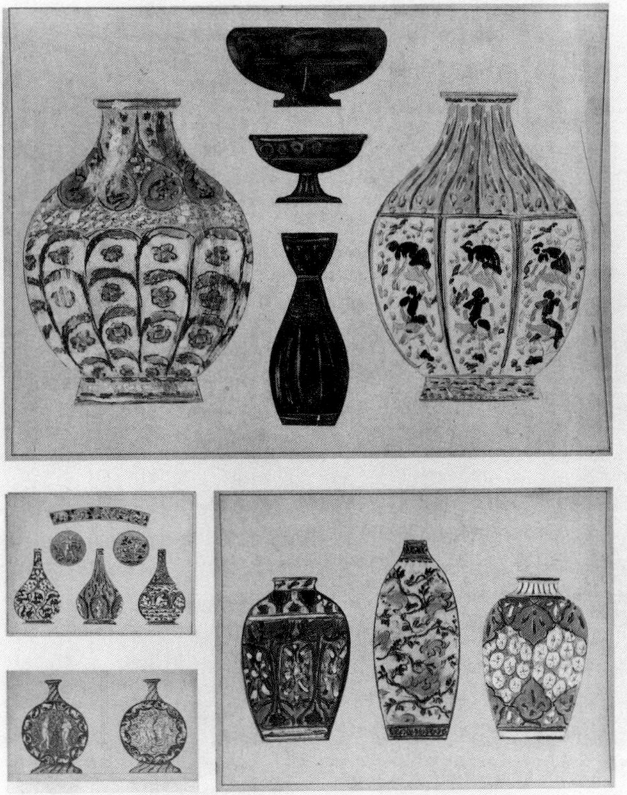

into Renaissance maiolica and seventeenth- and eighteenth-century French faience led him to believe that he could create a new art, given vigour by the use of truly local materials and beyond the historicism and pastiche of preceding styles. Vollard acted as catalyst for the experiment, but it was the sense of equality and genuine collaboration between Metthey and his artist friends that gave it vitality. The artists had no direct involvement in the making of the forms that they were to decorate, as Jean Puy recalled:

Vollard had the enterprise of reinvigorating the painting of faience, and we were sent to Asnières where a colleague had started a little pottery for faience and occasionally stoneware. Vollard sent Laprade, Derain, Vlaminck, Matisse, Rouault, Jean Puy and the older Rousseau there. The potter Methey [sic] gave us bisqued vases, plates and cups covered with a white glaze...

The artists were to paint on these three-dimensional canvases.

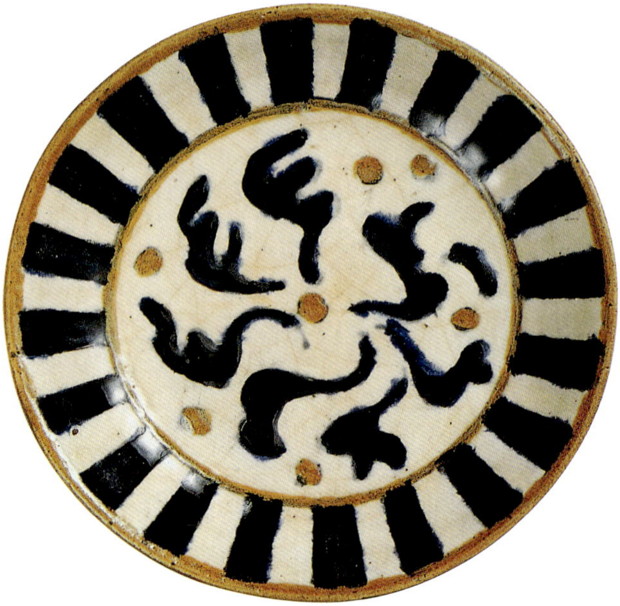

29 **André Metthey**, plate with striped edges, *c.* 1908 (earthenware, d. 21 cm/8¼ in) Metthey, who had 'an almost physical horror for cold and pompous ceramics', began by using the newly fashionable stoneware, but his passion for colour led him towards faience.

30 **Maurice de Vlaminck**, *Feuilles bleues*, *c.* 1907–9 (earthenware, h. 28 cm/11 in). Vlaminck uses only one colour, a deep blue-black cobalt, to paint two leaves onto a gently swelling pot. They are painted with a gestural abandon with only two dozen or so marks, one leaf wrapped around one 'side' of the pot, the other on the alternate 'side'. It becomes a play on flatness and volume.

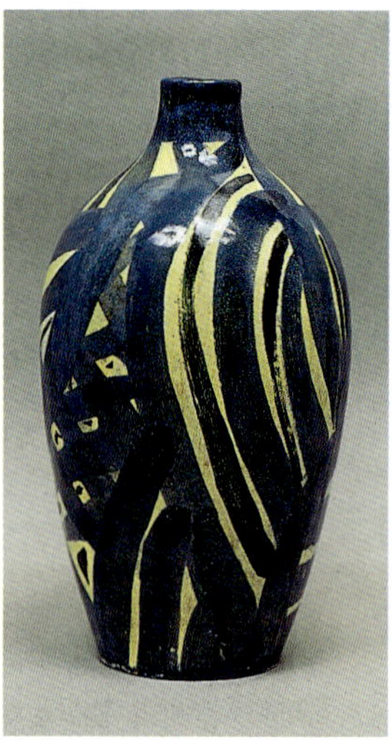

The colours' richness has all the directness of country faience. Because these colours were painted onto a white ground and were not poured or dipped glazes, the brushmark is given primacy. Maurice de Vlaminck (1876–1958), the creator of more than three hundred ceramic works, for instance, employed a rhythmical repetition of brushstrokes that delineate the space. Sometimes this follows conventions, a repeated border of leaves entwined around a plate or cup, but more often there is a capriciousness that suggests a freedom to play with decorative traditions. Metthey noted that instead of the relegation of a decorator into the role of repeating the same motif, these painters initiated designs in a novel way. In the treatment of the vases, for instance, Henri Matisse (1869–1954) found a suggestion of a larger space, 'a true plastic space'. Matisse, Ernst Ludwig Kirchner (1880–1938) and Gauguin added complexity to their pictures of interiors by incorporating depictions of their own (painted) ceramics on the canvas.

Many of these ceramics were widely exhibited between 1907 and 1910 alongside the paintings of the Fauves. At the Salon d'automne of 1907 one hundred pieces were shown and received gratifying attention. Indeed French contemporary critics, like Tristan Glingsor writing in 1907, who found abstraction difficult to defend within painting, found it 'happy and appropriate when

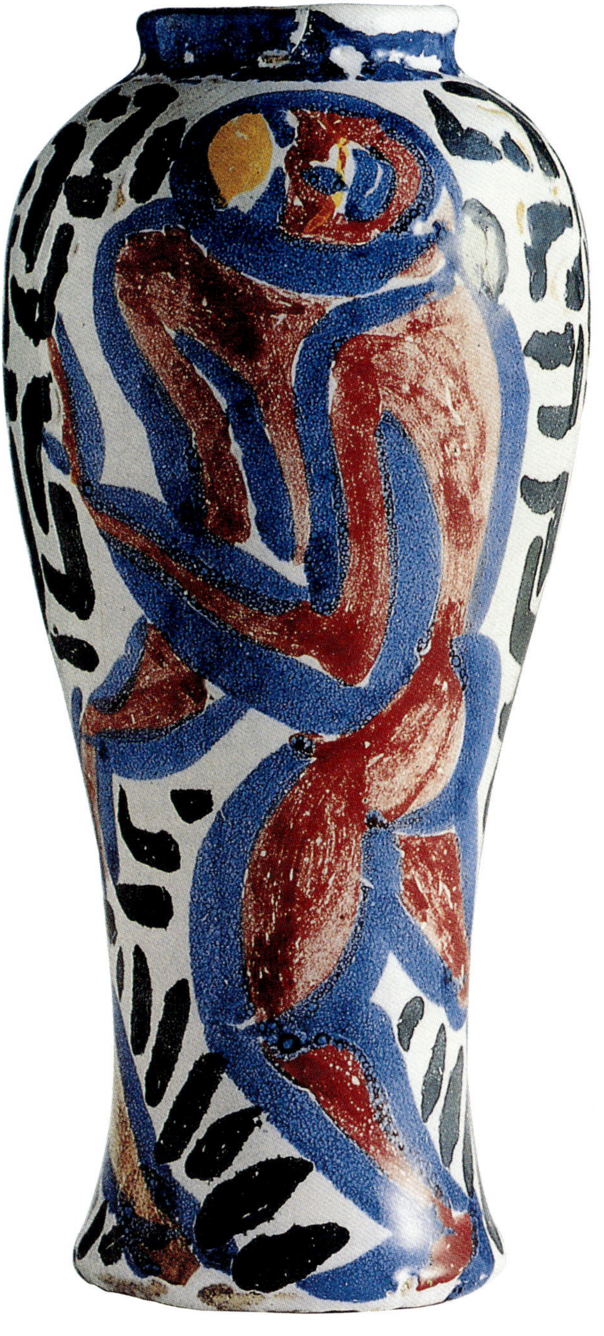

31 **André Derain**,
Danseuses, *c.* 1907 (earthenware, h. 19 cm/7½ in).
The correspondence between parts of vessel and human body is close, the feet of the dancers touching the foot of the pot, their waists depicted at the thinnest section, their heads reaching the lip. The pot enacts the painting with economy and verve.

applied to ceramics.' Such criticism reflected that there was a process of abstraction that could be deemed necessary to pattern-making.

Metthey himself continued to make faience, after his collaboration had ceased, for the ten years until his death in 1920, his work becoming more elaborate, showing Moorish forms with heavily patterned grounds across which stylized figures dance. Within France Fauve ceramics continued to have its admirers, led by Vollard. Its influence on the English art critic Roger Fry, however, led to the foundation of the Omega Workshops, and a rather dilettante experiment in the creation of ceramics in a bohemian setting. It was also pivotal in the creation of new aesthetics for ceramics, a mode of criticism that would define how pots were discussed for the next thirty years.

Fry was a heterodox figure within English artistic life. He came from a conservative middle-class background but trained as a painter. By the 1880s he had started to write as well as paint, and rapidly acquired a reputation as an authority on contemporary art, a position strengthened by his involvement in the founding of the *Burlington Magazine* in 1907. Fry organized the two exhibitions that introduced Post-Impressionist paintings and ceramics to England, the first chance for the paintings of Gauguin, Cézanne and Matisse to be properly seen, and the introduction of Derain and Vlaminck, among others, to a largely sceptical public. Fry and his colleague Clive Bell helped establish a new canon of ceramics enshrined in approving critical terms of vigour and economy. Both men had a genuine enthusiasm for the decorative arts, and saw the possibilities for connecting the new art of the Post-Impressionists with whatever earlier arts seemed to share their first principles. Thus when English medieval pots were rediscovered Bell could easily assimilate these ruggedly made and freely decorated objects into his aesthetic: 'Not that there is any fear of a modern critic… despising a rude and primitive school.' Fry wrote an anonymously published critique of the savagely received Post-Impressionism exhibition of 1910, which suggested how highly he regarded the ceramics of Vollard's painters:

I would instance as a proof of the direction in which the post impressionists are working, the excellence of their pure design as seen in the pottery in the present exhibition. In these there is often scarcely any appeal made through representation, just a hint at a bird or an animal here and there, and yet they will arouse a definite feeling. Particular rhythms of line and particular harmonies of colour have their spiritual correspondence, and tend to arouse now one set of feelings, now another…

In support of this apprehension that it was non-representational art that allowed for the free play of the emotions, Fry also turned to the pottery of China. In 1910 an exhibition of *Early Chinese Pottery and Porcelain* was held in London, the first chance to see in quantity the pots of the T'ang and Sung dynasties unearthed during the building of the Chinese railways. These pots overturned many previously held truths about the canon of Oriental ceramics. Here were monochromatic jars and bowls of unparalleled discretion, with decoration of an economy and vigour that appealed to his aesthetic: 'All the astounding skill of hand of the potter is here devoted to the refinement of the rough, primitive pot, not to its elaboration into something quite different, as happened in later ceramics.' The assimilation of these two kinds of art – early medieval ceramics and those of the Sung Dynasty – into a coherent aesthetic was rapid. By 1914, Bell could write with assurance that ' no one ever doubted that a Sung pot or a Romanesque church was as much an expression of emotion as any picture that ever was painted'. This welding of historic ceramics into the heart of the discourse about the value of contemporary art was to provide the theoretical basis for the foundation of the Omega Workshops, an experiment where art would be 'purified of its present unreality by a prolonged contact with the crafts.'

32 **Roger Fry**, collection of domestic ware, 1914. Monochromatic ceramics such as these from the Omega Workshops were destined for bohemian settings. A journalist wrote in 1916: 'Imagine how perfectly gorgeous tomato soup would look in a black soup-tureen! Why, one would have tomato soup every day! And the plates are obviously waiting for salad – vivid green lettuce, shy radishes, and magenta beetroots! Fruit would be a Futurist feast in those black bowls…'

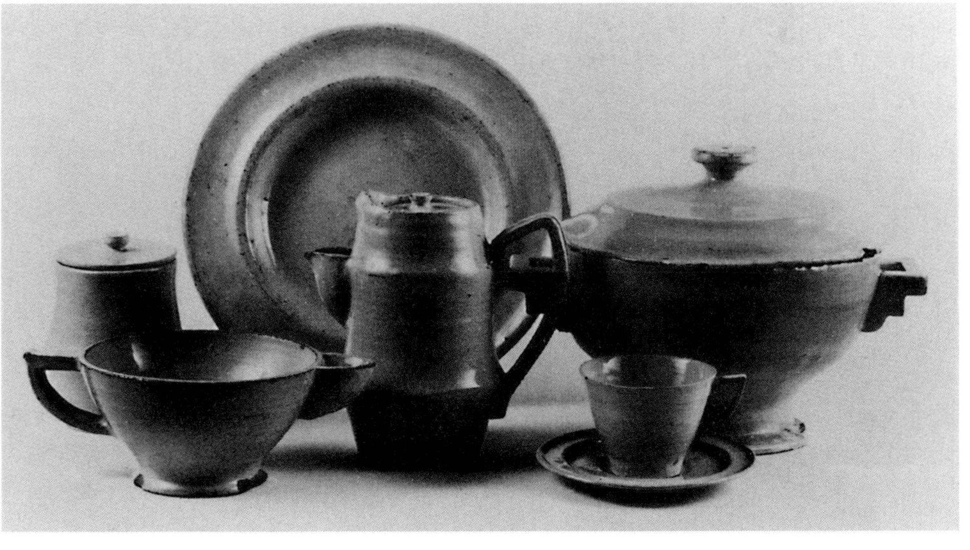

Omega was a scheme of Fry's that would offer a guaranteed income to a group of his friends, including Vanessa Bell and Wyndham Lewis, who would decorate simple bought-in furniture, textiles and ceramics. According to the prospectus of 1914 they would be involved with 'almost all kinds of decorative design, more particularly those in which the artist can engage without specialized training in craftsmanship… Substituting wherever possible the directly expressive quality of the artist's handling for the deadness of mechanical reproduction.' They would 'refuse to spoil the expressive quality of their work by sand-papering it down to a shop finish.'

The place of ceramics within this enterprise was clear. Certain shapes would be made at Carter's Pottery in Poole under the direction of Fry whilst he himself took throwing lessons and achieved a modicum of skill, enough to make 'expressive objects', if not technically proficient ones, that still carried the 'nervous tremor of the creator'. They were decorated with gusto by the Omega artists, sometimes with sub-Vorticist designs and sometimes with patterns that derived from Mediterranean sources seemingly in keeping with the tin glazes they used. Fry also created monochromatic pots, though the impulse behind them was certainly not one of austerity. Fry lamented the social standing of the potter ('a vague idea that a man can still remain a gentleman if he paints bad pictures, but must forfeit the conventional right to Esquire if he makes a good pot'); his construction of an alternative canon of 'good pottery' was to continue to be significant. The idea of bohemian living, of a cultivated interior where all objects corresponded to an ideal of decorative cohesion, threw a challenge to the accepted hierarchies of art. But Omega ceramics never remotely reached the heights of the Fauves' collaboration with Metthey or the Viennese experiments in the *Gesamtkunstwerk* (total work of art).

Native styles: reinventing the vernacular

It is possible to see the search for 'authentic' vernacular traditions that occupied many ceramicists at the turn of the twentieth century as a reflection of the highly charged question of how to define cultural identity. This was partly due to the increasing commodification of ceramics. The internationalism of trade, the ubiquity of art magazines, the Grand Expositions in which American, Scandinavian and European ceramic firms would jostle for attention, all contributed to a need to create an identifiable, exportable set of coherent national images. It was also due to an

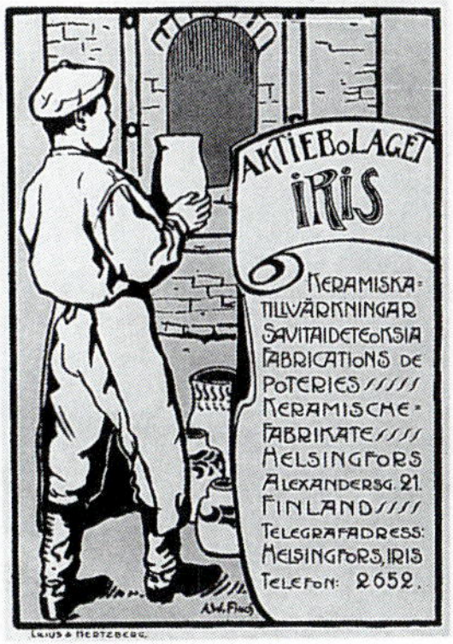

33 Cover of an **Iris** catalogue, 1901.

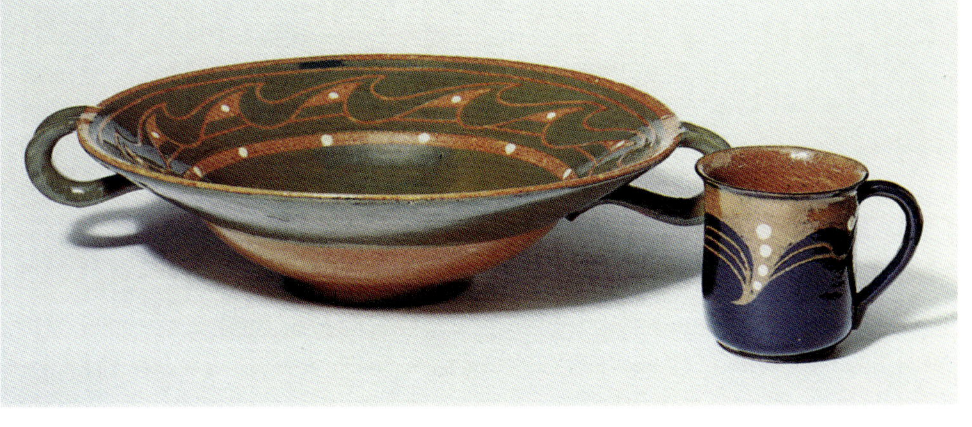

34 **Alfred Finch**, dish and mug, earthenware, 1897–1900 (dish: d. 34.7 cm/13½ in, mug: h. 9.5 cm/3¾ in). The forms seem suited for everyday living: there are mugs rather than cups and saucers and decoration is spare with repeated abstracted foliate patterns set off by punctuation dots of coloured slip: the impression is given of 'essential' pattern. These pots perform as examples of a new highly sophisticated simplicity, adept at demonstrating both 'roots' and knowledge of the contemporary.

excitement about a 'return' to a less complex, more 'grounded' form of ceramics. The idea that a particular local clay or woodash was more 'real' than another was central to the evocation of traditions in the 1920s and 30s.

Finland at the end of the nineteenth century was a province of Russia whose semi-autonomy was increasingly threatened by the growth of pan-Slavist ideas. Debates about independence were led by artists and intellectuals. The nationalist cause found a heady image in the vast wilderness of Karelia, the supposed location for the epic poem the *Kalevala* ('Land of the Heroes'). The combination of 'untrammelled' nature and mythic beginnings added to the potency of the use of native materials: stained Karelian birch and roughly hewn stone became carriers of romantic nationalist feeling. In 1894 the painter Akseli Gallen-Kallela (1865–1931), a cosmopolitan artist who had studied in Paris and travelled in Germany and England, gaining knowledge of the English Arts and Crafts Movement, designed a log studio that combined these materials. Together with the part-Italian and part-Swedish designer Louis Sparre (1863–1964) he founded the Iris Workshops in 1897, a company dedicated to refining public taste by producing domestic objects that reflected Finnish identity. They invited the Anglo-Belgian potter Alfred William (Willy) Finch (1854–1930) to join them. Finch's work at the Iris Workshops, though it was short-lived (they closed in 1902), is compelling. At the same time the Arabia factory in Finland consequently brought out a range of earthenware called 'Fennia' in 1902 with geometric patterns derived from Karelian sources, that was intended for export to the American market.

35 **Reginald Wells**, bowl and jug, earthenware, 1909 (bowl: d. 14.9 cm/5¾ in, jug: d. 17.5 cm/6¾ in). On these pots produced in 1909, Wells uses slip to inscribe 'Coldrum', a site of great significance in the history of English vernacular pottery. When he moved to London he established the 'Coldrum Pottery', marking some pots 'Coldrum Chelsea', perhaps the first example of a metropolitan potter making deliberately ruralist pots.

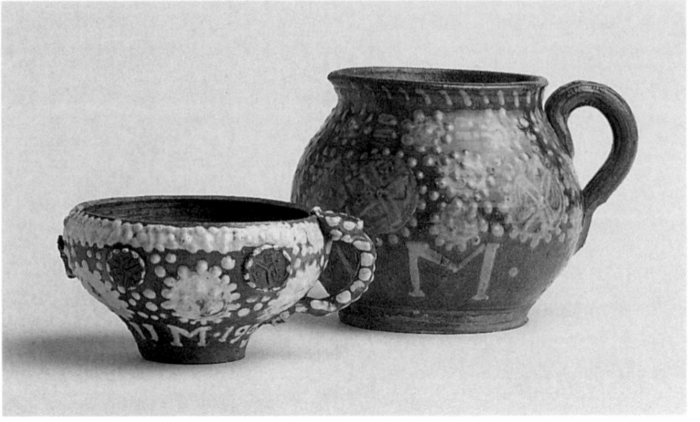

The mining of vernacular traditions can also be seen in England in the early career of the potter Reginald Wells (1877–1951). Wells trained as a sculptor before studying ceramics at Camberwell School of Art. Around 1900, according to an account from 1919, 'He set up his first kilns at Coldrum Farm, near Wrotham, Kent, employing the same bed as the seventeenth-century Wrotham potters'. The Wrotham potters were not only makers of slipware, they were regarded as the progenitors of distinctively English pottery. There could be no greater way of authenticating these new 'Coldrum Wares' than by using such powerful antecedents.

National style was an important commodity and it was a commonplace to proclaim just how specific local materials were (the notable Rookwood Pottery of Ohio, USA, used 'native clay' for instance) or how decoration reflected local foliage. This commodification was necessary because of how widely these ceramics travelled. It was as if the very intensity of these international contacts created a greater demand for obvious local or vernacular stylistic difference. Ceramics from the Iris Workshops were sold in Paris at Bing's L'Art Nouveau and in Meier-Graefe's La Maison Moderne, while the Iris Workshops themselves also acted as agents for Liberty of London. Bing acted as European agent for Grueby ceramics, selling examples of his work to the Museum of Decorative Art in Copenhagen. Liberty's sold Zsolnay ceramics from Hungary. Many of the protagonists in this modern world were cosmopolitan and knew each other personally. Finch was a friend of Henry van de Velde, Gallen-Kallela a friend of Gauguin, Van de Velde the designer of Meier-Graefe's salon.

The products of both the Iris Workshops and Reginald Wells participate in a revolt against the 'excesses' of art pottery. Sometimes this was expressed in the language of the Arts and Crafts Movement as a search for ceramics for everyday life that would obey the twin precepts of fitness for purpose and a transparency in their making: 'a happiness for the maker and the user', as Morris put it. The evangelical demand for simplicity was stated forcefully by the Belgian designer Henry van de Velde (1863–1957) in his highly influential *Les Formules de la Beauté* (The Formulae of Beauty) through his fierce analysis of an ornate Meissen soup tureen full of extraneous curves and extravagant decoration: 'Our reason is insulted by such lies, by such follies'. Van de Velde was introduced to the ideas of Ruskin and Morris by Finch in 1892, leading him away from painting to the decorative arts. In Van de Velde's designs for furniture, silver, tapestries and interiors, as well as ceramics, he attempts to reconfigure from first principles. In his cutlery designs of 1903 each handle was made differently as each would be held differently; so in 1905 the teapot lid for a porcelain service for Meissen has a sweeping extra tongue that fits into the handle to prevent movement. His keen interest in engineering led him to state in 1901 that 'The same laws which guide the work of an engineer also guide ornamentation'. It was a progressive naturalism: Van de Velde was not trying to invoke the heady metamorphic forces of Art Nouveau where forms and images appear unstable. Rather he was

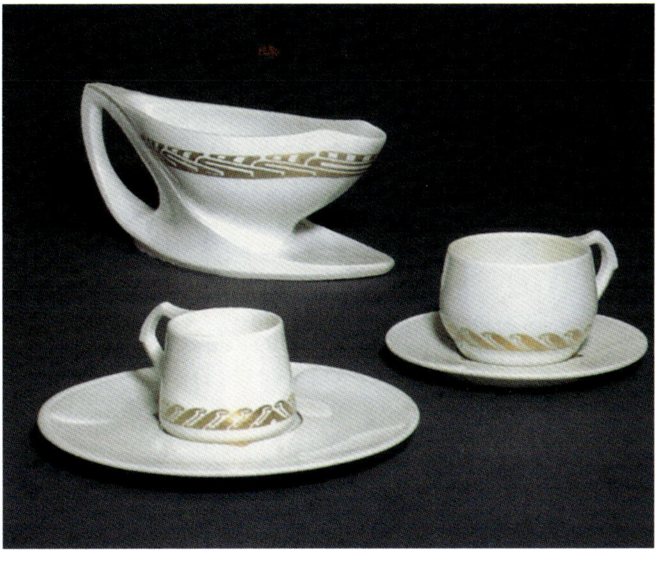

36 **Henry van de Velde**, tableware designed for Meissen, 1903.
With his tablewares there is an obvious manifestation of what a contemporary critic described as a 'a rhythmic interlacing of line, a circumspection of form, a purely musically experienced variation of figures, a flow of movement. It is the most strongly architectonically experienced ornament of the whole modern movement.' Here Van de Velde was using strongly articulated form in an attempt to make lines of force visible.

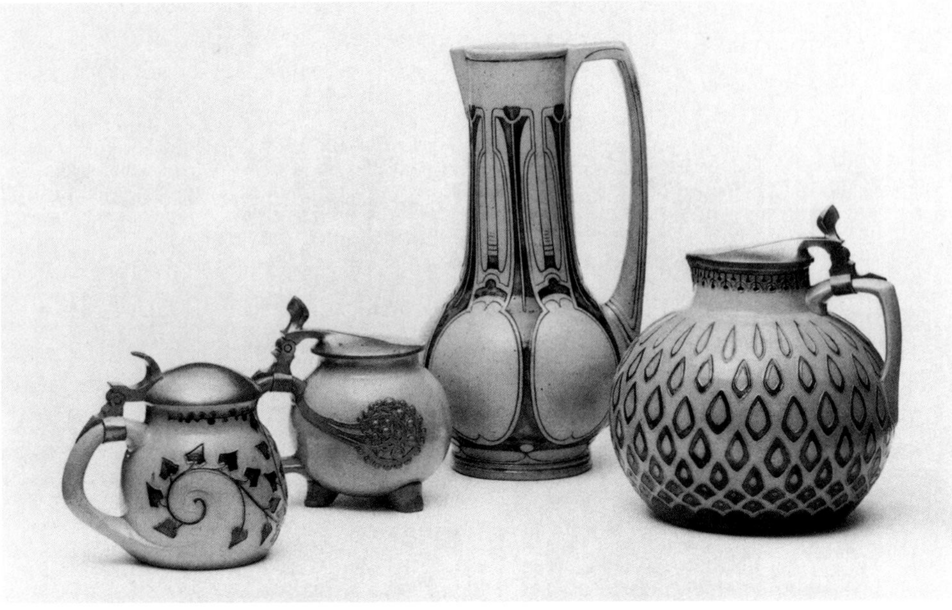

37 **Richard Riemerschmid**, tankards, 1902 and 1903, **Peter Behrens**, jug, 1904 (stoneware, salt-glazed and with enamel respectively; max. h. 24.6 cm/ 9⅝ in).
'The practical object does not seem any longer entirely subservient to mere utility, but combines therewith a certain degree of pleasure.' Peter Behrens, 1901

attempting to connect his engineer's sense of structure with the skeletal structure within a natural object: his ceramics are eviscerated forms.

A founding member of the influential Deutscher Werkbund (German Work Federation), Van de Velde also established the School of Applied Arts in Weimar from which sprang Walter Gropius's Bauhaus in 1919. His presence signified the direct links between the emerging architect-designers whose influence spanned Art Nouveau and industrial design.

The need to revitalize traditional forms and decoration led the stoneware companies at Hohr Grezhausen in the Westerwald district of Germany to employ the designers Richard Riemerschmid (1868–1957) and Peter Behrens (1868–1940). In doing so they were following a pattern across Europe of all kinds of manufacturers bringing in architects and designers to bring new life to standard designs. There were no technical innovations – the factories still used salt-glazed stoneware with ribbed and moulded decorations and pewter mounts – but the results were startlingly fresh, with rhythmical patterns accentuating the forms. These were designs for rich craft traditions, and both Riemerschmid and Behrens seemed sensitive to working with the traditions. This sensitivity reveals much about these designers: design was seen to be at the core of the matrix of the different worlds of education, handicraft, art and industry. The 'demands of aesthetic expression in handwork, and industry's need for an artistic impulse' were to be addressed through radical new schools of applied arts.

Ceramics and interiors: Vienna and Prague

Architects also led change elsewhere. Vienna saw, in the words of Kirk Varnedoe, 'the conquest of applied art by architecture.' In the crucible of Viennese art the idea of the *Gesamtkunstwerk*, the total work of art, grew powerful. The *Gesamtkunstwerk* demanded that that the whole environment in which one lived should be

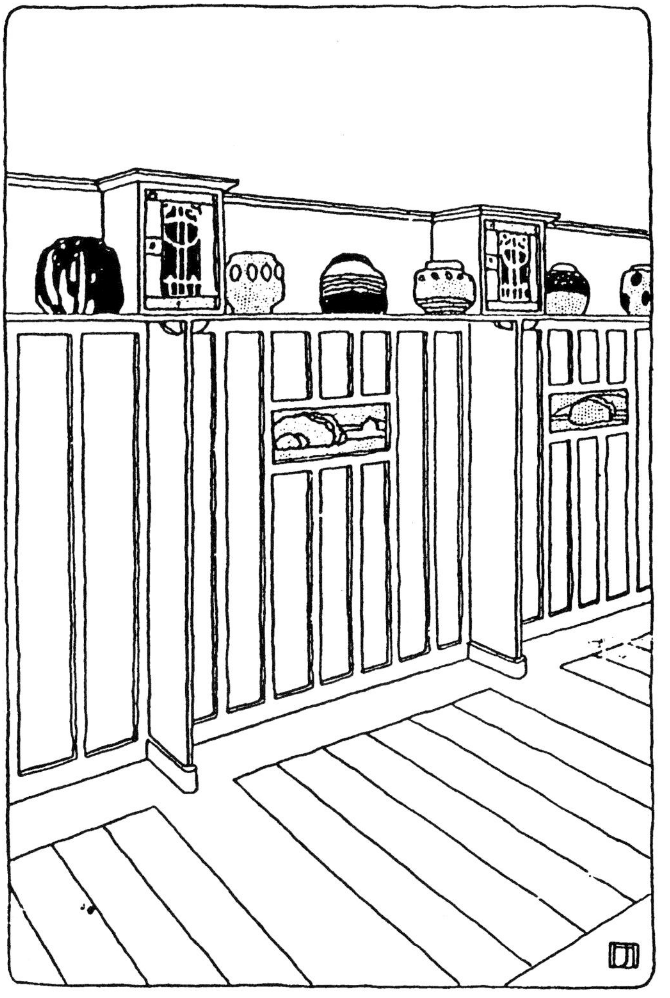

38 **Josef Hoffmann**, design for ceramics in a house.
'So long as our cities, our houses, our rooms, our furniture, our effects, our clothes and our jewelry, so long as our language and feelings fail to reflect the spirit of our times in a plain, simple and beautiful way, we shall be infinitely behind our ancestors.' Wiener Werkstätte Manifesto, 1905

designed as a piece, that there should be harmony between exterior and interior, furnishings, paintings, ceramics – even clothing would contribute to an almost operatic intensity of aesthetic living. While people would animate these spaces, the objects they used would act as a sort of living still life. Architects were held to be the impresarios of these works of art. The foundation in 1903 of the Wiener Werkstätte, the Vienna Workshops, by the painter and designer Koloman Moser (1868–1918) and the architect-designer Josef Hoffmann (1870–1956) was to shape this concept. Their aim was unequivocal: 'We wish to establish intimate contact between public, designer and craftsman, and to produce good, simple domestic requisites... usefulness is our first requirement.' In practice, the Wiener Werkstätte was driven by anything but such Ruskinian evangelism and soon Hoffmann had to concede that 'it is absolutely no longer to convert the masses. But then it is all the more our duty to make happy those few who turn to us.' The applied arts were to be unhampered by the need either to proselytise – or the need to be seen as cheap. Such economies were at the expense of the worker and 'we... regard it as our highest duty to return him to a position in which he can take pleasure in his labour and lead a life in keeping with human dignity.' Behind this sense of duty was the fierce aspiration that 'the work of the art craftsman is to be measured by the same yardstick as that of the painter and sculptor.' The production line was banished, and each worker was to sign what they made. 'Usefulness' was never really a determinant within this world: objects were selected for their symbolic weight, and materials were often lavish.

39, 40 **Jutta Sika**, Mocha service, c. 1901 (porcelain plate, d. 24.9 cm/9¾ in). 'Jutta Sika's coffee and tea service is original in form and decoration; without depending on the help of a border, it is relaxed and light in form and ornament', wrote a critic in 1902. These designs, with their severe pierced handles echoing the dots of the abstracted decoration and their placing of the cup off the centre of the saucer, were conceived to be part of the new drama of the domestic. This can be seen by their incorporation into **Carl Moll**'s painting *Breakfast* (1903) depicting a scene in a Hoffmann villa.

This interest in the display and presentation of ceramics led to some remarkable experiments. At the most simple level Hoffmann was to design coherent shelves and niches for the integral display of ceramics within his buildings, rather than placing the ceramics in separate vitrines. Functional tableware, too, was to receive the same attention as architecture: each place setting was conceived as a discrete installation. Moser was active in designing these kind of architecturally influenced ceramics and also in making links between young designers and the ceramics industry.

To launch their new showroom in 1906 the Wiener Werkstätte mounted an exhibition, *Der Gedeckte Tisch* (The Laid Table), in which several tables were themed for a birthday, wedding, artists' gathering and so on, with tableware, cutlery and

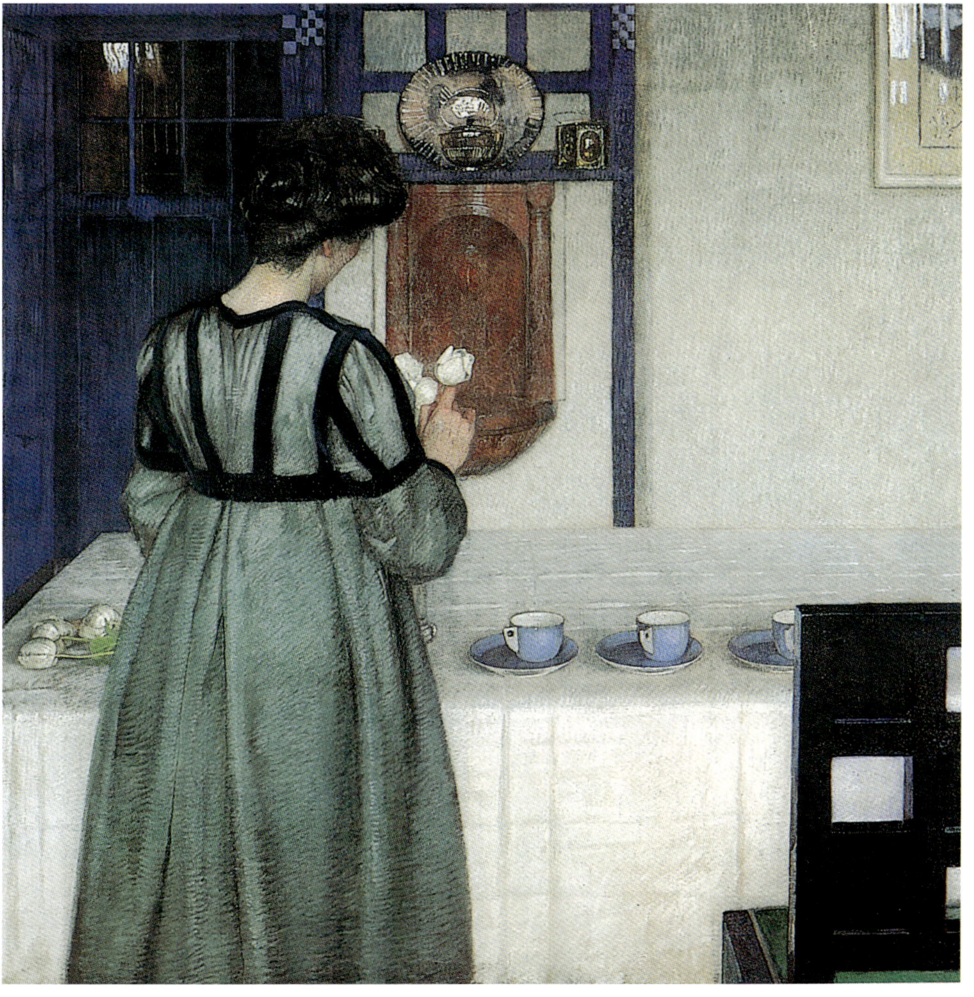

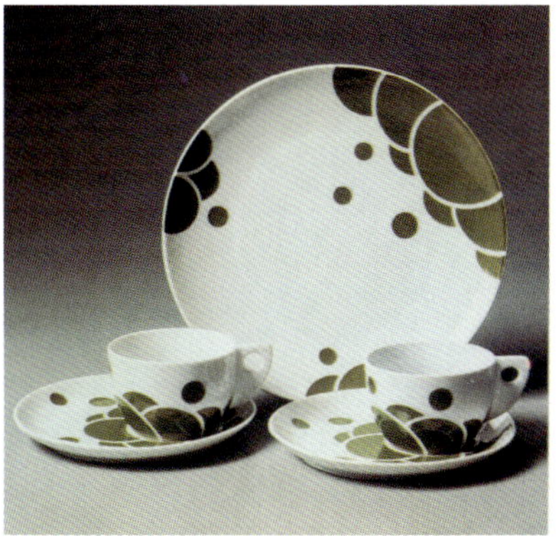

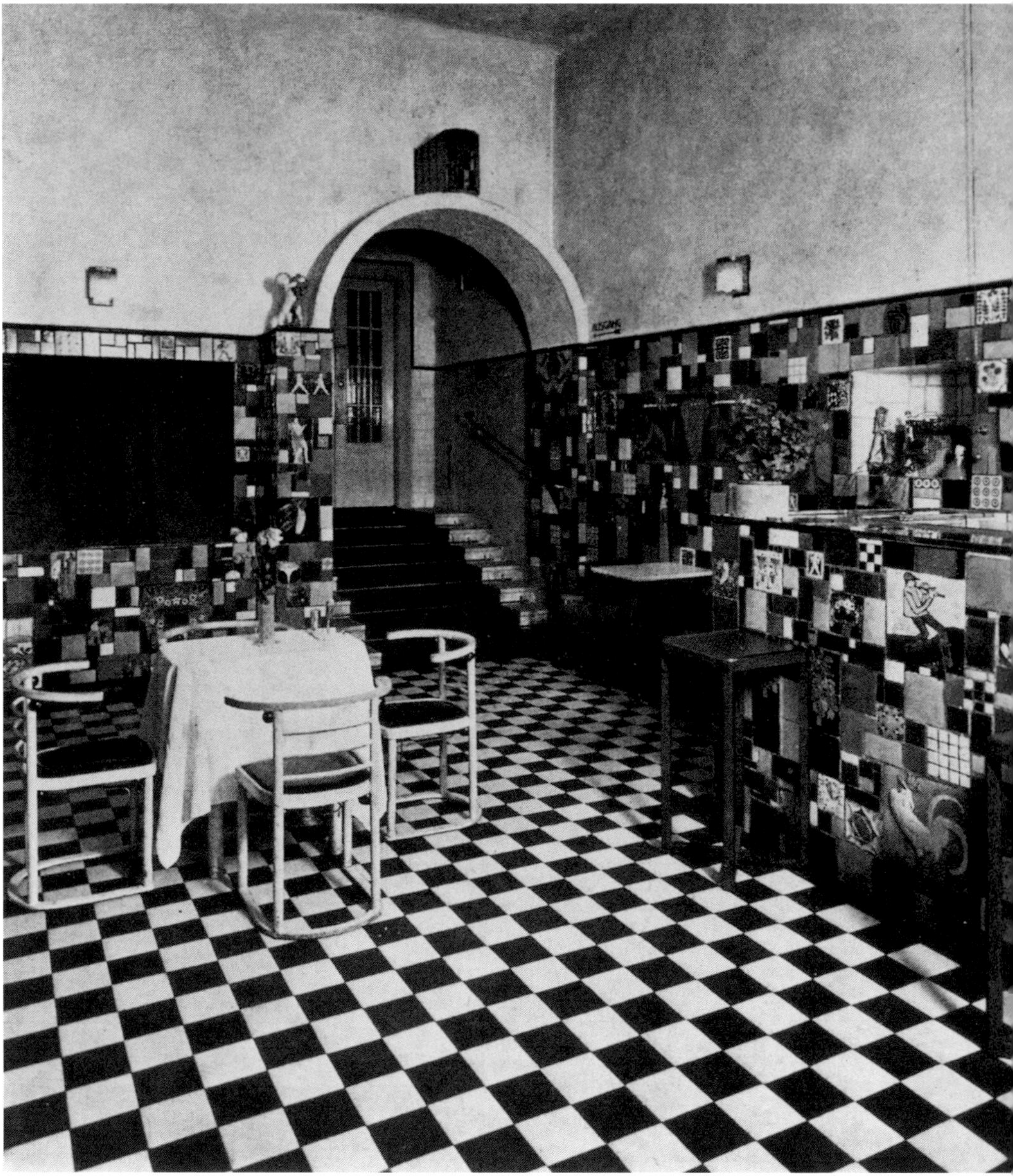

41 **Josef Hoffmann**, Cabaret Fledermaus, view of the foyer and bar, 1907.
Seven thousand maiolica tiles made up a continuous frieze of ornamental design, caricatures and mythical animals. According to the critic Ludwig Hevesi, writing in 1909, it was 'as colourful as colourful can be, as fantastic as fantasy. An irregular mosaic... seemingly composed at random.' It was nicknamed the 'paperhangers' nightmare'.

42 **Michael Powolny**, 'Autumn' and 'Spring' putti, *c.* 1910 (stoneware).
The putti hold cascading swags in dramatic Secessionist black and white – playful historicist 'Kleinkunst' for the cabinets of the well-off patrons of the Wiener Werkstätte. It was to this kind of ceramics that contemporary experiments in Prague were to respond so vigorously.

flower arrangements. Moser even designed the food: according to a sceptical critic, 'the dumplings are hand-turned by a craftsman and the only stylistically pure black-and-white desserts are the poppy-seed puddings improved by Koloman Moser... here madness marries geometry.' The 'symphonic' nature of the *Gesamtkunstwerk* was closely scrutinized. This can be seen in the creation of the Cabaret Fledermaus in 1907. Hoffmann designed this café-theatre as an informal headquarters for the Viennese avant-garde, a place that staged modern dance, semi-surreal masked plays against a background as vivid as the performances. It was this element of the dramatic and the fantastic that was to lead away from the austerities of Hoffmann's early work towards what became known as Viennese whimsy.

The Wiener Werkstätte provided the model for the foundation of the Artěl Co-operative in Prague in 1908. It comprised a group of architects and designers in the vanguard of a progressive nationalism. Since the turn of the century there had been a call, in the words of the architect Jan Kotera (1871–1923), to open the windows into Europe and to free Prague from Vienna: 'the creation of space and construction,

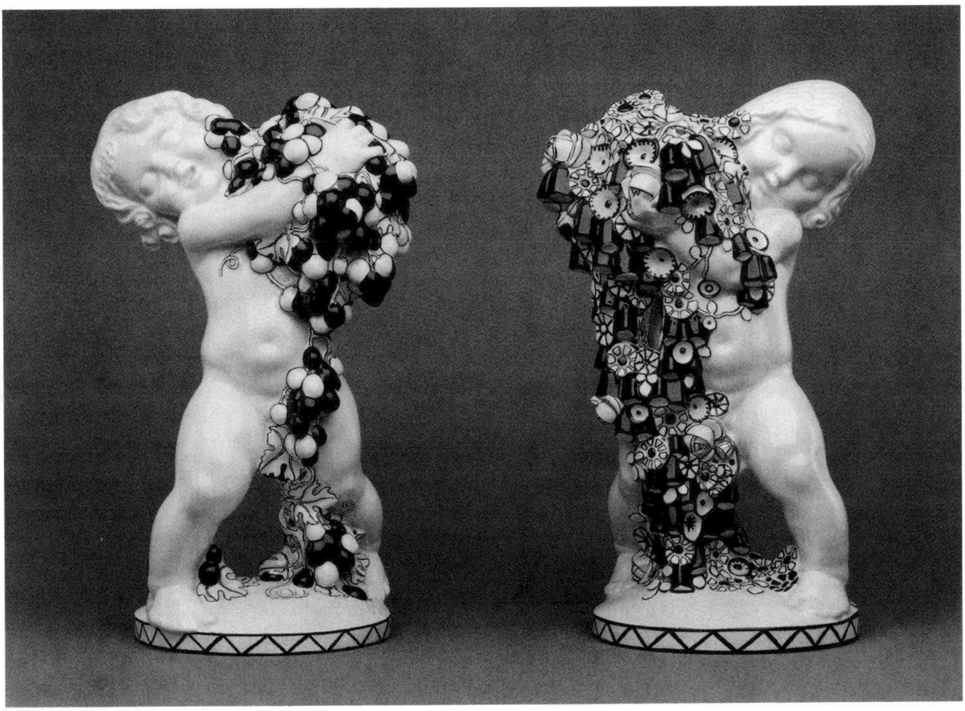

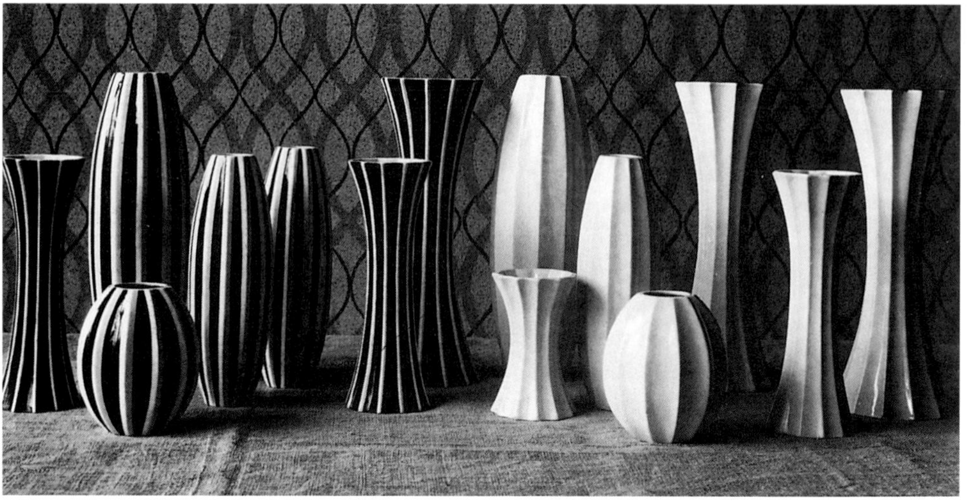

43 **Pavel Janák**, vases, 1911 (contemporary photograph). 'While architecture expresses plastically certain large entities and more complex encounters of forces, the candle holder, the bowl, and the jug offer an opportunity for simple dramatic situations, actions and volumes... which... provide the conditions to realize our cubist notion of matter and the volume of matter.' The stripping away of colour so that the hard cubist planes of these ceramics were revealed through shadow remains startling.

44 **Vlastislav Hofman**, ashtray, 1912 (earthenware, h. 4 cm/1⅝ in). Czechoslovakian Cubists translated some features of Cubist paintings (simplistic geometric forms, facets and angles) into the objects all around them. This ashtray was made while Hofman, who trained as an architect, was a member of the avant-garde Skupina Vytvarnych Umelcu (Group of Fine, or Plastic, Artists).

not shape and decoration, must be the purpose of the new movement.' As with many of these 'new movements', there was much proselytising and minting of manifestos. In contradistinction to the Wiener Werkstätte, Artěl's designs were tougher and more uncompromising, less in thrall to the lavish Viennese market: as Josef Chochol wrote in 1913,

We want to replace ornamentalism with an intellectualized vitality of form, and whatever we reject in decoration and ornament, we try to make up for by the power of concentrated and total effect. Its signs include a taste of a certain mathematical exactness, unpolished curtness and hearty roughness, which we prefer to the former starched quality of perfumed, fallow dandyisms and perversions, and the falsely naive geniality of the petite bourgeoisie.

In practice, this embracing of 'unpolished curtness' meant making objects on which to project the excitement of cubist design: the historicist tendencies of Vienna were to be disregarded too. The major protagonists of Artěl were architects for whom the applied arts were a testing ground for their theories. In Pavel Janák's (1882–1956) drawings for ceramics in his journals there is a wilful pushing at the boundaries of utility – even stability is dismissed. These are ceramics that not only prefigure Malevich's Suprematist vessels of 1923 [48] but also the idea of ceramic installation which would appear in the 1970s and 80s.

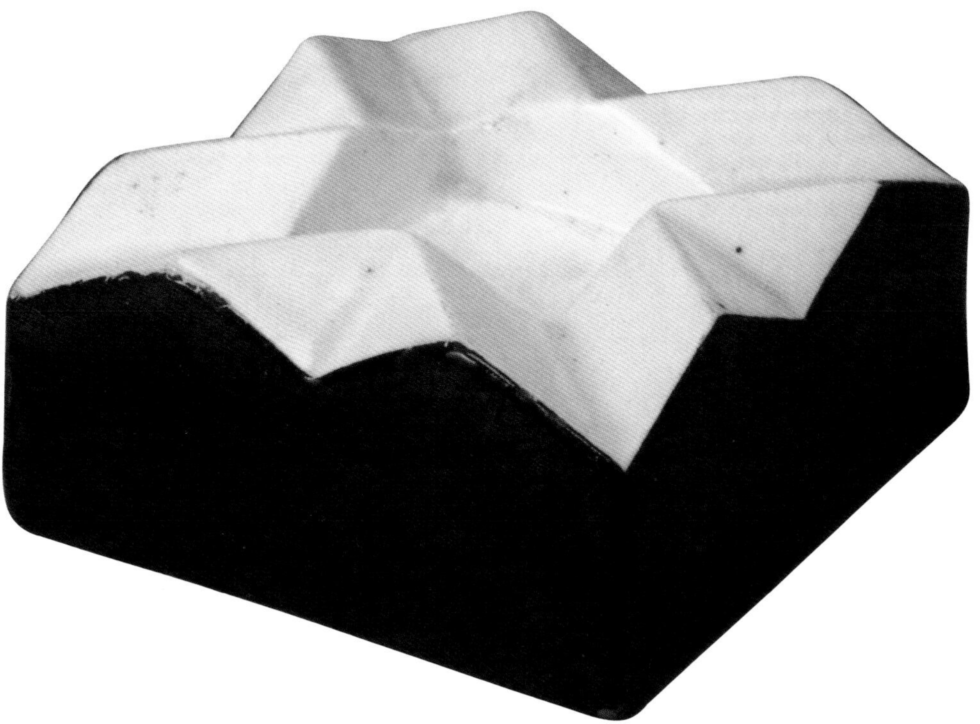

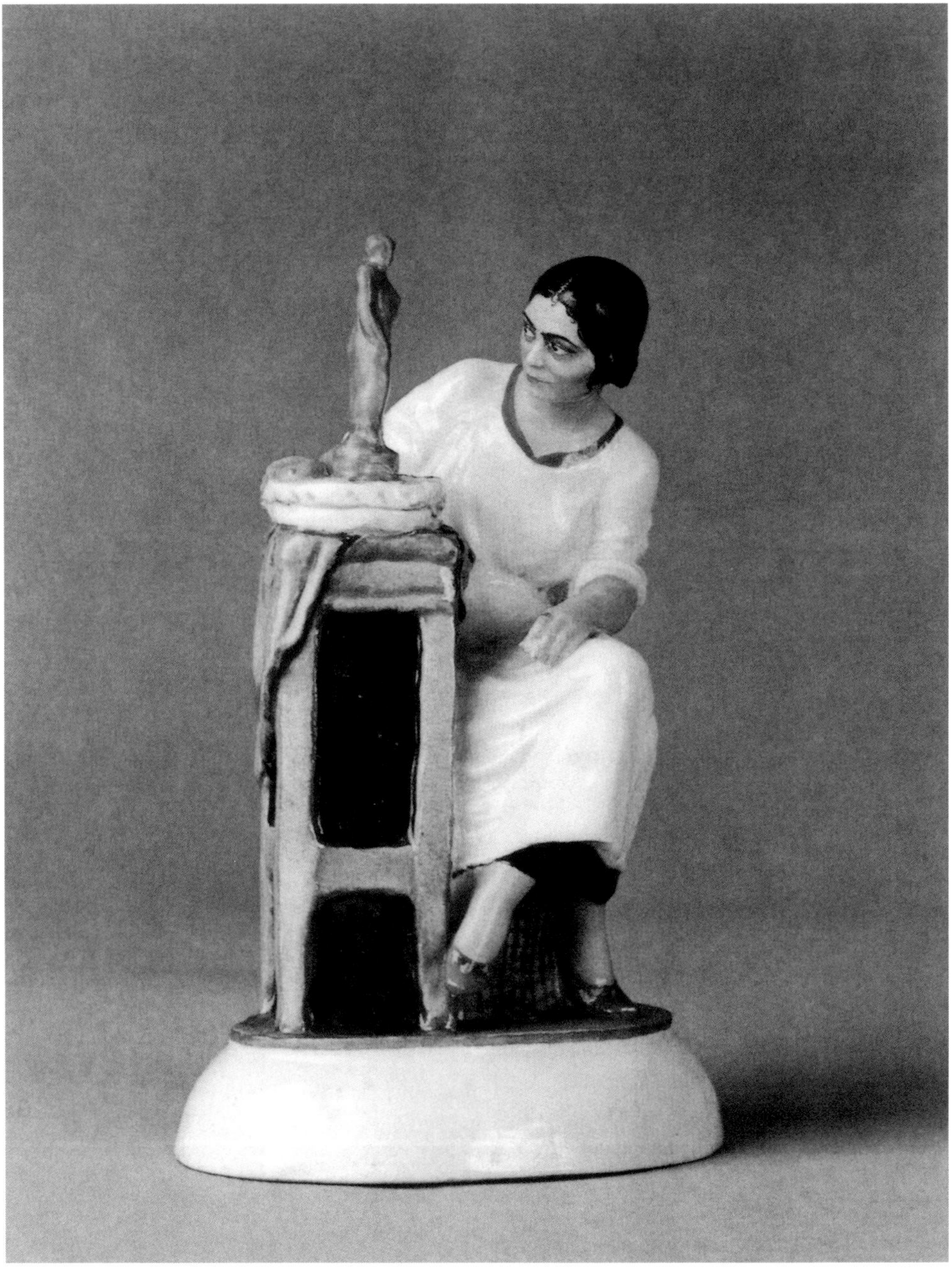

Chapter Two 1920–45

After the Russian Revolution: 'the parade of objects'

Ceramics between the two World Wars can be categorized as an era of manifestos and new groupings. From Soviet Russia to the Bauhaus of Weimar Germany, the *mingei* (folkcraft) movement of Japan to the social art movement of Sweden, quotidian objects were shown to be radical in their role in the 'organization of a new life'. Their means of production was radicalized too: potters, designers, architects and social commentators alike attempted to find new ways of making ceramics that fitted the age of unequivocal modernity. The relationship between art and industry had been scrutinized before; now the relationship became politicized.

Looking back at the early years of the Russian Revolution Anatoly Lunacharsky, the first Soviet People's Commissar for Education and head of the People's Committee for Public Enlightenment (Narkompros), a body responsible for the administration of both education and the arts, wrote:

It seemed that the great revolution in its titanic struggles ought to have utterly destroyed things of a brittle and fragile nature, things, like porcelain, which were totally alien to the great mass of the people. But this did not happen. One could only be amazed, by the care, one might even say gentleness, with which the great revolution protected things of artistic value, including the most breakable and fragile objects.

His pride in the way porcelain was valued in a time of civil war, chronic cultural upheaval and material shortages is indicative of how successful revolutionary ceramics were seen to be. The objects themselves became 'political representatives' of the new Soviet culture when shown abroad and treasured at home.

The role of art within Soviet revolutionary society was to agitate for the transformation of all aspects of life through the dissemination of propaganda. Lunacharsky involved artists directly in the planning of the regeneration of the applied arts and industry as well as in commissioning propaganda. The graphic arts and films were employed to express this new artistic language, while trains, ships and trucks were painted. Ceramics were to play a significant

45 **Natalya Danko**, *At Work* (self-portrait), mid-1920s. Danko was the principal figure modeller of the early Soviet epoch. Her iconic figures chronicled the characters of the time: the poet Anna Akhmatova, partisans, sailors with banners.

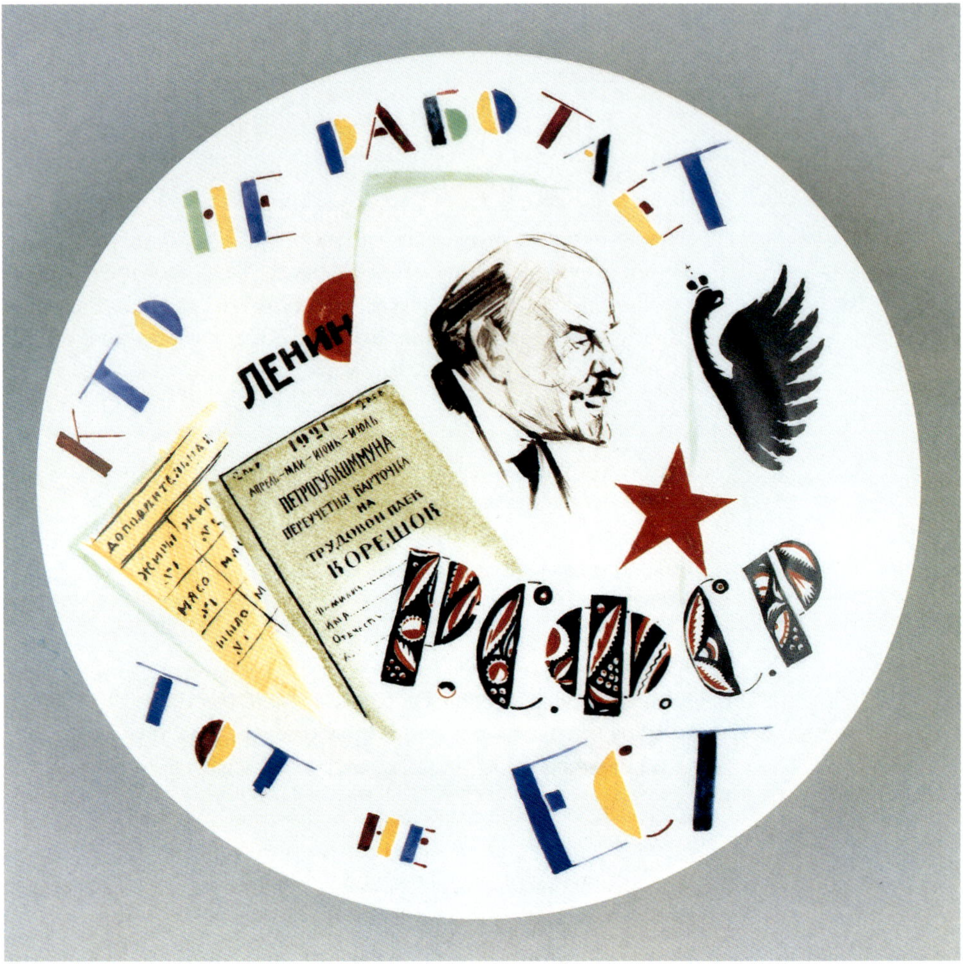

46 **Mikhail M. Adamovich**, *He who does not work does not eat*, 1921 (porcelain, d. 25 cm/10 in). Lenin is shown surrounded by ration cards, the monogram of the state, a red star and part of the Imperial eagle. In the prototype the red star obliterated the eagle; in subsequent versions the painters evidently felt that it was a shame to cover up such a good symbol and left it exposed.

part in this agitation. Within two months of the October Revolution in 1917 the Imperial Porcelain Factory in St Petersburg, founded in the eighteenth century to produce porcelain exclusively for the court, was renamed the State Porcelain Factory and reorganized to 'serve and not alienate the state'. Soon its remit was transferred to Narkompros. The artists and sculptors who worked there were classed as workers and were allowed to stay on. Coupled to the fact that the State Porcelain Factory had a huge stock of porcelain blanks from its previous incarnation, this meant that the 'porcelain nursery for a new state' had an impeccable foundation. It also meant that many of the greatest pieces of agitprop are marked with the monogram of the Tsar.

Pieces were made to commemorate the festivals and anniversaries of the new republic, figures were sculpted to symbolize the new types of worker. Slogans and aphorisms from Marx, Ruskin, Cicero and the Gospels were pressed into service on plates: 'Struggle gives birth to heroes', 'He who is not with us is against us'. After a report in 1920 to Narkompros, artists were encouraged to express subjects as diverse as 'modern life and ideas; daily life and culture; story-telling, epics and poetry; local interests and local life; social types and costumes.' Particularly appropriate images from folklore were corralled to emphasize themes of eternal Russia and motherhood.

This chronicle of Soviet life was the focus of the sculptor Natalya Danko (1892–1942). She worked on ceramic architectural reliefs for the Russian pavilions at the Turin International Exhibition and the Rome World Exhibition of 1910–11 before joining the Imperial Porcelain Factory in 1914, subsequently running its sculpture workshop from 1919 until her death. Genre figurines of artisans had been popular in the nineteenth century, but Danko's subjects were cooperative farmers, dockers, soldiers and sailors, partisans, women sewing banners, a factory worker making a speech: all the panoply of revolutionary activity. These pieces were hugely popular – *The*

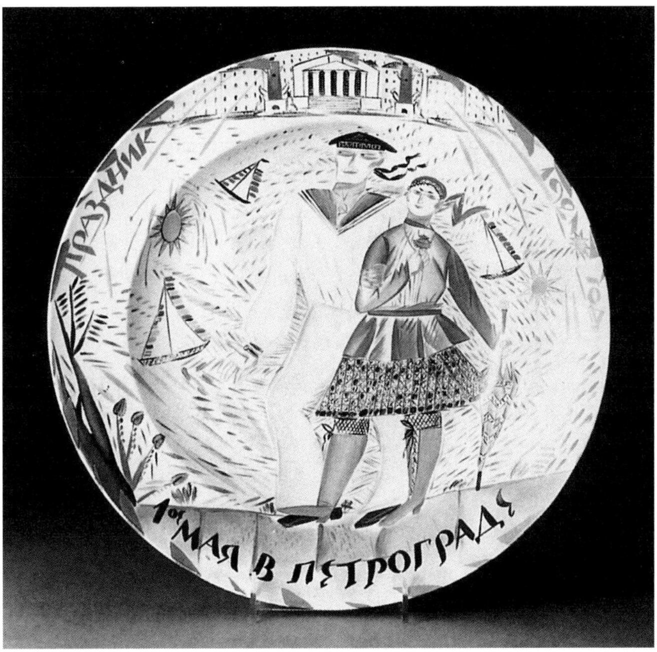

47 **Alexandra Shchekotikhina-Pototskaya** (1892–1967), *The Sailor Takes a Walk*, 1921 (porcelain, d. 34.5 cm/13⅝ in). Her designs for the factory essentially affirm an almost mythic Russianness: her figures are given religious or folkloric overtones. Peasant women are seen like madonnas surrounded with motifs of growth and abundance, the flatness of perspective connecting the images to the icon tradition.

Partisan was bought in quantity by the Red Army to be handed out in the place of medals. The success of Danko's work lay partly in its contemporaneity – she modelled subjects of the moment, responding to a famine, to an influx of gypsies into Leningrad one summer, or to a particular congress. Her most complex piece was the *Red and White Chess Set* of 1922. The Red pawns are modelled as workers at harvest, the Red Queen a peasant with a sheaf of corn and the Red King as a worker with a sledgehammer. Unsurprisingly, the White pawns become workers in chains, the White Queen is a demi-mondaine with a cornucopia of gold and the White King becomes a skeleton. This was made to be exhibited and sold abroad to raise much needed hard currency – and to show the artistic credentials of the new state.

Sometimes the demands of agitprop seemed to be at variance with the decorative impulses of the artists at the State Porcelain Factory. Sergei Chekhonin (1878–1936), the first artistic director of the Factory, was keen to bring in artistic innovation but was not driven by a programmatic ideology and was not above reusing pre-revolutionary designs if they fitted. Gregory Zimin (1875–1958), who had worked at the Imperial Factory since 1893, simply went on painting as before, inserting farming implements into his classicized landscapes. The wide and eclectic range of stylistic treatments of this porcelain – often incorporating both fragmented avant-garde patterning and highly conventional framing devices – reveals how free the factory was from outside interference. There are plates with elaborate cobalt-blue borders and complex interlacings of flowers and fruit surrounding gilded Soviet symbols: futurist motifs jostle with the classical. This also meant that there were artists at the factory whose work was distinctly heterodox.

For the Suprematists the whiteness of porcelain made it an ideal material for their experiments in 'economic geometry', forms that through their balance of masses and articulation of volume were intended to be free from any historic or stylistic reference. White symbolized weightlessness and carried a sense of the absolute. The founder and leading theoretician of the Suprematists Kazimir Malevich (1878–1935) attempted to create in three dimensions what had first been drawn as idealized architectural studies. Both Nikolai Suetin (1897–1954) and Malevich made designs at the State Porcelain Factory in 1922–23, Suetin decorating plates and coffee services with Suprematist designs. When these were shown at the Paris Exposition in 1925, they were to be a revelation for the Italian Futurist potter Tullio

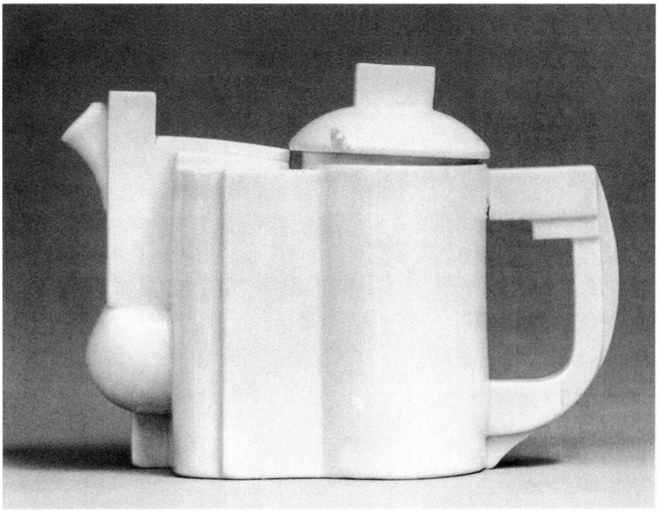

48 **Kazimir Malevich**, *Suprematist Teapot*, 1923 (earthenware, h. 16.5 cm/6½ in). Like his half-cup (a divided cup form with an angular rectangle plane for a handle), the *Suprematist Teapot* is not so much a functional object, but rather a study in how to achieve dynamic tension between complex forms.

d'Albisola and lead him towards 'Aeroceramica', Futurist ceramics (see pp. 76–78).

Agitprop and Suprematist porcelain was produced in small numbers and its impact on Lunacharsky's 'great mass of the people' was limited. In the winter of 1919–20 Narkompros organized a competition, 'Crockery for All', asking artists to submit designs for mass production. In the newspaper of the Soviet Young Communist League on 28 July 1928 there appeared an article entitled 'What do we want from a plate?' The first answer was that 'we want it to be right for its purpose, that is for serving food, we want it to be of good quality and style. These are the first requirements of an ordinary china plate.' But the article went on,

all is not well... Both sides forget, or at least play down, the educational significance of the things that surround us, and the role they play in the organization of a new life, a new man, a new society... The cultural revolution, like the buglers' trumpet, is summoning for examination and revaluation everything which mobilizes or poisons our consciousness, our will and our readiness for battle! In this 'parade' of objects there are no non-combatants – nor can there be! Plates and cups, i.e. things we see daily, several times a day, which can do their bit for the organization of our consciousness – these occupy an important place. We demand that a plate should fulfil its social function. We demand that the role of everyday objects should not be forgotten by our young... artists and the bodies in charge of our industry.

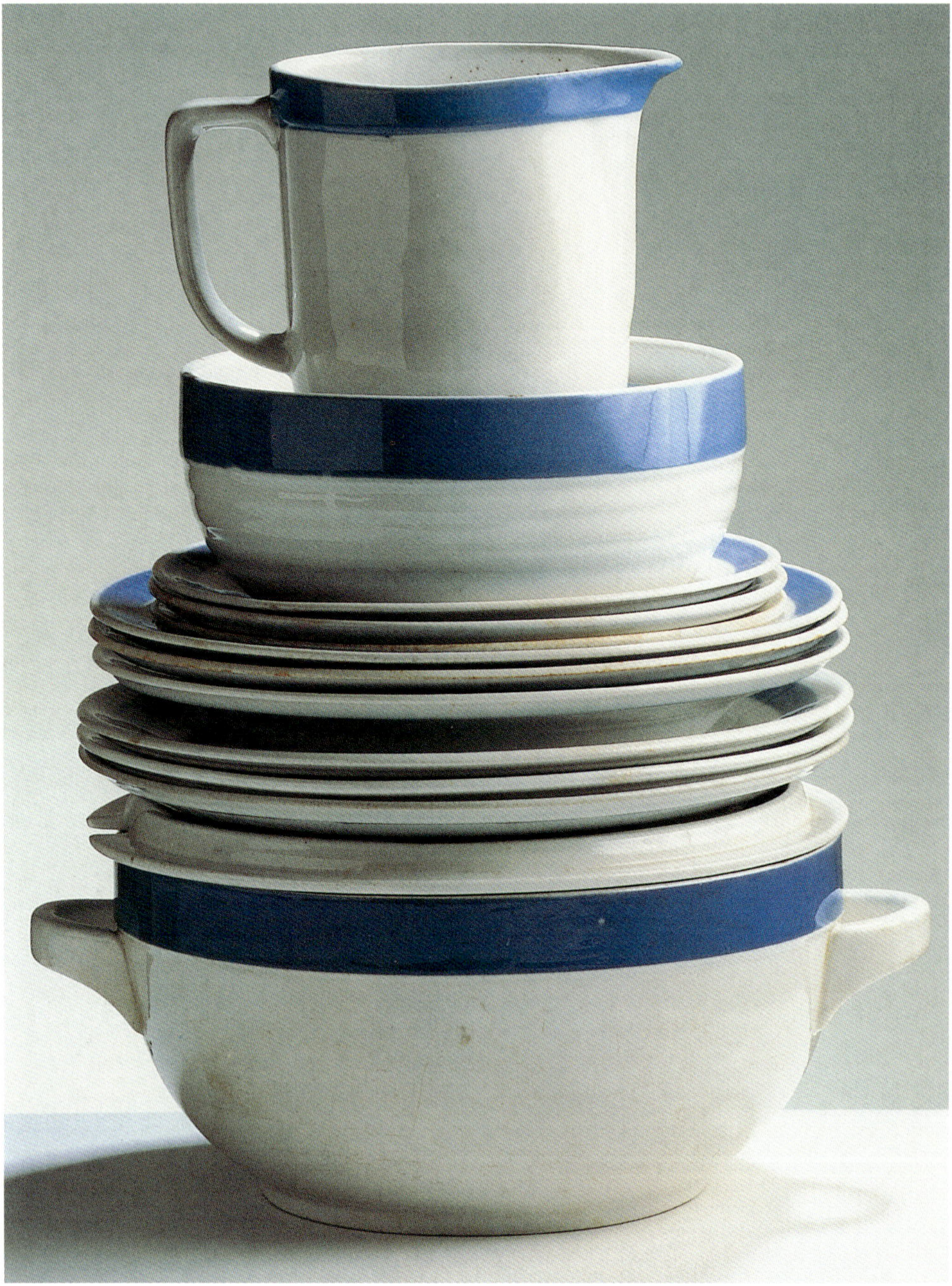

Scandinavia

It was not only in Soviet Russia that the social responsibility of the artist and designer was the imperative. At the 1917 Stockholm *Hemutställningen* (Home Exhibition) organized by the Svenska Slöjdföreningen (Swedish Society of Industrial Design), twenty-three interiors were displayed with the explicit aim of showing how to solve the problems of cramped and impoverished contemporary urban living. Furnishings were designed to be affordable for the ordinary working man: this was to be the meeting point of practicality, beauty and economy. For this seminal exhibition the young Wilhelm Kåge (1889–1960), in his first year as a designer for the Gustavsberg factory, created the *Liljeblå* service, quickly known as the *Arbetarservis* (Workers' Service). The exhibition helped to foster a growing enthusiasm for a new place for the arts as a vehicle for societal change. In 'Vackrare Vardagsvara' (More Beautiful Things for Everyday Use, 1919), a document that became central for this generation, the Danish critic and lighting designer Gregor Paulsson made this impassioned plea:

Dear craftsmen friends! How can you expect us to go on respecting you, while this swindle continues in the name of art, and while you ignore all your obligations to the modern world? WE have no proper tumblers, plates, water-sets, spoons, knives, or forks, while richer homes are flooded with trash and rubbish at fantastic prices! Think a little, and consider your obligations to make things for the delight of your fellow men in their daily life! Throw away your artists' berets and bow-ties and get into overalls!

49 **Kurt Ekholm** (1907–75), *Sinivalko* (Blue ribbon) service for Arabia Finland, 1936.
Born in Finland, Ekholm studied in Stockholm, Sweden, where he became influenced by the prevailing interest in functionalism. Like Wilhelm Kåge's *Praktika* service for Gustavsberg of 1932, it uses the appearance of function as a guiding aesthetic. It features bowls that can stack or double as covers for side dishes, and has overtones of cheerful informality.

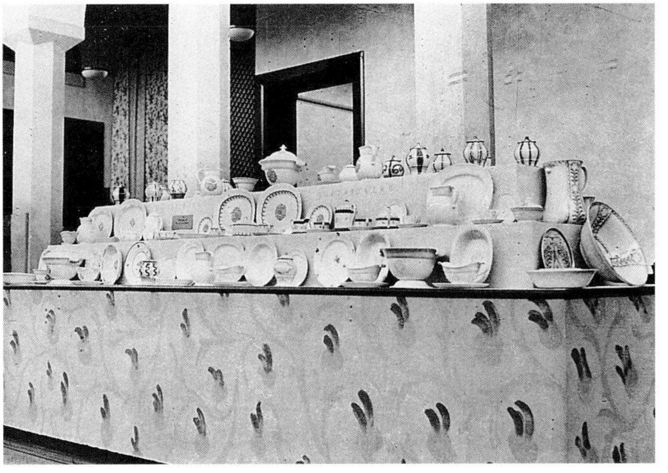

50 Photograph of ceramics from **Gustavsberg** displayed at the Liljevalchs Art Gallery, Stockholm, 1917, including the *Liljeblå* service by Wilhelm Kåge.

In Scandinavian ceramics of the 1920s and 30s this impetus was given momentum by factories such as the Arabia factory in Finland giving studio potters their own ateliers. There was also governmental help: the development of studio ceramics in Denmark owes much to the establishment of the Kunsthåndværkerskolen (school of craftsmen) in Copenhagen in 1930. However it was the influence of the small Saxbo workshop that continued in production from 1929 to 1968, and headed by Nathalie Krebs (1895–1978), that was most substantial. Saxbo became renowned for its subtly modulated Orientally inspired glazes over strong, simple forms. Saxbo was the training ground for many of the leading Scandinavian ceramicists. Alongside Krebs were a number of collaborators, principally Eva Staehr-Nielsen (1911–76) who threw many of the forms, and Axel Salto (1889–1961) who spent two years working with Krebs in the early 1930s.

The appearance of function and the actual performance of an object are quite distinct. At the 1930 Stockholm Exhibition the designs of Ewald Dahlskog (1894–1950) were described as 'functionalist'. Shown in London a year later, they profoundly influenced the British architect and designer Keith Murray (1892–1981), whose work for Wedgwood reveals this debt. This 'functionalism', apparent in Murray's basalt and moss-green lathe turned vases, bowls and boxes, meant that the work could be employed didactically as examples of good ceramic design by an architect. A handbook for children, *The Things We See*, stated: 'Simplicity, economy, precision and geometric harmony are the

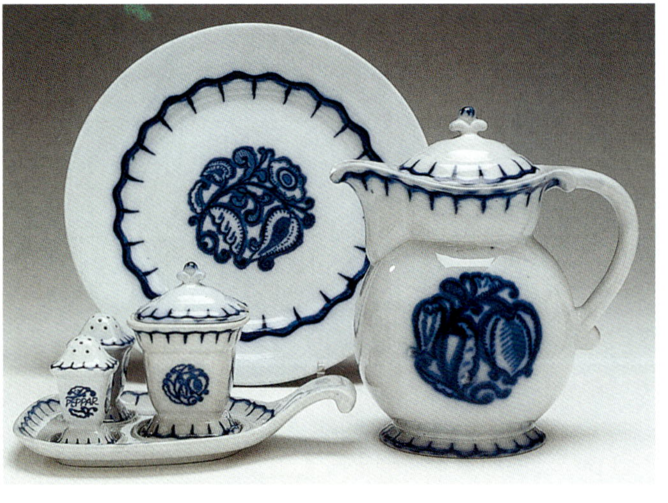

51 **Wilhelm Kåge**, *Liljeblå* (Blue Lily) service (also known as *Arbetarservis*, Workers' Service) for Gustavsberg, 1917. The service was of strong and simple forms made from earthenware with bold printed blue and white decoration to avoid costly hand-painting. Unsurprisingly, with its unimpeachable aura of the functional and vernacular, its reduction of the extraneous in form and decoration, the service made its appeal to the critics rather than to the workers.

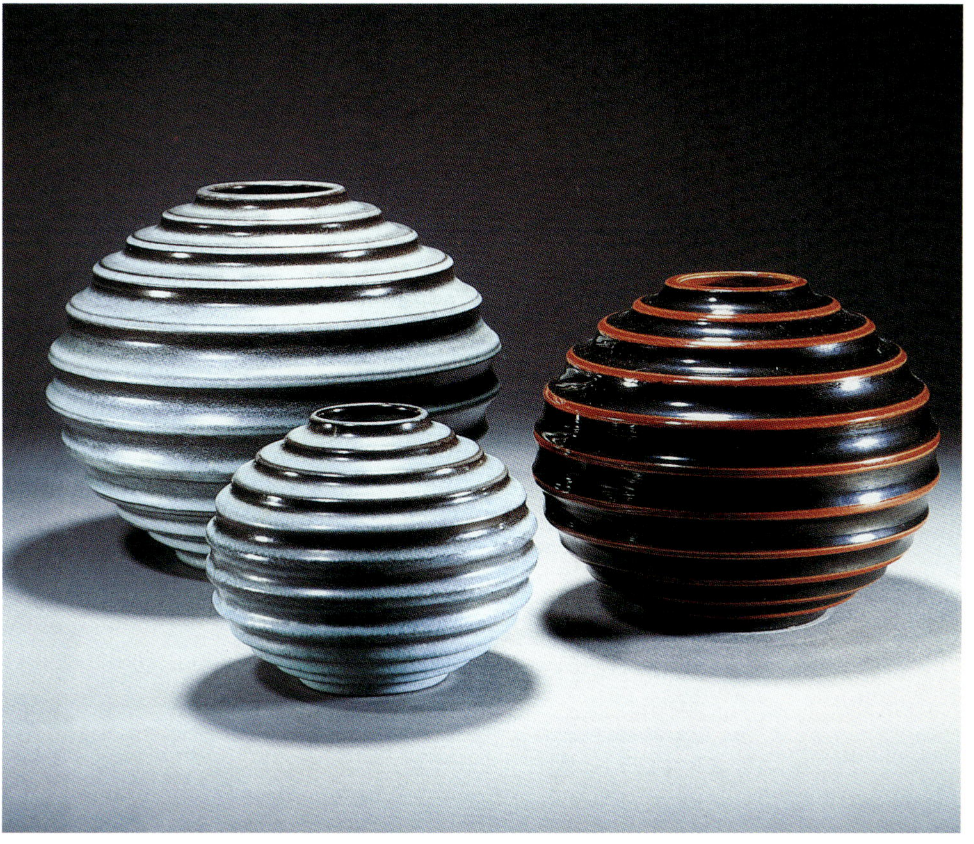

chief qualities exhibited. The clay forms suggest machine processes and have an austere and dignified beauty.' Both Murray's and Dahlskog's vases have only a toehold in the world of actual function, but in their stylization of elements from industrial production they reveal an interesting new possibility: commodities – often inessential – that could look like necessities.

52 **Ewald Dahlskog**, vases for the Bo Fajans factory (earthenware), *c.* 1930.
These vases were exhibited at the important Stockholm Exhibition of 1930, where the new Scandinavian design ideology became internationally recognized. His vases showed highly ribbed surfaces reminiscent of electrical transformers and were described as 'functionalist' in the Swedish press.

The Bauhaus

Walter Gropius, a radical architect and member of the Deutscher Werkbund (German Work Federation), was made the Director of the Bauhaus in Weimar in 1919. The Bauhaus was an amalgamation of the existing School of Arts and Crafts and the Academy of Fine Arts: its aim was to bring together the arts under the symbolic aim of 'Bauen', building. Handicrafts were to be the basis of all the teaching: the hierarchy of apprentice–journeyman–master was modelled on the medieval crafts. In each discipline there was to be both a Master of Form and a Master of Craft: according to Gropius's manifesto this would 'raze the arrogant wall between artist and artisan, and clear the way for the new building of the future.' There was, he admitted, a practical reason to work with two teachers too: 'since there were neither craftsmen with sufficient imagination to solve artistic problems nor artists with sufficient technical skills to take charge of workshop operations, a new generation first had to be trained who were able to combine both talents.' The teachers at the Bauhaus were a stellar grouping of talented artists (by 1922 Paul Klee, Oskar Schlemmer and Vasily Kandinsky were all Masters) and equally talented craftsmen. For the ceramics workshop, Gropius appointed Gerhard Marcks (1889–1981), a figurative sculptor with some experience in a porcelain factory, as Master of Form. Max Krehan, a traditional production potter, was appointed Master of Craft and the decision was made to use his workshop in Dornburg, 30 kilometres (19 miles) from Weimar. This meant that the ceramics students were exposed straight away to a busy, well equipped, functioning environment, learning how to throw pots, glaze and fire them while working on 'commercial firings' of pots to bring in money. It is not mere chance that the first Bauhaus designs for industry came from the ceramics workshops as the 'Dornburgers', removed from the febrile ideological intensities of the main part of the Bauhaus, proved themselves as 'down-to-earth' artists.

Bauhaus ceramics have a distinctive character. Earthenware was used, allowing for a clarity and hardness of profile: this meant that the pots could have convex rims or fine raised handles as sharp as any modern metal container. It was a clay body that did not warp, and this allowed for exact and complex combinations of components. Many of the pots exploit this aptness for creating objects expressive of structure above all things. Glazing was simple, with a single monochromatic glaze used on each pot, and brush decoration was rare. Theodor Bogler (1897–1968), a journeyman who took over the commercial side of the Workshop in 1924, used these possibilities with verve. His *Mocca machine* consists of no fewer than four components stacked together. Given the technical difficulty the Bauhaus had in actually producing quantities of any object, it was a useful presentational trope to display a unique object in a 'laboratory' situation and explain that it was a 'prototype for future mass production'. Lucia Moholy's photographs of Bauhaus objects often emphasized this.

53, 54 **Theodor Bogler**, Combination teapot, 1923 (h. 12.7 cm/5 in).
Bogler illustrated, in fine Bauhaus pedagogical style, how it was possible to create numerous variants from a set number of parts, echoing in ceramic form Gropius's idea of architecture as a 'large-scale building set.' They looked unequivocally modern and purposeful.

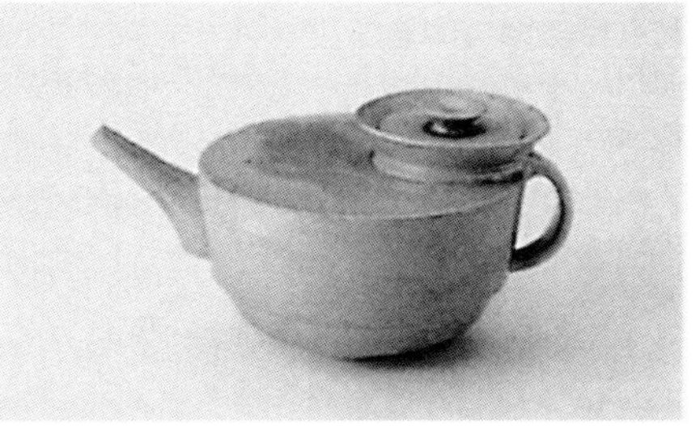

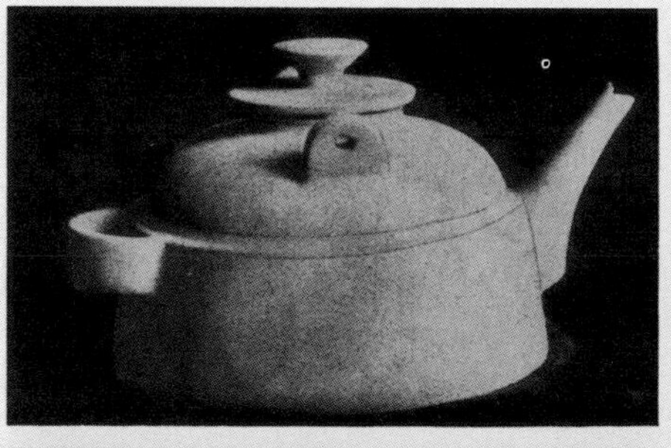

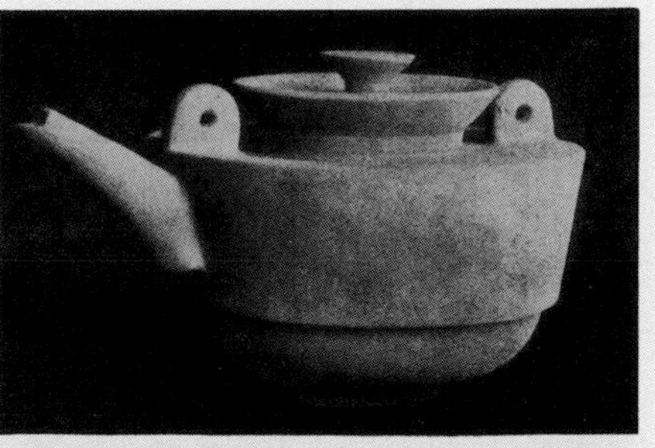

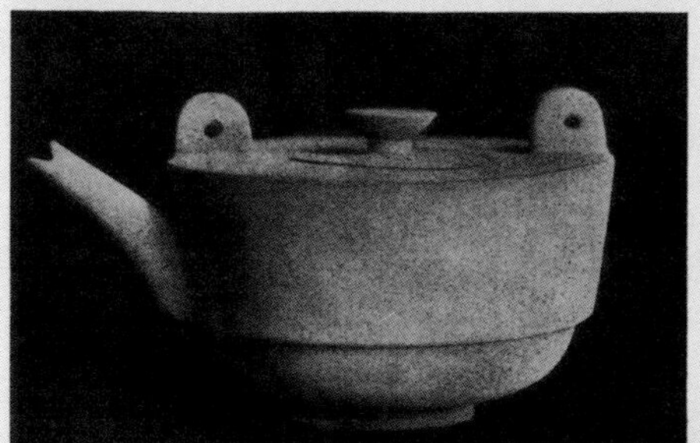

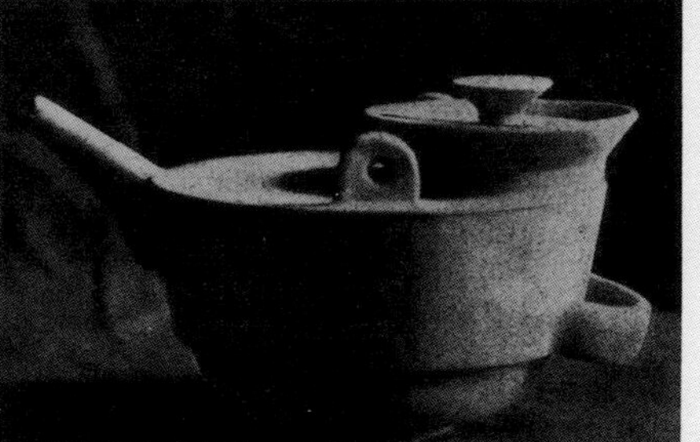

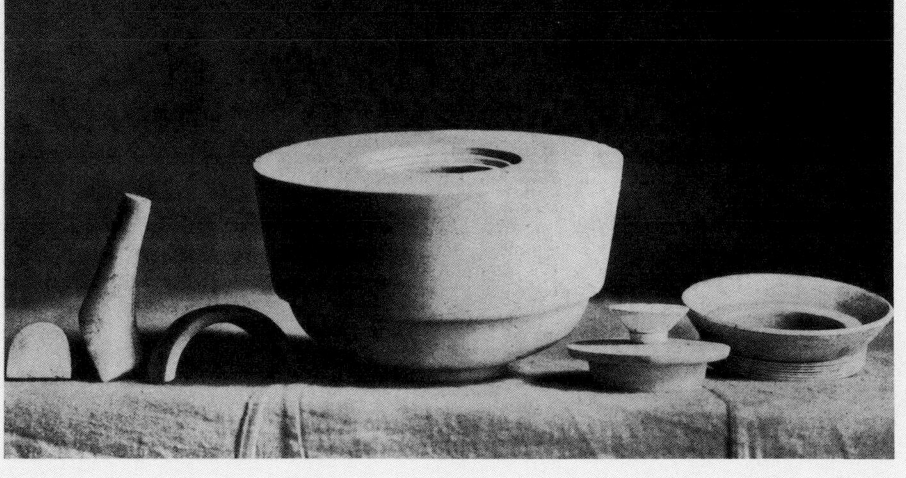

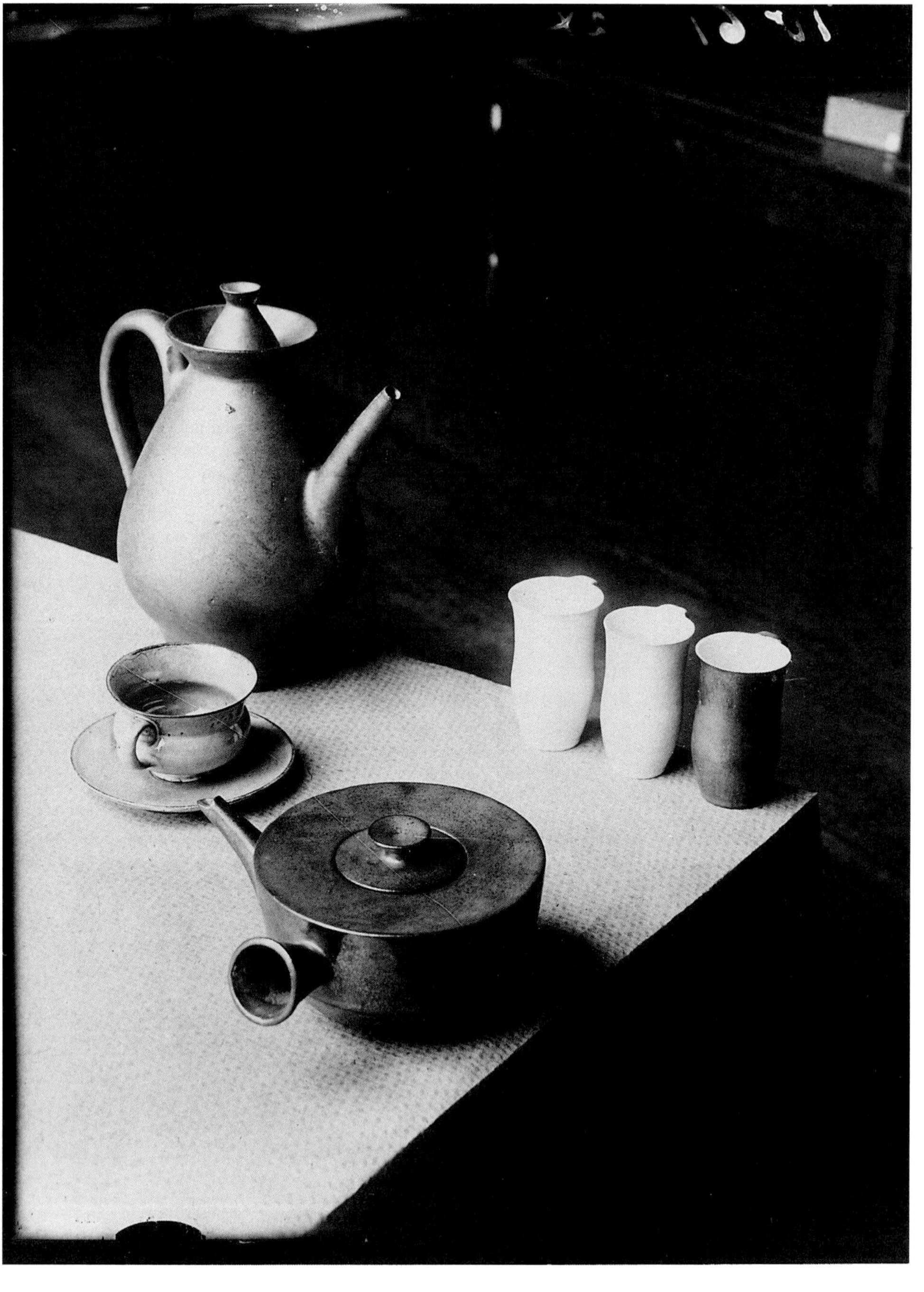

Gropius was clear on the possibilities. As he wrote to Marcks in 1923, 'Yesterday I had a look at your many new pots. Almost all of them are unique, unrepeatable; it would be positively wrong not to look at ways of making the hard work that has gone into them accessible to large numbers of people... We must find ways of duplicating some of the articles with the help of machines.' Marcks' reply shows a firmness of purpose against this imperative: 'We must keep in mind the fact that the Bauhaus is meant to be a place of education... We believe practical production is the right path towards this goal. But production must never be allowed to become the goal itself. Otherwise the Bauhaus will just be another factory.'

Otto Lindig's (1895–1966) work was not so driven by the 'goal' of production. Symbolism and a distinctive archaicizing strain was evident within the Bauhaus, particularly in the early years under the influence of the mystic radical painter and

55 Photograph by Lucia Moholy, showing coffee pot and cup by **Otto Lindig**, Combination teapot by **Theodor Bogler**, mugs by **Marguerite Friedlaender-Wildenhain**, all 1923.
In a complex transposition of values, ceramics for the kitchen aspired to the status of those of the laboratory bench: teapots recall 'water gauges', as a critic remarked of the 1923 Bauhaus exhibition. But these modern objects in fact took a huge amount of labour. Wilhelm Wagenfield ruefully noted that 'dealers and manufacturers laughed over our products... Although they looked like cheap machine production, they were in fact expensive handicrafts.'

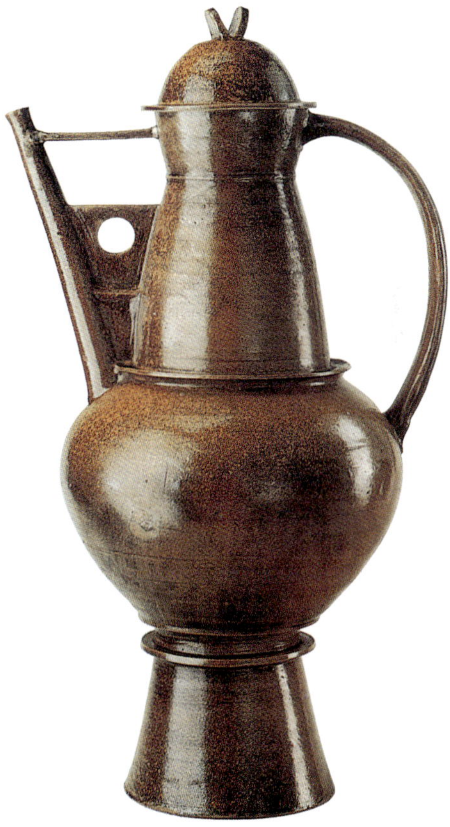

56 **Otto Lindig**, *Tall Lidded pot*, 1922 (h. 59 cm/23 in).
On the one hand Lindig's pot can be read as a Bauhaus homage to the balance of discrete geometric forms of cone, circle and cylinder within one vessel, but its character owes much more to the archaic than to the contemporary. Its role appears to be more hieratic and esoteric than functional.

theorist Johannes Itten. In an article in *Die Form* in 1929, 'Keramik in der Gestalt der Zeit' (Ceramics in the Form of the Age), a critic argued that 'we don't live in a time when the cultural face is determined by ceramics. The preferred material of the 1930s is not clay but metal... concrete and architectural glass. How can ceramics survive under these circumstances, ceramics that aren't... mass-produced household products?' The answer lay in going against technological change, by carrying on with 'true forms'. This reaction to the image of contemporaneity was also a part of the Bauhaus legacy.

The Bauhaus closed its ceramics workshop when it moved from Weimar to Dessau in 1925. In the short history of Bauhaus ceramics the importance given to clay as a material capable of expressing modernity was significant. And in making ceramics look as if they were 'essential', it meant a separation from the realm of the unique craft object and a connection to the multiple object of the industrial world. In the promotion of Marguerite Friedlander's porcelain for the Staatliche Porzellan-Manufaktur (State Porcelain Factory) in Berlin, published in *Die Form* in 1930, it is shown stacked as if recently unpacked from the kiln – and by its side is a photograph of other 'new porcelain', this time distilling vessels and a mortar. These distilling vessels acquired iconic status when they were chosen by Herbert Read for his book *Art and Industry* 1934 to illustrate 'severe practicality'. There was an absence of names of the makers or designers of objects in the

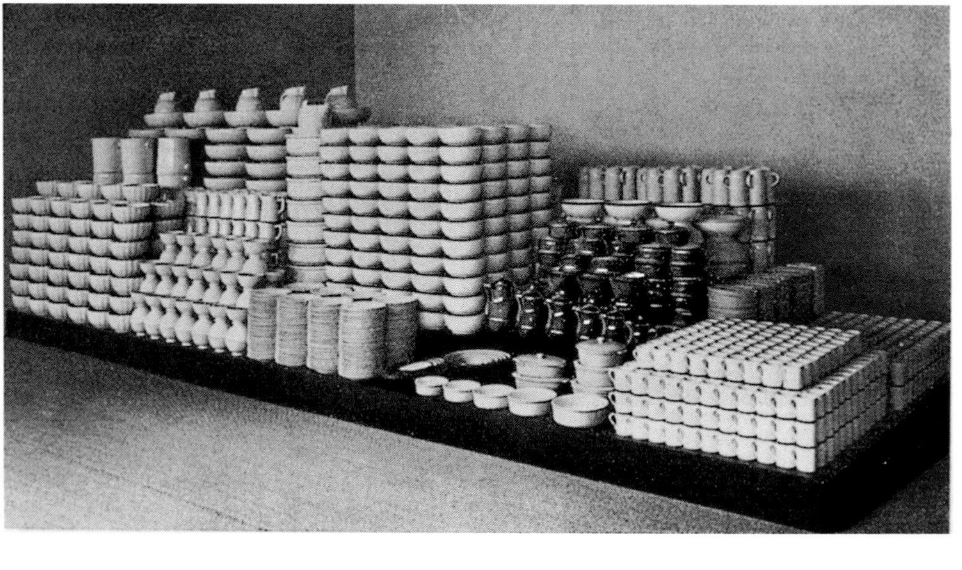

57 **Lily Reich**, *Bright Earth, Fired Earth*, installation at the *Deutsches Volk – Deutsche Arbeit* (German People, German Work) exhibition in Berlin 1934. Reich's installation is a hymn to the aesthetics of repetition.

magazine *Die Form Ohne Ornament* (Form Without Ornament) to emphasize their closeness to the anonymity of industrial production. This aspiration towards anonymity and severity was really an aspiration towards the 'type', an object whose form was so perfectly married to its usage that it could not be bettered.

This preoccupation reached beyond Germany. But looking for the 'type' in the work of studio potters was, as the British poet and critic Geoffrey Grigson trenchantly put it in a review in 1935, completely pointless: 'The best modern analogues for the medieval earthenware or the Siamese stoneware bowl of the tenth century, the T'ang earthenware jar [or] the Chinese stoneware bowls of the twelfth or thirteenth centuries... were not pots by Mr Staite Murray, Mr Bernard Leach, Miss Pleydell-Bouverie or Mr Cardew... but the Doulton fire-clay crucibles, the stoneware ginger-beer bottles, the mercury-bottle and bung-jar by Messrs Joseph Bourne'.

'Necessities' found their ultimate moment of authentication in the American Museum of Modern Art exhibition *Machine Art* held in 1934. Curated by architect and critic Philip Johnson, its purpose was to reveal an aesthetic of complete adaptation to purpose and lack of extraneous ornament present in industrial production from propellers and springs to the austere porcelain of hotel kitchen ware and beakers and dishes from the chemistry laboratory [58]. 'In spirit', Johnson wrote in his introduction, 'machine art and handicraft are diametrically opposed. Handicraft implies irregularity, picturesqueness, decorative value and uniqueness... The machine implies precision, simplicity, smoothness, reproducibility: plain textiles, vases as simple as laboratory beakers.' In keeping with the fierce didacticism of the enterprise each photograph in the catalogue is priced: these are objects to buy rather than collect. *Machine Art* stands as a summation at the end of fifteen years of exploration of the relationship between the artist and industry. The difficulty of making ceramics by hand that were as 'simple as laboratory beakers' had been fully recognized by the end of the Bauhaus ceramic workshop. The gap between the trenchant and highly politicized aspiration on the part of the designers and ceramicists to reeducate the public through such modern ceramics and the 'capriciousness' of the public in choosing to buy ceramics that represented other images of modernity was to remain considerable. In the ceramics of this period some of these images were also considerably less benign.

395

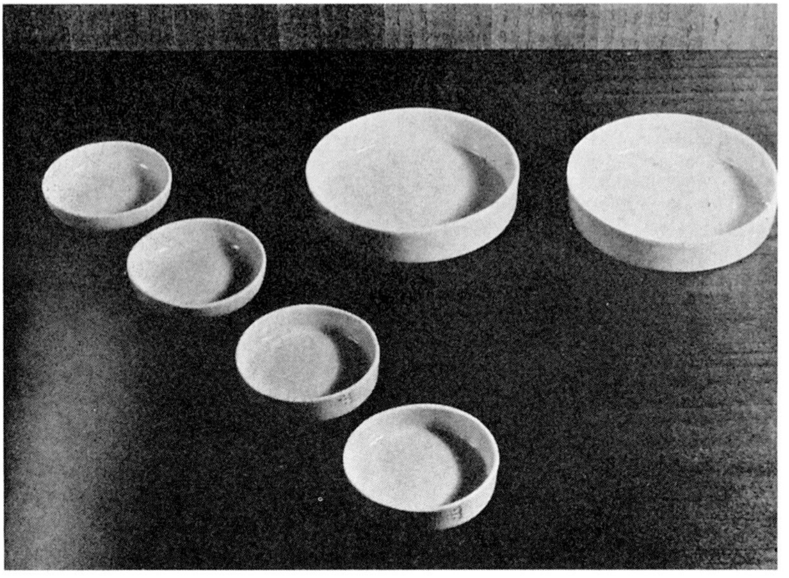

Capsules
Used for drying or incinerating chemicals
Coors Porcelain Co.
15¢ to 25¢. Eimer & Amend

397

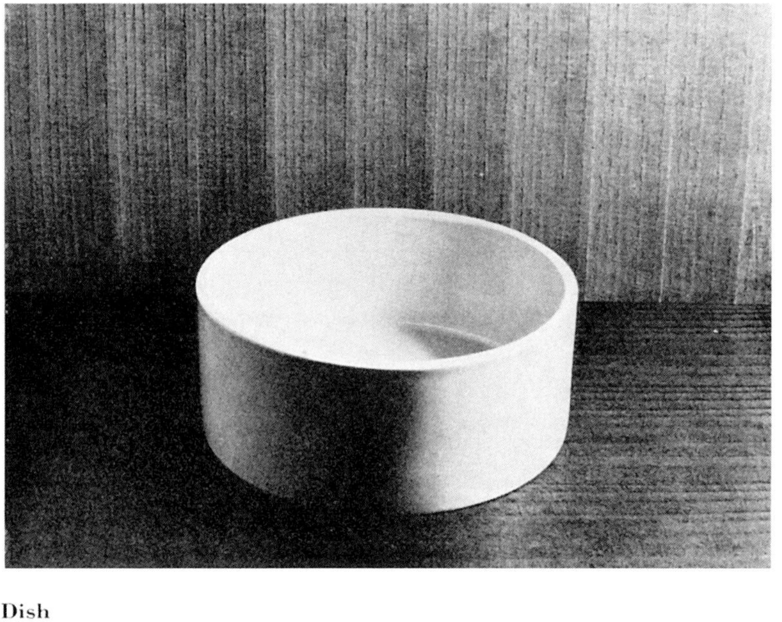

Dish

58 Capsules used for drying or incinerating chemicals. Page from catalogue of **Machine Art** exhibition held at Museum of Modern Art, New York 1934. 'The Exhibition contains… no purely ornamental objects; the useful objects were, however, chosen for their aesthetic quality' (Philip Johnson, *Machine Art* catalogue). The care with which the objects are displayed aesthetically in Johnson's polemical catalogue contrasts with the inclusion of such utilitarian details as price.

59 **Josef Hoffmann**, design for a coffee pot, *c.* 1925–28. Hoffmann was nicknamed 'Quadratl' ('little square') for his love of geometry. This severity was also present in his designs for furniture, silver and glass.

60 **Josef Hoffman**, Sonja Knips House, Vienna, view of glazed cupboards in the kitchen, 1924–25. The display of ceramics reveals how it was possible to aestheticize the type or the everyday object. Massed together within floor-to-ceiling glazed cabinets, they provide another powerful example of the removal of ceramics from the collectors' vitrine into a different kind of architectural space.

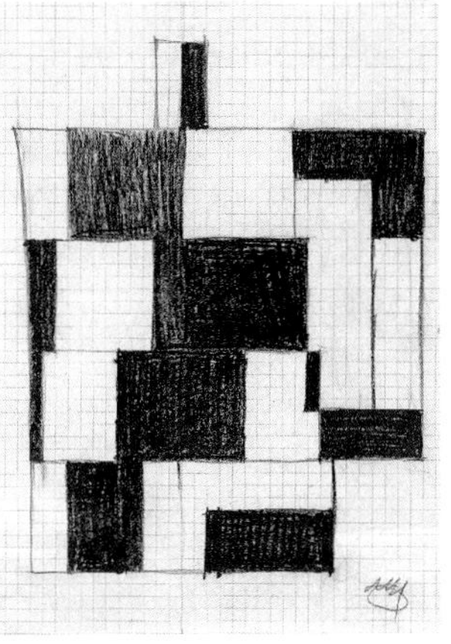

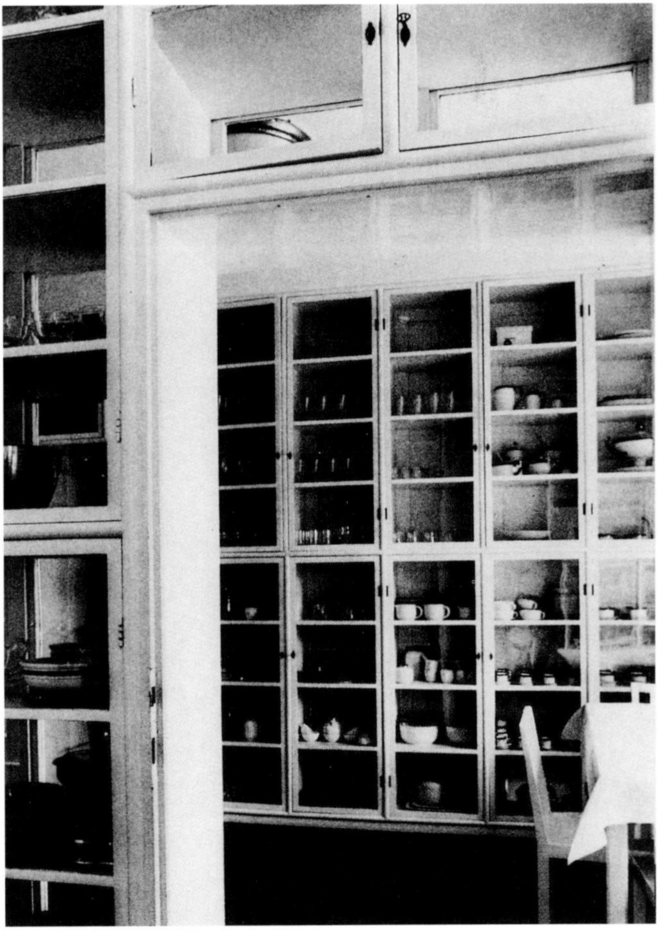

Italian Futurism

Proponents of the Italian Futurist 'aeroceramica' movement asserted its superiority to all other contemporary ceramics. In their bombastic Futurist Manifesto *Ceramica e Aeroceramica* of 1930, the potter Tullio d'Albisola and the leader of the Futurists F.T. Marinetti wrote: 'we confront our colourful Deperiani arabesques with the cold decoration of the Russian Suprematists' state schools; our plastic sportive complexes are more provocative, more beautiful and more similar to the rational furniture of Sant'Elia architecture than the affected sculptures of Viennese ceramicists'. As with other aspects of Futurism, decoration was to be 'inspired by Fascist events, by aviation and sport', and colour was to be lavish. True to these extravagant imperatives it was a movement that during its ten years produced, amongst other objects, a gilded terracotta gasmask and a dinner service of fifteen plates depicting the life of Marinetti from the 1909 Futurist Manifesto to the birth of 'Aeroceramica'.

The major protagonists in the group were Tullio d'Albisola (1899–1971) and the artists Vittorio Tommasini (1881–1964), known as 'Farfa', and Luigi Colombo (1904–36), known as 'Fillia'. Other poets (the name given by Futurists to multi-media artists),

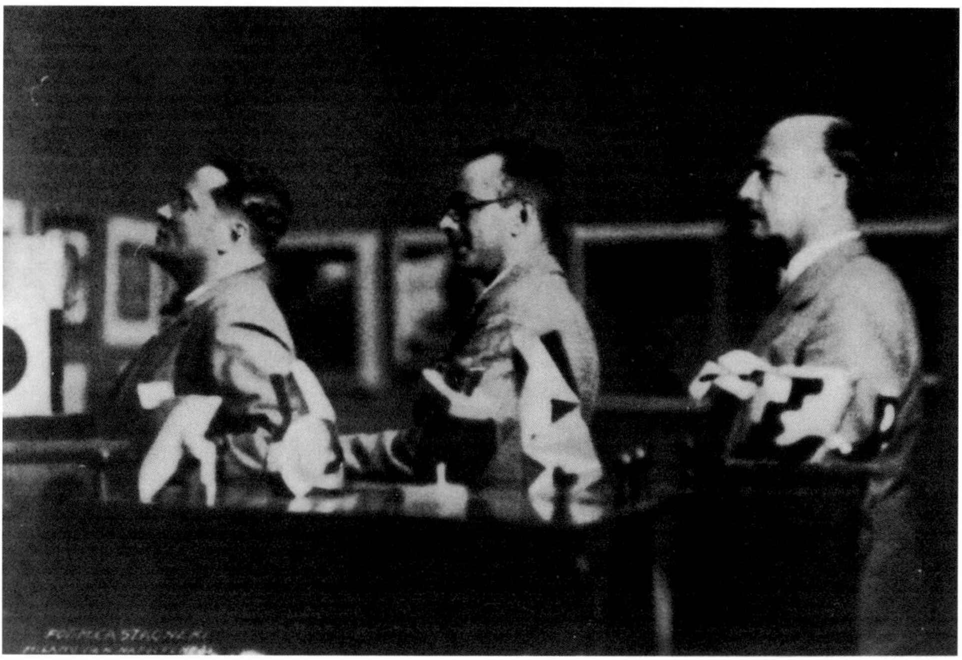

61 **Italian Futurists** at an exhibition in Milan, October 1930: (from left to right) Farfa, Tullio d'Albisola, F. T. Marinetti, the leading proponents of Aeroceramica. Their Manifesto declared, '[our ceramics] have everything to gain by comparison with Copenhagen, Meissen, Wedgwood and Sèvres, ceramics that don't know how to follow the speed of the times.'
The display in the foreground shows work by Farfa.

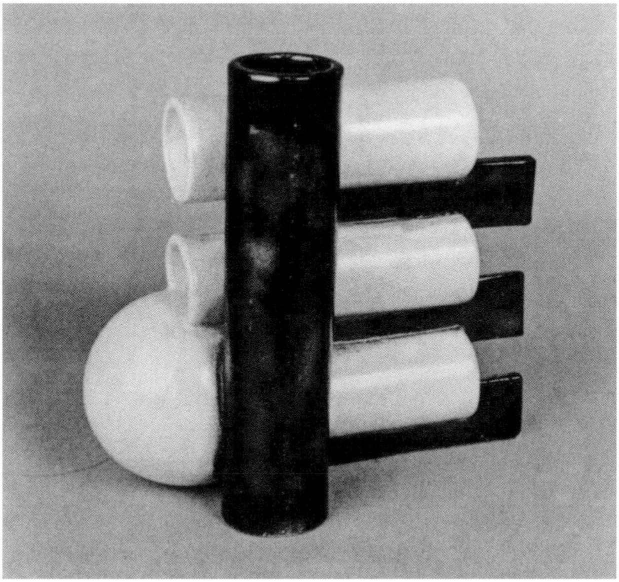

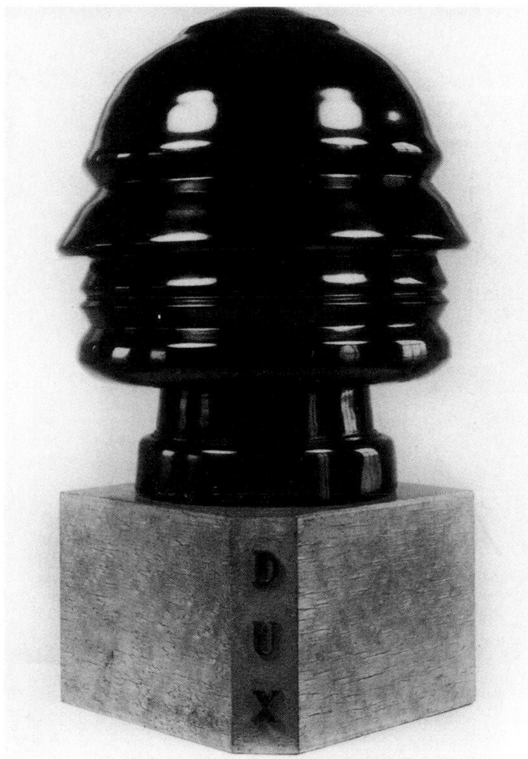

62 **Fillia**, *Aerovaso*, *c.* 1932 (earthenware, h. 25 cm/10 in). The Futurist relish for architectonic construction is clear: volumes are held in space by thin straps of clay.

63 **R. A. Bertelli**, *Head of Mussolini*, 1933. Mussolini's desire for self-commemoration found many willing contributors among Futurist artists, under orders to produce work that was dynamic and new. Bertelli's ceramic bust is an ultra-modern interpretation of a noble tradition of portraiture, in polished Fascist black.

painters and sculptors also worked with ceramics during the period, using the high technical skills available in the ceramic towns of Faenza and Albisola. D'Albisola's work displays a heady momentum of geometric patterning and figuration. Names, numbers and dates are prominent in most works, giving pieces like the tea service of 1933, whose decoration consists solely of numbers, the modernistic appearance of an advertising hoarding. Other decoration is more programmatic: a honey jar inscribed 'Italian honey' shows bees buzzing round the symbol of the fasces, or axes, that gave the Fascists their name. One lidded jar is even shaped like a falling bomb. With tubes instead of handles for cups and triangular plates instead of round ones, these are ceramics in love with their own modernity, 'ceramics which surprise the ceramicists themselves', as the manifesto puts it.

Futurist ceramics are a homage to the machine – some even look like the radiator of a car. Fillia's tea service of 1932 is an almost comically exacting tribute to speed, the lid of the teapot like Mercury's hat, the spout a truncated piston. They show an enjoyment of abstracted and rhythmical form that recalls the work of the Czech Cubists or the 'cold' Suprematists.

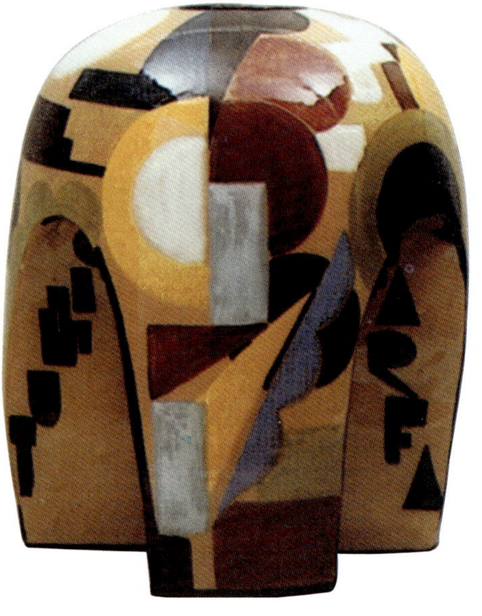

64 **Farfa** and **Tullio d'Albisola**, *Anteater Vase*, c. 1931–32 (terracotta, h. 26 cm/10¼ in). These ceramics play with hidden volumes; the proboscis creates a hidden space underneath the pot. The incorporation of names (Tullio/Farfa), dates, or slogans into the design is characteristic of the energy of Futurist ceramics.

Art Deco

The Art Deco or 'moderne' style, which combined a relish for angularity with sleek surfaces clad with geometric patterning, reached its zenith at the 1925 'Exposition Internationale des Arts Décoratifs et Industriels Modernes' in Paris. Its impact was considerable, as Leon Werth was to comment in 1927:

Since the 1925 Exposition of Decorative Arts... surfaces have been covered with regular or staggered, symmetric or asymmetric geometric figures – juxtaposed, interlocking, or overhanging. In a word, ornamentation has become Cubist. Cubist ornament was a compromise between the need for ornament and its satisfaction by means that seemed outdated. Whereas the arbitrary use of a rose might have appeared intolerable, the arbitrary use of a triangle or a sphere gave the illusion of rigour and necessity. The caprice was disguised as geometry. The caprice of fashion itself.

The susceptibility of ceramics to changes of style became an issue of critical debate. Here were ceramics that were far from the modernist ideal of a seamless unity of form and function, a unity of social purpose and artist. They were ceramics for a new market, suited to the needs of a changing demography, a younger and more stylistically aware urban population. Decorative ceramics that during the efflorescence of Art Nouveau might have been vases entwined with foliage, pots that still showed a connection with ceramic history, were now more likely to be book-ends shaped like ziggurats or teapots shaped like racing cars. As one British critic put it in a book aimed at educating taste, these are 'amusing toys – by-products of the potter's craft – which are too often made (and sold!) as genuine ceramic products for daily use'.

The most popular of the designers of 'distracting' ceramics was Clarice Cliff (1899–1972). Cliff was brought up in 'the Potteries', the name given to the traditional pottery-producing area around Stoke in the English Midlands, and at thirteen years old started as an enameller. She trained as a lithographer and her ability was rapidly recognized, after she received the encouragement to design her own work: 'The warehouses of the Newport Pottery Co. were stacked with bowls, vases, jugs and candlesticks, mostly of the Art Nouveau period. This huge stock had always interested me, and presented a challenge. Eventually in about 1924–25, I was allowed to experiment...' These first experiments were a huge success and soon Cliff was designing new geometric shapes for her aspirationally named patterns

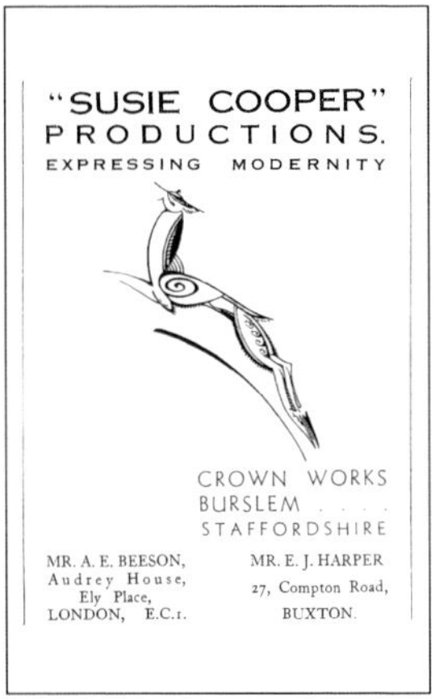

65 **Susie Cooper**'s introduction of *Early Morning* sets and *Breakfast in Bed* sets reflected her openness to new domestic realities: these were ceramics for families with few if any servants. It was noted that 'Miss Cooper is a lady who designs from the standpoint of the lady'.

66 **Russel Wright**, *American Modern* service for Steubenville, designed 1937, produced from 1939. Thought to be the most popular dinnerware ever produced, it seemed to respond to the need for casual but stylish living. Salad bowls were asymmetric with turned-in rims, jugs and carafes streamlined as if to emphasize the liquidity of their contents; handles were dispensed with where possible.

67 **Viktor Schreckengost**, *Jazz Bowl*, 1931. One of five bowls commissioned as 'something modern' for the New York Governor's mansion in Albany by the Governor's wife, Eleanor Roosevelt. Made as punch bowls in an era of Prohibition, with their sgrafitto of turquoise glaze over black, they conjure up night in the metropolis. Images of a saxophone, cocktail glasses, musical notes, and skyscrapers are interspersed with zigzags and stars, and like nightclub signs the words 'jazz', 'follies' and 'café' emerge from the black background.

Bizarre, Fantastique and *Biarritz*. That these were ceramics for collecting was emphasized by having Cliff's facsimile signature printed onto the base of each pot.

Susie Cooper (1902–95), the English designer of sophisticated modernist table ware, was also credited by her contemporaries as someone who 'has found, if not actually created, a market for her productions'. She established her own ceramics firm in 1929, decorating wares made by other factories, but within three years was employing forty women decorators. Committed to the idea that contemporary design could be affordable, Cooper developed ranges of streamlined and ergonomic shapes (*Kestrel, Falcon* and *Curlew*) with focused decoration of banded colour or polka dots. The cohesion of these designs, their sense of 'rigour and necessity', was approved of by those who were appalled by Cliff's *Bizarre*: 'Form, decoration and even texture in the Susie Cooper ware are part of a considered scheme; it is not merely a case of sticking a decoration on to a pot regardless of context', said the *Pottery Gazette and Glass Trade Review* in August 1935. Indeed, a reason for both Cliff and Cooper's enormous popular and enduring appeal lies in exactly their intelligent assessment of the change in the market for domestic ceramics.

In America, the industrial designer Russel Wright (1904–76) also designed ceramics that were more organic than geometric. These were ceramics to handle – far from the dinnerware of formal meals; Wright even named one service *Casual China*. Frederick Rhead, the erstwhile colleague of Adelaide Robineau, stressed this change in context for ceramics by giving his *Fiestaware* of 1936 mix-and-match settings and selling them through the mass-market chainstore Woolworths. Five deep colours were originally produced and more added: these ceramics were as 'capricious' as the images of the Fiesta with which they were marketed.

The modernity of the work of Viktor Schreckengost (b. 1906) – like that of Wright and Cliff – was expressed through an engagement with the culture of the moment. His compelling set of *Jazz bowls* integrated the imagery of the Jazz Age into ceramics. An American, Schreckengost studied after graduation at the Vienna Kunstgewerbeschule under Michael Powolny. On his return he joined the Cleveland School of Art and became a designer for the Cowan Pottery Studio. These were not agitprop ceramics: their agenda was far from that of the Scandinavian polemicists or Bauhaus propagandists. How they were made was of little consequence in comparison with how they could perform.

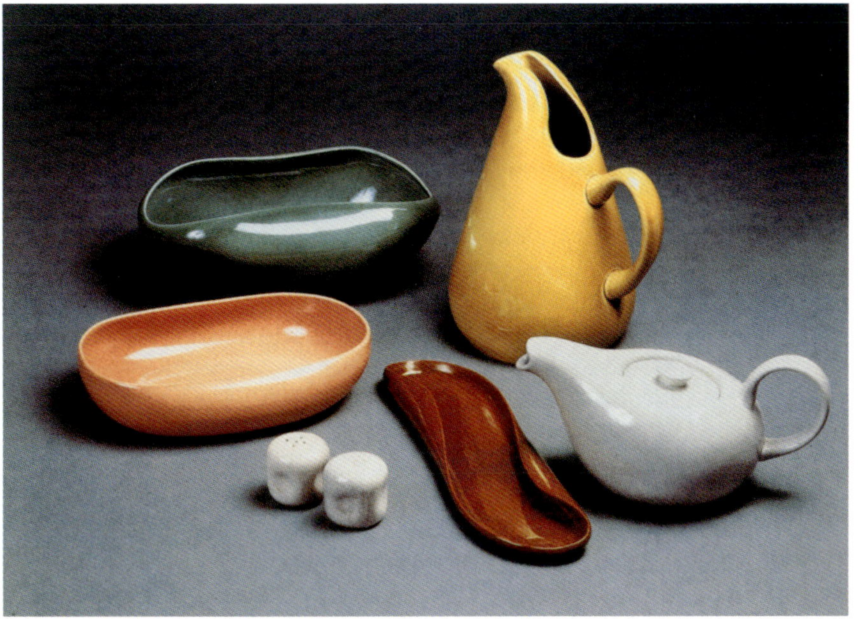

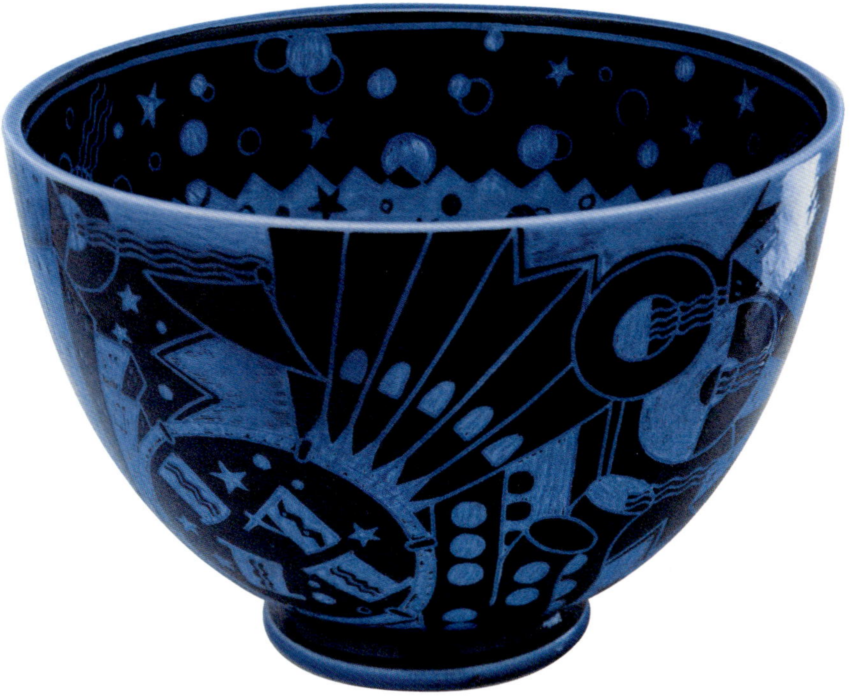

Women and ceramics; figures and figuration

The place of women working in ceramics was highly particular. At the Bauhaus women were not admitted to train as architects and were channelled towards the pottery or weaving studios. In England it was difficult for women to learn to throw at the few art schools that admitted them, the assumption being that they would be decorators. In Vienna at the Wiener Werkstätte, architecture and the furniture design studio were closed to women, meaning that women of a certain social class – the Viennese upper middle classes – were also most likely to train as potters or as textile designers. By the mid-1920s this 'preponderance' of women was subject to much comment. That ten out of twenty-five Austrian potters exhibiting at the 1925 Paris Exposition des Arts Décoratifs et Industriels Modernes were women caused interest. And in the heated atmosphere of Viennese art politics this meant that such critics as Adolf Loos and Julius Klinger had their knives out. The Wiener Werkstätte was pejoratively dubbed the 'Wiener Weiberwirtschaft' (the Viennese Women's Business), or even the 'Wiener Weiberkunstgewerbe' (the Viennese Women's Arts and Crafts). There were comments by Loos about 'Fräuleins who regard handicrafts as something whereby one can earn pin money or while away one's spare time until one can walk up the aisle'. Even the decline in prestige of Viennese art was laid at their door.

'Handicrafts' for the modern Viennese ceramics craftswomen meant one of two things: either it meant pots for display or figuration. The pots for display are baroque, with pierced panels, exaggerated multiple handles, undulating rims and complex profiles. They were far from the Hoffmann ideal – and were thus unequivocally dismissed by some American critics as redolent of 'frivolity'. But in other contemporary criticism these 'excesses' were regarded as expressions of a specifically feminine approach to handling clay: they 'demonstrate the free, voluptuous handling that is the familiar speciality of the Neue Wiener Keramik [New Viennese Ceramics]. It is no coincidence that they should echo the rococo vocabulary of form, for they share the same uninhibited, playful, sensuous spirit. One sees the world take shape around these objects, a cheerful, light-hearted, friendly world.'

The sensuality and spontaneity of these ceramics was particularly noted in the work of Vally Wieselthier (1895–1945) whose lack of 'worry over the usual potter's concerns for texture, detail or finish' was applauded. The growth of figuration

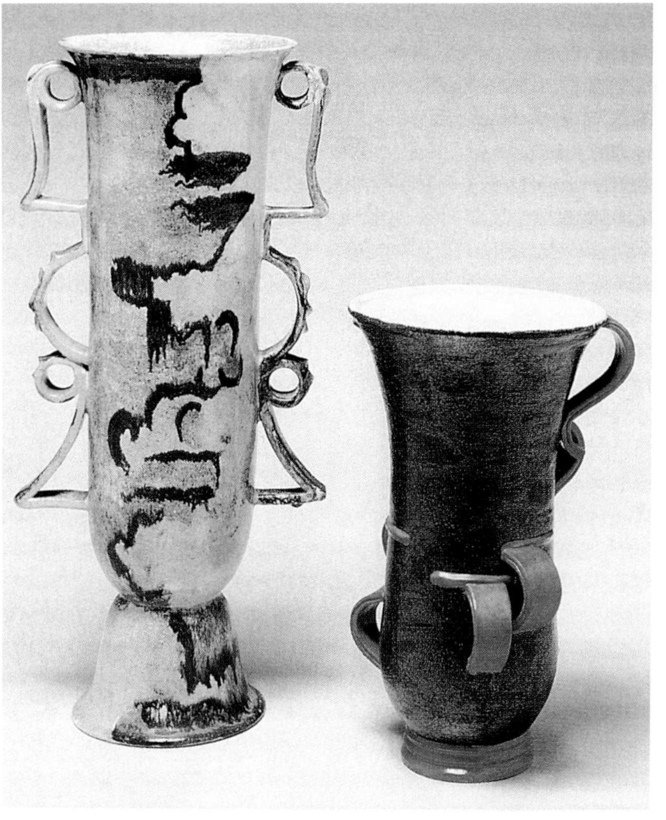

68 Wiener Werkstätte vases by **Vally Wieselthier** (left) and **Gudrun Baudisch**, *c.* 1920–25 (glazed earthenware, h. 39.4 cm/24 in, and 25.4 cm/10 in respectively). Wieselthier's ceramics show an excitement about the process of making: they are vessels where the surface is not unitary but disturbed, broken by fragmentary pattern or 'extraneous' handles. In 1929 she wrote that 'Every touch of the finger on the clay as it is rolled out from the kick-wheel reveals new possibilities, so plastic is the material.'

in ceramics had its inception in Powolny's putti (see p. 55), a staple of Viennese ceramics from early in the century. But the change from putti (or models of women in crinolines) was due entirely to women artists, in particular to Wieselthier, Gudrun Baudisch (1907–82) and Susi Singer (1895–1949). Their figures owe little to the light-footed figures of Parisian Art Deco inspired by modern dance – they are grounded and solid, not types or indeed archetypes so much as modern women.

But the figures from the Vienna school were the exception: most of the ceramic figures of the period were the middle-class (and respectable) versions of the luxury ivory and bronze sculptures of Demetre Chiparus. These idealized dancers surrounded by swirling scarves were popularized in America by R. Guy Cowan (1884–1957) who set up the Cowan Pottery Studio after the First World War. His first figurines were designed to be used decoratively in table arrangements, but, concerned with the lack of critical appreciation for them, he subsequently started

69 **Waylande Gregory**, *Woman's Head*, c. 1933 (earthenware, h. 61 cm/24 in). Gregory's career spanned many of the concerns of 1930s figuration: he made portrait busts (Henry Fonda, Charles Lindbergh, Albert Einstein), sleek stylized heads, and later monumental public works.

70 **Gudrun Baudisch**, *Head of a Girl*, 1927 (stoneware). More 'flapper' than nymph, Baudisch's *Head* sets this kind of figuration apart from the chryselephantine Art Deco statuettes of dancers and sportswomen, with sleek surfaces so reminiscent of car mascots.

hiring sculptors and recent graduates from the local Cleveland School of Art. The Cowan Pottery Studio acted as a training ground for many ceramic sculptors, amongst them Alexander Blazys and Waylande Gregory (1905–71). Gregory joined in 1928, making figures based on mythological or Biblical characters (*Diana and Two Fawns*, *Salome*). Gregory's figures, highly popular at the time, with their high-glaze finish, can be read as a transposition of expensive materials into cheaper clay, a democratization of figuration. But this transposition was also predicated on a diminution in scale – the figure becomes the figurine.

Vally Wieselthier moved to America in 1929 after a successful appearance at the significant International Exhibition of Ceramic Art held in New York in 1928. The scale of her figures increased,

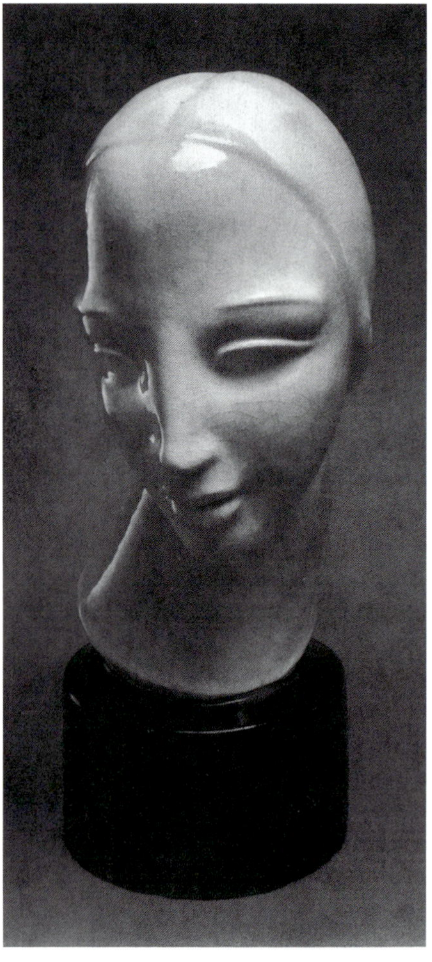

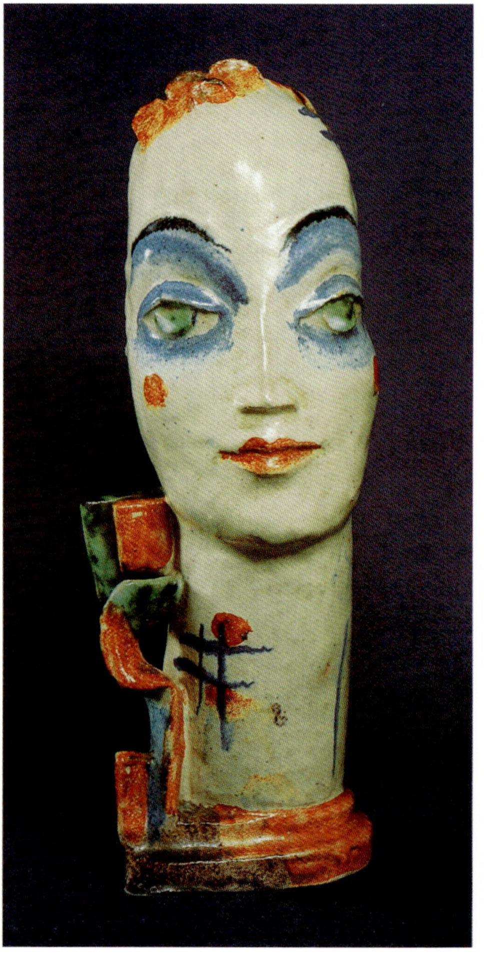

71 **Waylande Gregory**, model for 'War' (terracotta, h. 79 cm/31 in), one of six symbolic figures commissioned in 1937 for a monumental fountain, *Light Dispelling Darkness*, in New Brunswick, made with the aid of unemployed workers from a nearby terracotta factory. With their six symbolic figures of Death, War, Famine, Pestilence, Greed and Materialism surrounding reliefs of heroes of technological advancement, it was a positivist hymn to the future.

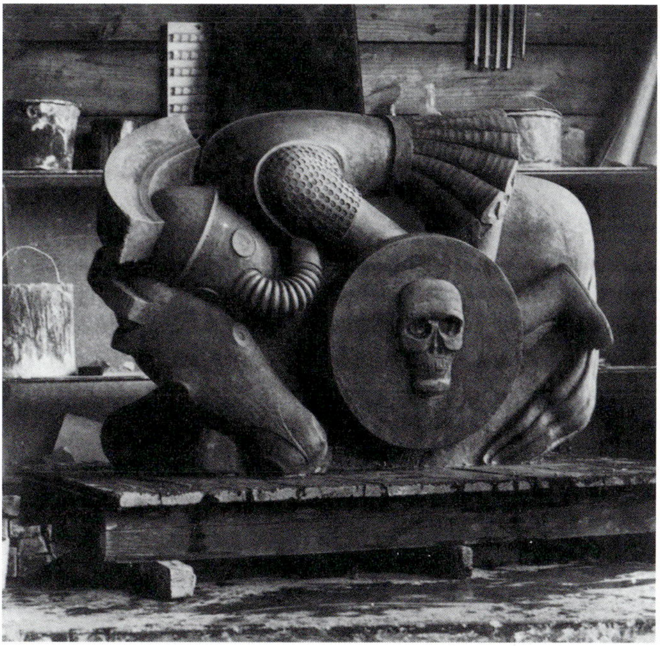

72 **Viktor Schreckengost**, *Apocalypse*, 1942 (earthenware, h. 40 cm/15½ in).
Figures of Death dressed as a German soldier, Hitler, Hirohito and Mussolini are shown clinging to the flanks of one of the horses of the Apocalypse as it straddles the Earth.

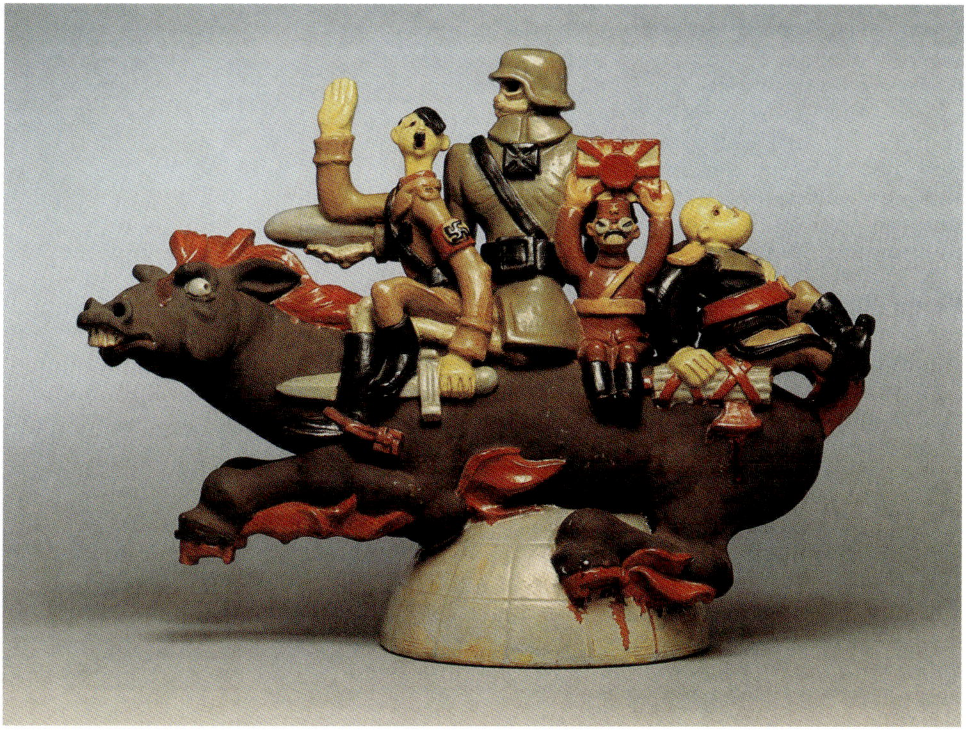

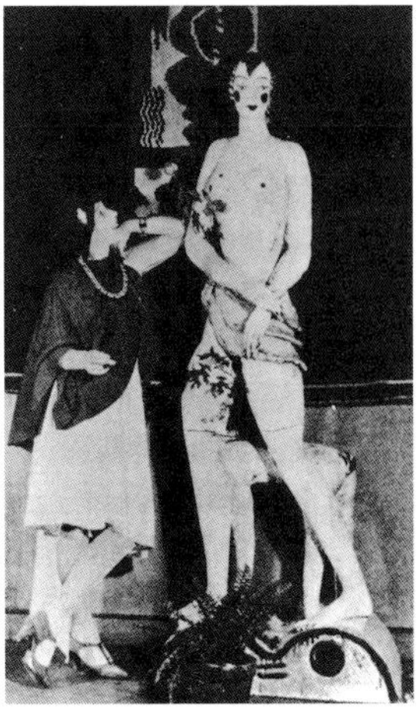

73 Photograph of **Vally Wieselthier** beside one of her garden figures, *c.* 1929, the year she emigrated to the United States of America.

74 **Treadle wheel** on sewing machine base, used at the University of Southern California, during the 1930s and 1940s. The technology used in art colleges and universities was often basic and limited. These wheels severely restricted the scale of thrown work.

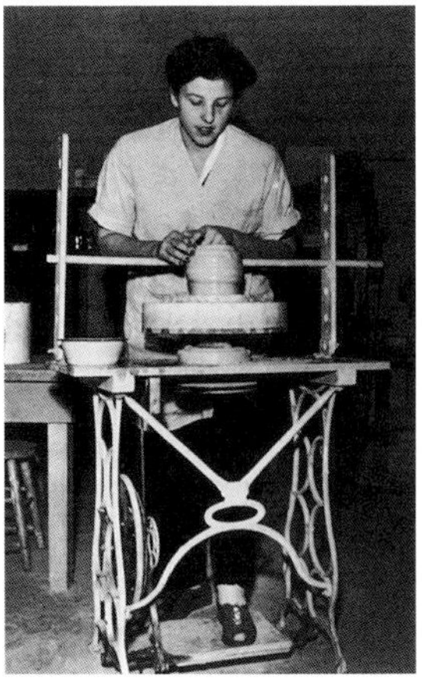

some of them to more than life-size. That there was a more expressionist handling of clay in figuration reflected the growing links made between Vienna and America in American ceramics in the 1930s. Schreckengost received a scholarship to study with Powolny in Vienna in 1929, and was followed by Russell Aitken (b. 1910) in 1932. Schreckengost's work was wide-ranging, embracing black culture and powerful political commentary.

In Britain the field of ceramic figuration provided a genre in which women were conspicuously successful. The reasons for women forming the vanguard for ceramic figuration were partly practical. Unlike the demands of making of functional vessels, it was possible to have a small urban studio with a kiln, an image of bohemian living so commonplace as to be found in the fictional portrait of 'Miss Marjorie Phelps', a Chelsea sculptor who 'made figurines in porcelain for a living' in Dorothy L. Sayers' 1930s novels.

For women who wanted to use clay, figurines also provided a usefully ambiguous midpoint between the worlds of sculpture and fine art, and that of craft. This ambiguity was needed as women who were studying ceramics in the few art colleges of the day were actively discouraged from learning to throw and encouraged to become decorators. Consequently the stress in the practical handbooks on pottery-making of the day is on making with exigent materials or kilns, on hand-building rather than throwing: in short, how to get by (and improve) away from the academy. The fact that most of these handbooks were written by women (including Denise Wren, Dora Lunn and Dora Billington) suggests their awareness of the need for information and encouragement; these were not intended as aesthetic treatises. Their tone was inclusive: Dora Billington (1890–1968), for instance, championed decorative traditions like maiolica that were disparaged by Leach.

The radical art critic Frank Rutter in the Government Report on 'British Studio Potters' exhibiting at the 1925 Paris exhibition commented that there was a lack of virility to be seen in the work on display: 'it is inclined to be affected or to err on the "pretty-pretty" side', but he noted an exception in Miss Gwendolin Parnell, 'a most versatile designer, and... one of the most distinguished studio potters we have yet produced.' Often mentioned approvingly by critics, Parnell made figures of 'colourful' characters and types, romanticized views of a popular culture peopled by gipsies, hawkers and lovable rogues. They were finely modelled and painted with strong colours in the traditions of eighteenth-century Chelsea genre figures.

This tradition also lay behind the figurines of Charles Vyse and

Nell Vyse, Charles doing the sculpting and Nell (in the words of a critic in 1943) 'adept at the painting of them.... a delicate and tedious business.' As interest grew in the work of studio potters during the 1930s, ceramic figuration began to be seen as of less interest. The popularity of the work of Stella Crofts, whose figures were mostly animals, was noted, but with the concomitant criticism that her work was more meretricious than original: 'Miss Crofts is rather too easily successful on the zoological side and would gain from some drilling in what is called "abstract" composition – designing in shapes that have no illustrative meaning'. It was the continuation of the debate about the value of skill within ceramics that had been so much rehearsed in French ceramics at the turn of the century.

75 **Denise Wren**, sketches of ceramics made by women, 1923, showing coil pots typical of the kind encouraged on the teacher-training courses she ran in the 1920s.

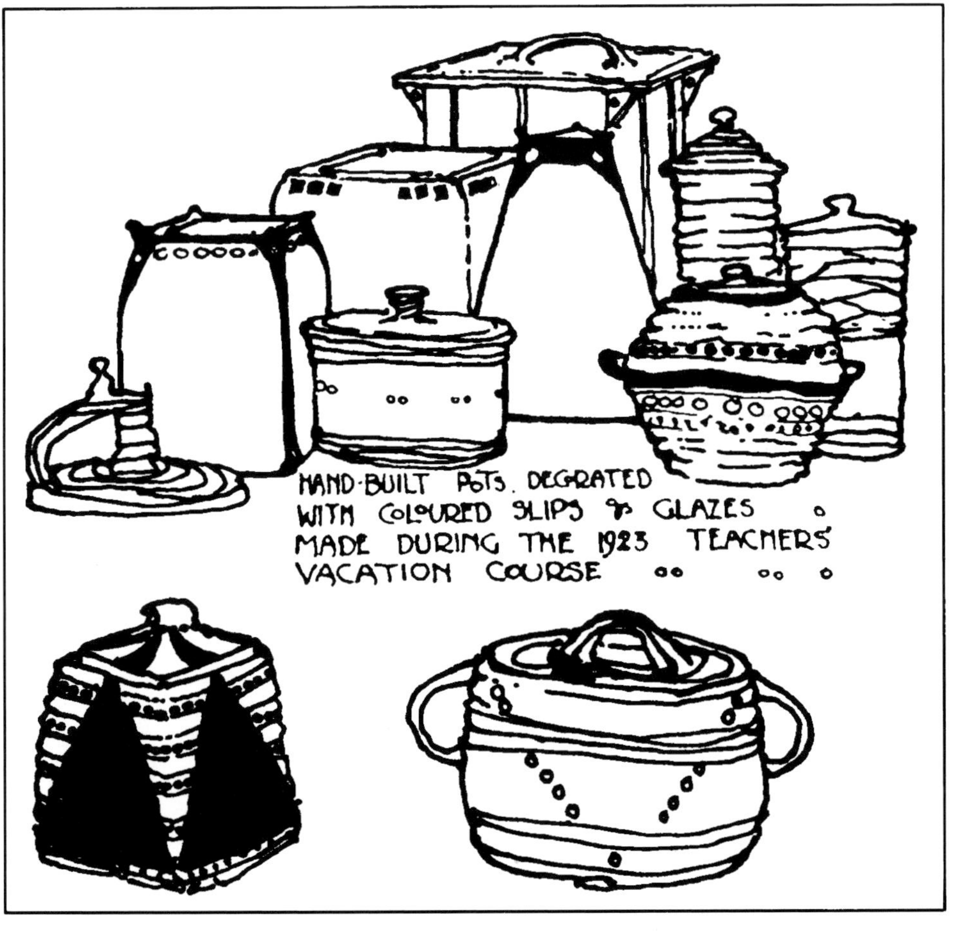

Romantic Nationalism: Bernard Leach and Japan

Modernity could be expressed in powerfully heterodox ways. In the 1920s and 30s in ceramics it was expressed in 'functionalism', through the imagery of metropolitan living and through avowedly political messages. But in parallel – and often in opposition – to this embrace of the technocratic was a strong vernacular revival. This often manifested itself through the use of emblematic national forms, glazes or imagery. The support for the crafts in Nazi Germany, the growth of the *mingei* (folkcraft) movement in Japan and the rise of the studio potter in Britain, were all based in the apprehension that an increasingly urban and industrial society was losing a powerful value system. These were the values found in the crafts, values that were projected as being based around continuity and closeness to the natural order. Many of these themes were played out in the figure of Bernard Leach (1887–1979), the potter and writer whose (changing) evangelism for the role of pottery in society was to dominate aspects of the middle century.

Leach was born in Hong Kong and brought up partly in Japan, before going to England to be educated. He studied art at the Slade School of Art in London and in 1909 he decided to return to Japan to make his life as an artist and to teach etching. Leach

76 Photograph of **Bernard** and **David Leach** and **Shoji Hamada**, at Lake's Pottery, Truro, 1923 watching a potter pulling a handle on a pitcher. Leach had an ambivalent relationship with the few remaining country potteries, feeling that they were debased versions of great vernacular traditions.

77 Handbill advertisement for the **Leach Pottery** at St Ives, *c.* 1924, showing large slipware plate. The stress on locality, in both materials and imagery, was crucial to the Leach Pottery's economic survival when it started.

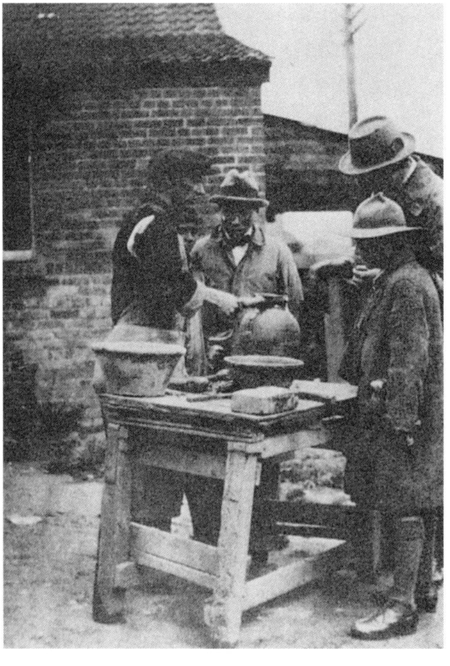

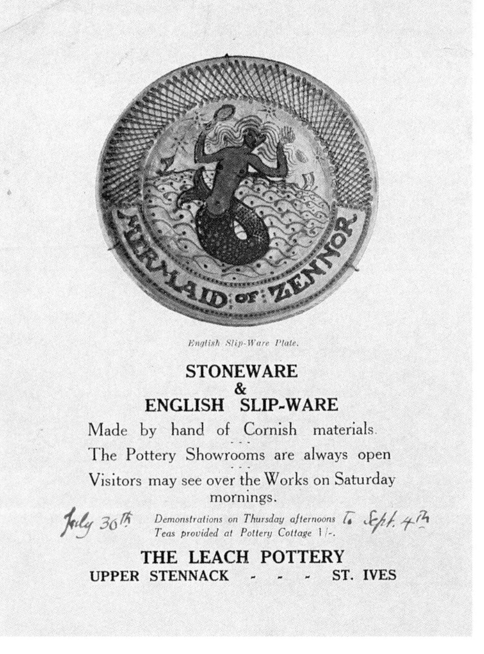

rapidly found himself in a milieu of similarly well born young men, an avant-garde of writers, artists and thinkers in which fervid ideas about the value and place of art were commonplace. Leach soon forged a great friendship with Soetsu Yanagi, a critic and the editor of the magazine of the 'Shirakaba' (White Birch) movement. His first encounter with ceramics came at a raku party at which young artists and writers were painting pottery. Within this world, raku (low-fired earthenware) was an accomplishment, as common as watercolour painting or the piano would have been to an European gentleman of the same time. Leach was 'enthralled…
on the spot seized with the desire to take up this craft'. Further tutelage came from an elderly potter, Urano Shigekichi (1851–1923) known as Kenzan VI, the undistinguished last member of a great lineage of potters noted for their use of calligraphy and painting on pottery.

Leach's first pots were direct copies of Chinese ceramics. But Leach soon built up a highly allusive decorative repertoire, finding

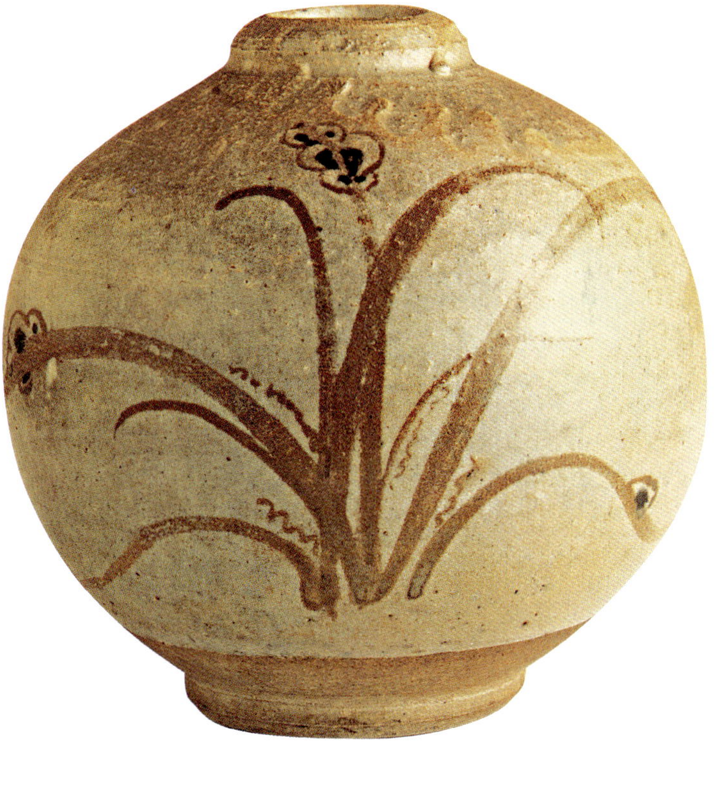

78 **Bernard Leach**, *Globular Pot*, 1927 (stoneware, h. 14 cm/5¾ in). Leach's subdued tonality was highly influential. He was passionate about revealing the qualities of the clay, and often left a significant part of the pot unglazed. The gestures used in throwing, trimming, glazing and decorating this pot are all still apparent: Leach emphasized their congruence.

in pottery the chance to synthesize his current excitements. He began to spend an increasing amount of his time making as well as decorating pottery. An abortive attempt to settle in China was brought to a quick end by Yanagi's invitation in 1917 to live next to him in Abiko, a hamlet near Tokyo. Here Leach built a new studio and rebuilt Kenzan's old kiln. His ceramics now included imitation English slipware made in raku; 'my first attempt after having started making pots in an alien country to get my feet on the ground of English tradition.' It was at Abiko that his interest in vernacular crafts grew: in them he saw the opportunity for an artist like him to supervise the making of everyday objects by local artisans, who 'stumble badly when it comes to modern things.'

By 1920 when he returned to England Leach's experience of ceramics in Japan was a very particular one. It was confined to making decorative pieces for an urbane Westernized audience; it also depended on having capable technical help. Leach's technical knowledge was limited: in the world where he exhibited these ceramics, technical deficiencies were subordinated to what Yanagi described as his 'naive power'. In deciding to start a pottery in the Cornish artist's colony of St Ives, he was fortunate in having in Shoji Hamada 'a good Japanese assistant'.

Leach's return to England was described by Yanagi as a 'mission'. The evangelical imperative behind his pottery was clear: it was to introduce to a world habituated to the display of skill apparent in 'art pottery' or in industrial ceramics a new aesthetic. This new kind of pottery would depend on an understanding and

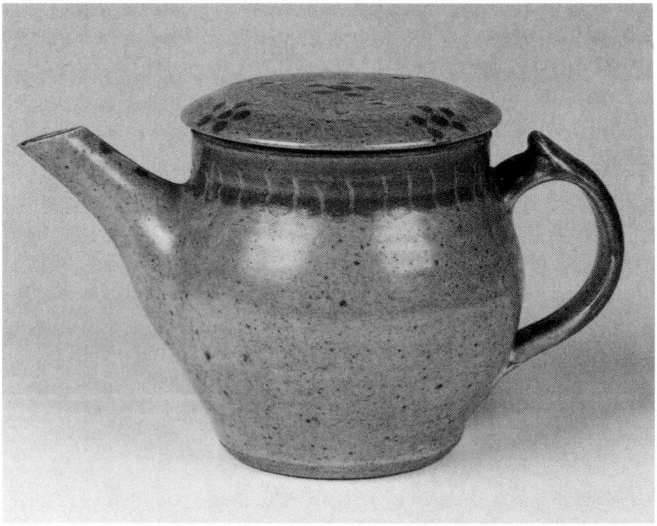

79 **Bernard Leach**, *Teapot*, 1930 (stoneware, h. 12 cm/4¾ in). A reviewer wrote in 1928 of Leach's domestic pots that 'Mr Leach abandons what may be called the museum attitude, and comes down into the living room, with jugs, tea sets, porridge bowls, what not. They are sensible and friendly in shape and pleasant in colour... in these wares Mr Leach has pushed down the possibilities of the private kiln about as far as they will go to meet the factory on economic costs.'

an appreciation that 'even clumsiness is preferable to suave dullness', that the expressiveness of a pot lay in the visibility and tactility of the marks of the potter's hand on the clay and glaze rather than a successful effacement of the hand. The particularity of the materials used was to be brought to the fore: rather than a glaze completely covering up the base of the foot, the unglazed clay would be left as a 'symbol, here do I touch earth, on this I stand, my Terminus.' His use of local materials went beyond economic expedience: it acted as a guarantor of authenticity. Glazes themselves were austere, irregular and 'natural' rather than employing decorative 'Art effects'.

Leach made three main kinds of pottery at St Ives: raku wares, slipware ('Made by hand from Cornish materials') and the stoneware pots made in emulation of Sung dynasty wares. In all of these there is a projection of the pot as a serious carrier of tradition, of continuity: in the slipware dishes, for instance, there is a heavily stylized use of medieval imagery of griffons and other heraldic emblems. He found the audience for all these kinds of pots almost non-existent and throughout the 1920s and 30s his struggles were as much economic as aesthetic. This led to confusions for Leach. His evangelism for studio pottery was a declaration of belief in independence, a romantic identification with 'real craftsmen'. It was a passion that led to numerous articles, a pamphlet and ultimately the influential *A Potter's Book* of 1940: all ways of making a larger public for handmade pots. But more than any other potter of the period, Leach enjoyed the combative role of defender of his ideas against others. One crucial way of securing notice was to emphasize his authority as a lifeline to an oriental tradition, to put a distance between his pots and those of other potters who used the oriental canon, such as Charles Vyse (1882–1971) or William Staite Murray (1881–1962). His disparagement of the French pioneers, whose aesthetic was often close to his, was particularly vitriolic.

In 1927 Leach showed his collector's pieces and his domestic ware in two separate galleries simultaneously. He knew which audience he wanted for the domestic ware: ' "This is the sort of jug a working man would want to have beer in", said Mr Leach, pointing to a magnificent example of modern stoneware...' But, the critic went on, 'I am afraid members of the working class will not be able to buy any of the beautiful things shown in the exhibition'. Leach' s angry reflections on the seeming impossibility of surviving as an artist-potter were published as a pamphlet, 'A Potter's Outlook', in 1928: 'What kind of person is the craftsman of our times?' In forceful language he argued that factories had degraded the folk art of England and now

the trade offers us crockery which is cheap, standardised, thin, white, hard and waterproof – good qualities all – but the shapes are wretched, the colours sharp and harsh, the decoration banal, the quality absent… We have been supported by collectors, purists, cranks or 'art' people, rather than by the normal man or woman… and consequently most of our pots have been still-born: they have not had the breath of reality in them: it has been a game.

The etiolated nature of the market that Leach described led him to consider the possibility of using machines. He never did, preferring to work in more ad hoc ways with his 'local lads' and the increasing number of students who came to St Ives. Some became remarkable potters, amongst them Katherine Pleydell-Bouverie (1895–1985), Norah Braden (1901–2000) and Michael Cardew (1901–83). In the 1930s his ceramic work became more disrupted, with extended stays away from St Ives and a long visit to Japan. It was his writing that was to have the most impact.

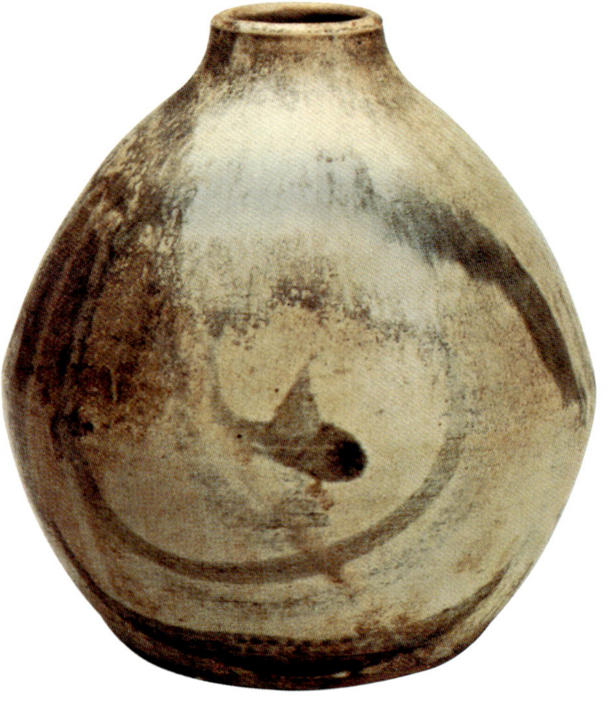

80 **Norah Braden**, stoneware vase (h. 16.2 cm/6⅜), c. 1932. See caption opposite.

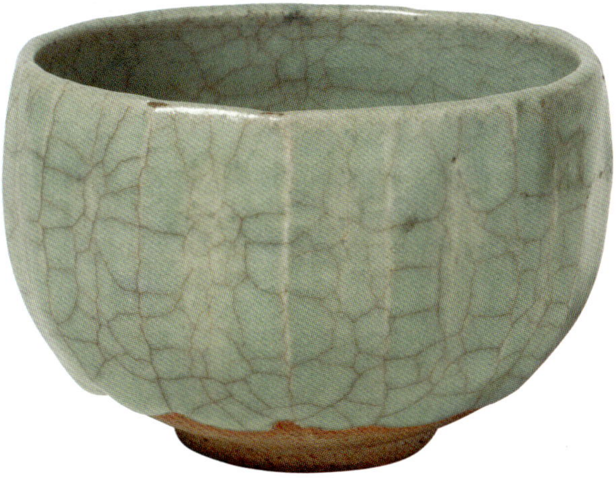

81 **Katherine Pleydell-Bouverie**, small stoneware bowl, 1936.

'The idiom which begins in form is carried on into glazes, the most experimental and original aspect of the work of Miss Bouverie and Miss Braden. The glazes are original because they open the art of pottery to a ceramic expression of English sentiment. ... The chief function of pots or vases... is to hold flowers; and flowers grow in landscape. The pot which is to support them should be a bit of landscape brought indoors and turned off in the round... Miss Bouverie and Miss Braden do not try to copy the rich Sung glazes, but limit themselves to a low-tone scale of white, grey-green, brown, yellowish-brown and the like – the colours of stones and grass and burnt fields and overgrown pools. This is both good naturalism and good decoration.' (1930 review)

The popularity and influence of Leach's *A Potter's Book*, finally published in 1940, have been colossal. The book is both a manual and a polemic, a drawing together of technical information on making, glazing and firing pots within the mantle of Leach's values. His first chapter, 'Towards a Standard', took as its premise the need for a common standard for potters. In the absence of any in the West, they should look to the East and 'accept the Sung standard without hesitation. As it is there are a few English craftsmen potters today who do accept it, and their work is incomparably the best that is being turned out.' This meant an 'appropriateness': glazes should have the qualities of melted stone, forms be true to clay, potters themselves should immerse themselves in hard work. Such a modesty of ambition would produce healthy work. Examples of such work are illustrated in the book, canonical pots of the Sung dynasty, tea-ceremony wares, pots by Hamada and Leach himself. The reason for the success of the book lies partly in the image of independence that it projects, an image of a potter as symbolically independent of contemporary society. For many people after the war, it provided a blueprint in how to make pots and what kind of pots to make. Contemporary critics were more divided, some complaining of the gaps in Leach's canon (all figurative ceramics, most European decorative traditions, all the French pioneers). The most damning – and prescient – criticism of all was that Leach was in danger of formulating a 'new academicism. Not only are many other sorts of past ceramic achievements dismissed by it as debased or at best misguided, but the future is closed. It will admit only hand made ware of the kind produced by the author... for a precarious market of rich and cultured people, and those few commercially produced wares that illogically conform to the same standard.'

Leach's travails were most closely echoed by those of his potter friends in Japan. The porcelain of the Japanese potter Kenkichi Tomimoto (1886–1963) showed an attempt to make ceramics that responded to a contemporary situation as complex as that in Britain. For though there was a 'precarious market of rich and cultured people' prepared to support his ceramics, and a much higher literacy in ceramic history in Japan than in Britain, the specificity of Tomimoto's work made it a rarified art. Tomimoto had studied architecture and interior decoration at the Tokyo Academy of Fine Arts, before travelling to study in England between 1908 and 1910. A passionate and rebarbative writer, he published some of the first accounts of the ideas of Morris and Pugin on the decorative arts when he returned to Japan. He became a friend of Leach and they shared many early fervent experiments in making not only ceramics, but also furniture and textiles, exhibiting these 'modern' hybrid objects in Tokyo galleries to a select group of artists and intellectuals. For instance, in 1915 Tomimoto started making *toban* (porcelain boards), flat pieces of either round or rectangular porcelain that were intended to be hung on the walls of modern houses. Conscious that his ceramics were a rarified, not a demotic, art he commented in 1917 that 'what has been called craft are toys... for a limited number of people. Those, of course, include my works.' Tomimoto's sophisticated eclecticism shows in his description of a particular porcelain jar from 1918 as inspired by a figurine by Aristide Maillol with a 'soft, rounded back'. He was a singular figure in Japanese ceramics in the 1920s and 30s: his critiques of the orthodoxies of his contemporaries, his development of new techniques of decorating porcelain and above all his advocacy for the design of new patterns ('don't make patterns from patterns') made him well known. His porcelain jars, boxes and dishes expressed their contemporaneity not through a choice of modern motifs, but through his conviction that the potter was an expressive (and intellectual) artist.

This metropolitan view of where ceramics belonged contrasted with Hamada's decision to move to the pottery village of Mashiko on his return in 1923 from his three years with Leach in St Ives. Mashiko was to remain his home until his death in 1973, and it became a place of pilgrimage for both Japanese and Western potters. His choice of a small and undistinguished pottery village was based in his perception of the innate 'health' of country pots, something that had been important to him since his 'discovery' of the quotidian unglazed *namban* jars of Okinawa during his travels with the potter Kanjiro Kawai in 1917. These jars seemed to him to reveal the 'real true life' of these potters. His time with Leach and their joint exploration into vernacular English slipware compounded this vision of an integration between self-effacing maker and pot. Into this also came the memory of his 'numerous visits made to see the life and work of the weaver Ethel Mairet and the sculptor Eric Gill in Ditchling, Sussex': examples of a successful aesthetic life. The significance of these experiences in England was expressed by the Japanese critic Jiro Aoyama in 1933 when he commented that Hamada 'went to England and trained himself to be Japanese'. For Hamada, Mashiko meant a 'letting go of what I had learned at schools in Tokyo and at the laboratory in Kyoto, I set out wholeheartedly in search of health in my work and in my lifestyle'. This meant making real his oppositional view of an unhealthy (Westernized and academic) metropolis and a 'healthy' (Japanese and instinctive) rurality.

Hamada's search for health meant 'limiting' himself to local raw materials for glazes and local clay for the pots: an identification with place through direct working with the 'stuff' of its composition. It was a 'limitation' in which he revelled. His pots were an expressive re-interpretation of country pots from Japan and Korea and medieval England. The Chinese Sung pots and English slipwares that had been his model in St Ives developed into vigorously thrown, facetted and trimmed bowls, teapots and vases. The iron and ash glazes rarely lie still on the surfaces; they are animated by fingers pulled through, splashed with overglazes, incised with patterns. Even bright enamels inspired by the pots of

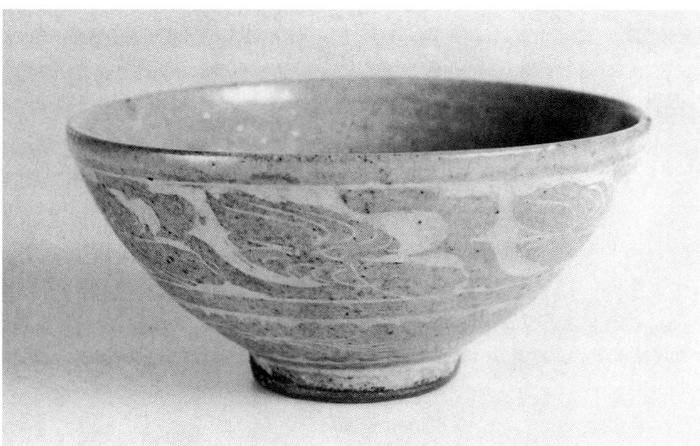

82 **Shoji Hamada**, bowl, 1923 (stoneware, d. 19.5 cm/7⅝ in). Early reviewers were struck by Hamada's facility with different decorative techniques. While working at St Ives he used sgraffito, slip-trailing and inlaid slips. This bowl is made in emulation of Sung Dynasty Chinese T'zo Chou wares.

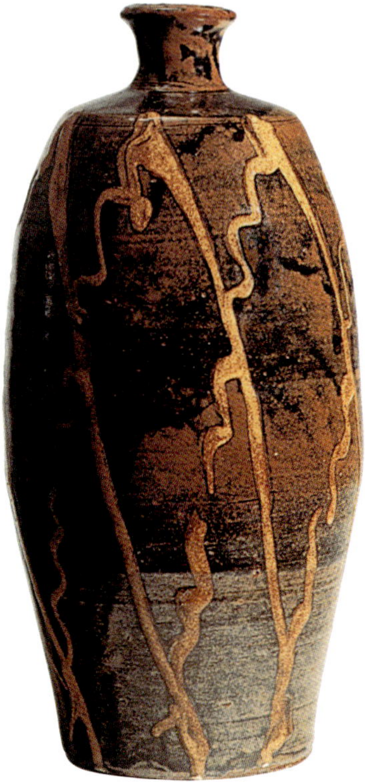

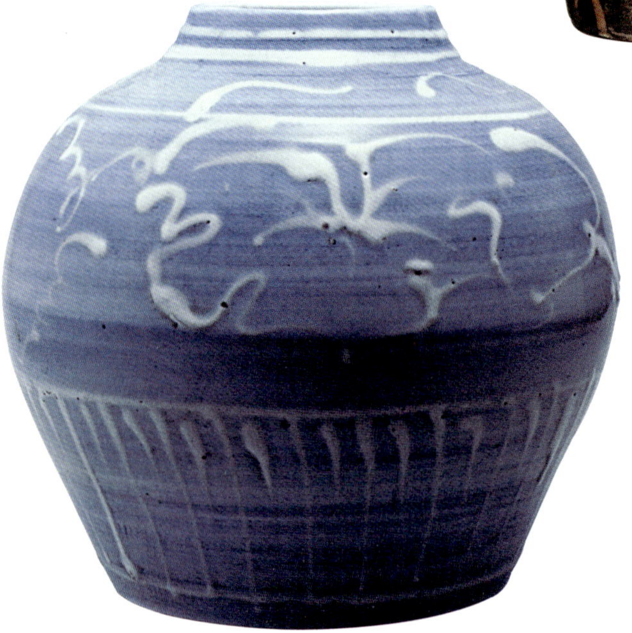

83 **Shoji Hamada**, bottle, *c.* 1929 (stoneware, h. 35.5 cm/14 in). This vigorous bottle shows how adept Hamada was at synthesizing different pottery traditions. The form is Chinese, the pattern Japanese and the trailed slip a technique he learnt in England.

84 **Kenkichi Tomimoto**, jar, 1925 (24.5 cm/9⅝ in). Tomimoto's commitment to developing new patterns was dogged: 'During the ten years or more since I decided to make my own patterns, I have drawn thousands of pattern designs… [but] there are only twenty to thirty patterns that I use today… if I compare them with one pattern from an old ware, I feel that all my works degrade into nothing while the old piece continues to shine.'

the Okinawa islands to the south of Japan were employed. These were modern pots for a convenient metropolis, powerful expressions of a belief by a modern potter in how particular traditions could authenticate a potter's practice. For Kanjiro Kawai (1890–1966), like Hamada the scion of a well-to-do family and graduate of Kyoto University, the mediation of tradition and contemporaneity was expressed through the development of a complex palette of rich glazes and overglaze decoration.

In April 1926 Hamada, Kawai and Tomimoto met under the auspices of Soetsu Yanagi to discuss the 'intention to establish a museum of Japanese Folk Art', and an arts organization, a guild of artisans connected to a 'common belief in correct crafts aesthetics'. Yanagi, a philosopher, literary critic and aesthetician, had been Leach's great interlocutor between 1912 and 1919 when Leach returned to England. As the editor of an avant-garde magazine he had introduced to Japan an eclectic melange of the ideas of Tolstoy and Ruskin, the poetry of William Blake and Walt Whitman and the art of Rodin. He had also provided much needed moral and financial support to Leach by subsequently exhibiting his work in Japan. Now Yanagi's attention, once fixed on Western mysticism and art, now became focused on what he called *mingei* or the 'arts of the people' of Korea and Japan. For him the beauty of everyday ceramic, wooden and lacquer utensils provided a corrective to the ego-driven arts of the present with their stress on self-expression. *Mingei* was best seen in the work of the Korean peasant potters, or the craft workers of Okinawa, who made things 'unknowingly' and self-effacingly, unconcerned by an imperative to innovate. As a movement its aim was to preserve some of the threatened native local traditions of handwork through inspirational contact with artist-craftsman leaders.

The first manifestation of this was in 1928 when artist-craftsmen associated with the nascent movement contributed to both the exterior and interior of the Folkcrafts Pavilion (Mikuniso) at the Tokyo Exhibition. It was 'Japanese in nature and also extremely suitable for contemporary life', with Hamada showing not only pots, but also a Gothic fireplace revealing the continuing influence of his life in England. By 1934 when Leach again visited Japan the *mingei* movement was substantial, with a monthly illustrated journal, a regional network of associations, patronage from the powerful Tokyo department stores, and annual exhibitions. As Leach put it: 'they have their shops and press and sales and their work is on the point of really entering the households of taste of new Japan as an antidote to the wretched half caste and modern products which so sicken Western visitors to this country.' At its best, the *mingei* movement nurtured renewed interest in the 'old kilns' of Japan, those making work for an immediate locality or for the tea ceremony. Bizen, for instance, once famous for its unglazed wood-fired vessels for the tea-ceremony, was almost defunct before the renaissance of interest in the early 1930s. The potter Toyo Kaneshige of Bizen, credited as the 'father' of this revival, became nationally known – and eventually was named a 'National Living Treasure'. The continuing strength of regional potteries can be traced back to this period. The 1930s provided a background of increasing militarism and fervent nationalism, against which the idea of a distinctive Japanese culture seen in the 'healthy' arts of everyday people was seductive.

The *mingei* movement was not unified: there was a class division between the university or art school-educated leaders of the movement, Yanagi, Hamada and Kawai (Tomimoto soon having departed from the group), and the artisan recipients of their advice. Leach wrote of Hamada:

Take that tea-cup alone – that handle… there is only one man in Japan who can put a handle on properly. He knew his own culture before he came to the west to study ours. When he knew both he began to put handles on cups in a way of his own, the real new Japanese way… Under his guidance a few country potters are beginning to learn and perceive what is needed.

In the pottery village of Fujina in the south of Japan, one of the few places where lead-based glazes were used, Yanagi and Leach encouraged the production of a version of English slipware. Large 'medieval' jugs, in the English spirit, began to be made for the new taste.

Britain in the 1930s

For the British potter, the practical as well as ideological complexities of making contemporary pots in a vernacular idiom can be seen in the early career of Michael Cardew. A passionate exponent of the innate vigour in English slipware, he frequently visited one of the last folk-potteries in North Devon as a child, and fell in love with its 'generosity'. In 1923, after graduating from Oxford, Cardew joined Leach just as Hamada was leaving for Japan, and spent three years at St Ives. In 1926 he took over an abandoned pottery at Winchcombe in the Cotswolds, employing local potter Elijah Comfort to help. A contemporary sketch shows aesthetic dereliction. The pottery had impeccable vernacular credentials, having supplied large washing pans and flowerpots for the local community. There was a vast kiln that took 3500 to 4500 pieces to fill if fired three or four times a year. The scale of this enterprise, coupled with the fact that Cardew intended to make his pots as cheap as their industrial counterparts, meant that he was throwing quantities and sizes of pots unthinkable at St Ives. There was an element of the heroic in these huge grain jars and cider flagons: they suggest a generosity in living, an expansive view of what he thought were 'necessary pots'.

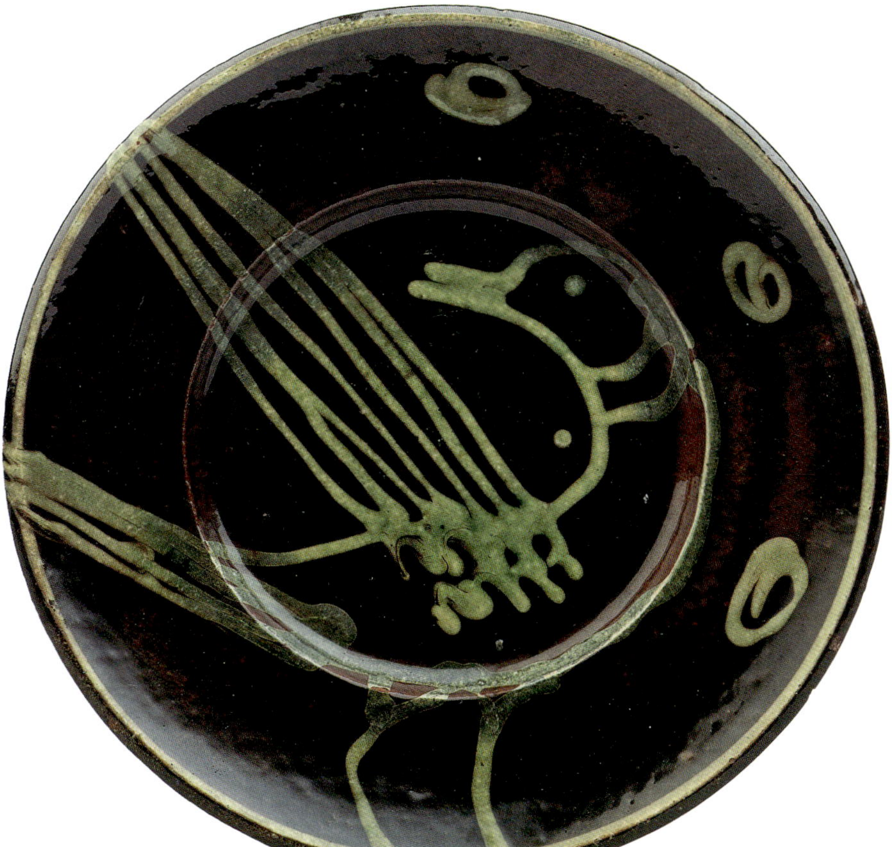

85 **Michael Cardew**, *Bird Dish*, c. 1932 (earthenware, d. 30.2 cm/11⅞ in).
Cardew learned to sliptrail – pipe liquid coloured clays – with great facility and spontaneity; his imagery of birds, fish and deer were less studied and symbolic than that of Leach's pilgrims, mermaids and well-heads.

Although Cardew had a vision of his pottery as part of an organic community, it was London collectors and exhibitions that were supporting him in his precarious experiment. Earthenware harmonized, as Leach had said, 'with the whitewash, oak, iron, leather and pewter of old England'; to make it appeal to all but the cognoscenti was impossible. To critics like Charles Marriott, what Cardew was doing was 'to lift this peasant tradition into the region of conscious art, and still keep its native character and relation to utility.' But even Henry Bergen, one of Leach and Cardew's most supportive collectors, was driven to complain 'peasant work is quite out of place in the modern kitchen... Practically all the slipware I have begins to lose its glaze after a short time. Much of it is porous.' In 1939 Cardew decided he could no longer pretend that it was economic to run Winchcombe and decided to move to Cornwall. Cardew's experience at Winchcombe framed some essential questions for him for his later life as a potter in Africa and Cornwall. His emphasis on self-reliance in technology and an understanding of local raw materials came from his bruising encounter with the realities of his attempt to revive slipware. His optimism about the possibilities for pottery remained intact.

Not all pottery in Britain in the 1920s and 30s was so embattled, nor so defensive. For William Staite Murray, the Head of Ceramics at the Royal College of Arts since 1925, it was self-evident that pottery was the equal of the other arts. Perhaps because he had worked making pots on the fringes of the Vorticist movement after basic training in pottery at Camberwell Art College, Staite Murray was more confident of their reach. His stoneware pots rapidly moved from an emulation of Chinese forms and brushwork decoration to a more complex repertoire of incisions and abstracted markings. They are vigorously thrown and trimmed, often with prominent foot rings and deep throwing marks enhanced by the spontaneity of the decoration, a process that he described as 'rhythmic plastic growth and form, abstract and sculpturesque.' The effect of these pieces is of the monumental, close to what the poet and critic Geoffrey Grigson noted in relation to the work of Henry Moore: 'what is typically English in pottery seems to me never out of touch with the roundness and solidity of natural forms, the human breast or thigh, the tree trunk, the boulder, the flint block, if you like, the turnip.' In exhibiting with Henry Moore and in becoming a member of the Seven and Five Society with Ben Nicholson in 1927, Staite Murray's work was seen to be in the vanguard of 'canvas-free artists', as Herbert Read called them. Just as Moore was exploring direct carving in English stone, where, as Rosalind Krauss has pointed out, the organic form of the sculpted object is close to the organic development of the material from which it was made, so in Staite Murray there was an engagement with pottery as direct making with clay.

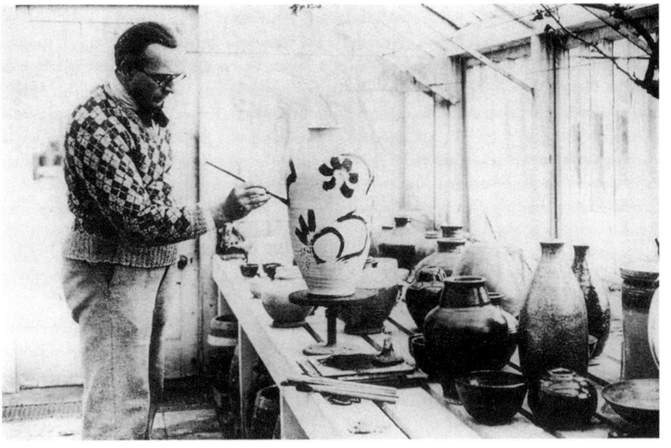

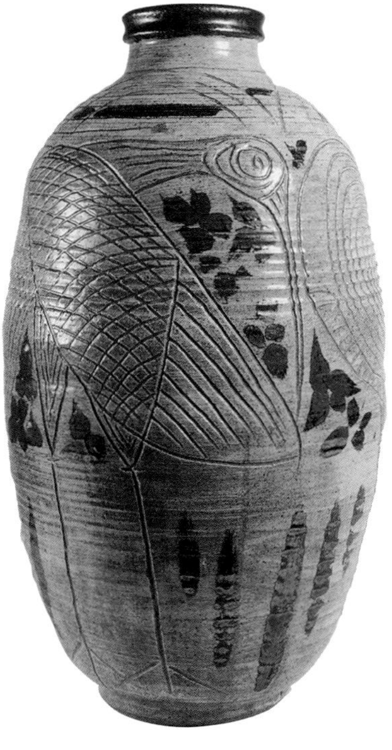

86 **William Staite Murray**, decorating a pot at Bray, *c.* 1930. Herbert Read called him a 'canvas-free artist'; Staite Murray aimed to set pottery on a par with painting as an art form.

87 **William Staite Murray**, *Persian Garden Jar*, 1931 (stoneware, 56.5 cm/22¼ in). For Staite Murray, well read in Zen Buddhism and the philosophy of Henri Bergson, pottery was 'practical theology', a deeply spiritual process of attunement to the act of creation. Pots were conceived as experiments in 'pure form', their names acting as indicators of mood rather than as directions to source material: *Persian Garden*, *Wheel of Life*, *Kwan Yin*. 'Staite Murray would roundly refuse to sell you one of his masterpieces... if he imagined that you might stick geraniums into it. Such pots are really abstract sculpture under accepted limitations'.

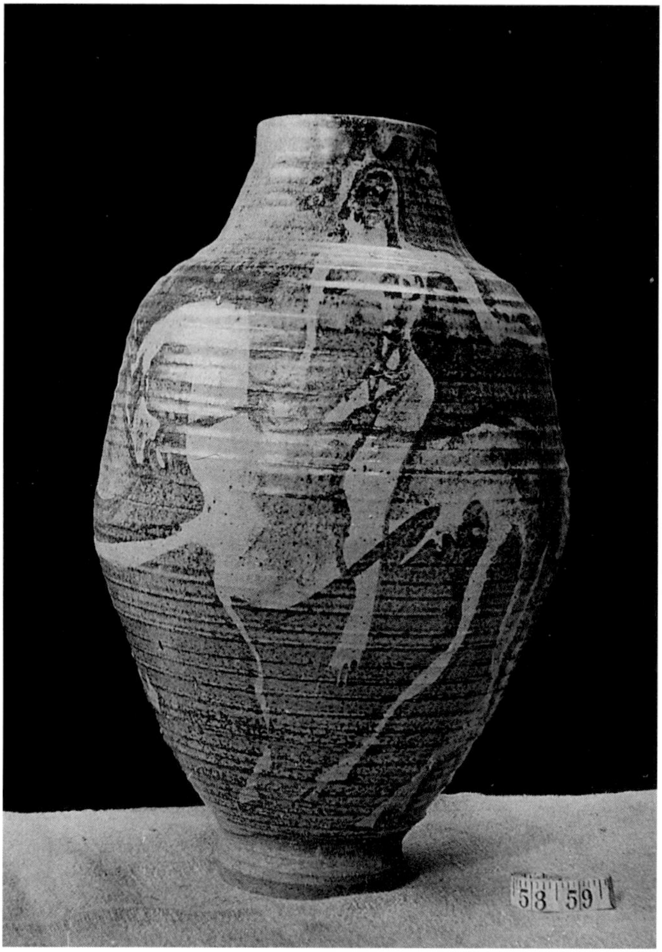

88 **Sam Haile**, *Triumphal Procession*, 1937 (stoneware, h. 42 cm/16½ in).
Haile's pots turned the quietist appropriation of English traditions on their head. Where Leach or Staite Murray made reference to vigorous freedom in throwing, or quoted in their decoration from vernacular sources, Haile made direct expressions with vast, loose anthropomorphic forms and Dionysian decorations.

Staite Murray left England in 1939, was stranded by the war in Rhodesia and for complex reasons never made pots again. Unlike Leach, his written output, though interesting, was scattered. His pupils, the best of whom were Henry Hammond (1914–89) and Sam Haile (1909–48), had only a limited impact, Hammond due to his immersion in teaching, and Haile because of his early death. Haile was both a painter and a potter, a quixotic visionary whose imaginative grasp of source material was searching and intense. The titles of his pots indicate the gap between Leach's and Haile's readings of English tradition: in the place of Devon harvest jugs are the pots with such titles as *Cerne Abbas Giant* and *The Long Man*.

Haile was a pacifist and, as war approached in 1939, he decided to move to America, where he rapidly gained exhibitions and landed jobs teaching, first at Alfred University for a year and subsequently at Ann Arbor. Here his interest in the archaic developed through Mediterranean sources (*Cretan Feast* and *Blood Rite* showing his visceral approach) to those of Mexico and pre-Columbian sources. The large jar *Chichen Itza* of 1942 was described by a critic in 1946 as showing that Haile

perceived some imaginative relationship between the barbarism of the past and the present war situation, of which this pot is really an expression.The painting, boldly divided horizontally into three layers, shows the savage figure of a sacrificial priest, uniting all three zones in a design of great power. Round the other side totem animals appear above and below, and the severed arms of sacrificial victims in the dark central band.

Haile's time in America amounted to only four years before he was drafted into the army, but in this compressed period he managed to expose the rather bloodless attitudes to decoration then prevalent in ceramics and to open up a view of forms previously unapprehended – intensely symbolic, sexual and transgressive.

Germany and the USA in the 1930s

If Leach was struggling in England to make a new kind of vernacular ceramics popular beyond a metropolitan elite of collectors, in Germany traditional ceramics were being used in

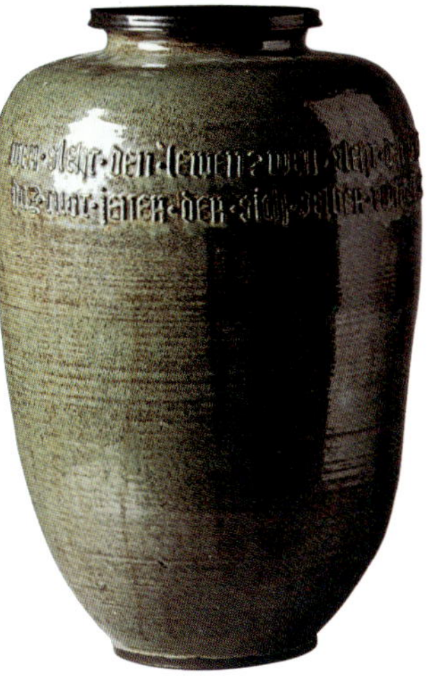

89 **Hubert Griemert**, vase made as a prize for the Berlin Olympic Games of 1936 (stoneware, h. 60 cm/23½ in).
Griemert's large, high-shouldered jar shows how the use of a form redolent of sturdy country-ware, steeped in vernacular traditions – the 'volkisch' – could be made official. The verse in German blackletter script around the shoulder comes from a famous medieval poet, Walther von der Vogelweide. The pot brings together powerful cultural images and traditions to serve a specific political ideal.

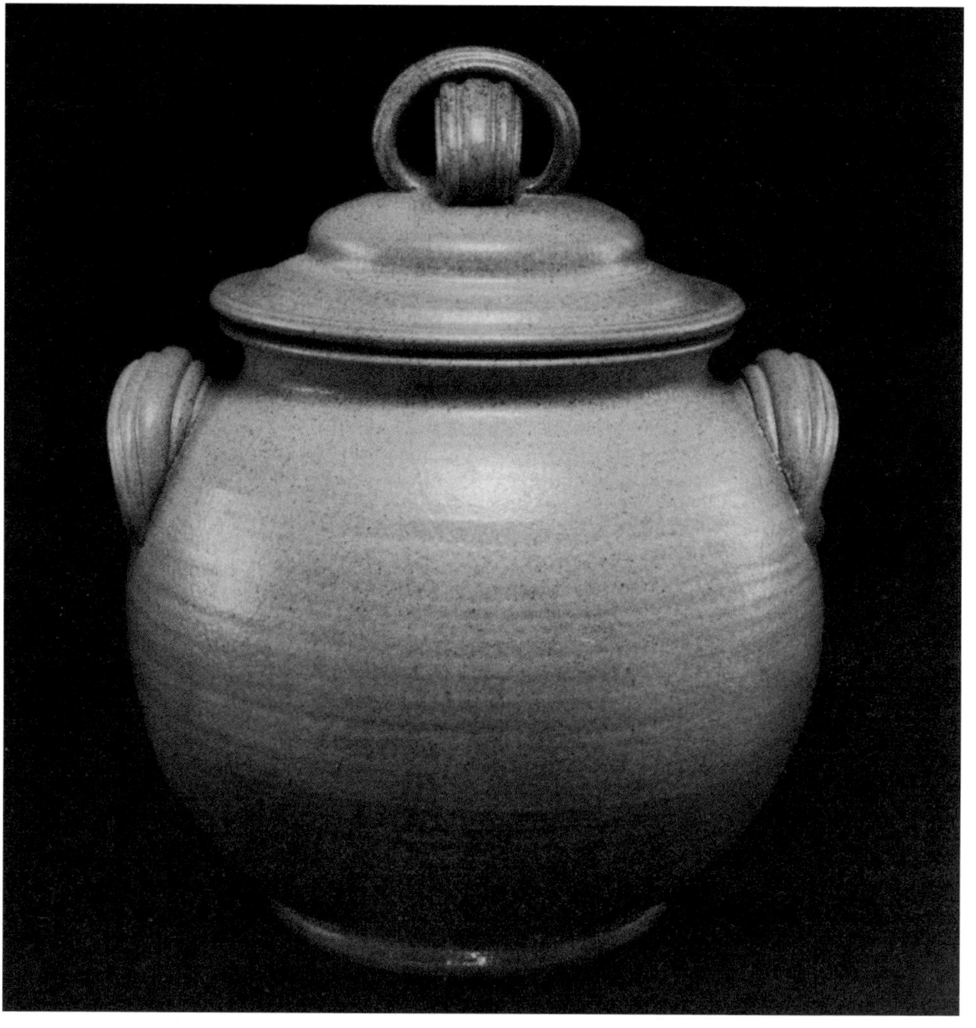

90 **Arthur A. Baggs**,
Cookie Jar, 1938 (salt-glazed stoneware, h. 33.3 cm/13 in). The title of this pot is suggestive of domestic comfort, rather than indicating its actual intended use: it was the prize-winning exhibit at the National Ceramic exhibition. With its generous proportions, salt-glazing, throwing-marks and pulled handles, it is a sophisticated interpretation of traditions of rural pottery presented in nostalgic terms.

many ways, some of them powerfully politicized. Particular materials and techniques, like wood panelling in larch or the use of wrought iron, were considered indigenous and thus correct for the new German state. In 1939 the Deutsche Warenkunde (or German Index of Goods) was published as a 'guide to a racially pure material environment, free of foreign influences, of stupidities and deformations, that corresponds to our whole German renewal, and in addition stimulates designers and manufacturers of our objects of use to produce beautifully formed, well made and functional creations'. In Hitler's words, 'the German Handicrafts rooted in a dignified tradition, will proceed to a new blooming, sheltered by the People and State'. Hitler's twisting of 'tradition' to suit his political aims of racial purity took on chilling associations of 'earth' and nationhood.

However, not all the ceramics of the period followed such politicized styles. Otto Douglas-Hill (1897–1972) and the Dutch-born Jan Bontjes van Beek (1899–1969) both used Oriental idioms in a decidedly modern way. Both of these potters were critical of the Nazi regime and suffered as a consequence, but they were able to continue to work and exhibit because their pots were not deemed to be 'decadent'.

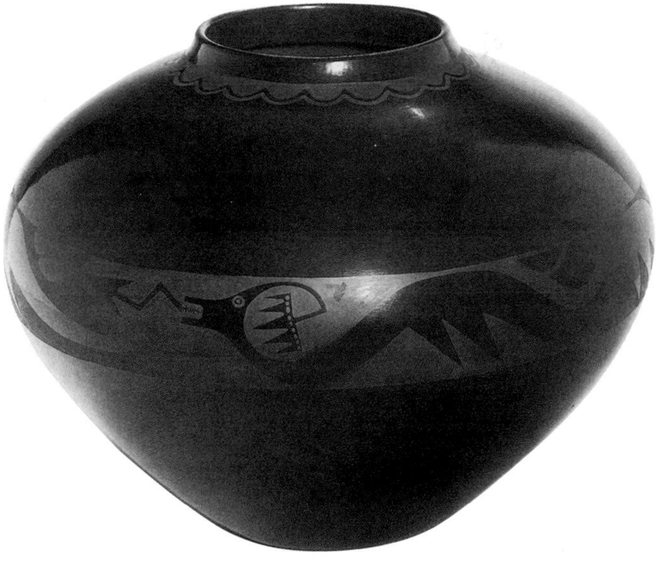

91 **Maria** and **Julian Martinez**, *Cartier Jar*, 1935 (black on black, h. 38 cm/15 in).
With growing interest in a revivified, or reinvented, folk pottery whose aesthetic of repeated geometric patterning on simple forms appeared so contemporary and close to Art Deco style, Maria and Julian Martinez of the San Ildefonso Pueblo of New Mexico abandoned traditional polychrome wares and concentrated on the burnished blackwares. Modern motifs appeared with indigenous ones; from 1925 their work was signed, putting further distance between the anonymity of older Pueblo pottery and this new kind of 'romantic nationalist' ceramics.

In America during the Depression a few attempts were made to encourage waning indigenous ceramic traditions, with a 1934 directive that all National Park shops with a government concession were required to sell regional handicrafts. Traditional ceramics, like those of the Carolinas or the American Indian pueblos of New Mexico, were adapted to survive. It was a request from the Smithsonian Institution and from archaeologists working on excavated black shards that encouraged Maria Martinez (1884–1981) to develop the 'black-on-black' wares that became so popular in the 1920s and 30s. Though the integrity of design was hers, the imperative to change from polychromatic wares was entirely driven by others' apprehension of greater 'authenticity' lying in earlier styles.

In North Carolina a co-operative pottery called Jugtown was established in 1921 to make traditional domestic wares – but not for traditional domestic interiors. Their distributor was the Tiffany Studios of New York, and gradually Chinese glazes were added to the decorative repertoire.

A more complex representation of Americanness is to be found in the work of Glen Lukens (1887–1967). In 1933 a new ceramics department was established at the University of Southern California in Los Angeles and Lukens, self-taught, and with only a limited technical knowledge, was made chairman. His work goes well beyond a heady, romantic appropriation of landscape and cultural source material. In his ceramics, with their use of rough unglazed surfaces in tension with rich glazes, he achieved an intensity of expression that prefigured the organicism of postwar European ceramics.

The passionate search by potters in the 1920s and 30s to find an appropriate reflection of fundamental national characteristics, to encapsulate aspects of a landscape, or to animate a vernacular tradition, was a search for a way of giving new meaning to the art of pottery. The correspondence between pottery and national character was expressed most cogently by Herbert Read in *The Meaning of Art* (1931):

the art [of pottery] is so fundamental, so bound up with the elementary needs of a civilization, that a national ethos must find its expression in this medium. Judge the art of a country, judge the fineness of its sensibility, by its pottery; it is a sure touchstone. Pottery is pure art; it is art freed from any imitative intention.

92 **Glen Lukens**, *Death Valley Plate*, 1941 (earthenware, d. 47.7 cm/18¾ in).
Lukens was noted for his use of bright crackle glazes and glazes that pooled or fluxed on the rims of his bowls, properties that he connected to the forces of nature: 'I used to watch lightning across the sky and think, if we could control that, it wouldn't be beautiful anymore.' Lukens used the minerals of the desert within some of his glazes, and named them accordingly: Death Valley Yellow, Mojave Golden Amber.

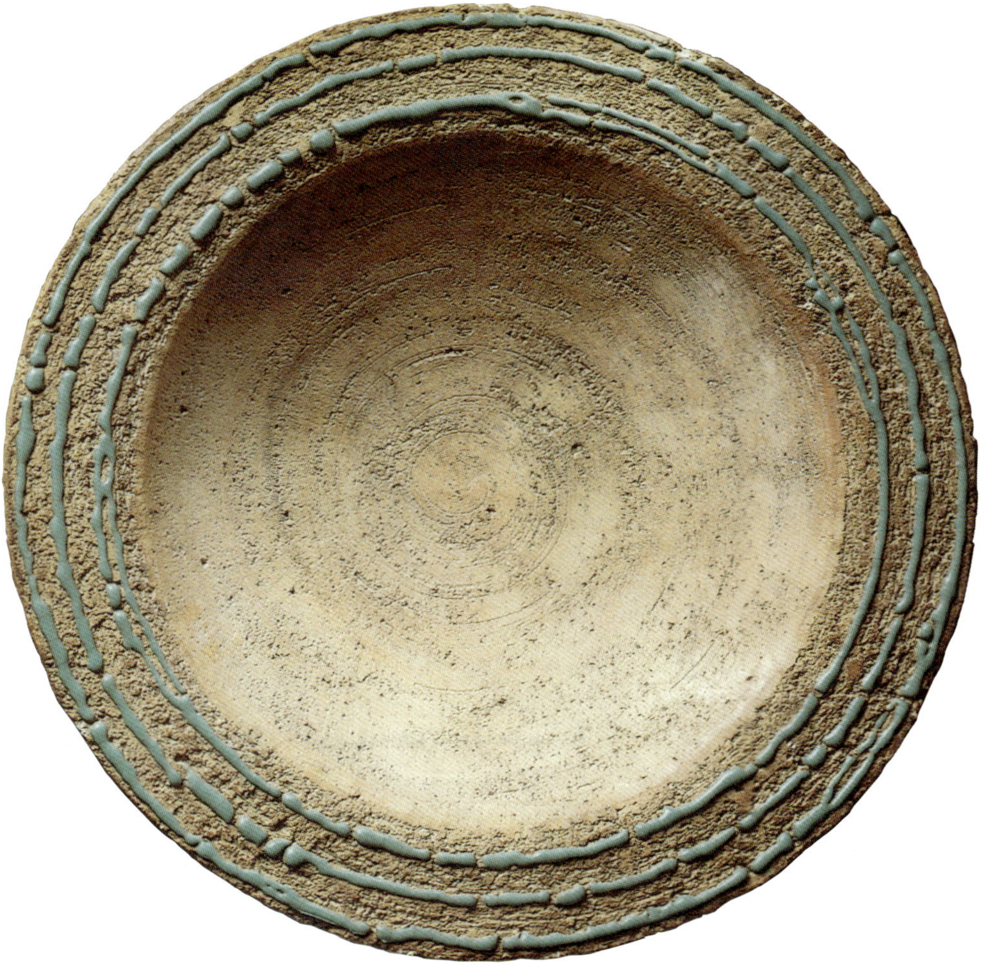

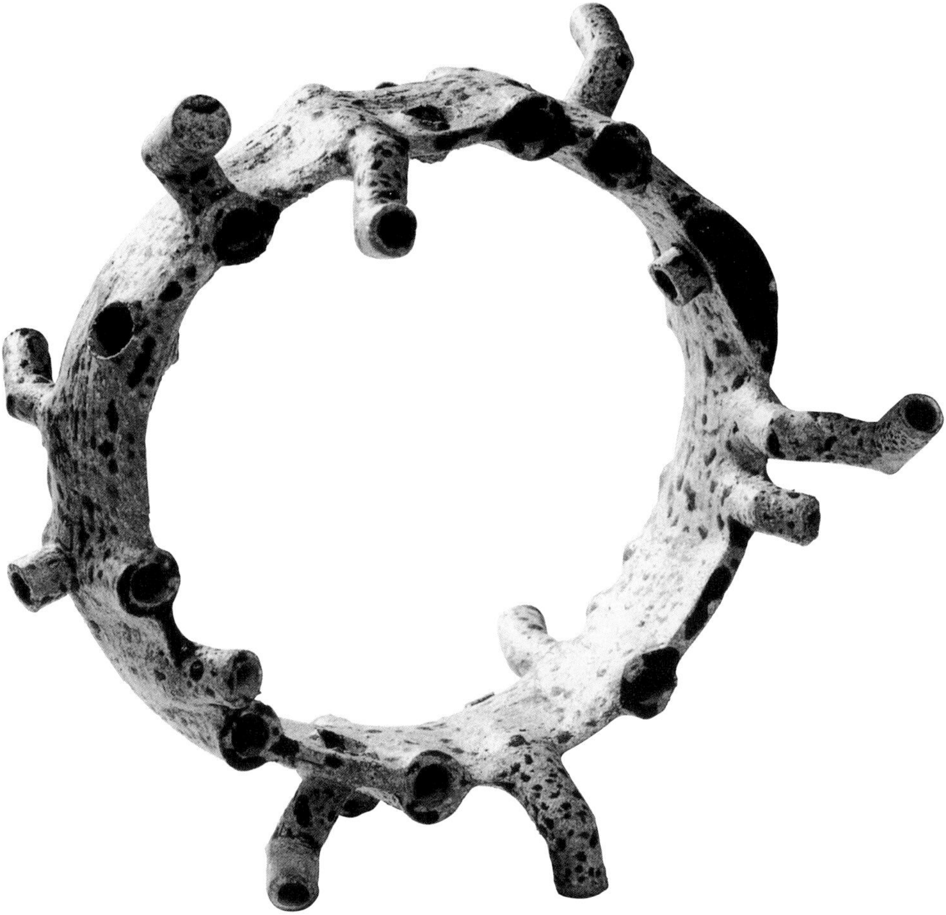

Chapter Three 1945–65

Japan: radical beginnings

For a generation of young Japanese potters, returning to the highly stratified world of salon exhibitions after the cataclysmic events of the Second World War was inconceivable. Japan lay in ruins. Many cities had effectively stopped functioning and, for the first time in its history, Japan was occupied by a foreign army; yet the art world that they were confronted with seemed unchanged, stultifying and unreal in its adherence to pre-war conduct. There remained a clear separation between sculpture and ceramics, and the deep prevailing hostility to modern Western art that had been fostered during the highly nationalist 1930s persisted. Furthermore, due to the chronic shortages there was 'no clay for making, no firewood for firing, no ceramics for selling'; it seemed a time to begin again and to return to first principles. The ferment of ideas that led to the formation of new groupings, in particular the Shiko-kai in 1947 and the Sodeisha in 1948, is reflected in their manifestos with heady talk of new eras: 'A harmonious group of young ceramic artists have been born out of the decayed plain fields. Since we have been brought up by the earth which is warmer than a mother's heart, we will efface ourselves by means of the earth', as the Shiko-kai manifesto put it.

The formation of the Sodeisha by Kazuo Yagi (1918–79) and four friends, all sons of Kyoto potters, was built on two principles. One was simply to stop submitting their works to the salons and to initiate their own independent exhibitions with no category divisions, thereby liberating themselves from having to submit to genres they disliked. The other was to stop using canonical forms. These were the shapes that underpinned the gentle modulations in traditions deemed acceptable by the critics and curators that ran the prestigious national exhibitions. The choice of name, 'sodei' referring to an earthworm wriggling in mud, was a palpable expression of their powerful absorption in an elemental relationship with clay. These young potters were 'returning' to clay, being 'effaced' by it: in doing so they expressed their feeling that the older generation of potters had betrayed and smothered the material. That much of the Sodeisha's early work is unglazed is

93 **Kazuo Yagi**, *Zamsa no sampo* (Walk of Samsa), 1954 (stoneware, h. 27.5 cm/11 in). This work provoked hysteria when first exhibited in a Tokyo exhibition. With its reference to Franz Kafka's *Metamorphosis*, a classic story of twentieth-century angst in which Gregor Samsa is turned into a gigantic beetle, the work can be read as a 'walking sculpture', the small thrown pipes acting like myriad disorientated legs. All the normative properties of the vessel – the singularity of its opening, its volumetric clarity, its stability – are upended and symbolically broken.

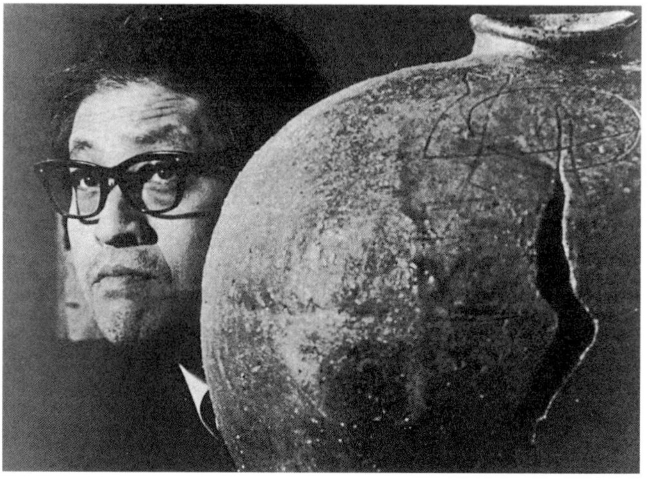

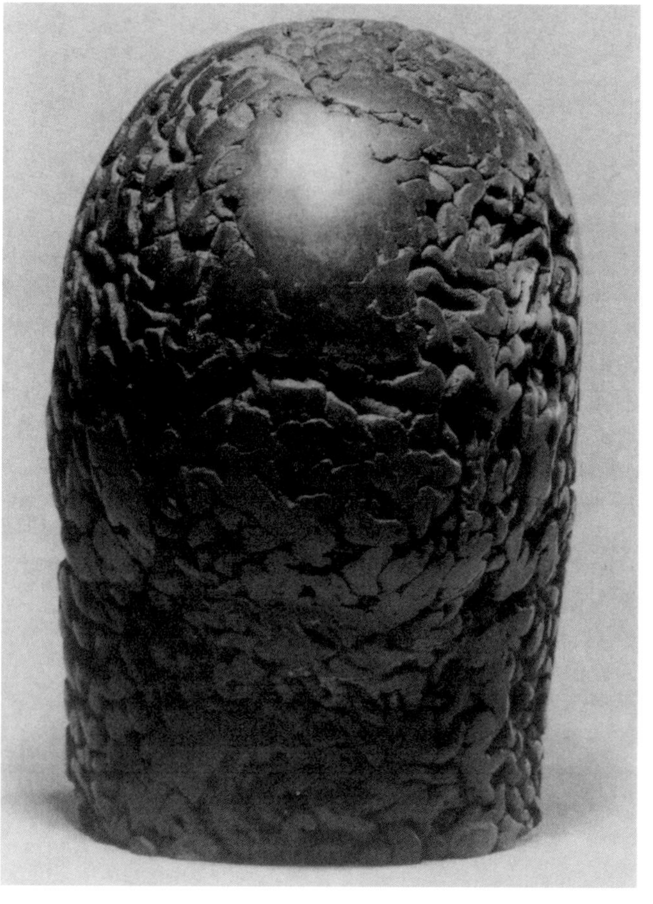

94 **Kazuo Yagi** with his large pot fired at Shigaraki, 1969.
Yagi often inscribed his vessels with distinctive doodles that recall the work of Paul Klee.

95 **Kazuo Yagi**, *Shozo* (Portrait), 1964 (h. 19 cm/7½ in).
Yagi's 'Kokuto' or black earthenwares fired without glazes such as this piece formed a major part of his sculptural output in the 1960s. A Japanese critic wrote of their 'inorganic gleam… the furthest thing possible from the qualities of chance and *aji* [good taste]'.

no coincidence: it reflects this passionate, almost phenomenological, identification with clay itself. The choice of what to reject was more complex.

For a young avant-garde potter the postwar world of Japanese ceramics was beset by traditions, from the rural 'old kilns' of Bizen and Iga that produced pottery for the tea ceremony to the great centres of tableware production like Seto. Traditions were not, and could not, be ditched wholesale. It was one thing to choose to exhibit independently, but to work in Kyoto – or anywhere else in Japan – necessitated working alongside more traditional potters. It is telling that Yagi was firing his new ceramics in the traditional communal wood-fired kiln at Gojozaka in Kyoto: this very close proximity to old practitioners would mean that any deviation from the norm in their ceramics was to prove shocking. Then to lay claim to parts of ceramic history as 'modern', as the Sodeisha group did, was an even greater iconoclasm for this older generation of potters. For one of the key strategies in the work of these avant-garde potters was the animating of diverse parts of ceramic tradition. For instance, in 1950, when some of Yagi's pots, inscribed with images derived from the work of Paul Klee and Pablo Picasso, were exhibited in New York, Yagi declared that these vessels, with their intense graphic scribbles, showed a powerful connection between Klee and Korean Mishima wares. They both possessed what he described as 'pure, autonomous lines'. In claiming this connection, Yagi was declaring that it was possible to be an avant-garde Oriental potter, that modernity could be built on Oriental foundations. In a description that captures the intensity of their identification with modernity, they adopted the French word 'objet' to describe these new kinds of ceramic object.

In searching for the modern within tradition these potters often looked to the archaic. Osamu Suzuki (b. 1926), another founding member of the Sodeisha, made work whose titles referred to the prehistoric Jomon period (10,000–300 BC) figures: 'deizo' (clay image) and 'dogu' (clay figure). Mutsuo Yanagihara (b. 1934) would claim in the early 1970s that his gold and silver vessels were derived from ancient Japanese Sue wares (AD 300–600) [140]. It was clear that in making a connection with elemental ceramic history contemporary 'objets' acquired a depth of significance that was comparable to the use of Primitivism in the work of Picasso or Die Brücke.

In a way that echoes the Parisian avant-garde's rediscovery of African masks the Sodeisha became interested in 'haniwa', small earthenware archaic figures decorated with highly abbreviated patterns and marks from the Jomon period. Their 'modernity' and 'new immediacy' lay in the fact that they had not been considered as part of the formal ceramic canon by a previous generation. The American-Japanese sculptor Isamu Noguchi, who was working in ceramics in Japan between 1950 and 1952, gave them even more gravitas: they crossed over from the archaic to the modern, from pottery into sculpture – and indeed from the national to the international.

The fierce valorizing of the unorthodox and non-canonical is clear in the work many of the potters of these young movements. Junpie Sugie (b. 1936), a student of Tomimoto's at Kyoto brought up in the ceramic town of Tokoname, described how he used his inheritance in this new spirit: 'in Tokoname, the main product is the clay pipe, and the technology we had was concerned mainly with large-scale products. Many of the works produced there have diameters of more than a metre, whether they are giant jars and flower pots... Such an environment naturally made me want to produce large-scale works in ceramics.' This was an avant-garde that knew how to search for the non-aesthetic in ceramics and how to re-employ ceramic techniques, from industrial clay pipes to wood-firing.

Yagi's *Zamsa no sampo* (Walk of Samsa) [93] is an ambitious animation of what had been grounded and still. The disjunction of seeing the gentle effects of wood-firing and the striations of the

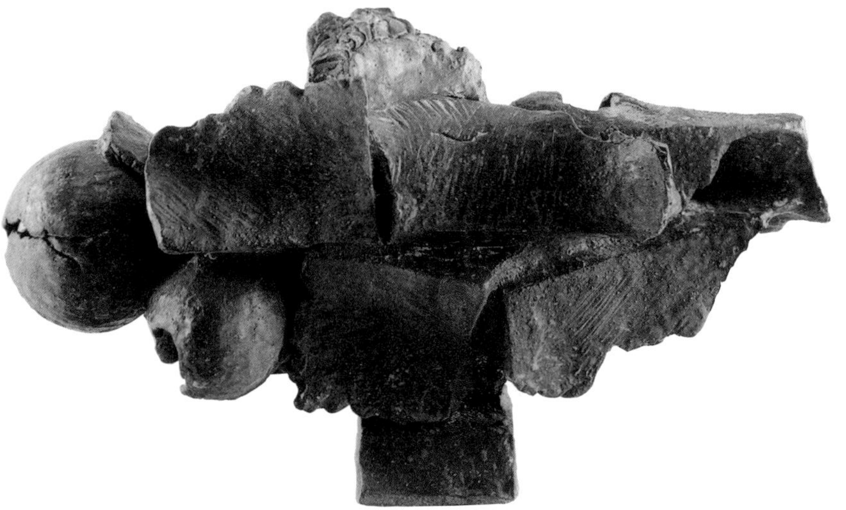

96 **Junpie Sugie**, *Action*, 1965 (clay/coil building, h. 43 cm/17 in). The solidity and grounded nature of vessels was questioned by Sugie's work in the 1960s. They are often composed from broken elements: Sugie seems to be implying that the certainties expressed by a central volume can no longer be upheld.

throwers' hand used to such new purposes was powerful. The reorientation of a wheel-thrown section was greeted as an iconoclastic way of thinking about the wheel: it was as if the almost spiritual correspondence between the potter's wheel with the traditional potter had been upended. Here was a potter using the wheel 'as a machine', as a starting point for a process of fragmentation and reconstruction.

Much of the early work of Yagi, Junkichi Kumakura (1920–85) and Shindo Tsuji (1910–81) followed a process of fragmentation of wheel-thrown forms, and their collaging into new works. These 'objets' lie down, are broken, have multiple openings. Decoration seems incoherent and arbitary.

The very closeness of familial and pedagogic relationships, the proximity of studios and kilns, was to make the suggestiveness of these new ceramics even greater. Such closeness allowed for – or

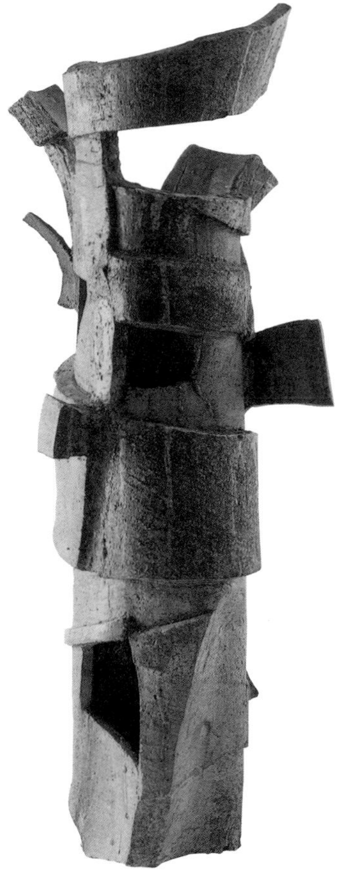

97 **Junkichi Kumakura**, *Frozen Flames*, 1956 (earthenware, h. 81.5 cm/32 in).
Kumakura's career led him through a number of different avant-garde groupings. This work shows the fascination with fragmentation and the opening up of interior space common to many of the early members of the Sodeisha group.

even necessitated – parody: these young potters were making their own work in contradistinction to their forebears. Yanagihara, who had studied under Tomimoto with Junpie Sugie and Shoji Kamoda (1933–83) at the Kyoto Municipal Art College in the late 1950s, made work that commented directly on his mentor's famous directive, 'No patterns from patterns'. This iconoclasm was often blunt and personal: Tomimoto's view of decoration was savagely satirized in Yanagihara's *Work a* of 1960. In a comment on the complex Japanese aesthetics of the 'accidental' in which some marks of the hand or the firing are considered particularly beautiful, Yanagihara 'accidentally' threw lumps of clay onto a rough base before blanketing the whole construction with an Oribe glaze. Yagi's development of 'kokuto' (literally 'black fire') in the early 1960s – a way of burning materials within the kiln to create a completely black surface on the object – also acted as a brutal effacement of the gentle austerities of wood-fired surfaces.

Although images of Picasso's pots and other contemporary Western painting and sculptures were known and admired, this was a revolution within and about Japanese ceramics. The connection that many avant-garde potters made with the new flower-arrangement schools of Ohara and Sogetsu which came to prominence in the 1950s reveals this. In opposition to the highly stylized conventions of flower arranging for the tea ceremony, these schools, catering to an increasingly affluent young generation of urban women, developed a new and dramatic aesthetic that needed new and dramatic ceramics: it was common for potters to make both so-called ' "objet" flower vases' alongside sculptural forms. It was as if after a period of almost convulsive dislocation these potters were involved in a cultural relocation, finding a new audience and new patrons.

The Sodeisha, too, achieved recognition for their works. In 1959 some of its members exhibited in a prestigious exhibition at the Tokyo National Museum of Modern Art, and the critical commentaries of the early 1960s suggest that they were taken seriously. By then the map of the Japanese art world had been reconfigured. There were new museums, new art colleges, new magazines: the positioning of hegemonic tradition against an avant-garde had broken down. At the time of the Tokyo Olympics in 1964 Japan had its first major international ceramics exhibition, the first opportunity for Japanese potters to contextualize their work with their international contemporaries. For many young Japanese potters, American West Coast ceramics, with their bravura brash colour and scope of non-ceramic reference, would be startling. The impact of these American ceramics in Japan was to be great but not revolutionary. The revolution – led by Yagi's generation – had already occurred.

Isamu Noguchi

The presence in Japan of Isamu Noguchi between 1950 and 1952 made a considerable impact in the ceramics world. In the vivid words of Osamu Suzuki, 'We felt his work to demonstrate the nature of clay itself; it was like throwing a rock into the seemingly unstoppable system of pottery.' Noguchi's work with clay mattered to the young potters of the Sodeisha in two ways. It connected them – as Suzuki put it – to the 'nature of clay itself', it seemed to be concerned with an essential materiality: just as the Sodeisha pioneers had tried to recover the rawness of clay so did Noguchi. Just as they had tried to 'efface' themselves through clay, so Noguchi, in his own words, wanted 'to exhaust one's hands in [Japan's] earth'. Secondly Noguchi seemed to have stepped outside the interminable movement of ceramic history by adopting whatever aspects of the canon he liked, a wildly liberating eclecticism for the Sodeisha. Noguchi, the son of an American mother and a Japanese father, had spent his childhood in both America and Japan. He studied with the sculptor Constantin Brancusi in Paris in the 1920s and had worked with clay, stone and bronze in New York. In 1931 he spent five months working in Kyoto in the studio of Uno Ninmatsu, a successful commercial mass-producer of popular lamp bases, and first saw archaic haniwa figures. Noguchi led a varied existence, both as a set designer for contemporary dance working with Martha Graham, and designing for industry, alongside his role as a sculptor. On his return to Japan in 1950 he 'jumped right into the world of Japanese pottery' as the critic Shuzo Takiguchi wrote in the introductory essay to an exhibition of his in 1953. He was

devouring the Japanese clay, firing in the traditional kilns of Karatsu, Shigaraki, Seto and Bizen; he has become a potter… this is an exhibition of pottery. Nevertheless Noguchi is firing his pottery as sculpture, or, at least they are being fired in a manner that captivates the fancy of the sculptor… He finds rightful justification in the primitive haniwa sculpture; no modern potter shall deny the sculptural position of the haniwa. The haniwa is ultimately united with the ancient earthenwares and pottery; Noguchi's aim is the revivification of this primitive relationship.

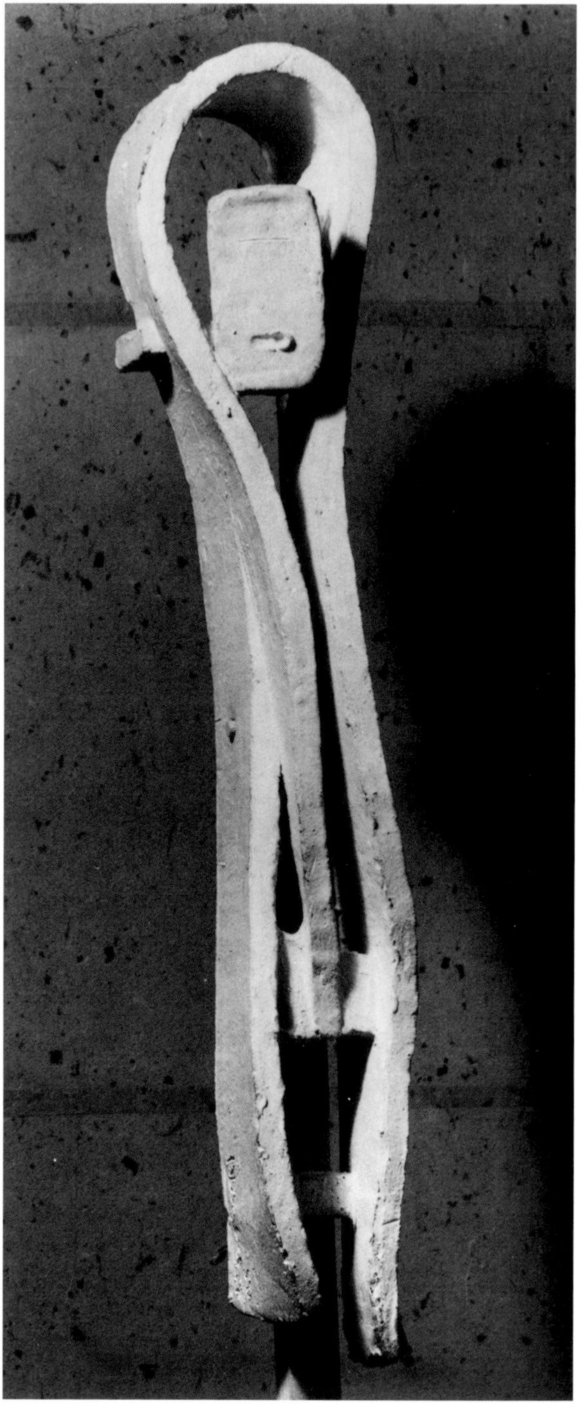

98 **Isamu Noguchi**, *Mrs White*, 1952 h. 100 cm/39 in).
A slab of Shigaraki clay over two metres long folded over into a sinuous loop, the work resembles a transparent structure, an abstracted figure whose interior is open to the viewer's gaze. Figures such as this one are, in fact, abstracted haniwa, something that Noguchi hinted at in his catalogue essay: 'Abstractions themselves are rooted in associations as potent as anatomy.'

The list of kilns Noguchi worked at gives an indication of why his impact was so great: he was playing fast and loose with Japan's ceramic heritage. This international sculptor was choosing to work not just with clay, but with particularly symbolic ceramic traditions. The kilns he used were wood-fired, his sculptures unglazed and often roughly modelled: their connection with the primitive was undisturbed by decorative surface associations. His use of a multiplicity of clays and of different ways of firing, as a starting point for a process rather than an aesthetic destination in itself, parallelled the ways in which Yagi was using traditional techniques of throwing and firing. In his exhibition in 1952 at Kamakura, Noguchi showed a great range of vessels and sculptures, quick figurative clay studies and fragmentary totems ranging from the scale of a hand to over six feet (two metres) high. They were often displayed on wooden or metal stands like exhibits from an ethnographic display. They possessed what Noguchi called an essence of sculpture, tactility: 'we may bump into it, bleed from its rough surface, or delineate its contours with our fingers'. Noguchi was claiming for sculpture something much more than sensual touch: this was sculpture that through its association with the primitive and the bodily, could threaten and even draw blood. Sculpture could – and should – connect with the ritualistic. Given this potent intermingling of themes and images, it is no wonder that Yagi should write, 'It was probably with Isamu Noguchi that I first started to feel close to sculpture and think about the actual process of making [sculpture] and its structure. When I looked at Noguchi's ceramics, I had the feeling, "Out of the blue he's really bloody well gone and outdone me!" '

Noguchi's freedom with traditions and his eclecticism was read by some Japanese critics ignorance of the cultural specificity of traditions. This discontent found a particular focus in his choice of collaborator – the potter Kitaoji Rosanjin (1883–1959). A maverick in the ceramics world, a calligrapher, restaurateur and gourmand, Rosanjin chose to work in a diverse range of styles encompassing most traditions and making work that possessed a passionate intensity. Critically, he felt free from obligations to regional styles: he functioned as Noguchi was said to do, 'firing in a manner that captivates the fancy of the sculptor'. Aloof from the ceramics hierarchies (he turned down the award of 'Living National Treasure' as meaningless) Rosanjin offered Noguchi not only a place to live on his estate near Kamakura, but also the use of his kilns.

99 (following pages) **Isamu Noguchi**, earthen wall, studio of the Noguchi/Yamaguchi House, 1951–52 (destroyed).
One wall of the studio was of beaten clay with a fireplace and a crude alcove cut into it for a haniwa (archaic clay image). The manner in which he conceived of his studio, carving some of it out of the hillside and using earth to create the key focal points of the room, 'ties me further into the soil', as he put it.

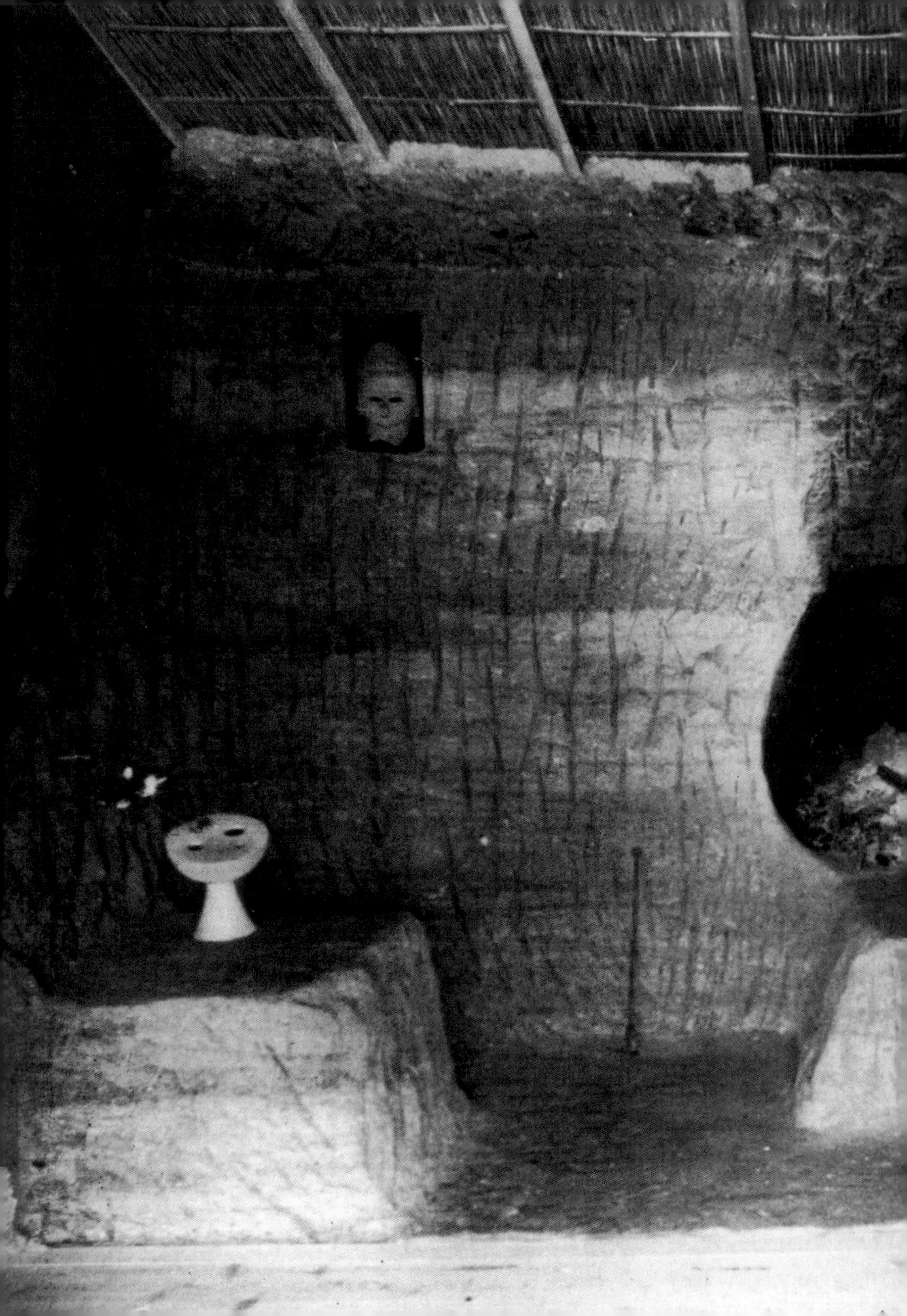

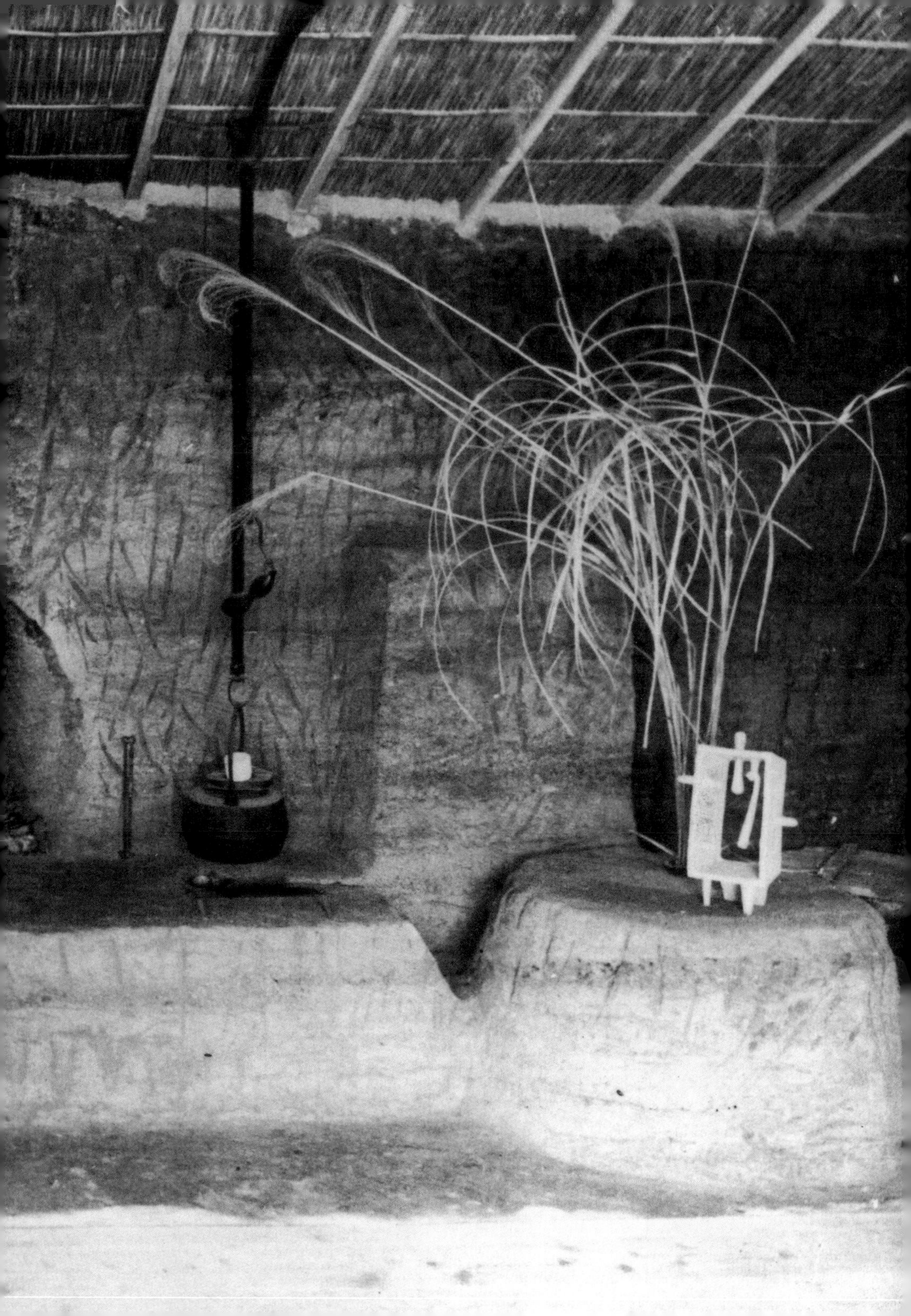

With Martha Graham Noguchi had thought about figures moving on a stage; now in a very literal way he was making a home, or a stage, for himself and his sculpture. His studio showed his way of thinking about clay as both medium and environment. It was seen by American magazines like the *New York Times Magazine* and *Interiors* as an example of distinguished Japanese taste; in Japan it was considered novel and mystifying. His terracotta of 1952, *The Apartment*, shows a similarly theatrical approach. It is an open box form with three 'floors' on which are placed small figures: in a telling comment on the back of a photograph of this work, Noguchi wrote that 'its secret and real name is *The Life of the Artist*.' Just as the interiority of Noguchi's figures is revealed through the openness of the sculpture, so he suggests that figures come alive when moving through architectural spaces. His later work creating sculptural environments, gardens, playgrounds and plazas, share this passionate identification between artist and the need to define space.

When Noguchi's ceramics were exhibited in 1954 at the Stable Gallery in New York the critic Hilton Kramer saw them as works of 'high unseriousness' and *Time* magazine described them as 'the gingerbread cookies of a playful and somewhat inebriated baker'. They were regarded as frivolities, as if Noguchi was on a Japanese holiday from his responsibilities to high seriousness, responsibilities that could only be achieved with other materials. Noguchi certainly felt this reproach. He had no exhibition after this for five years, and in his next show didn't exhibit clay works, but continued his concerns through his marble, granite and bronze sculpture.

The excitement about archaic pottery visible in European ceramics of the 1950s and 60s reflected a reclamation of 'intrinsic' Europeanness similar to the evaluation of cultural beginnings seen in Sodeisha and Noguchi's reclamation of Japanese haniwa. One of the strongest connections between contemporary ceramics and the more general field of contemporary sculpture lay in a claim on the prehistoric past. Sculptors like Alberto Giacometti, Marino Marini and William Turnbull and potters like Kylliki Salmenhaara, Hans Coper and Axel Salto drew from a common well of both images and thought about the archaic. The cave-paintings of Lascaux in France, discovered in the 1940s, had provoked new thinking about the origins of art. These origins suggested that art could have a ritual status in the centre of people's lives, reflecting the immediacy of fears or dreams. Pottery was seen to have this status too. To be a contemporary potter in the 1950s was to be able to make objects that had an immediate and identifiable sense of cultural beginnings.

Postwar Europe: Salto, Coper, Duckworth

For David Sylvester, writing anonymously in *The Times in* 1955, 'The most obvious difference between the art of today and the art of the inter-war period is that rough surfaces have taken the place of smooth ones.' He ascribed to smoothness the outward sign of aspiration to order and impersonality, whilst roughness was the aspiration to freedom. Roughness was a signifier of emotion, unchecked feeling, and unsubdued materials that felt appropriate to a postwar generation less able to subscribe to positivist humanist values. Herbert Read famously wrote, in his catalogue essay on sculpture for the 1952 Venice Biennale, 'These new images belong to the iconography of despair, or of defiance… Here are images of flight, of ragged claws "scuttling across the floors of silent seas", of excoriated flesh, frustrated sex, the geometry of fear'. The parallels between primitive and modern sculpture were strong, thought Read. The primitive 'religions of

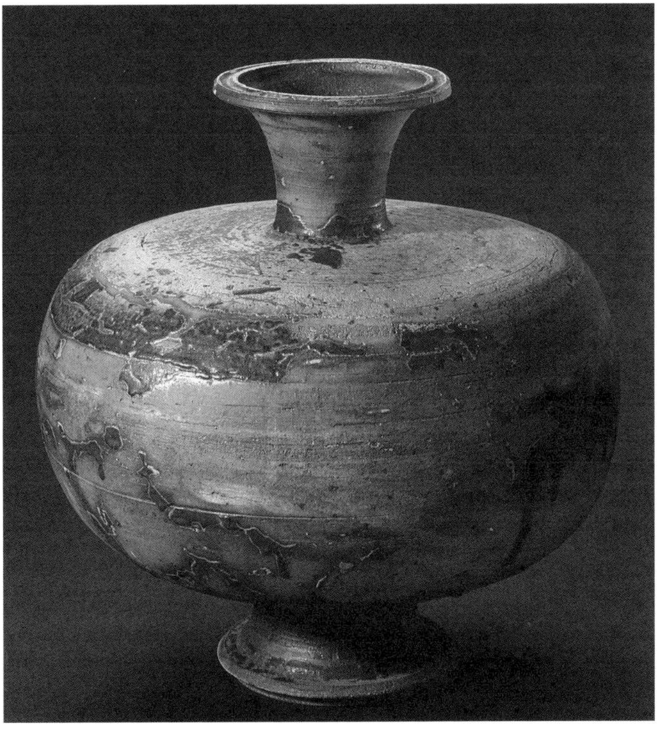

100 **Kyllikki Salmenhaara**, stoneware pot, 1958 (stoneware, h. 43 cm/17 in). Salmenhaara's pots were described by a Danish critic in 1963 as reflecting 'impressions from the Finnish landscape in a way which appears completely instinctive and uncalculated. Her glazes create impressions of birchbark, primeval mountains, or autumn leaves.'

101 **Axel Salto**, *Jar*, stoneware with solfatara glaze for Royal Copenhagen, 1943.
Salto believed it was possible to make objects that reflected changes of state: like Acteon metamorphosing into a stag, ceramics could catch moments of transition, or 'the painful processes of transformation', as he put it.

102 **Axel Salto**, *Interior Strength*, 1956 (stoneware, h. 127 cm/50 in). A textured plinth raises up three smooth tapering forms: the glazing is sombre and arcane. It looks as if it must once have had some use but is now an abandoned ritual object. This piece incorporated many of the stylistic devices (including a reference to archaic Mediterranean sources – in this case a Cretan tripot) that were to become commonplace in the 1950s into a single bravura effort.

fear, terror, propitiation and retribution' corresponded to the existential anguish and unease of modern man. 1950s ceramics show a profuse number of standing forms, totems, memorialized offerings, winged pots. Vessels have plinths to raise them up as if they had ritual uses or fragmentary attachments as if they had been recently unearthed. These were pots that aspired to the status and condition of grave goods.

The propensity of certain objects to cause unease was characterized by the Danish potter Axel Salto (1889–1961) in 1949 as 'Demonic things… objects possessing not only apparent but also other, concealed properties that mark them off completely from their surroundings: things which carry a curse or have a special fate, things which rub you the wrong way.' Salto, famed for his subtle Oriental glazes used over organically patterned vases with which he won the Milan Triennale in 1951, made vessels that tried to capture this 'demonic' unease.

To refer to ritual became for some potters a way of aggrandizing vessels that had no apparent utility, just as to use

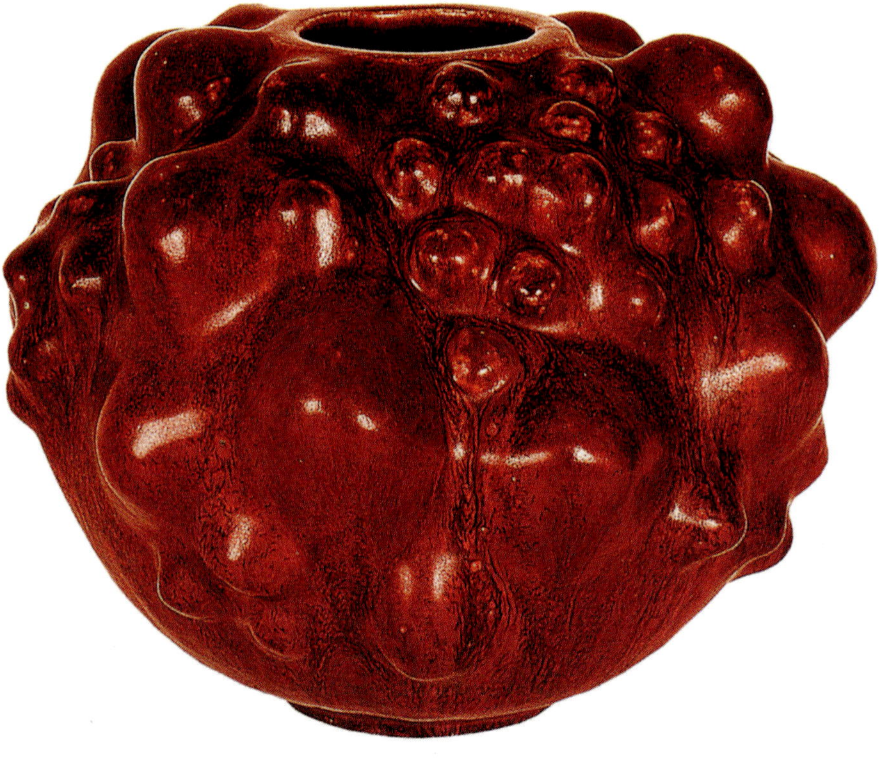

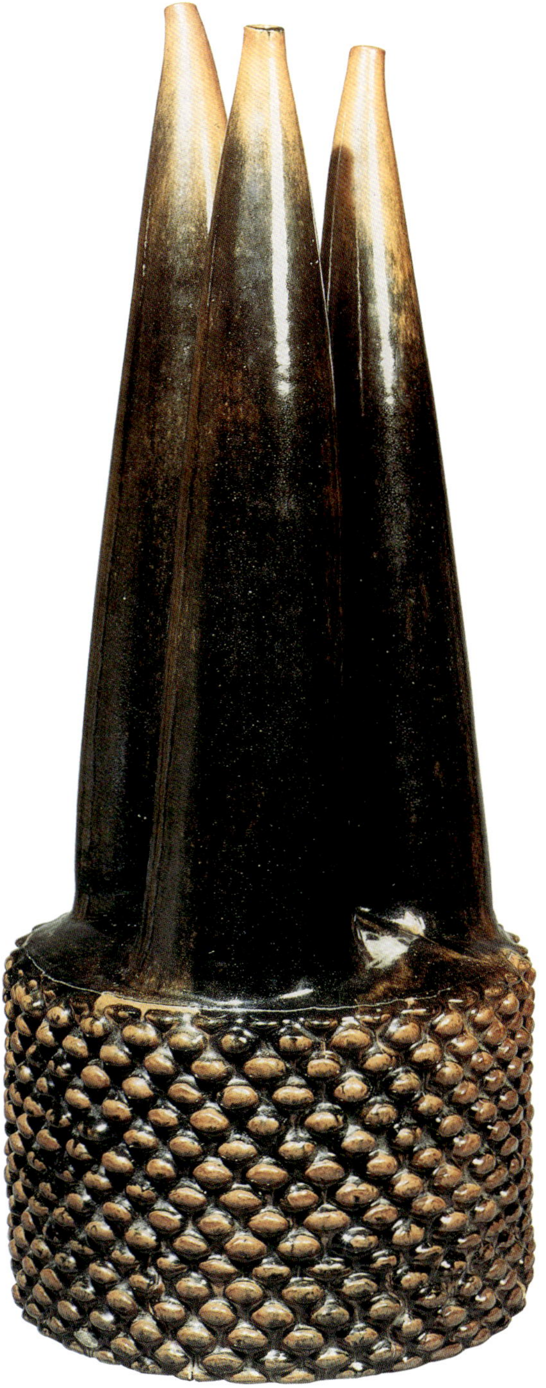

Totem as a title for a work was to show a sense of contemporaneity that acknowledged such works as Freud's book, *Totem and Taboo*. Freud used pyschoanalytic terms to connect primitive practices and the structure of modern relationships. The totem was, in the words of critic Rosalind Krauss describing the American sculptor David Smith, 'not an archaic object. Rather, it was a powerfully abbreviated expression of a complex of feelings and desires which he felt to be operative in himself and within society as a whole.'

From the very first, the work of Hans Coper (1920–81) showed this excitement. Coper, a young Jewish engineering student, had been forced to emigrate to England in 1939 from Germany. He joined Lucie Rie (1902–95) in her London studio in 1946 to assist in making ceramic buttons for the fashion industry. Rie's studio was a meeting place for émigré architects and artists and in this urbane atmosphere Coper was encouraged to learn to throw and to help make Rie's finely thrown porcelain tablewares. Soon Coper started to make other pots alongside these tablewares.

Coper's pots made a considerable impact when exhibited at the 'Festival of Britain' in 1951, and subsequently at exhibitions with Rie in the 1950s at the Berkeley Galleries, noted as dealers in primitive art as well as painting. Surfaces grew more complex, with white slips used in contrast to black manganese slips to give greater depth to the textured markings. He soon began to make simple compound shapes where two or more forms were brought together to make vessels – three amphorae joined together to create a 'tripot', for instance – recalling Cretan tripod pots. The compound shapes grew more complex, with bowls joined edge to edge supported on high thrown feet: forms that had no precedent yet gave a feeling of almost totemic significance.

Coper was, in effect, making objects suffused with the passions of his period, the attraction towards ancient art as a signifier of the elemental, and of the graphic mark on surfaces as more 'real' than the unmarked, implacable surface. He was exploiting the surfaces of his ceramic objects much as a sculptor might use the patination of metal, to lead the viewer to move round the whole object. He expressed this belief in the complete contemporaneity of his occupation (or vocation) as a potter by invoking this connection between the modern and the archaic. His choice of two iconic figures of the time, a sculptor and an engineer, cited in the following description of an archaic pot, is very telling:

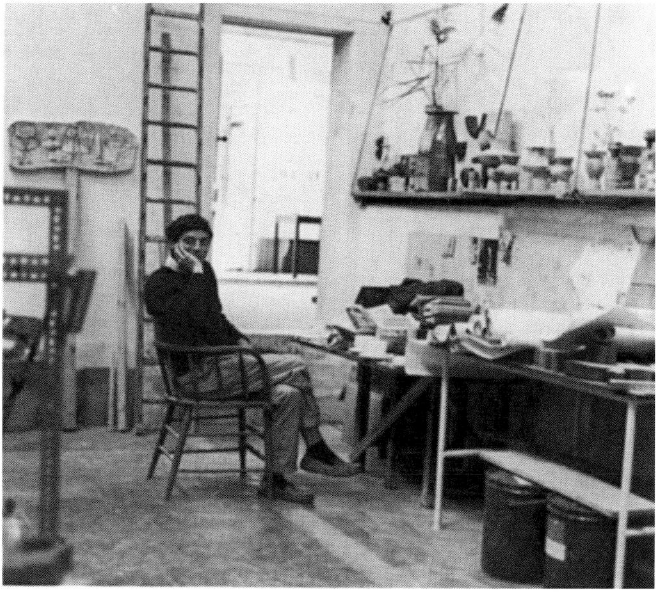

103 **Hans Coper** in his workshop at Digswell, *c.* 1960.
The simplicity of Coper's studio – and his living space beyond – reflected his engagement with contemporary architecture. He designed ceramic cladding for walls as well as making candlesticks for Sir Basil Spence's new Coventry Cathedral (installed in 1962).

A pre-dynastic Egyptian pot, roughly egg-shaped, the size of my hand: made thousands of years ago, possibly by a slave, it has survived in more than one sense. A humble, passive, somehow absurd object – yet potent, mysterious, sensuous. It conveys no comment, no self-expression, but seems to contain and reflect its maker and the human world it inhabits, to contribute its minute quantum of energy – and homage. An object of complete economy made by MAN; Giacometti man; Buckminster Fuller man. A constant. This is the only pot which has really fascinated me. It was not the cause of my making pots, but it gave me a glimpse of what man is.

His sense of 'complete economy' can be seen in the work of his final years with his small 'Cycladic' pots, named for their resonance with Cycladic figures. Standing on drums or plinths, these pots with their vestigial wings, stand as an endpoint of the interest in aestheticizing the archaic.

A more visceral and rugged approach was apparent at the Central School of Art in London in the 1950s. This radical art college, maintained no hierarchy between the fine arts and crafts, and allowed considerable fluidity between departments. The sculptors Eduardo Paolozzi and William Turnbull taught a Basic Design course there, and many ceramicists were taught by them. With no agenda for potters to acquire 'proper' skills, students

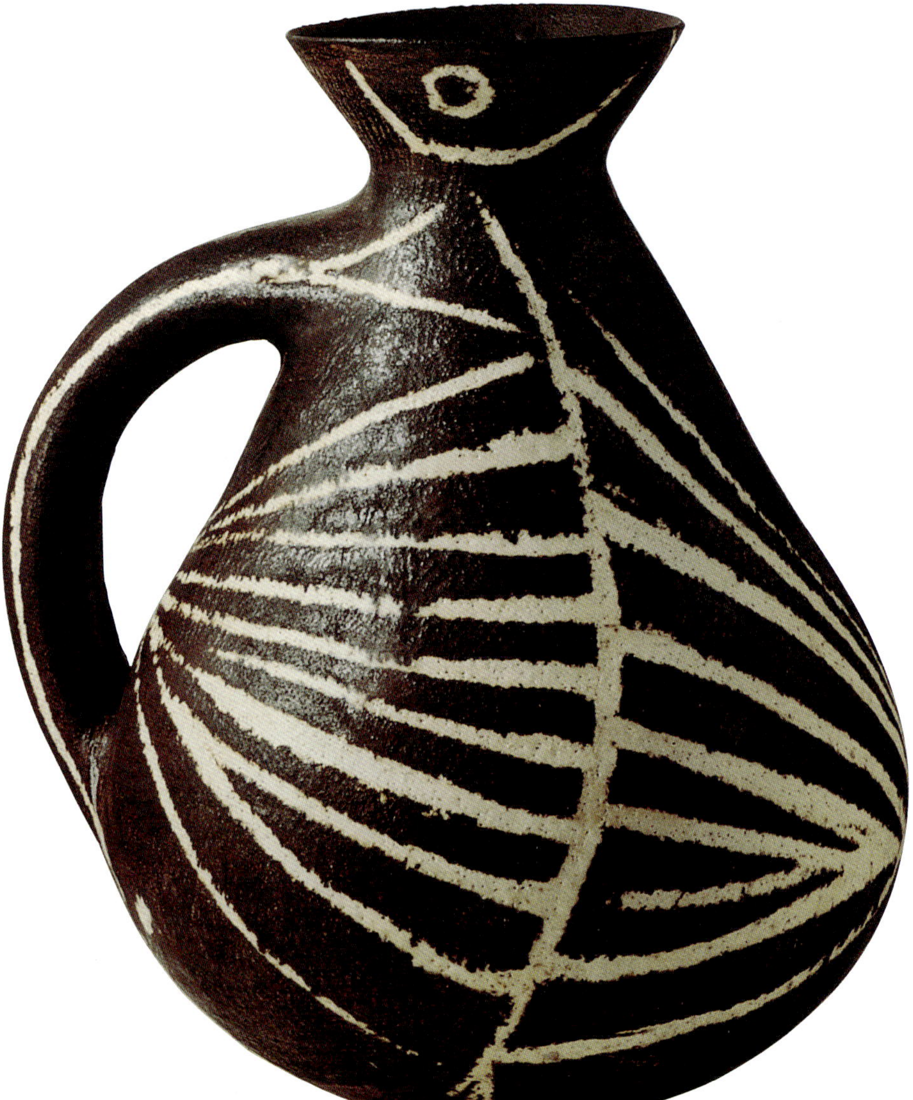

104 **Hans Coper**, stoneware jug with sgraffito design, 1951 (stoneware, h. 35 cm/13¾ in). Coper's pots were thrown, but were heavy and bold with a sort of willed archaicism that showed in the thick strap handles and the semi-abstracted designs of birds and fishes, each with a single fierce eye. These early decorations, where a sgraffito design was cut through manganese and a shiny white glaze applied, were soon abandoned in favour of an intense preoccupation with unglazed surfaces.

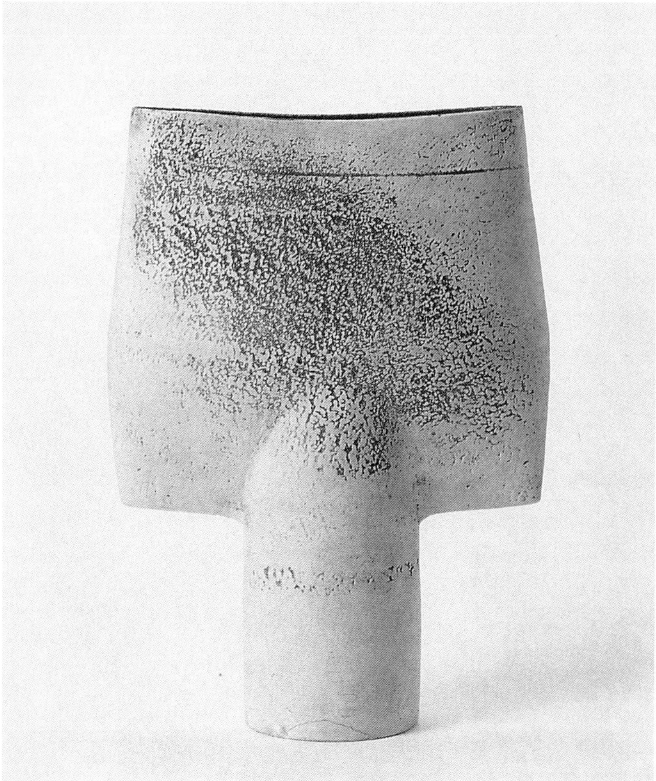

105 **Hans Coper**, spade form on cylindrical base, 1966–68 (stoneware, h. 23 cm/9 in). Coper expressed his passion for ancient Minoan and Cretan pots: their unglazed exterior surfaces had the dry abraded and scarified surfaces of archeological vessels, or of objects made from stone. Into these surfaces lines were scored – fine circling networks and webs of lines that seemed to suggest lost meanings. This also connected Coper to the mark-making of contemporary painters like Ben Nicholson, or sculptors like William Turnbull.

were encouraged to hand-build their pots – the potter's wheel being seen as an impediment to direct handling of material. Gordon Baldwin (b. 1932), who studied there between 1950 and 1954 and taught from 1956, remembers Paolozzi 'not worrying two pennies about ceramic quality and feeling for clay', but just 'bending bits of clay and glazing it.' The 'messiness' of the new sculpture reached exhibition design, with the 1957 *This Is Tomorrow* exhibition in London compared to 'a shed...excavated after an atomic holocaust.' Baldwin was unafraid of making pots that lacked formal coherence: rather than achieving resolution they could exist as violent or untidy accretions of forms and marks attesting to energetic process. [107]

Other potters from the Central school, such as Ian Auld (1926–2000), Gillian Lowndes (b. 1936) and Dan Arbeid (b. 1928), also made work that reflected this fiercely experimental mode of making. In abjuring functional vessels in favour of aysmmetrical, roughly made expressive objects, they revealed what Tony Birks wrote of Lowndes in 1967, that there was 'no easy relationship

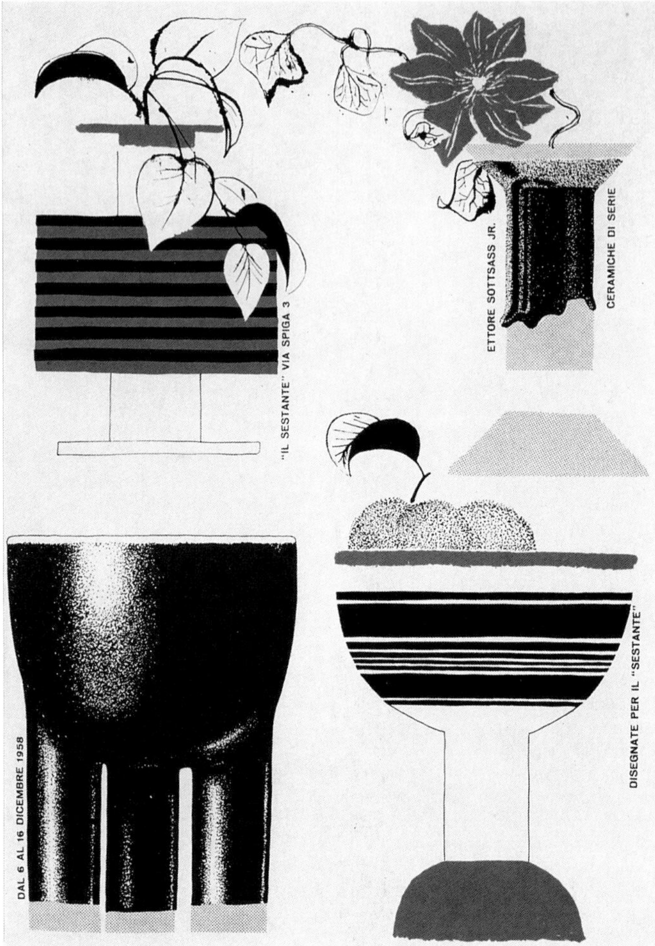

106 **Ettore Sottsass**, *Designs for Rocchetti*, 1956–59. Many of the ceramics that the Italian designer designed from 1956 were strongly influenced by archaicism, amongst them his *Ceramics of Darkness* and *Menhir, Ziggurat, Stupas*. This illustration shows the *Rocchetti* series: 'the forms are simple, very popular, as one might describe… ancient bowls with very primordial colours, or ancient chalices such as may have been used at Mycenae or in Galilee or at Ur or wherever for drinking water from springs. It seemed to me that it might be possible to find some sort of archetypal forms.'

107 **Gordon Baldwin**, *Standing Form*, 1961 (multifired stoneware, h. 61 cm/24 in).
Baldwin uses a Coper-like combination of forms, but with his immediacy of treating the surface of the clay changes them into something considerably more threatening. The 'sinister' impression, noted by a critic, is perhaps due to the fact that the vessels often looked as if they had been attacked or broken.

with clay, no ingrained rhythm of work.' This work was rough in Sylvester's terms: it was born out of uneasiness and made the viewer uneasy. This was most apparent in the work of Ruth Duckworth who joined the Central School in 1957. Duckworth (b. 1919), a German émigré to England in 1936, used both porcelain and stoneware clays with a wide variety of techniques. She made craggy hemispheres by collaging slabs of clay together, leaving visible suture-like joins and tall thin cylinders with vestigial knobs and lugs. [109] Indeed Duckworth also made small pinched porcelain biomorphic forms that showed a fascination with what could be described as structural organicism, the skeletal forms of creatures and plants. Some are like bones, others like membranes.

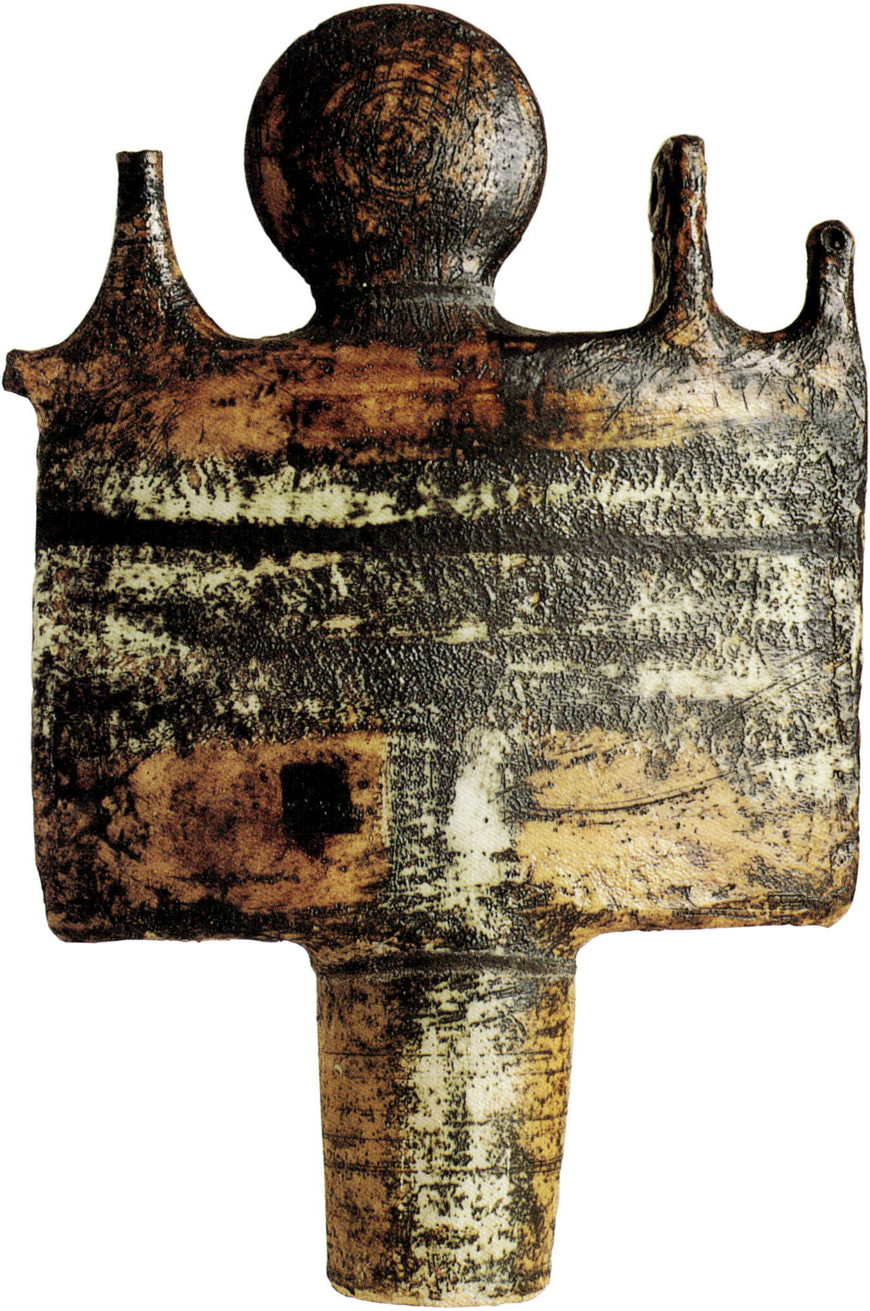

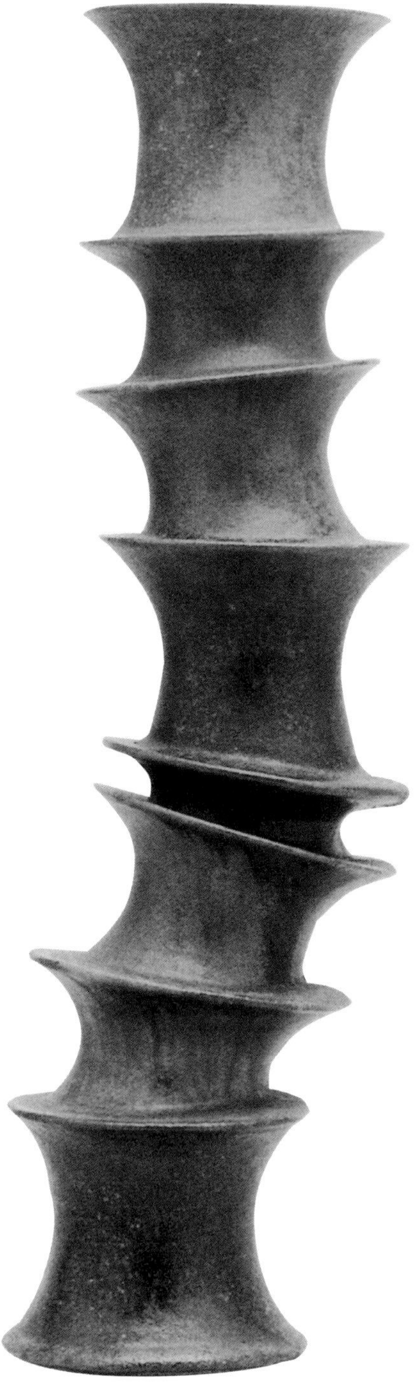

108 **Beate Kuhn**, *Vertebral Column*, 1973 (stoneware, h. 46 cm/18 in).
In Germany Beate Kuhn (b. 1927) made severe work which shared these concerns, (biomorphic/ structural organicism/ skeletal forms of creatures and plants) some pieces based on vertebra, others with complex structures constructed from multiple repeated elements.

These pots had a widespread influence in Europe during the 1960s and 1970s. In Austria Kurt Spurey (b. 1941) also worked within this biomorphic style. The work of the British potters Mary Rogers (b. 1929), Peter Simpson (b. 1943) and Geoffrey Swindell (b. 1945) were also extremely popular at this time. But in the main the mass of small hand-built ceramic sponges, corals and fruit were derivative and slight and lacked the uneasy qualities of Duckworth's work. In 1964 Duckworth moved to America and began to make a series of highly ambitious ceramic wall pieces alongside her vessels.

These disparate forms strongly asserted an alternative way of thinking about a corpus of work: it was no longer necessary to have a sustained normative style, or body of work reflecting an 'ingrained rhythm of work.'

109 **Ruth Duckworth**, *Porcelain Forms*, 1967. Duckworth's 'assertive geometry' was noted by a critic at the time. The anthropomorphism of her pots, unlike those of many contemporary potters, tended to disturb rather than console.

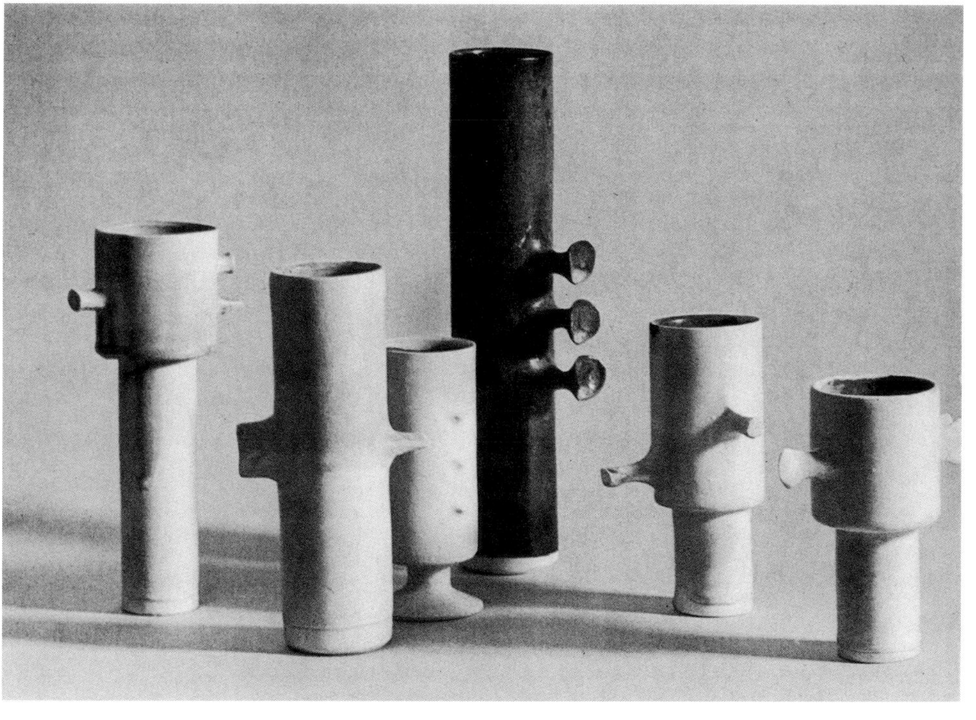

'High unseriousness': painters and clay

In the period between 1945 and 1960 acknowledged masters of painting, including Pablo Picasso (1881–1973), Joan Miró (1893–1983), Marc Chagall (1887–1985), Georges Braque (1882–1963) and Fernand Léger (1881–1955), were all involved in ceramics. Hilton Kramer wrote in a review of a 1955 Léger exhibition,

The digression into ceramics which has lately occupied the elder generation of painters in Paris has tended to isolate certain decorative and frivolous aspects of their talents at the expense of their expressive powers. ... this digression has caught some of these artists in moments of relaxation if not actual decline.

'Decoration' was seen by formalist critics such as Clement Greenberg as a secondary activity, disguising rather than revealing form. Greenberg's advocacy of 'optical' sculpture that appealed to the intellect not to the touch was rapidly becoming an orthodoxy in the 1950s. Clay, messy, inchoate, sensual, had none of the putative clarity of steel. Yet a major corpus of ceramic work was made by Noguchi, Miró, Picasso, Lucio Fontana and others,

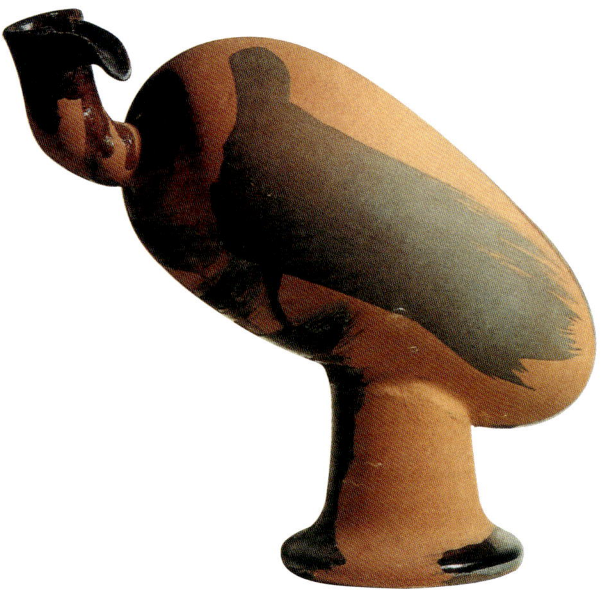

110 **Pablo Picasso**, *Condor*, 1947. In Picasso's ceramics objects are often other objects simultaneously. His zoomorphic forms, the condors which were amongst the first forms made at Madoura, are still amphorae with unlikely spouts.

suggesting that this element of 'high unseriousness' constituted a release from the expectations of modern convention. There was an element of play in the ceramics of these artists that could not be appropriated into normative critical discourse, and could not always be understood by contemporary critics.

In all of these four artists' cases the technique played a significant part, in each case mediated through a collaborator working within a tradition. The word 'collaborator' implies a relationship of equality, and that was certainly true of Noguchi's relationship with Rosanjin, of Miró's work with the Catalan potter Josep Lloréns Artigas, and, to a lesser extent of Picasso working in the south of France at the Madoura Pottery in Vallauris. The case of Fontana was different from the start, as his use of ceramics predated his use of other materials and gave him an immediate access to the technics; his use of the Mazzotti studio in Italy was thus more that of a ceramicist working with a technician. Traditions were active forces: Picasso knew about Etruscan pottery and Renaissance Pallisy wares and used his knowledge, and Noguchi knew what it meant to wood-fire his sculpture in particular kilns. For Noguchi, Miró and Picasso, pots were thrown not just to be decorated but to be metaphorically as well as physically altered and manipulated. Vessels were in some ways found objects, susceptible to the conditions of surrealist exchange. Much of their influence on studio pottery came not from style or vivid colour, but from this radical freedom create clay vessels that reached beyond cultural allegiances.

Pablo Picasso

The large runs of indifferently produced, yet officially sanctioned, editions of Picasso's ceramic work have given the impression of a simple decorative transposition of ideas from paper or canvas into clay. The look of these ceramics, the brevity of his brushwork and his choice of imagery (owls, bacchanals, still life) have obscured the scope of his passionate engagement with ceramics. In fact in the twenty years from his first visit in 1946 to Georges and Suzanne Ramies's Madoura pottery in Vallauris, a town in the south of France with a once strong tradition in vernacular pottery that stretched back to antiquity, he made over four thousand objects from clay. They range from freely formed figures to complex appropriations and commentaries on ceramic traditions. Though he did use ready-made dishes and jars as the ground for decoration (six hundred designs were made on the standard Madoura meat plate) Picasso was also immediately taken by the

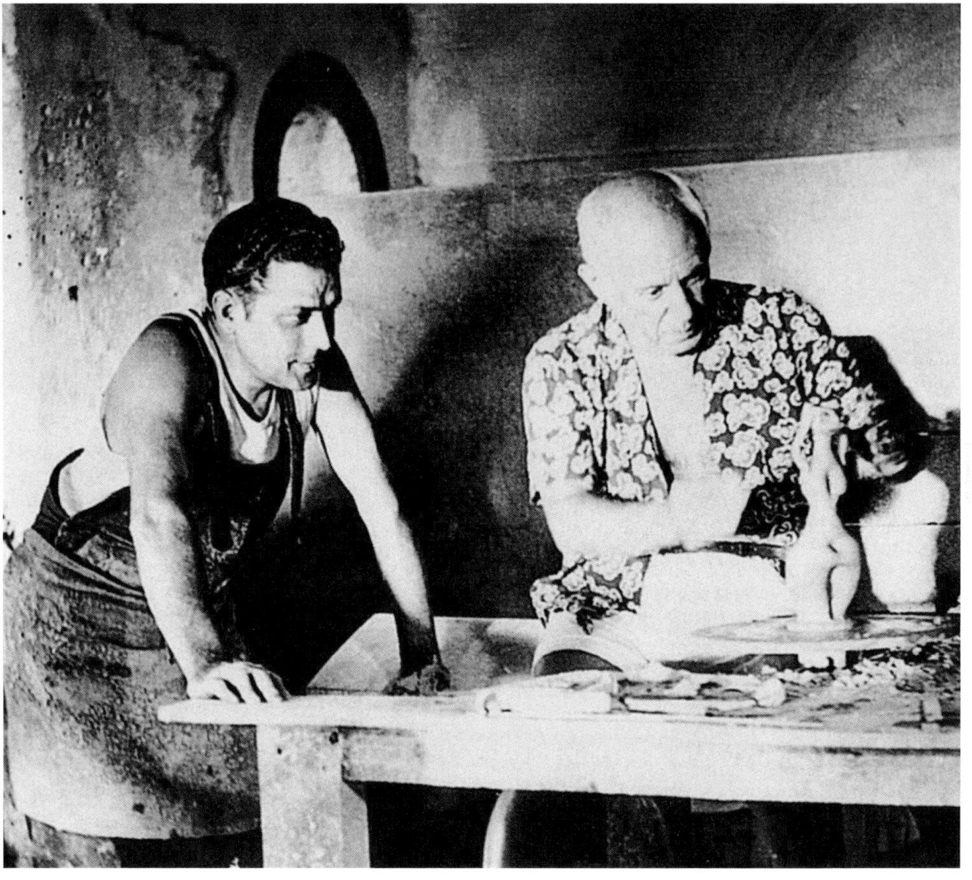

111 **Pablo Picasso** and **Jules Agard** at Madoura, 1947.
Picasso at work on a 'tanagra' Hellenist sculpture. Agard would throw these as simple closed bottle forms, which Picasso would then model.

112 **Pablo Picasso**, *Head*, 1948 (h. 30 cm/12 in).
Thrown pots when still damp can be manipulated, dented or warped and Picasso used this attribute often, bending the tall neck of a bottle over to make a face or squeezing a jar to indicate a woman's body.

formal possibilities implicit in vessels, turning up at his next visit in 1947 with drawings for composite thrown and joined pots. These were made for him by Jules Agard, the talented thrower at Madoura. The Ramies workshop, where 'contemporary' versions of local pots were produced, was quickly turned over to servicing Picasso's voracious needs for thrown pots of all kinds and blank press-moulded dishes.

Picasso's interest in the found object, something to be appropriated and manipulated, led him to use discarded kiln fragments and shards, the detritus of the studio. In this interest his ceramics developed in parallel with his other simultaneous sculptural activities – he rented a sculpture studio near Madoura and from 1949 went to and fro between the two places. This is where he made *The Goat* (1950) from plaster, pottery and a wicker basket, before it was cast in bronze. But the vast majority

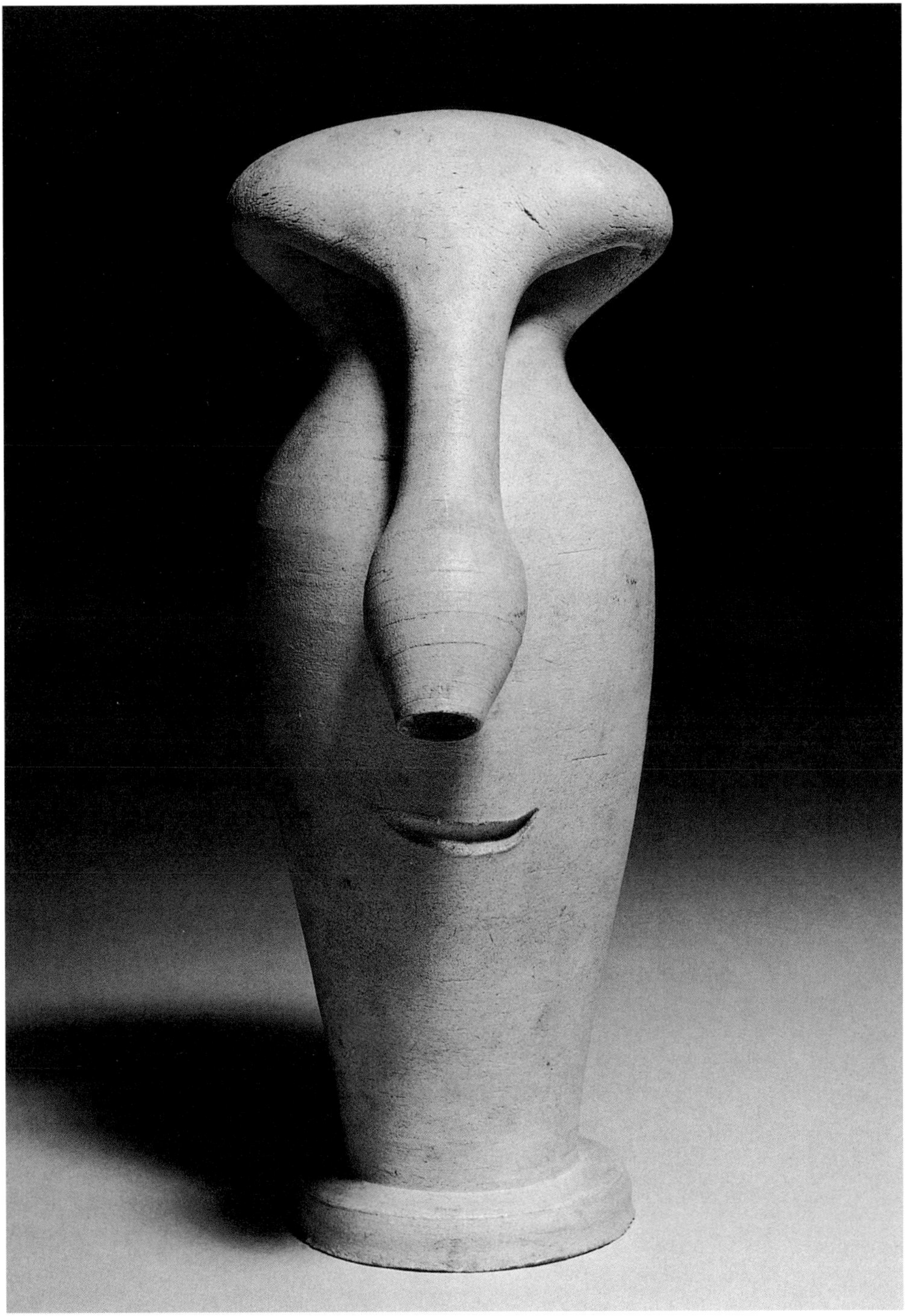

of his ceramics were envisaged as finished clay objects within the realm of ceramic traditions. He relished using the vernacular pots of Vallauris, the two-handled terracotta 'marmite' or casserole, chestnut roasters and tiles, alongside the meat platters. Some of these marmites were painted with black figures in the manner of Etruscan antiquities, some of the tiles broken to give the impression of archeological finds. They are knowing commentaries on the inherent archaicism of painting terracottas, something also present in his use of the 'tanagras', figures that recall Hellenistic terracotta figurines. He was as combative in his ceramics as in his paintings: these are not respectful recontextualizations of ceramic history but a full-blooded taking on of artistic forebears. This was also true of his imagery: in rich fluxed colours painted onto the meat dishes are not just doves and epicurean still lives but also sexual dramas and the violent theatre of bullfights.

Transformation took place at different levels of seriousness, humour and complexity. A handle can become a snake, or a spout a phallus. The border of a meat dish can act as the crowd for a bull fight, the nest of a bird, a woman's hair. A terracotta vase becomes a gallery wall on which images are pinned: the interleaving of two and three dimensions is often vertiginous. The framework is unstable, a handled jug 'contains' the painted image of a flower vase, another vase already 'contains' a painted bouquet of flowers. And in one of the most bizarre of these, a terracotta vase was surrounded by a mould made from corrugated cardboard, and plaster was poured into the space between the two: a vase was thus made into a larger plaster jug. For much of these ceramics are rooted in what André Breton described as the most fundamental of all Surrealist visual techniques, the suppression of the word 'like'. In Surrealism a tomato is no longer 'like' a child's balloon, it is also a child's balloon.

In some of his last ceramic works made in 1962, Picasso stood corrugated terracotta roof tiles and brick fragments upright, painting faces onto them with customary speed and brio. They show Picasso's 'catalytic' use of materials: his ability to apprehend the possibilities of upending and destabilizing the world of objects.

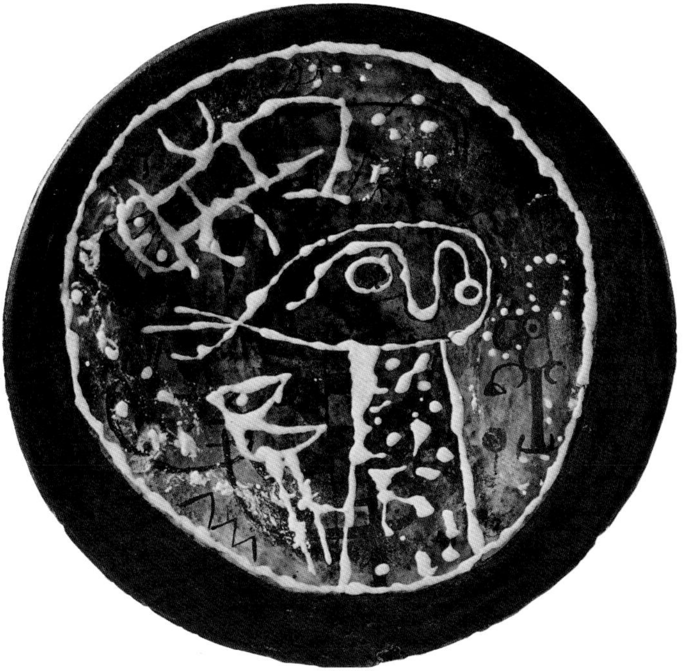

113 **Joan Miró** and **Josep Lloréns Artigas**, *Green Plate*, 1956 (stoneware, h. 37 cm/14½ in). Just as his painting was connected to childhood mark-making through his use of stains and traces and scratches, so Artigas instructed Miró to give up on the idea of accuracy in drawing on ceramic surfaces and to inscribe the clay with a sharp stick, scratch through slips or trail glazes.

Joan Miró

Ceramics for Miró were embedded within Catalan culture, and within its landscape. For him pots had an iconic value as objects that belonged to the people who had made them: they had the power of simplicity, of being uninflected by art. And as he said, 'The simplest things give me ideas. The plate that a peasant eats his soup out of is more interesting than the ridiculously rich plates of rich people.' Simple pots, 'plates that are not even signed', were charged with the clarity of everyday things: they possessed a luminosity lacking in rich art objects. He was the son and grandson of craftsmen and placed himself within this continuity of making these kinds of things: 'I do nothing else than what my ancestors used to do in this land of Catalonia. Most of them were craftsmen and potters. They did what they did to the best of their abilities. They did not see themselves as artists, but they were proud of their craft. They belonged to the aristocracy of craftsmanship.' Miró had simultaneously an unromantic apprehension of what was involved in the making of objects, the discipline of the crafts, and a powerfully romantic apprehension of the symbolic value of what the crafts meant. His collaboration with the potter Josep Lloréns Artigas was grounded in this respect. Miró always credited Artigas as a full partner in the creation of the ceramics. Because they were friends and art school contemporaries it was a collaboration of equals.

For Miró the excitement of using ceramics lay in their unpredictability, the consigning of the work to the transformative process of the firing, where clay and glaze changed into mass and colour. This transformative element connected with his sense of how his art came into being, the way in which in dream figures and landscapes and symbols change and become 'other'. It was also present in his admiration for Neolithic art, where organs and limbs interchange, and for children's art where objects recede in and out of focus in the picture plane. In his small ceramic sculptures of women, this transmogrification is most clearly visible, with an almost studiedly archaic transposition of mouth and sexual organs. Other works were more complex. When he saw the outcome of a disastrous firing of Artigas's ceramics, with broken detritus and pots stuck together and to shelves, it was for Miró a surrealist symphony of melted or fragmented forms. Materials, he said 'always excite me and give me points of

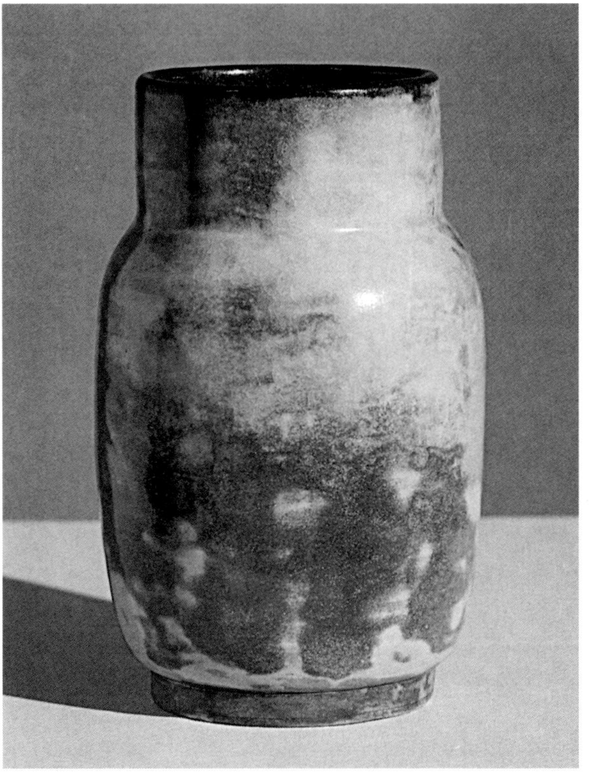

114 **Josep Lloréns Artigas**, *Clair de lune* (Moonlight), 1927 (stoneware, h. 25.5 cm/10 in). This early jar of Artigas shows his preoccupations: forms were predominantly Chinese in inspiration, their strong uninflected silhouettes a foil for his glazes. This was as true for his early works as those being made up to his death in the 1970s.

115 **Joan Miró** and **Josep Lloréns Artigas**, *Double Figure*, 1956 (earthenware, h. 44 cm/ 17½ in).
By 1942 when Miró approached Artigas to ask if he could work with him, Artigas was already well known for his carefully modulated undecorated pottery and needed convincing that it was a worthwhile project. 'You must not become Miró – but I, Miró, must become a ceramicist.' They worked together in 1944 and then again in the three years between 1953 and 1956. Their sustained collaboration resulted in over 200 pieces and an exhibition in New York and in Paris.

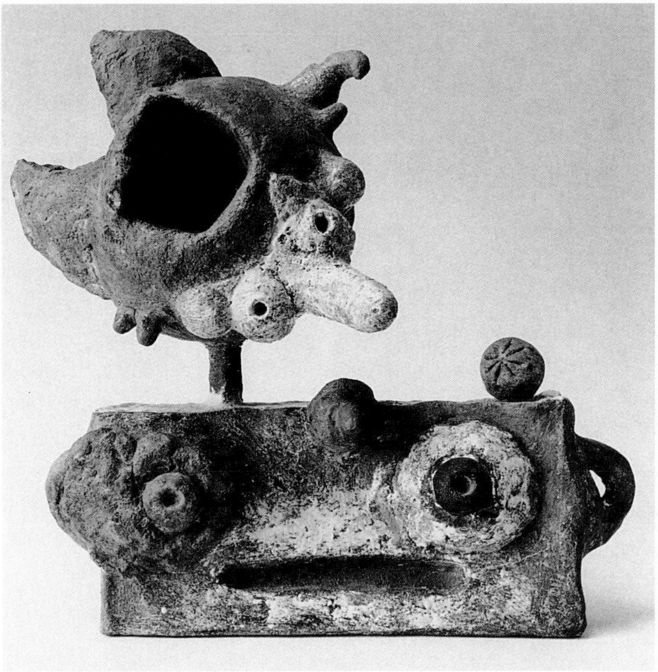

departure of great richness'. His own ceramics often employ these transformations and disjunctions as 'points of departure'. There is either an almost violent syncopation of different forms or the bringing together of different ways of handling clay within the same piece, all to the end of keeping alive the febrile energy of making and painting. Indeed, in a notebook of 1948 he counterpointed the deadness and academicism of 'frozen porcelains of decadent dancers' against his ambition to have 'ceramics that one can throw in the face / during the ecstasies of LOVE.'

Where a form is unitary, as with his use of Artigas's large jars or dishes, the images are placed so as to pull the form off centre: the smoothness and opacity of a glazed surface, its tactile coherence, was a 'point of departure' rather than a terminus. Because these ceramics were wood-fired there was an unevenness of tone and colour in the surface that pleased Miró. Indeed the rougher the surface, the better. Just as Picasso was to do at Vallauris, Miró picked up broken kiln shelves, discarded shards and even kiln bricks to work with. Their brokenness gave them an immediate correspondence with the surrounding rocky landscape. Some of these painted fragments of kiln shelf, with

116 **Corneille**, Untitled vase, 1954 (h. 57 cm/22½ in). Corneille used the surfaces of his plates and vases like a canvas, scribbling, painting and over-painting.

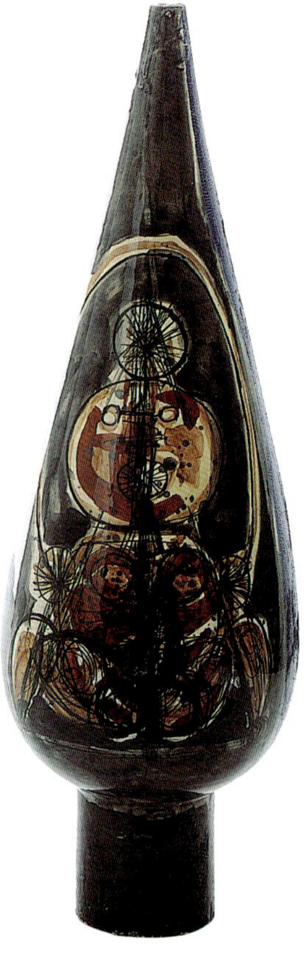

their condensed ideographic figures, stars and animals, look as if they might have been removed from the prehistoric caves at Altamira. Miró's identification with the landscape extended to his painting of the boulders outside Artigas's hillside studio, and finished ceramics were placed outside to see if they had the necessary aesthetic force to survive the challenge.

There is a robustness about these larger works, comprised of ceramics, wood, metal rods, and kiln bricks, a refusal to meet any polite criterion of material, that has led them to be overlooked. The challenge to the formal properties of 'high art' is shared with other contemporary art movements of the 1940s. Jean Dubuffet's 'Art Brut', with its deliberate retention of clumsiness and messiness, its emphasis on a direct handling of materials, recalls many of Miró's ideas. Dubuffet's rejection of formal canons of beauty ('I don't worry about [objects] being ugly or beautiful') was intimately bound up with the immediacy of his use of 'only the most common materials in my work, those that one does not dream of at first because they are too crude and close at hand'.

CoBrA

Similarly for CoBrA, a group formed in 1948 of Danish, Belgian and Dutch artists, sculptors and writers, improvisatory assemblage was a way of escaping from the strait jacket of high art. Determinedly experimental, they believed in an approach to materials that was unhampered by anxieties about technique. In this, like Dubuffet and Miró, they took their cue from an expressionism they located in the work of children, those with mental problems, or in 'primitive societies'. It was not surprising that those involved in CoBrA should work with ceramics: Miró's and Picasso's new work was already well known to them.

In 1948 the Dutch artists Karel Appel, Corneille, Anton Rooskens and Constant experimented with ceramics. The Danish artist Asger Jorn worked in Sorring, a small town in Jutland, decorating vernacular pottery in the hope – as he explained in an article in 1954 – of revitalizing its traditions as Picasso had done at Vallauris. Jorn, the most experienced of the CoBrA artists to work with ceramics, initiated the plan of working in Albisola with Tullio Mazzotti, or d'Albisola, as he called himself. D'Albisola had been deeply committed to the idea of artistic exchange for twenty-five years, working as the leader of the Futurist ceramics movement and as the erstwhile collaborator of Lucio Fontana. In 1954 Jorn organized 'International encounters in ceramics', inviting amongst others Fontana from Italy, Corneille and Appel

117 **Asger Jorn**, Untitled, 1954 (33 × 31 × 10 cm/13 × 12 × 4 in). Jorn's work in ceramics – often taking a simple vessel form and energetically remodelling it – was paralleled by his 'detournements'. In these situationist works he would use junk shop paintings as the basis for overpainted slogans and figures.

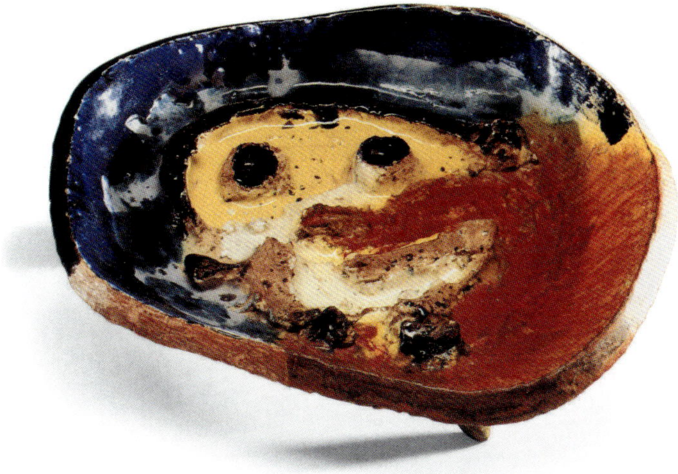

from the Netherlands and Matta from Chile to work collaboratively and experimentally in Tullio's workshop. Appel recalled: 'It was like opening the floodgates. We were allowed to make pottery at Mazzotti's factory. Everyone was busy painting pots and plates and vases, but I preferred to hit the bits of clay I pulled out of the dirt with an iron bar. I beat animal reliefs into the material, and once I had hammered out the shape, I painted it before firing the piece.'

Appel's work, with its bright poster paint colours and freely scratched surfaces, mostly consisted of an almost medieval bestiary of animals and birds, graphic and emotional. He also made small squeezed heads from clay with punctured eyes and mouths, an intense and cursory engagement with clay that emphasizes the anti-aesthetic. If playing with clay constituted a crime against the ideals of modernism, then there was true radicalism in CoBrA's involvement in ceramics at Albisola. In a decisive reversal of hierarchies one hundred plates were decorated by children and illustrated on the covers of Jorn's treatise *Structure et Changement* (Structure and change): 'The results…seem to reveal that any child, before it has reached school-age, is better able to apply modern techniques to bring a particular surface to life than all the professionals in the field of decoration, both in the artistic sense and in terms of handicraft.'

This attempt to bring a surface alive can be seen in Jorn and Corneille's ceramics: surfaces are rarely treated as flat and inert but scribbled into, gouged out, and added onto to make even a dish a sculptural object. In endeavouring to release this necessary

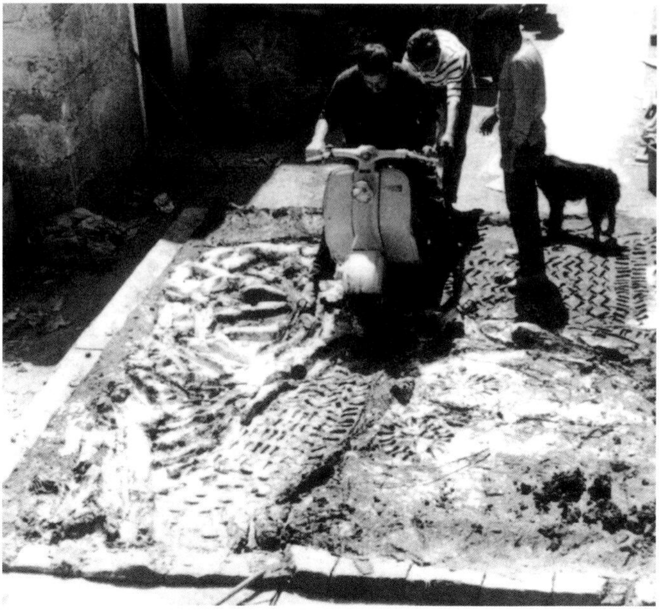

118 **Asger Jorn** on a scooter preparing the panel for Aarhus at the San Giorgio ceramics factory in Albisola, Italy, 1959.

spontaneity with clay, reliefs and murals were also made, their vast scale necessitating huge gestural markings: for a mural three metres high and twenty-seven metres long for Aarhus Grammar School in Jutland in 1959, Jorn even rode his scooter over the unfired clay. CoBrA artists continued to work with clay intermittently after the Albisola experiment, often using a Dutch workshop, 'Struktuur 68', that had been set up in the Hague in 1968 specifically to facilitate monumental ceramic work. The difficulties of keeping open the improvisatory impulses behind using clay when given great technical help and expertise can be seen in some of these later ceramics: they begin to look decidedly professional.

Lucio Fontana

Though he is now best known for his slashed canvases, Lucio Fontana did not begin to paint until 1949 when he was fifty; before this his reputation was based on his sculpture. 'I am a sculptor, not a ceramicist. I have never thrown a plate on a wheel nor painted a vase. I detest lacy designs and dainty nuances.' Like Gauguin, Miró and Picasso, he hated the academicism of ceramics, rolling up this dislike into Sèvres and Copenhagen with their delicacy, fragility, exquisite firing, and 'amazing technical achievements'. What went on in these places was the satisfaction of the taste of collectors. It was not art.

Fontana was born in Argentina, the son of a sculptor and an actress, but was sent to Italy as a boy. He trained as a sculptor, making acclaimed academic sculpture in stone and bronze. In 1931 he made his first polychrome terracotta reliefs, and then in 1936 starting working intensely in Albisola at the workshop of Tullio Mazzotti (d'Albisola). The common element in his work with different materials was polychromy: 'The forms I made, right from the beginning, have never been disassociated from colour... [they] cannot be separated, they are born out of the same need.' Fontana seemed to relish his transgressive vigour, reflecting, after he had accepted an invitation in 1937 to work at Sèvres, on 'their astonishment at my vast consumption' of materials, making one hundred pieces in a month: 'Into these workshops where the tableware of all the kings of France had been made I brought a minotaur on a lead – to crash about amongst the dainty porcelain baskets and the allegories in biscuit-ware'.

Vigorous gesture was close to violent gesture. In his *Natura* series ('natura' being an Italian slang word for female genitalia) Fontana pushed a long pole into the middle of a huge boulder of soft clay and opened up a void. Puncturing surfaces, gashing them open with a knife, as he did with his *Concetto Spaziale* series of canvases and ceramic objects, was a way of revealing a 'new dimension of space' through sudden action. By opening up this dimension he could 'escape symbolically, but also materially, from the prison of the flat surface', as he put it. The gesture was highly

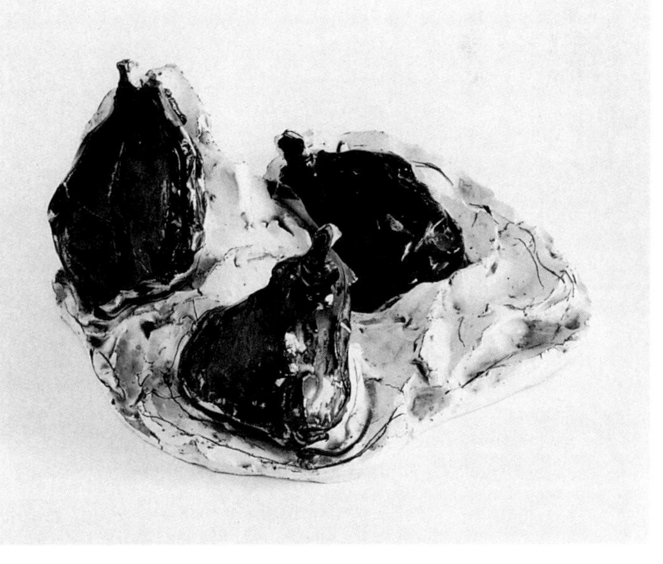

119 **Lucio Fontana**, *Natura Morta*, 1938 (17 × 32 × 28 cm/ 6¾ × 12½ × 11 in).
Fontana could shape 'a submarine landscape, a statue or a tangle of hair and press pure pigment on to it which the heat of the kiln would then amalgamate. The kiln was a kind of intermediary: it made the form and colour permanent.' Forms were pulled and pummelled out of solid lumps of clay, images scratched deep into the surface. After working it the material 'looked as if it had been hit by an earthquake, yet it was motionless'. Sometimes it is as if he was attempting to see how much he could do to a form before it collapsed into formlessness. *Ceramica spaziale* of 1949, for instance, is a rough cube of clay, two feet wide, into which a pole has been pushed: the external surfaces are so gouged and battered that it is more mass than form.

sexualized, the climactic point of drama in the making. This excitement with basic form and with condensed movement manifested his desire for an art of the instinctual, an art based on what he called 'the first artistic experiments' of the prehistoric. But in his ceramics of the 1950s Fontana appeared to be trying to see how little he could do to create this 'escape' into a different dimension.

Fontana's passionate refusal to be defined by his work with one material – the *Concetto Spaziale* title was applied across all the media he used – must be seen in the context of his great knowledge and interest in the particular properties of the materials he used, whether clay or neon. His long friendship with Tullio d'Albisola, revealed in thirty years of letters, shows him to be endlessly particular about the minutiae of glazing and firing. As with Miró's work with Artigas and Noguchi's work with Rosanjin, the vigour and iconoclasm of these artists' ceramics lies in their fierce independence from expectation about what ceramics constituted coupled with courageous collaborators who made it happen.

120 **Lucio Fontana**, Untitled, 1968 (porcelain, 16.5 × 43.2 cm/ 6½ × 17 in).
In 1949 Fontana had remarked that he wanted to work in highly polished ceramic 'in reaction' to Picasso, and certainly after this time his vessels display a use of deep monochromatic tones rather than rich colour and a different sense of gesture. He punctured holes into strange, almost biomorphic, pod shapes, or quickly slashed plates.

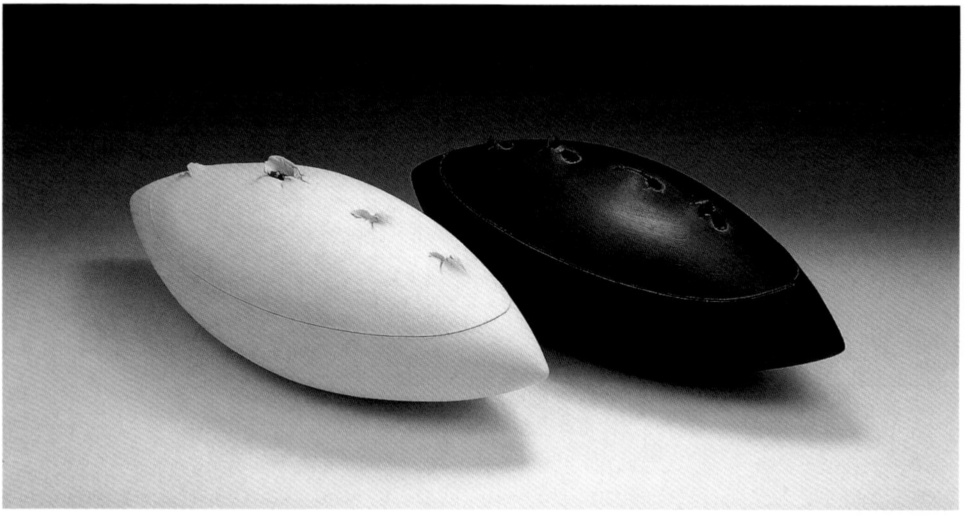

Reactions to Picasso in the 1950s

The reaction to Picasso's ceramics was immediate. Leach was antagonistic and defensive, writing of the Vallauris pots that 'the ware is of no interest as ware. Picasso simply manages to express Picasso, grand acrobat that he is.' Leach dubbed those young potters in Britain who responded favourably 'Picassiettes', punning on the French word 'assiette' for plate, whilst both feminizing and belittling them simultaneously. Reviewing the exhibition 'Picasso in Provence' that toured Britain in 1950, the trade journal *Pottery and Glass* called Picasso's ceramics 'slap happy', whilst a curator in Stoke-on-Trent wrote that 'Picasso's use of slip in broad washes is not altogether happy; it is a painter's approach and not effective as pottery decoration. Doubtless he felt the limitations of a poor body material and it would be interesting to see what he could do with a good Staffordshire earthenware.'

The positive reactions, on the other hand, came from a generation to whom the possibilities afforded by Oriental ceramics, whether or not mediated through Leach, seemed nugatory. Picasso opened up figuration, Mediterranean culture, colour and a diffused sexuality noticeably absent from the Orientalist canon. The Mediterranean effect could be detected in the designs of industrially produced tablewares. When wartime austerity restrictions on the production of decorated ceramics were finally lifted in Britain in 1952, the Stoke-on-Trent Midwinter factory produced the Primavera range designed by Jessie Tait with images of provincial French market life.

The effects of Picasso's influence on European and Scandinavian studio ceramics were considerable. In French ceramics of the 1950s, most notably in the work of the sculptor and ceramicist Georges Jouve (1910–64), there was a self-conscious modernity that showed in its adoption of much of the vocabulary of doves, minotaurs, and harlequins of Vallauris. Jouve's ceramics from the early 1940s were freely modelled versions of vernacular sculptures of saints and animals: later that decade Picasso's influence led to his peasant jugs and cups sprouting horns, breasts and faces. The use of faux-naif imagery – often of animals or mythological beasts – became widespread in Scandinavia too. In Finland at the Arabia factory Michael Schilkin (1900–62) made both monumental reliefs and small wall plaques whose expressive use of drawing into the clay combined with strongly delineated areas of rich glazing used the Vallauris idiom. The acclaim for Picasso's ceramics opened new possibilities for established potters too. In Sweden, Wilhelm Kåge's *Surrea* series of manipulated cut vases and bowls which he had exhibited in 1940 with the title *Idyll and Panic in the Furnace*, were produced again in 1953 to considerably more acclaim:

Surrea, Kåge's most recent chalky artware, is an adventure in pure, glaze-less ceramic sculpture. With the split personality of a Picasso half-face, a vase may be only half a vase, a branch blooming where its mirror image should be. Bowls, the raw material of many of his whimsies, are sliced and mended awry, as if the glazed edges had slipped... He pastes the cracked pots into new, surreal forms which tease the eyes and fingers like melting watches in a dream desert.

In Britain one young potter remembered the Picasso exhibition as 'stately galleries pulsating with vitality and liberation'. Other artists were encouraged towards ceramic experiment by the Vallauris example: at an exhibition at the Redfern Gallery in London in 1952, young artists and sculptors including Victor Pasmore, Kenneth Martin and Eduardo Paolozzi showed decorated ceramics alongside works by the ceramicists Margaret Hine, Nicholas Vergette and William Newland. Architects commissioned ceramic murals for metropolitan coffee and milk bars. The use of tin-glaze, like references to Minoan ceramics, was part of an unassailable attempt to reclaim 'intrinsic' Europeanness in the face of the dominant Oriental canon. The image of Picasso's Mediterranean quickly became as crucial to this generation as Leach's Sung bowls had been to their predecessors.

It was, however, Picasso's way of working with clay, his 'catalytic use of materials' in the words of the American potter Robert Arneson, that was to have the most profound effect. For Dora Billington, writing in 1956 on 'The New Look in British Pottery', Mediterranean influence was behind a new 'experimental attitude of mind', a desire to 'preserve freshness of handling' that she located in the liberation from Oriental orthodoxy. She suggested that 'Every pottery studio in this country might well have inscribed on its walls, 'Craftsmanship is not enough'. To be a truly contemporary potter, she suggested, was to travel, to be eclectic and to resist the dogmatism of the previous generation: this was the gateway from convention to an 'exciting mixture of sculpture, painting and potting'.

121 **Nicholas Vergette**, ceramic mural for the Moo Cow bar, Victoria Street, London, late 1950.
Decorative ceramics for the urban interior reflect an assured contemporaneity unseen since Vienna.

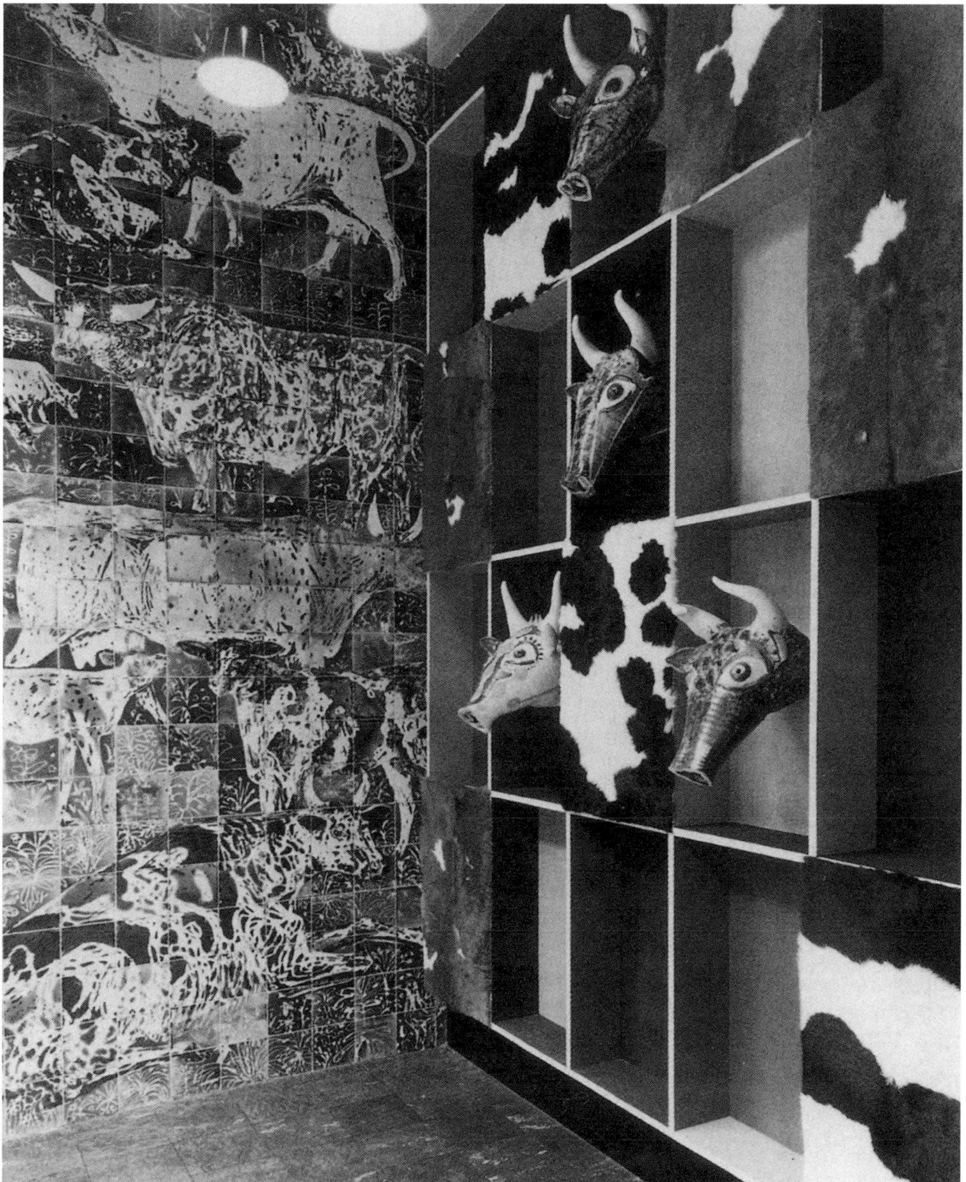

Studio pottery after 1945

There were makers of vessels in the middle of the twentieth century for whom the attraction of pots from early cultures was consolatory rather than an expression of angst. Pots could stand as markers of continuity in a hostile technocratic society. Whereas Leach valued vigour and found it best expressed in the quotidian, these potters valued understatement but avoided the everyday. These were rarely pots for the kitchen table, but rather vases and bowls for collectors. This kind of pot had been made in Scandinavia since the 1920s where the synergy between industry and studio potters allowed potters to design functional ceramics for industry and still make individual pieces. In Denmark Nathalie Krebs (1895–1978) had established the Saxbo studio in 1930 where she had worked with and trained many potters (see p. 66). This kind of vessel tradition continues in Denmark in the work of such potters as Beate Anderson (b. 1942), Bodil Manz (b. 1943) and the Turkish-born but Danish-trained Alev Siesbye (b. 1938).

In America the work of the Finnish born potter Maija Grotell (1899–1973) stood out for this belief in the uninflected vessel. She made strong cylindrical forms with textured surfaces, onto which repeated geometric marks, almost like abbreviated memories of Native American or Aztec designs, were incised or painted onto the glazes. Grotell, who had studied under Willy Finch in Finland, was an influential teacher, running the ceramics at Cranbrook Academy of Art from 1938 until her retirement in 1966. The work of Gertrud (1908–71) and Otto Natzler

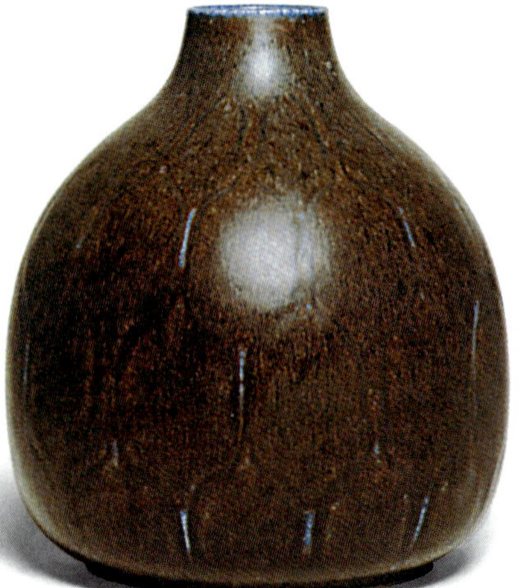

122 **Nathalie Krebs** and **Eva Staehr-Nielsen**, stoneware vase, 1951 (h. 15.2 cm/6 in).
Saxbo was central to Scandinavian ceramics from 1930 to its closure in 1968, training Axel Salto and Tias Eckhoff, among others. Krebs was the glaze chemist whose style was a restrained Orientalist palette of muted browns, ochres and greens. Staehr-Nielsen, who joined in 1931, designed and threw the uninflected stoneware flask and bowl forms.

123 **Gertrud** and **Otto Natzler**, *Pilgrim Bottle*, 1956 (earthenware with yellow crater glaze, h. 43.2 cm/17 in).
'The field we work in is ancient, yet little explored. It is hardly recognized by the public in general who do not associate pots made of ordinary clay with art, unless they happen to be old or decorated. Yet, the objects we make are pots, they are made of clay, they are made today and they are not decorated. Their possible function as containers is unimportant to us' (Otto Natzler). This shape is rare: bowls and flasks were their preferred forms.

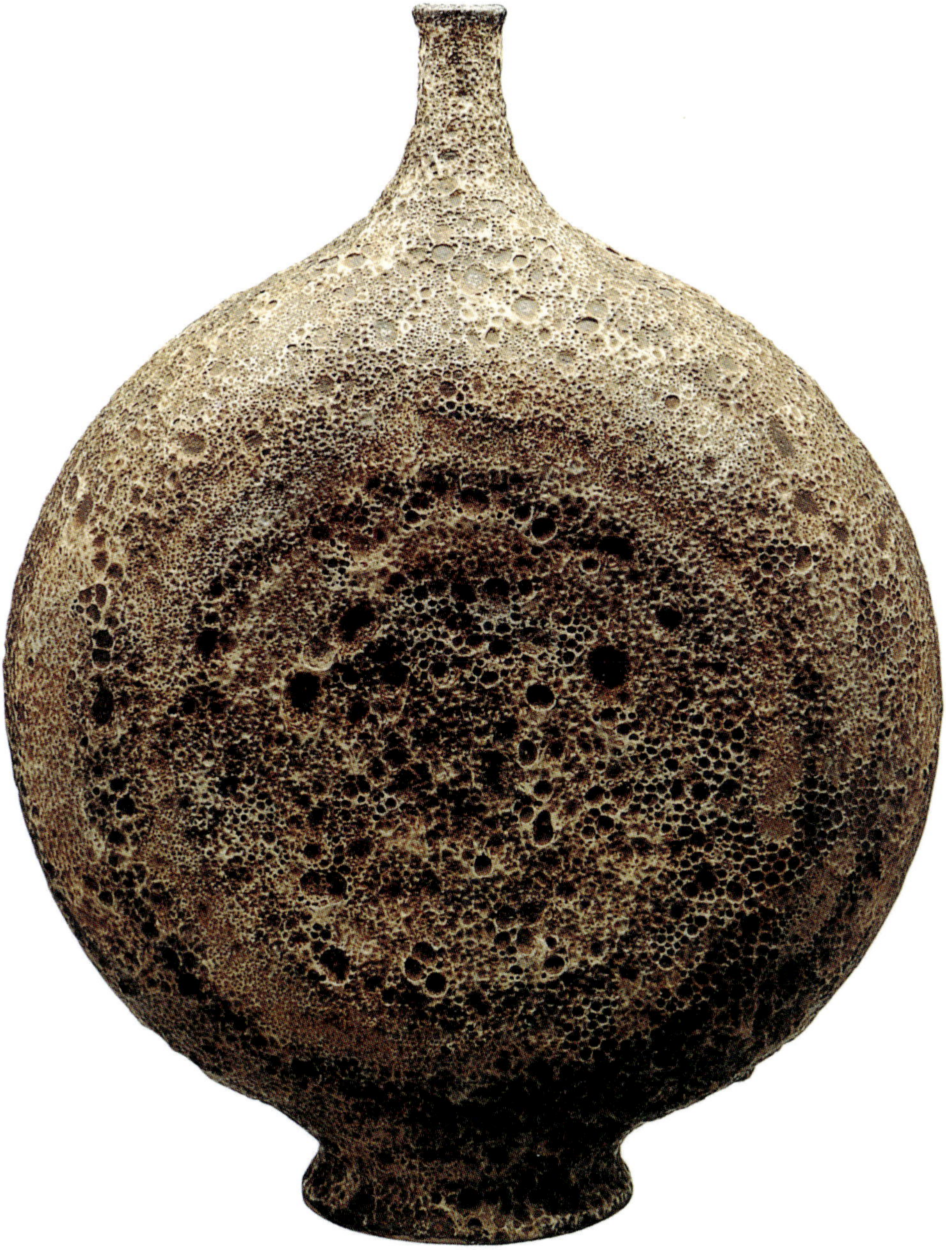

124 **Gertrud Vasegaard**, tea service for Bing & Grøndahl, 1955–57 (porcelain with white celadon glaze).
Between 1949 and 1957 Vasegaard designed for Bing & Grøndahl. This design, like others employing fluted lines, brought together Oriental styles and a Modernist sensibility.

125 **Lucie Rie** and **Hans Coper**, tableware, *c.* 1955 (stoneware).
At an exhibition held at the International Conference on the crafts at Dartington Hall, Devon in 1952, this tableware, designed by Rie and made by her and Coper stood out. A critic remarked that the 'general effect is of an ethnographic exhibit of the remains of a lost civilization, of a village and town community of highly aesthetic peasants. Only the stoneware of Hans Coper and the porcelain of Lucie Rie remains outside the prevailing atmosphere of rural quietism… They show that the artist craftsman is not necessarily an anachronism in our time'.

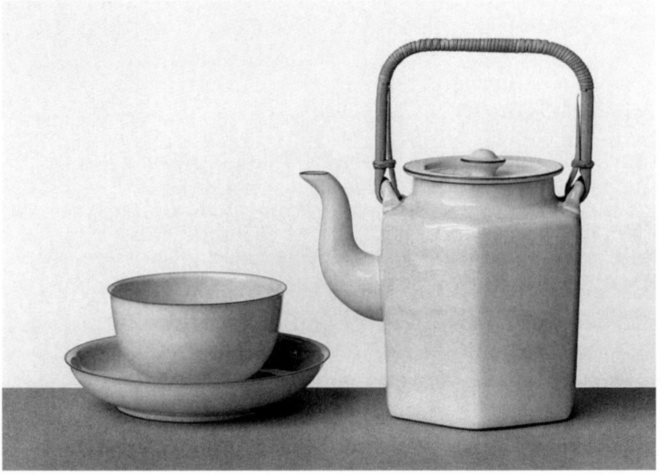

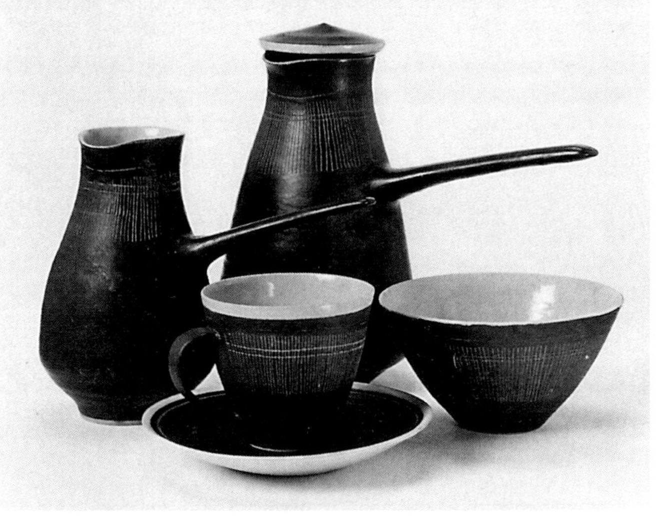

(b. 1908), pre-war émigrés from Austria, also showed this different sensibility. Working in Los Angeles from 1938 they produced their pots as a team: Gertrud threw the pots, thin walled bowls and bottles, and Otto prepared the glazes – cratered like lava or elaborately lapidary – and fired them. Their pots, as Otto Natzler put it, functioned within this 'ancient yet little explored field'.

The Natzlers' non-demonstrative and non-gestural way of making vessels reflected a great self-assurance about where pots belonged. These kinds of pots rarely emphasized the way they were made. With their studied balance of form, colour and texture, they were pots whose arena was a studied domestic interior: they fitted into modern homes alongside contemporary art and modernist furniture, carrying with them an aura of condensed modernity and a sense of private rather than public utterance.

Lucie Rie (1902–95) had trained in Vienna at the Kunstgewerbeschule with Powolny. The severity of her early work had displayed the influence of Hoffmann, setting her apart from the gestural extravagance of the Wiener Werkstätte. Her early pots, thrown and burnished cylinders contrasting with pitted and fluxing glazes, were exhibited widely and successfully in international exhibitions. Rie emigrated to London in 1938, but her work found little favour, her forms criticized by Leach as weak and 'feminine'. But gradually after the war she began to achieve recognition. Her tablewares attracted attention first, the austere designs of black and white glazed teapots and coffee sets decorated with minimal sgraffito cross-hatching rapidly achieved commercial success as products of a distinctively European aesthetic. Their controlled modulation of proportion and decoration was quite unlike the prevailing Orientalist fashions. With their almost engineered surfaces, no throwing lines, glaze runs or brushwork, they found favour with the interior decorative schemes of the time. Rie used sgraffito from the late 1940s, her interest apparently dating from an encounter with Neolithic and Bronze Age pottery at the museum in Avebury, Wiltshire. Sgraffito allowed her to articulate points of transition in forms, on the shoulders of jars or at the springing point of a bowl. But when used on the tablewares it also made a powerful connection between archaic vessels and modern ones. Indeed her forms in the 1950s often centred on beaker shapes, a form that is particularly amenable to this correspondence.

Rie provided a different axis for British studio potters from that of Leach. Her centre of gravity was 'metropolitan', as a critic of the time put it: she embodied interests in design and architecture, she lived in the city, used an electric kiln and was unbothered by anxieties about a 'truth to materials'. Her work, undemonstrative and focused, provided a bridge to pre-war European modernism. It had no aspirations to sculpture, it mediated its own place as a decorative art in the Viennese sense: it was neither cheap nor demotic but attracted collectors. In this way Rie was a crucial model as ceramics became increasingly seen as a part of a counter-cultural movement.

126 **Lucie Rie**, *Baluster vase*, c. 1960 (stoneware, h. 26.1 cm/ 10¼ in).
Rie's interest in ceramic surface led her to experiment with an enormous number of textured glazes. Her early experiments with cratered glazes while still working in Vienna prefigured her later repertoire of matt and pitted glazes.

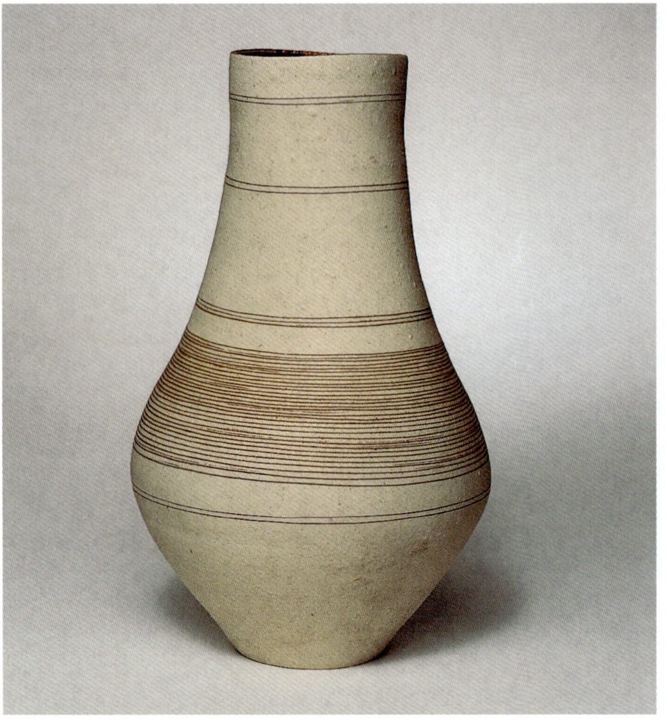

The publication of Leach's *A Potters Book* in 1940 had given an extraordinary impetus to his vision of a quietist, vocational workshop-orientated pottery. Many of Leach's students were now running their own workshops, and training their own apprentices. The introduction of 'standard ware', a repeatable range of simple domestic pottery glazed in celadon and tenmoku, gave the St Ives pottery a focus and method of training the eclectic group who came. The painter and critic Patrick Heron analyzed the effect of Leach's philosophy on this generation:

Even if their pots were bad, their choice of occupation – their chosen 'way of life' – would read as a gesture of protest against the present quality of life accorded us by our contemporary technocratic civilization. It is always the main danger of this movement that the social protest may annul the creative artistry: the craft may preclude the art... Bad hand-pottery may succeed in registering a protest – but it can do little more.

A Potter's Book had given a powerful vision of an integrated 'way of life' as a potter: Leach offered a view of pottery as a civilizing force.

What is intriguing is how widespread was the reach of Leach's message – and where its limitations were most felt. A reviewer in New Zealand in 1959 remarked on the 'preponderate influence of Bernard Leach in the work displayed. So much so that the derivative nature of much of the form speaks of over-much dependence. It is here, sadly enough, that the colonial spirit of self-reliance is weakest and thinnest.' The issue of self-reliance was seen as technical as well as aesthetic. Ivan McMeekin, who had first trained with Cardew at Wenford Bridge, published *Notes for Potters* in Australia in 1967 to encourage new expression in ceramics through a deeper knowledge of indigenous materials.

How to make and how to live were intimately connected. The international reach of this book was such that the description of the ruralist life of a craftsman in America in the late 1960s by Lee Nordness could equally describe one in Britain or Australia:

In nine times out of ten... the person involved with the handmade object is an intellectual who regards his home as a temple and has built within or nearby it a studio he regards as his adytum... To visit artist-craftsmen today, especially those of the post-war generation, is to know silent valleys, dirt roads, unhampered vegetation – and usually homes crafted by hands concerned with every surface.

There were potters of great quality working within the arc of Leach's influence – in England the work of Geoffrey Whiting (1919–88) and Richard Batterham (b. 1936) stand out – but many of the stereotypical pots of the 1960s read as pastiche Leach wares. Glazes were predominately orientalist with tenmoku, ash-glazes and celadons used indiscriminately, and forms were hybrid

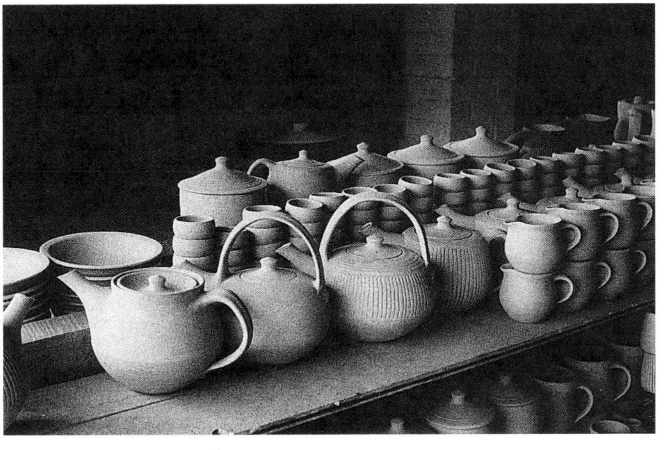

127 **Geoffrey Whiting**'s workshop, 1962.
Repetition tableware was the backbone of the Leach tradition. Whiting, like his contemporaries in Britain, Australia and America, attempted to make handmade domestic ware pottery accessible.

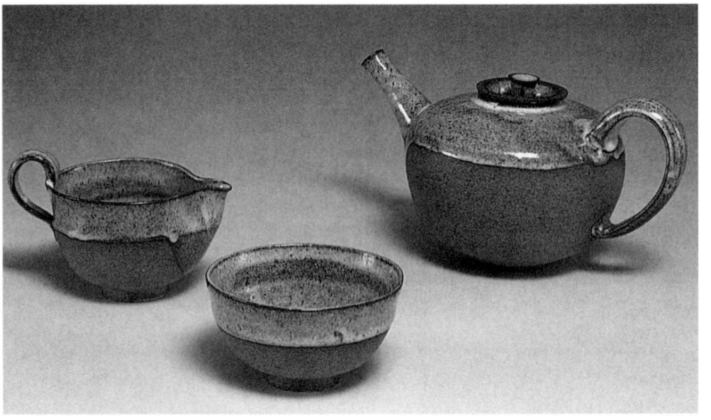

128 **Marguerite Wildenhain**, tea set, 1946 (stoneware). Wildenhain contradicted Leach: 'It ought to be clear that American potters cannot possibly grow roots by imitating Sung pottery or by copying the way of life of the rural population of Japan. Conscious copying of the works of a culture unrelated to the mind and soul of our generation would only produce dubious makeshifts and turn our struggling potters into either dilettantes or pure fakes.

English and Oriental. The mantra of 'truth to materials', an idea that had great resonance in the 1930s when Leach's work had correspondence with Moore and Hepworth, was by now often used to excuse a stridency in proclaiming the robustness of clay and the fluxing qualities of glaze. The idea that a pot had to function in an obviously utilitarian way led to a tidal wave of crudely made and conceived mugs, jugs and casseroles.

Postwar America

The issue of whether the 'standard' that Leach espoused was immutable across cultures, or was more provisional, was debated most strongly in America. Leach first visited America in 1950, a 'spare, tweedy, Hong Kong-born Englishman' in the words of *Time* magazine. He lectured and demonstrated and exhibited his pots. His analysis of American pottery, published in the American magazine *Craft Horizons* on his return to England, was predicated on a

thankfulness that I had been born in an old culture. For the first time I realized how much unconscious support it still gives to the modern craftsman. The sap still flows from a tap root deep in the soil of the past, giving the sense of form, pattern and colour below the level of intellectualization. Americans have the disadvantage of having many roots, but no tap-root, which is almost the equivalent of no root at all. Hence Americans follow many undigested fashions.

This view drew a powerful riposte from Marguerite Wildenhain. Wildenhain (née Friedlander, 1896–1985) had trained at the Bauhaus and was one of the school's brightest stars, designing for the Berlin porcelain factory. After emigrating to America in 1940 and establishing a workshop at Pond Farm, Guerneville,

California, she rejected her earlier engagement with industry, choosing to make functional pottery by hand. A passionate educationalist, she ran hugely influential summer workshops at Pond Farm, bringing a focus onto exactitude of throwing and design that reflected her Bauhaus years. Articulate and confident, her response to Leach, published as an open letter under the headline 'Potters Dissent', was characteristic in its assessment of where the value of tradition lay: 'Roots are, of course, useful to have, but who has the one, single "tap-root" you talked of. That single tap-root no longer exists in our day. It is probable that it never existed'. Some potters were nonetheless converted: Warren MacKenzie (b. 1924) and Alix MacKenzie (1922–62) became the first of many American students of Leach's in St Ives. On returning to America they proved effective evangelists for their master's voice, and developed a version of the Leach style, drawing on similar forms and glazes. Other potters managed to develop a more independent way of making pots that drew on Leach's canon without becoming Leach-styled. Byron Temple (1933–2002), another apprentice, made lidded porcelain boxes that related to Korean pots in their softness of handling.

When Leach returned to America in 1952 it was to tour with Hamada and Yanagi. The trio travelled extensively, giving workshops and lectures at Black Mountain College in North Carolina, the Archie Bray Foundation in Montana and in Los

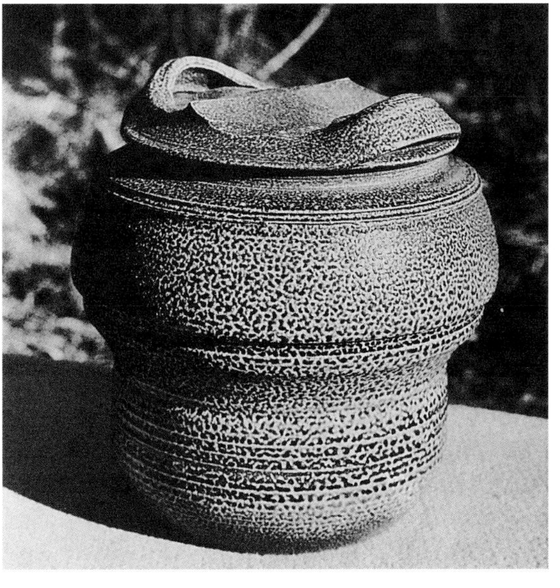

129 **Karen Karnes**, *Lidded Jar*, 1973 (h. 50 cm/20 in). Karen Karnes (b. 1920), who briefly taught at Black Mountain College in the early 1950s, developed a powerful style of facetting her salt-glazed pots. She and her husband organized two important ceramics symposia, bringing together Yanagi, Hamada, Leach and Wildenhain.

Angeles. Leach lectured on the St Ives pottery and Yanagi on aesthetics, but it was the vigour with which Hamada threw and decorated that impressed American observers. His relaxed manner of brushing slip onto a pot, or of trimming a footring, found an audience receptive to new and responsive approaches of handling clay.

For this postwar generation of potters and students watching Japanese potters use the wheel, not as an exercise in making perfect forms, but as a starting-point for other kinds of manipulation, seemed to show how academic American thrown pottery had become. The tension between the expected and planned, the centrifugal force of the pot on the wheel, and the spontaneous gesture that disrupts this, is central to many Japanese ceramic traditions. Pots from the Iga and Shigaraki kilns with their gaping rents from the firing, or pots from the Bizen kilns with their dented sides from gestural handling, were known through photographs. In the 1950s Hamada, Toyo Kaneshige and Kitaoji Rosanjin all visited California, and their pots, distorted, textured or inscribed whilst still wet from the wheel, were exciting manifestations of these traditions. Hamada at Black Mountain College in 1952 said he could 'make do' with the materials to hand; Paul Soldner remembered how Kaneshige 'trimmed the pots with a twig he had broken off an orange tree outside the studio'. This was pottery, and crucially the making of vessels, as an exploratory, improvisational art.

These Japanese potters also made a bridge with the burgeoning excitement of interest in Zen Buddhism. For America in the 1950s, Zen, mediated through the writings of D. T. Suzuki and Alan Watts, showed a world where spontaneity and sudden violent expression were markers of real communication, where conventions could be broken asunder at revelatory moments. It also meant 'looking in the opposite direction', as Suzuki put it, putting intuitive ways of doing something before over-considered ways, something seen in the approaches to making of Hamada and Kaneshige – and in the explosive marks of Japanese calligraphy. Zen became much talked about: knowing about Zen was a marker of contemporary savoir-faire. Ad Reinhardt even caustically anatomized one part of the 1950s art world as 'café-and-club-primitive and neo-Zen-bohemians'.

Peter Voulkos and Otis

It was in Peter Voulkos (1924–2002) that these vigorous and iconoclastic modes of thinking and acting would come together, and produce a ceramic movement of great importance. Voulkos had started to study painting before turning to ceramics. A preternaturally gifted thrower, he was soon making a considerable name for himself with his large and precisely thrown lidded vessels with their Miró-like decoration. Voulkos was fiercely and passionate eclectic, rapidly absorbing ideas and images from pottery and other arts and translating them into his own work. He had been at the Archie Bray Foundation when Hamada visited in 1952 but equally significant were encounters with John Cage and Robert Rauschenberg the following year at Black Mountain College and with the work of the Action painters of Abstract Expressionism in New York, including Franz Kline and Jackson Pollock. In 1954 Voulkos accepted an invitation to set up a ceramics department at the Los Angeles County Art Institute, later renamed the Otis Art Institute. His five years at Otis have become celebrated and, by some, mythologized.

At Otis Voulkos was unhampered by a prescriptive institution: there was no programme to follow, little equipment, and at first Paul Soldner was Voulkos's only student. As there was no separate studio for Voulkos at Otis, the classroom was the studio, and formal relationships between teacher and student were blurred. This suited his way of working. He negotiated for the studio to be open twenty-four hours a day and seven days a week, with much of the making taking place at night, with parties, music and firings adding to the liberating and ambitious atmosphere. Much of the mythic quality of these years centres on this

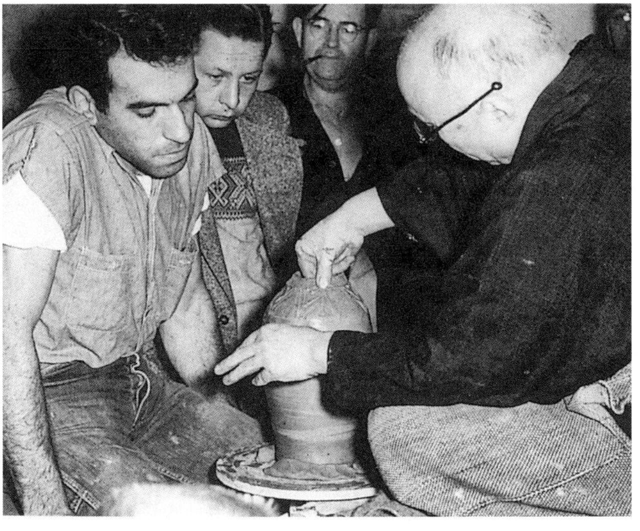

130 **Peter Voulkos** and **Shoji Hamada**, Archie Bray Foundation, Montana, 1952.
Hamada asked Voulkos to kick the wheel for him: 'I was right there, and had my head down with his, and he'd tell me to kick faster or slower, so I was just watching his hands… How often to you get close to a living legend like he was?'

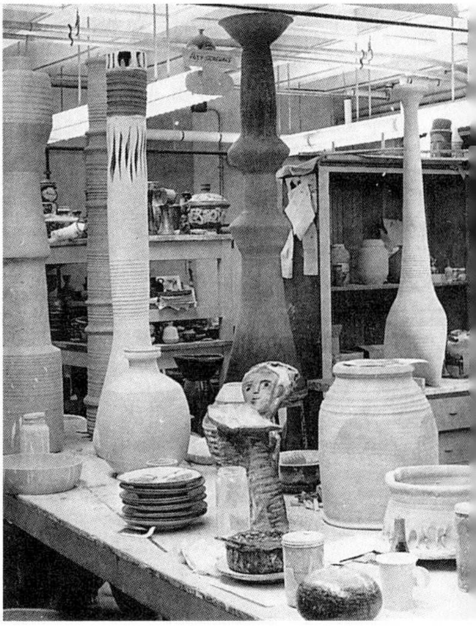

131 **Otis ceramics studio**, 1955–56. The tall vessels are by Paul Soldner, the pots on the tables and shelves are by Peter Voulkos and his students.
The idea of the radical campus ceramics studio, where tutors worked alongside students, gained its power from this period. When Soldner experimented with 'extended throwing', adding coils of clay to make six foot pots, Voulkos made yet taller ones.

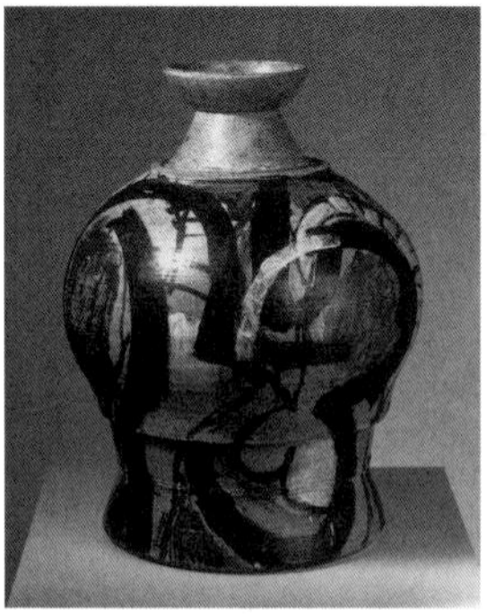

132 **Peter Voulkos**, *Tall Covered Jar*, 1956 (stoneware, h. 64.7 cm/ 25½ in).
'When you are experimenting on the wheel there are a lot of things you can not explain. You just say to yourself, "the form will find its way" – it always does... The minute you begin to feel you understand what you're doing it loses the searching quality... You finally reach a point when you are no longer concerned with keeping this blob of clay centred on the wheel and up in the air. Your emotions take over and what happens just happens.'

atmosphere, with Voulkos as protagonist, spurring on the students to greater expressiveness, larger pots and more open gestural movements into the clay. Experimentation was the defining experience of making pottery. This way of working, compared by the critic and editor Rose Slivka to the experiential and improvisational quality of jazz music, was valued as a release from anxiety over craftsmanship. Just as Cage at Black Mountain College had created 'happenings' where poets, painters and musicians were given prescribed amounts of time to perform in a spirit of 'purposeless purposefulness', where there was a breakdown in distinctions between chosen and accidental sounds and movements, Voulkos moved from the private 'theatre of skill' of the early art potters into the semi-public 'happening' arena of the campus studio. It recalled Harold Rosenberg, writing of Action painting, who famously described the artists acting out the drama of their state of mind in material. Although there were women students at Otis, most notably Janice Roosevelt, this atmosphere of iconoclasm was predominately male, with a strong emphasis on scale and prowess. In this it mirrored the canonical images of the Abstract Expressionist male painter, admired for his rugged, laconic individualism as much for his breaking of artistic conventions. At Otis there was a strong element of being, as in Greenberg's description of Jackson Pollock, 'radically American'.

Voulkos started to stack thrown pots together, disregarding fluid transitions between the discrete elements, and emphasizing the fact of assemblage by adding on strips of clay, like bandages or buttresses. Clay strips were also pasted onto the surface to make shallow relief patterns. Large brushstrokes (sometimes using housepainters' brushes) broke any remaining symmetry. Some were fissured or had abrupt apertures. Some still looked like vessels, in others thrown pots were cut and pasted together with slabs and 'nails' to make objects with several complex volumes. They owed something to Miró in the almost violent conjunction of the parts, something to Picasso in the disjunction of decoration and form, something to Japanese pottery in their gestural throwing, and a great deal to a whole-hearted attempt to give ceramics 'a kick in the pants', as he put it in 1957 in his statement as juror to the Fifth Miami National Exhibition.

In the same year Voulkos and John Mason rented a new studio and had a vast kiln built, allowing work on a still bigger scale. The titles of his works tells of the monumentality – and the 'radical Americanness' – of the impulse with which he was gripped – *5000 Feet* (1958), *Little Big Horn* (1959), *Camelback Mountain* (1959),

USA 41 (1960), *Gallas Rock* (1961). In these works the last vestiges of a centred volume disappeared and multiple compound elements were attached to an axis. In this displacement of volume – not its eradication – Voulkos showed how contingent his sculptural apprehension was on the idea of the vessel. But as a critic in 1966 was to put it, 'the upshot of the latter tendency was... clay sculpture'.

The idea of how clay could be used sculpturally was provocatively discussed by Rose Slivka, the editor of *Crafts Horizon*, in a 1961 article 'The New Ceramic Presence'. She analysed the effect that the developments in abstract sculpture and painting had on 'the formal environment of ceramicists everywhere'; the decision of the sculptors

to project intellectually devised forms with no objective reference inevitably enlarged the formal vistas of every craftsman and designer working in three dimensions. To pottery, sculpture has communicated its own sense of release from the tyranny of traditional tools and materials, a search for new ways of treating materials and for new forms to express new images and new ideas.... The sculptor today places greater emphasis on event rather than occasion, in the force of movement and the stance of the dance rather than in the power of permanence and the weight of immobility, in the metamorphosis of meanings rather than in the eternity of symbols.

Slivka's key apprehension in this densely argued essay was of the 'presence' of these ceramics. It is what ceramics did to the viewer that was more important than their style: ceramics could be 'event rather than occasion'. 'Event' implied action and reaction, the spirit of engagement that was present in happenings. 'Occasion' implied stasis, a viewer gazing – solemnly – at a perfectly achieved object. For her the 'New Ceramic Presence' reflected an important shifting of the weight of ceramics from being consolatory and reflective to being confrontational and self-consciously avant-garde. Ceramics took their place alongside the new art. Slivka's sense of this moment was highly optimistic: there was a movement of 'painted pottery to potted painting to sculptured painting to potted sculpture to sculptured pottery. And often the distinctions are very thin or non-existent.' In the future she suggested the ambitions of painters, ceramicists and sculptors would meet as one: the 'formal environments' of exhibitions, museums and criticism would coalesce.

Slivka's stress on the newness of the movement, its impeccable avant-garde credentials, gave an added heroism to her protagonists. At the expense of any contextualization of other kinds of abstraction in ceramics (most importantly those Japanese ceramics that take vessels as a theme) the new movement seemed to have thrown off 'the tyranny of traditional tools and materials.' In effect Slivka was claiming for the Voulkos school what Greenberg had claimed for Abstract Expressionism. The article produced a furore which continued for many issues of the magazine. Its validation of this movement seemed an affront to craftsmanship, to value introspection over ceramics' utilitarian roles.

The variety of Slivka's 'very thin' distinctions was present in an impressive group of 'independent contestants', as the fellow student potters at Otis were categorized. Soldner had been joined the following year by John Mason, who in turn was followed by Ken Price, Henry Takemoto, Michael Frimkess and Jerry Rothman. Mason followed a similar path away from the vessel towards powerful accretions of forms, collaging together slabs of clay to make fissured geological-looking sculptures. In the spirit of release from aesthetic and technical codifications he experimented with colours normally used on low-fire ceramics, using house brushes to paint bright reds and yellows onto the clay in great sweeps further highlighting the actual act of marking a surface. The surface became Mason's arena, with vast slabs of clay placed on the floor to be gouged, incised and textured in a way that invoked the automatism of Pollock's gestural marking of a canvas. Mason's *Blue Wall Relief* (1959), nine feet (2.75 metres) long, showed his ambitions to move beyond what in 1958 he had angrily anathematized as potters' 'Timidity of spirit, coupled with little real conviction'. Photos of Mason in a T-shirt straining to compact great handfuls of clay onto an easel to make one of these reliefs show the passage from discrete working at the wheel to the mode of contemporary sculptor. By the time of his exhibition at the Los Angeles County Museum of Art in 1966 his work had moved to include increasingly severe, geometric, cross and spear forms. A monolithic smooth-surfaced 'Red X' from that year, five feet (1.5 metres) wide, presaged his involvement in more minimalist uses of clay, culminating in the 1970s with his use of firebricks to make floor pieces. Mason was working, in effect, as a sculptor with clay: making work in series driven by ideas.

The model of the studio-potter, where stylistic change is incremental and – of necessity – slowed by selling work, was replaced by the model of the artist showing bodies of work in galleries and museums. Indeed the role of museums in the

133 **Peter Voulkos**, *Little Big Horn*, 1959 (stoneware, h. 157 cm/62 in).
For Voulkos size became a metaphor for his increasing ambitions. The scale of his ceramics 'confirms our sense that something big has actually happened in art in our time', as the critic E. C. Goossen wrote in 1958 of the Abstract Expressionists.

134 **John Mason**, Vase, 1958 (stoneware, h. 61 cm/24 in).
Mason criticized potters who had 'sacrificed inner experience in terms of results, spotlighted in terms of techniques and standards of good taste.' It was an imperative to act as if boundaries between sculpture, painting and ceramics were just not there, to make work that couldn't be easily accommodated into canons of taste.

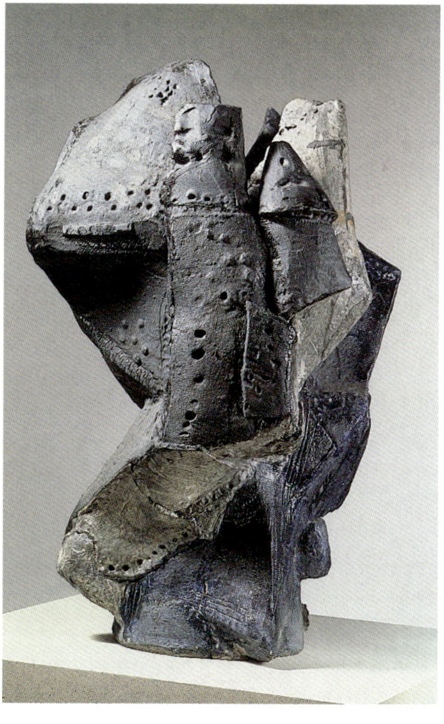

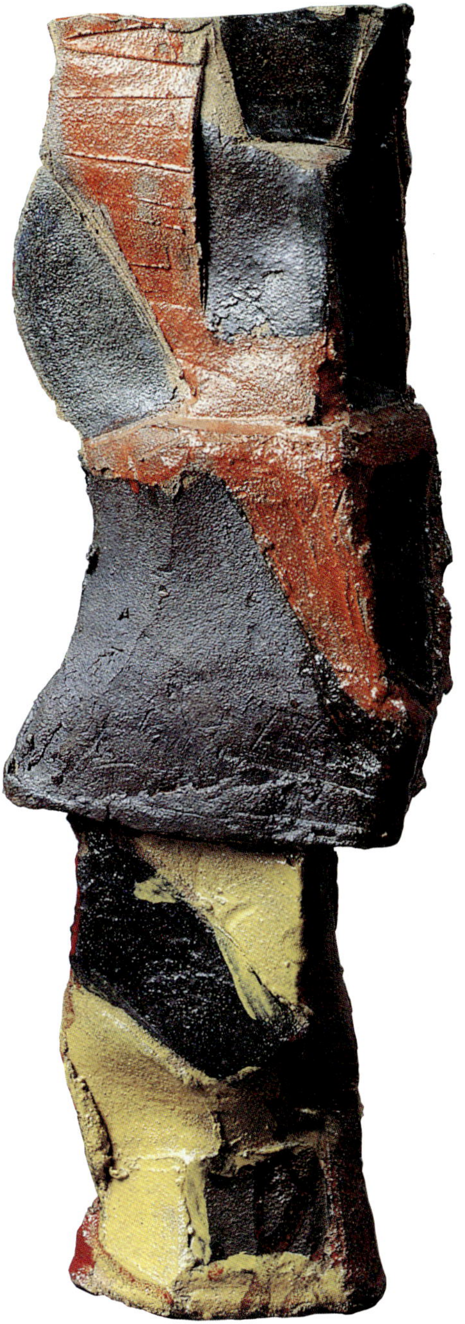

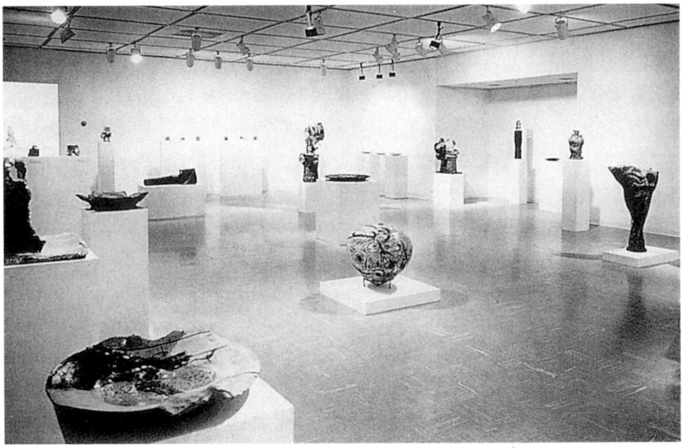

135 ***Abstract Expressionist Ceramics*** exhibition, 1966. This exhibition coupled together the two movements – Abstract Expressionism and the Voulkos school – almost inextricably. It included the work of Voulkos and Mason, Takemoto, Frimkess, Price and Melchert. The curator John Coplans called these ceramics 'the most ingenious regional adaptation of the spirit of Abstract Expressionism that has yet emerged.'

validation of this way of working was significant, with solo shows for Mason and Voulkos in Los Angeles, a small show for Voulkos at the Museum of Modern Art in 1960 and then in 1966 an exhibition at the University of California in Irvine, *Abstract Expressionist Ceramics*.

Abstract Expressionism's absence of a single focal point and the way that a composition became a field of diffuse energies has a correlation with Voulkos and Mason's ceramics. Mason's ceramic reliefs share the sense of 'event', the sudden explosion of energy, present in the paintings of Franz Kline or Robert Motherwell. But Coplans, by labelling these potters in relation to painting (and region), occluded the diversity of their inspirations. Their dramatization of parts of the ceramic canon – the ceramics of Picasso and Miró as much as of Japan – was subsumed in this relationship with part of the 'greater world' of painting. Certainly Voulkos's decision in 1963 to stop using clay in favour of other sculptural materials (though it was revoked later in the decade) could be seen as an attempt to gain greater recognition for himself as a sculptor, not a ceramic sculptor. When he did return to pottery it was to concentrate on two vessel forms, a stacked tripartite vase and an open dish, forms with which he continued to work until his death. These forms used in an intensive way a few kinds of marks, slashes and perforations, something that led Jim Melchert, writing of Voulkos's 'Return to Pottery' in 1968, to comment that 'The group is composed of the most haptic pottery I've seen in a long time; it wouldn't surprise me if the pots were made in the dark'.

The dramatizing of traditions continued after Otis. Soldner's pots, which had started out as experiments in 'extended throwing', changed after his first attempts to use raku in 1960. The intense theatricality of raku, with the visible metamorphosis of the red hot pots taken with long tongs from the kiln and plunged into leaves or straw and then water, provided Soldner with an arena where intuition and skill seemed in balance. He had taken the limited technical information about raku in Leach's *A Potter's Book* as a starting point, but disappointed by the subtle tonalities of the glazes that he found, he experimented with different materials to achieve a greater colour range. Raku, the most highly inflected of Japanese traditional pottery techniques, closely bound up with the aesthetics of the tea ceremony, was about to undergo an American conversion.

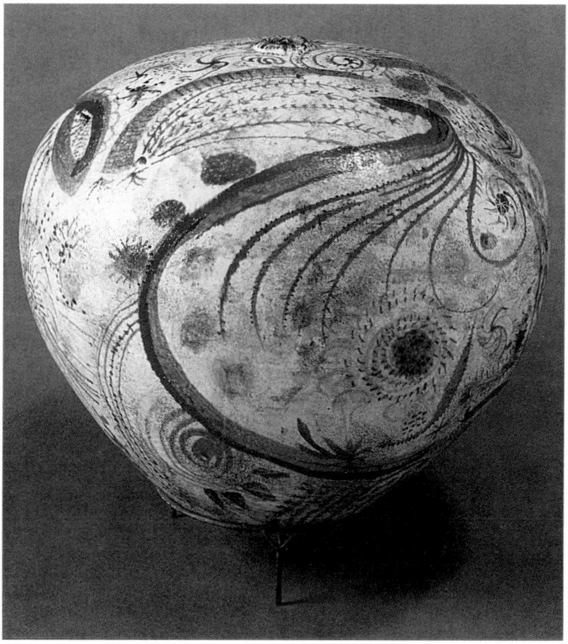

136 **Henry Takemoto**, *First Kumu*, 1959 (stoneware, h. 92 cm/36 in).
Henry Takemoto (b. 1930) started at Otis in 1957 after an art degree in Hawaii. He covered his pots with dense spiralling patterns, some faux-naif and vegetal, some almost sinister reworkings of Oriental blue and white styles.

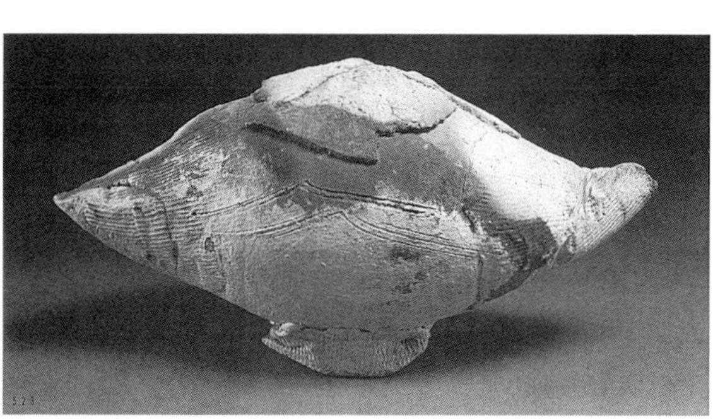

137 **Paul Soldner**, *Raku Pot*, 1962 (earthenware, h. 24.3 cm/9⅝ in).
Soldner developed a way of treating surfaces that allowed for a greater eclecticism in the making – vessels were cut or dropped, folded or creased or imprinted with found objects: many of his constructed objects bear the imprint of his sneakers. Invoking the spirit of Zen he regarded experimentation as the crucial imperative: 'In the spirit of raku: make no demands, expect nothing, follow no absolute plan, be secure in change, learn to accept another solution and, finally, prefer to gamble on your own intuition.'

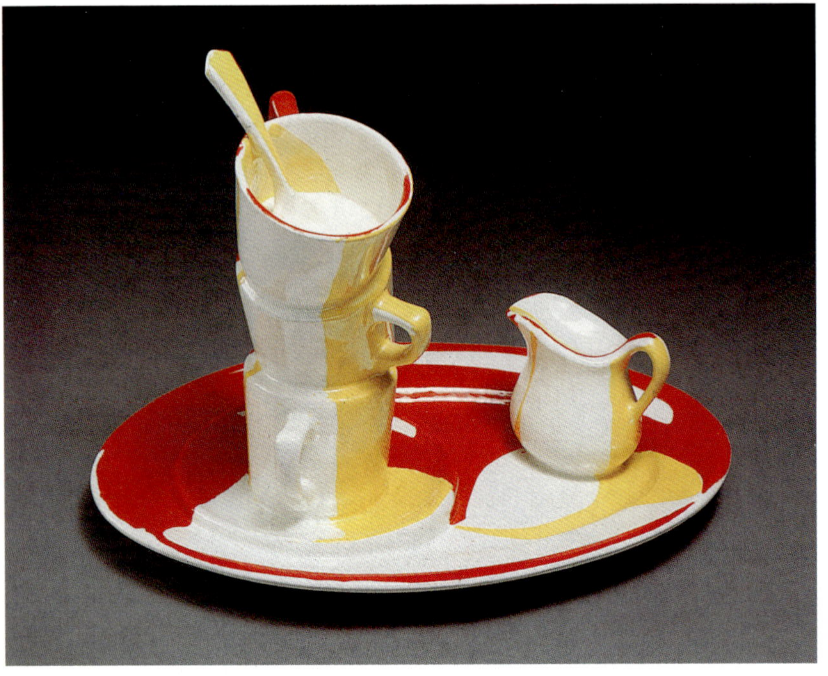

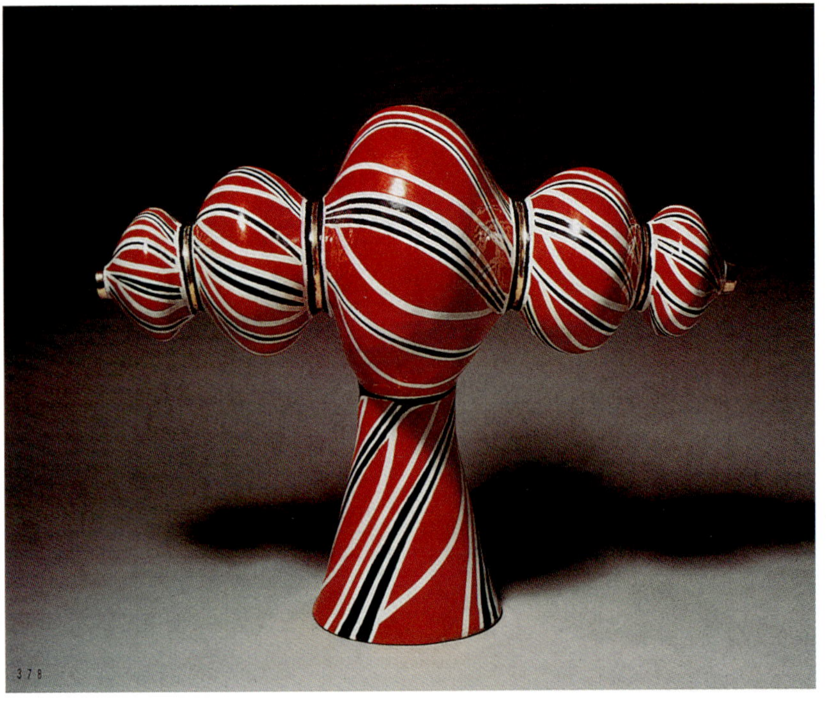

Chapter Four 1965–2000

138 **Roy Lichtenstein**, *Dinnerware*, c. 1967 (earthenware, h. 30 cm/11¾ in).
The most explicit of Pop's connections with ceramics was the collaboration in 1965 between Hui Ka Kwong and the painter Roy Lichtenstein. Small tableaux of precariously stacked cups, saucers and jugs were created using thickly potted bland hotel china wares – the ubiquitous ceramic equivalent of Warhol's Brillo boxes. Strong colours – the reds, yellows and blues of the comic strip rather than ceramics – stripe the groups. Each have the framing device of a tray or saucer: they exist as three-dimensional commentaries on two-dimensional images of three-dimensional objects.

139 **Hui Ka Kwong**, *Ceramic Form*, 1968 (stoneware, h. 55 cm/21⅝ in).
Hui's own constructed compound forms of the same period share the clarity of Lichtenstein's colours, and use thin strips of lustre to accentuate the geometries in the decoration. Hui described them as having a 'different kind of emotion' from his earlier work, 'kind of formal, accurate'.

Pop and Funk ceramics

Nineteen-sixties America saw a new kind of ceramics. Some were brash, highly finished objects whose surfaces and decoration seemed more akin to surfboards or Harley-Davidson motorcycles than pottery. Others were, as Donald Judd wrote of Claes Oldenburg in his 1965 essay 'Specific Objects', 'slick, flaccid and a little disagreeable.' Both Pop ceramics and Funk ceramics, as these two closely entwined groupings were called, came out of a preoccupation with the ordinary and the suburban, the imagery of consumer life that was already so highly inflected through film, television and advertising. In the words of the critic Henry Geldzahler, it was 'so pervasive, persistent and compulsive that it had to be noticed.' Pop Art had two distinct phases, one in England in the 1950s and one that came together in New York in the early 1960s around Claes Oldenburg, Andy Warhol and Roy Lichtenstein. Turning its back on the emotional theatre of Abstract Expressionism, in Pop Art the smooth and clean surface became the arena for a staged anonymity. Instead of the catalytic moment of expression between artist and material there was the considered and analytic use of materials. Warhol even referred to his assistants in 'The Factory' as production-line workers.

The proximity of Pop Art to avant-garde craft was closely considered in the American magazine *Craft Horizons* in 1965. The 'new object makers' Richard Artschwager (b. 1923) and Claes Oldenburg (b. 1929) were interviewed. Artschwager, a functional furniture maker who had recently turned to using formica to make highly finished colourful but useless wooden objects that seemed to refer to utilitarian objects, described his practice as a

sort of invasion. Nothing is safe, and everything is discovered in a limited way. The offense is that I'm spending time and money on things which should be good for something. I'm making objects for non-use; by use, I mean cups to drink out of, a spoon to stir with. By killing off the use part, non-use parts are allowed living space... Things in still life painting can have monumentality.

What Artschwager offered was a schema, one that many ceramicists took for their work – the re-presentation of ordinary things, as sculpture. Indeed it was this re-presentation, something he called the 'theatre of objects', that Oldenburg undertook with his installation *The Store* (1962), where he sold his everyday objects of painted plaster to the public.

In England Glenys Barton (b. 1944) made slip-cast cubes with geometric decoration in primary colours, her *Graphic Permutations* series, a cerebral puzzle that echoed this formality. Similarly Mutsuo Yanagihara (b. 1934), the Japanese ceramicist whose early work was so closely identified with the Sodeisha and who taught in America in the late 1960s and early 1970s, developed a style of work that employed lustres and rich overglaze colours of turquoise and mauve.

The use of colour is reminiscent of the work of Kenneth Price (b. 1935), who trained as a painter before studying ceramics at

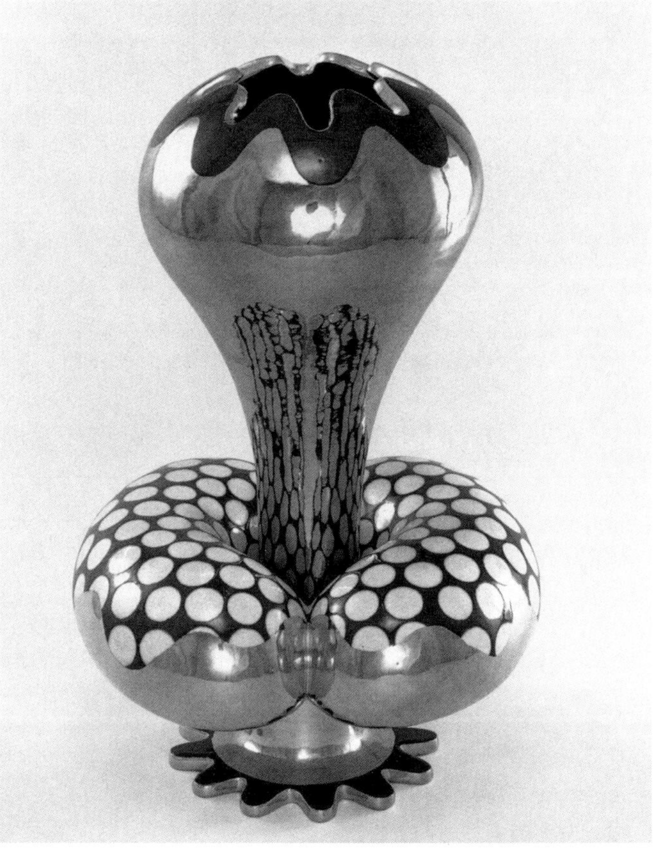

140 **Mutsuo Yanagihara**, vase with gold and silver pattern on dark blue base, 1971 (semi-porcelain and lustre, h. 62 cm/24½ in).
Yanagihara has suggested that his often overtly sexualized forms were derived from Prehistoric Sui wares. His work attempts to satirize the values of contemporary society by creating rich illusionistic surfaces that obscure an accurate reading of the vessel's form.

Otis and Alfred and returning to California. His application of almost violent colour – sometimes the result of acrylic paint and lacquer on the surface rather than glaze – gave his work a clarity allied to objects made from metal or acrylic, or indeed to the painters alongside whom he showed at the Ferus Gallery in Los Angeles. Many of them shared the so-called 'Finish Fetish', an emphasis on what the critic James Meyer has called 'the illusionistic qualities of shiny, synthetic materials'. These artists were at the forefront of an innovative art that Judd saw as 'neither painting nor sculpture', a collision between new synthetic materials and the depth of colour achieved in contemporary American painting. Price's work occupies a middle ground between painting and sculpture, offering colour as an integral rather than supplementary part of the work. Some of Price's objects were curious, almost biomorphic forms like eggs or mounds that John Coplans, writing in 1964, called

a strange interplay between the joyful and the ominous. His color is physically brilliant, almost gaudy: these colors are set off against an imagery which would seem to be least congenial to it – it is dark, murky, very elementary and primordial – the last in the world that one would think to use this coloration with.

It was not the sheer virulence of the colour on these forms that was so shocking, it was their conjunction with 'natural' forms. For Price was also interested in the shock effect of seeing specifically ceramic forms as a vehicle for his ideas. They were, as Judd had said of Oldenburg, 'a little disagreeable.'

If the iconic figure of Pop Art was the billboard artist, the replicator of smooth and clean and glamorous images of consumer culture, the iconic figure for Funk was the hobbyist, the amateur at sea in the mess of failed enthusiasms. If Pop Art was clean, then Funk was most definitely dirty. The work of Robert Arneson (1930–92) defined the movement. Trained at the California College of Arts and Crafts, he was an accomplished thrower briefly enamoured with Voulkos-style Abstract Expressionism. But in 1963 he created a series of toilets, ceramic objects that like Duchamp's urinal *The Fountain* of 1917, were the ultimate 'invisible' artefacts. Given the chance to exhibit with Voulkos and other 'greats', 'I made a toilet and cut loose and let every scatological notation in my mind freely flow across the surface of that toilet'. The work, *Funk John*, was removed from the exhibition. He followed this with others, a panoply of penile pipes and handles, ceramic excrement and stains. There was a

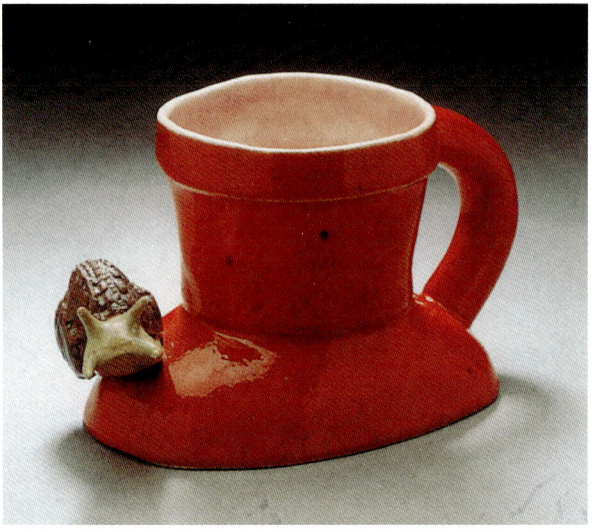

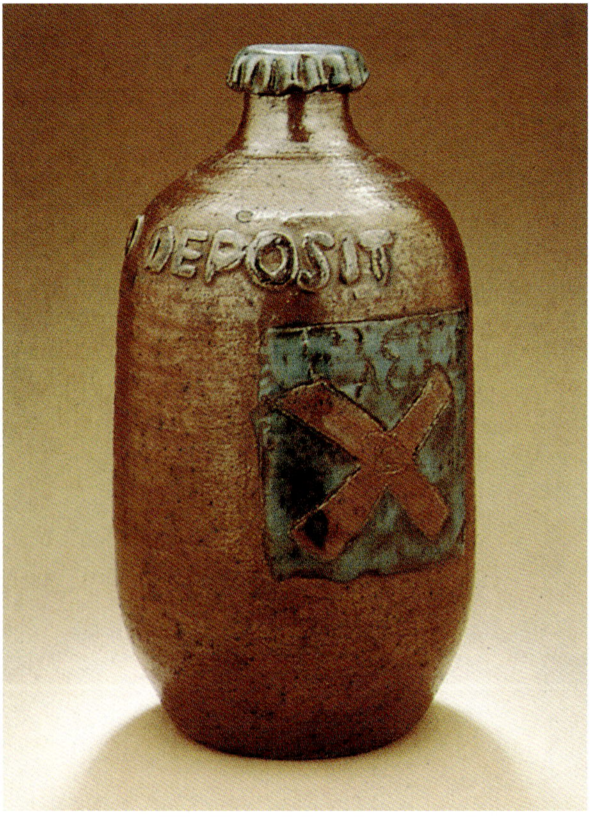

141 **Kenneth Price**, *California Snail Cup*, 1968 (h. 7.3 cm/3 in). Price has not so much collapsed definitions of artifice and the natural, but allowed one to invade the other: there is a dialectical pull between attraction and repulsion.

142 **Robert Arneson**, *No Deposit, No Return*, 1961 (stoneware, h. 27.3 cm/10¾ in). While demonstrating at the wheel Arneson threw a 'handsome, sturdy bottle about quart size and then carefully sealed it with a clay bottlecap and then stamped it No Return. That's what its really about, isn't it?' This was an act of liberation, an act of no return, a relocating of ceramics in the banal.

brashness and menace to these objects – the unsettling feeling that the material world could bite back, something noted by a critic in 1966 in Ken Price's work as 'prime examples of the aesthetic of nastiness.' Arneson's *Toasties* of 1965 has a burnt hand struggling out from the machine, while *Typewriter* of 1965–66 has long manicured fingernails in the place of keys, an image of woman as 'writing machine'. Much of the humour was played out in a highly elaborate series of visual and verbal gags, often dramatizing the ways in which repressed desires become manifest. Just as Oldenburg had talked of *The Store* as a place of 'dreams of the proletarian Venus, stifled yearnings which transmute into objects, brilliant colours and grossly sensuous surfaces', so Arneson offers obvious objects of desire like a six-pack of Coca-Cola bottles. Later in the 1960s he started to make work that was more concerned with suburbia, including elaborate depictions of his house: 'a monument, a sculpture, a wall, a trophy, a jar and a souvenir plate. It is a slab built, one-story, two-bath, three-bedroom, two-bath, two-car garage, California-style house. It is for sale'.

The exhibition *Funk* was held in 1967 art the University Art Museum at Berkeley in California. It included all the major

143 **Robert Arneson**, *Smorgi-Bob the Chef*, 1971 (h. 183 cm/72 in). Arneson created a series of absurd, mock-heroic self-portraits, including representations of himself with the Mona Lisa and as Van Gogh.

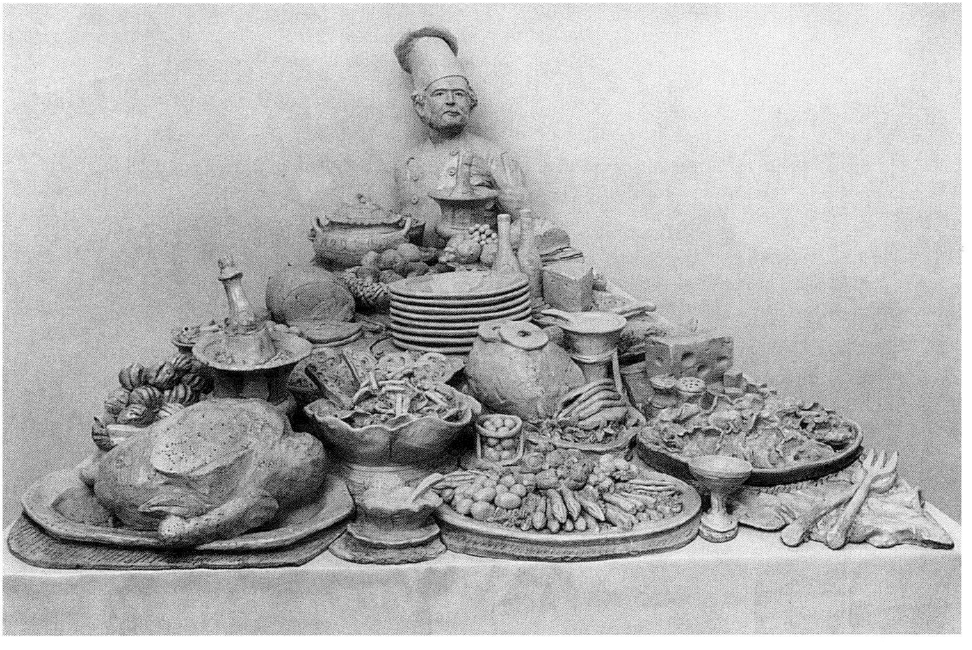

protagonists of the movement including Arneson, David Gilhooly (b. 1943), Jim Melchert (b. 1930) and Kenneth Price. Gilhooly's ceramics showed a sort of alternative world populated by frogs, a conceit that allowed for political, sexual and social commentary. Melchert, who had studied with Voulkos, produced work in defined series, beginning with his 'Legpots', where a sort of broken, archaic limb was attached to a rough block of clay. By 1970, after reading Raymond Queneau's *Exercises in Style* in which a story is retold in a hundred different ways, Melchert began to use the lower-case letter 'a' as a hook on which to hang different stylistic explorations – some gilded, some glazed, some left as raw clay. Crucially each piece was titled, placing it in the necessary verbal–visual matrix.

Many of these ceramics were modelled from whiteware, a recently formulated white earthenware clay. They were objects that owed no debt of 'truth to material'. Indeed it can be claimed that the invention of this clay was as important to the ceramics of the period as formica and fibreglass were to sculpture: all were new, neutral materials that provided a surface onto which brash colour could be applied. With these materials came the chance to produce the kind of unbroken coloured surface of the industrially manufactured object – the kind of object that looked like something out of a brochure or catalogue. 'Auto lacquer' and photographic decals could also be used with this clay and, as was noted in 1965, 'China paints, until recently relegated to hobbyist decoration or dime store china, have been rediscovered along with low-fire luster glazes. The signs and symbols of popular art and culture are expressed with appropriate sharpness through the use of these metallic or almost neon colored low-fire glazes'. The embrace of all the ornate, gilded, narrative, commemorative ceramics, often with written commentary attached, was totally antipathetic to the studio pottery movement. For this was not so much ironic commentary on popular culture, more an amused attempt to flatten distinctions between high and low cultures.

Unlike the heroics of the Voulkos school, Funk was concerned with the banality of making. Hence the image of the hobbyist and student potter in Arneson's work, spouting the words 'Well – yes I'd say that ceramics is the world's most fascinating hobby – but'. In *How to make the big dish*, four panels reduce the experience to

1. Exert Uniform Pressure' (Hands mould the blob on the wheel.)
2. Make a Well. (Firm hands, steady hands.)
3. Keep fingers stiff.
4. Spread the Opening. (By now the dish is wide open and well made.)

Though Michael Frimkess (b. 1937) had only a tangential relationship with Funk he shared this interest in pulling together the canonical and the clichéd. In *Things Ain't What They Used to Be* (1965), a large covered Chinese jar provides the backdrop for a ceramics class – rows of students throwing with their thoughts exposed: 'Mom'll be so proud', 'I wonder if he'll notice me?'

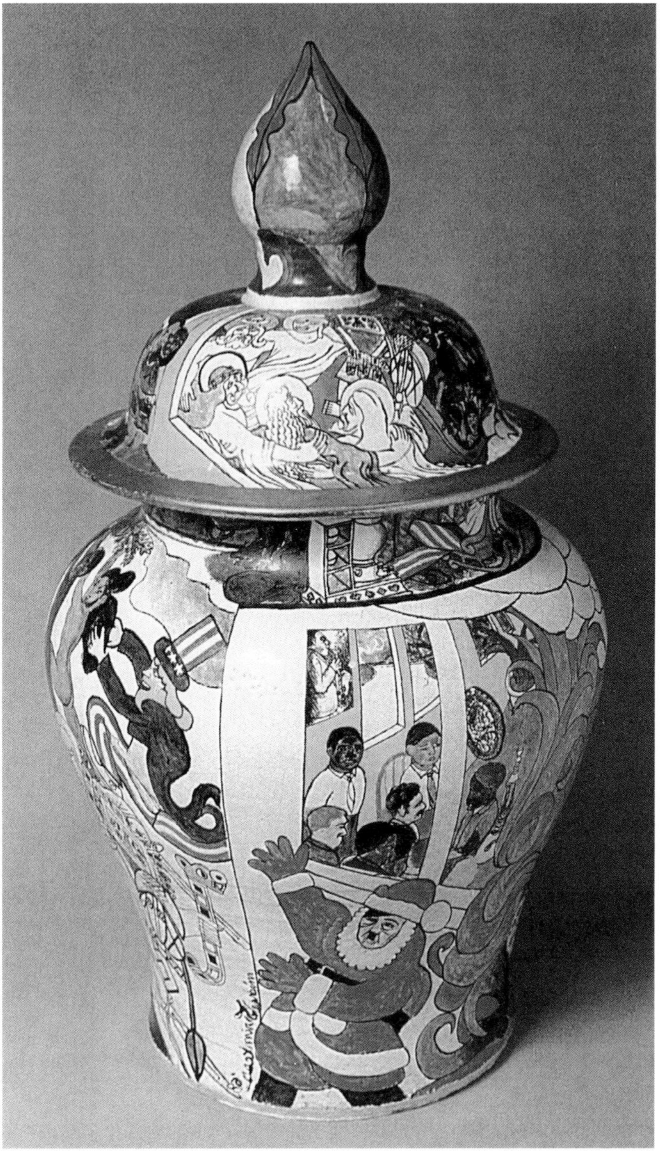

144 **Michael Frimkess**, *Jumpin' at the Moon Lodge*, 1968 (stoneware, h. 69 cm/27¼ in).
A student of Voulkos's at Otis, Frimkess moved towards his interest in using archetypal forms (the Attic amphora, Minoan vase and Chinese ginger jar) as the ground for involved social critiques – all captured in a comic book style. This jar is painted with depictions of Uncle Sam, Hare Krishna, Superman and Santa Claus with Hitler's face.

A more reductive view of the meanings possible in ceramics came in what the writer and historian Garth Clark has called the 'Super-Object', an obsessively crafted rendering of detail and trompe l'oeil that achieved great success in the middle of the 1970s. The Super-Object came out of Pop's obsession with surface and it found its most attenuated form in the assemblages of Richard Shaw (b. 1941). Shaw began his career making nostalgic objects (sofas and chairs with scenes painted on them) before moving to increasingly elaborate assemblages. Some were constructions of clay vessels out of bizarre faux materials – cardboard, twigs, antlers – that had some connection with baroque ceramics. Others were trompe l'oeil books, scraps of paper and houses of cards, which collected images and texts together in a kind of narrative. Both history and narrative were secondary to the projection of what one critic approvingly called their 'triumph in thinness, perfection of size, and appearance'. As the technology of transfer printing became more sophisticated, these objects lost even the faintest element of surprise. For some that was the point.

The work of Marilyn Levine (b. 1935), said the critic Harold Rosenberg, is 'essentially a conceptual art, that brings to the eye nothing not present in nature but instructs the spectators that things may no longer be what they seem.' Levine mixed clay with fibreglass or nylon fibres to produce meticulous ceramic versions of leather shoes, knapsacks or jackets. She was particularly drawn to things that were aged or scuffed, objects that contained what she described as '*Trace*... the accumulation of the marks left by the realization of man's intent, such as trampled grass, grease spots and dirt. In *trace*... we find richness, a humanity often omitted in intent'. These ceramics, like some Pop sculpture, seem to question whether any interpretative act has taken place at all beyond the choice of object to reproduce. But both Shaw and Levine were enormously popular in the 1970s: they seemed to affirm the place of craft in the making of an art object while still seeming conceptual.

In her 1971 essay 'Laugh-in Clay', Rose Slivka sounded the death knell for Funk. She acclaimed Funk artists and ceramicists' capacity to recontextualize through their 'new aesthetic of narrative and relic. They have created artifacts of our time as if it were already over, as if it were nostalgia anticipated, cast into the future.' But she questioned whether in the attempt to 'outwit the museum and the gallery', by being unclassifiable 'these extremely witty and clever and gifted and knowledgeable and deft university-produced, degree-laden artists and teachers of art have not themselves, in turn, outwitted art... and by doing so outwitted themselves?' The charge was that, like the Pop artists of the fine art world, these ceramicists had become assimilated into the institutions they had set out to interrogate.

Critical commentary, new contexts

The great majority of the ceramicists making 'disagreeable objects', work that set out to 'challenge', were eventually lecturers in either art colleges or university art departments. This was true in Britain and Japan as much as in America. There was a growing gulf between the kinds of ceramics supported by the academy and the studio potters who were making their livings from functional pottery and to whom this kind of institutional support was not forthcoming.

The growth of independent co-operative societies, exhibiting groups and magazines for the studio potter, all of which flourished in the 1970s, can be traced to this separation. A benign reading would be that it demonstrated a 'permissive pluralism', a happy co-existence between different kinds of ceramic practice. In fact there was considerable friction, conflict and anger, with distaste for 'brown mugs' from the more sculptural end of the spectrum, and disdain for 'personality cult' from the potters. Gerry Williams, the co-editor of the American magazine *Studio Potter*, suggested at a symposium in 1979 that the 12,000 potters making studio pots in America were part of a 'cultural continuity' that stretched back to the Indian potters of 2000 BC. Such continuity was threatened by this new momentum, where a slow maturation of forms was superseded by a turnover of style. In 1976 the British potter Geoffrey Whiting acidly commented on the 'established, rarefied craft circles' where there was a form of 'exhibition mania': 'each show must demonstrate some change of outlook, some difference, some broadening of view here... What next. The Pottery World Cup?!' Michael Cardew, on hearing the names of famous ceramicists, accepted they might be 'significant artists, but they are not potters. Are you a potter? Answer yes or no?'

There was a paucity of critical writing about ceramics. The kinds of writing published fell into two kinds – either technical, or commentaries on particular potters that were mostly uncritical, if not adulatory. Monographs published in the 1970s on Hamada, Maria Martinez and Voulkos all fell into this latter category, stressing their individualism at the expense of context.

The technical literature was often more radical, reflecting the changing interests in techniques of glazing and firing. Daniel Rhodes's *Clay and Glazes for the Potter* introduced in its second edition in 1973 new material on raku, salt-glazing, use of fibres and fibreglass in clay, fuming with metallic salts, and overglaze processes, all absent from the first edition in 1957. Hal Riegger's book *Raku: Art and Technique* (1970) and Cardew's *Pioneer Pottery* (1969) both encouraged technical exploration based on the knowledge of local materials.

There were informed British and American critics who were prepared to take ceramics seriously, but few ceramics exhibitions gained the kind of coverage that even a first exhibition by a minor painter would achieve. This was partly due to a (mostly misguided) perception as to the inward-looking nature of the discipline. Under the editorship of Rose Slivka, *Craft Horizons*, the magazine of the American Crafts Council, had provided an inspired forum for debate, with writings on all media, including on contemporary sculpture and painting; writers included John Cage and the poet-educator M. C. Richards. In 1966 it had 30,000 subscribers, and by 1976 400,000. In Great Britain *Crafts* magazine was founded by the Crafts Council in 1972 and, under the editorship of Martina Margetts between 1978 and 1987, it was particularly productive, with poets, sculptors and art critics all contributing illuminating texts on ceramics. In France *La Revue de la Céramique et du Verre* was first published in 1981, and *Keramik* magazine in Germany in 1978. In Britain, *Ceramic Review* was founded in 1970 to act across sculptural and domestic arenas, with extensive technical coverage as well as exhibition reviews and profiles. It also reflected the increasing internationalization of ceramics, something not seen since the eras of the International Expositions, with articles on the techniques of many kinds of traditional ceramics. These were mostly far less interested in *why* potters were making pots than *how*, something reflected in the frequent presence as 'spectacle' of potters from Africa and South Asia at pottery festivals. The staging of 'Potter's Camps', events in Europe and America where slide presentations, practical demonstrations, and kiln building all took place, became another arena for discussion.

One book did offer a more searching view of what ceramics might mean: Philip Rawson's *Ceramics* (1971). Rawson's book was the most significant attempt to create an aesthetics for ceramics since Leach's *A Potter's Book*. It took as its central precept the idea of the 'transformation image' in ceramics. For Rawson this was a 'focal point where strands of meaning related to life, use, and symbolic thought are knotted together [reflecting] back into the mind of each owner or user an image of himself as existing in his world.' All ceramics, whether overtly functional or not, played out this image. Rawson's book was passionate, and because of its measured prose and its inclusiveness (all of Leach's disfavoured traditions, from maiolica to Meissen, found a place in his book), it seemed magisterial rather than partisan. Rawson was concerned to suggest how ceramics could

re-establish its existential foundations. There is... no reason at all why fired clay should not be used, as other sculptural materials are nowadays, to explore... functions which have no basis in immediate life needs, with its own symbolic justification... there is no reason at all why lines of thought taking up from one or another of humanity's past ceramic achievements should not be picked up again, and developed along radical new lines.

Fifteen years later, Rawson's vision of a critically informed community of potters and ceramicists was severely tested by a British exhibition, *Fast Forward*. He found a 'Coper-esque retreat to silhouette' in the contemporary work of Carol McNicholl (b. 1943) and Elizabeth Fritsch (b. 1940), a ceramicist given to complex spatial games and optical illusions on flattened forms. The refusal of many in the exhibition to 'take possession of the three dimensions of space' seemed to Rawson to intimate a lack of guts: 'chillingly often we are nowadays given pots that retreat, flattening themselves and huddling back into diagrams'. Margetts, in the same catalogue, was more positive. She sensed that these kinds of pots 'need special interpretation. Categories of description and theories evolve, structuralist critics sharpen their dissecting tools. We see the beginning of the potted word'. The 1980s and 1990s was to see the making of elliptical and highly referential work that sought 'special interpretation': the interpenetration of contemporary theory and art practice, that is a constituent part of post-modernism, had arrived in ceramics.

'A Field of Possibilities': Politics, Performance and Environment

The beaten clay wall of Noguchi's Japanese ceramics studio in the early 1950s had offered an image of raw earth as an environment in which to make art, and a way of staging a visceral connection with materiality. How to create art that could keep these passions alive and resist commodification became an increasingly pressing issue. In 1969 the critic Barbara Rose wrote: 'A dissatisfaction with the current social and political system results in an unwillingness to produce commodities which gratify and perpetuate that system. Here the sphere of ethics and aesthetics merge.' Rose was indicating that the ways in which art was sold, displayed, and curated would soon be challenged. The rise of feminist art theory and politically inflected engagement with conventional modes of museum and gallery display also played their part. Land art, performance art, and installation all were manifestations of a critique of the limitations of the gallery and the museum as the principal sites for art during the 1970s. There were different ways of making art connect in new ways with their audience. By making the audience work for their experience – either by having to travel great distances to see it, by moving through the art work, or by participating in its creation – it was possible to make problematic the notion of the single, expensive and collectable art object. Recording the creation or destruction of the object, its reception by the public or its 'life-history' in the gallery through texts, photography or video became commonplace. The art object – and this was increasingly true for ceramics – was becoming 'dematerialized'.

The focus of the 1970s environmental movement on the degradation of landscape through pollution and stripping of natural resources led to a particular stress in ceramics on the value of their own raw material – the earth. The iconography of earth was potent – Robert Smithson had called the key 1968 New York exhibition *Earthworks* after Brian W. Aldiss' science fiction novel where, in a dystopian future, soil itself had become precious. This iconography was explored within the movement, loosely titled Earth Art, where many sculptors worked by displacing earth in the landscape or by removing it into galleries. Viewers of Walter de Maria's New York *Earth Room* (1977), where an even depth of earth was spread through the Dia Center for the Arts in Manhattan, could not enter the room but stood behind a glass panel. The effect, as with much of the movement, was dialectical, counterpointing the formless with the structured or framed. The viewer was left alienated by this, aware of their distance from the primary experience of, and involvement with, the earth. The opposite was true for artists where the element of sheer physical labour involved was significant, recalling Noguchi's sense of satisfaction at 'knowing nature again as an adult... [exhausting] one's hands in its earth'. In a 1955 performance, *Challenging Mud*, Kazuo Shiraga (b. 1924) of the radical Gutai group, founded in Osaka in 1954, had writhed around in mud until

145 **Victor Cicansky**, *Unfired Clay*, 1970 (earthenware, 15 cm/6 in).
The prospectus for this exhibition read:
'JURY: The Elements
The Exhibition of Unfired Clay, 1970, will be out-of-doors.
The last 10 pieces to withstand the elements (weather) will be declared the winners…
All pieces will remain at the exhibition site and become part of the site.'

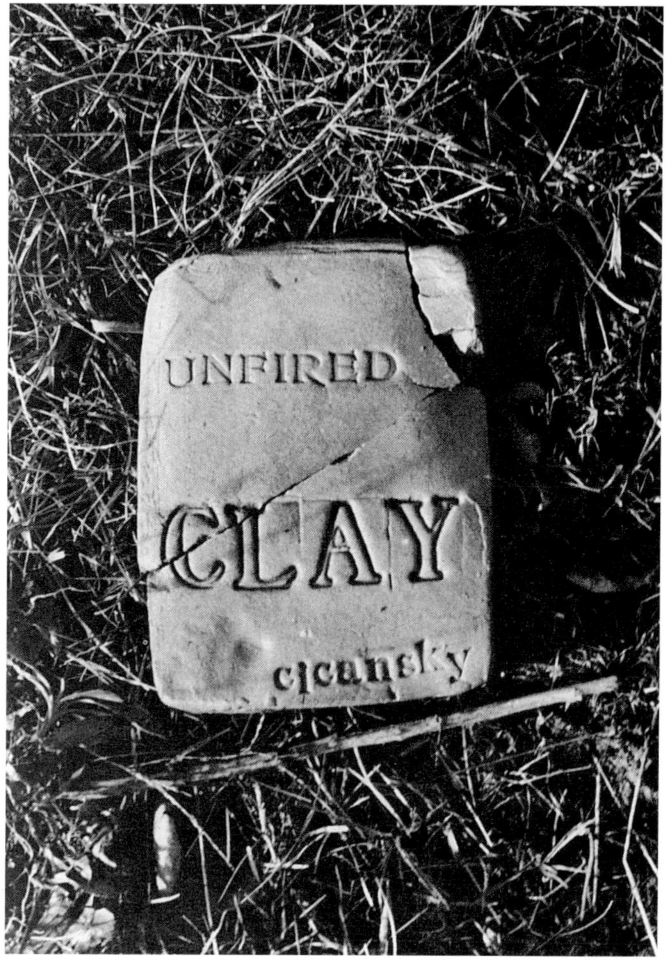

he was so exhausted that the earth had 'won'. Jiro Yoshihara (1905–72), the painter who had founded the Gutai, had said of these kinds of provocative performances that 'what we are trying to do is forge direct links with the earth and to yield to natural conditions'. Commenting on the 1970 *Unfired Clay* exhibition held at Southern Illinois University, Evert Johnson wrote that 'There is something spiritually appropriate in the implication of the pot returning to earth, of artists participating physically in the installation of their own exhibit, and of creative man being, for a short time at least, really at one with his work, the earth from which it was made and elements that besiege both'.

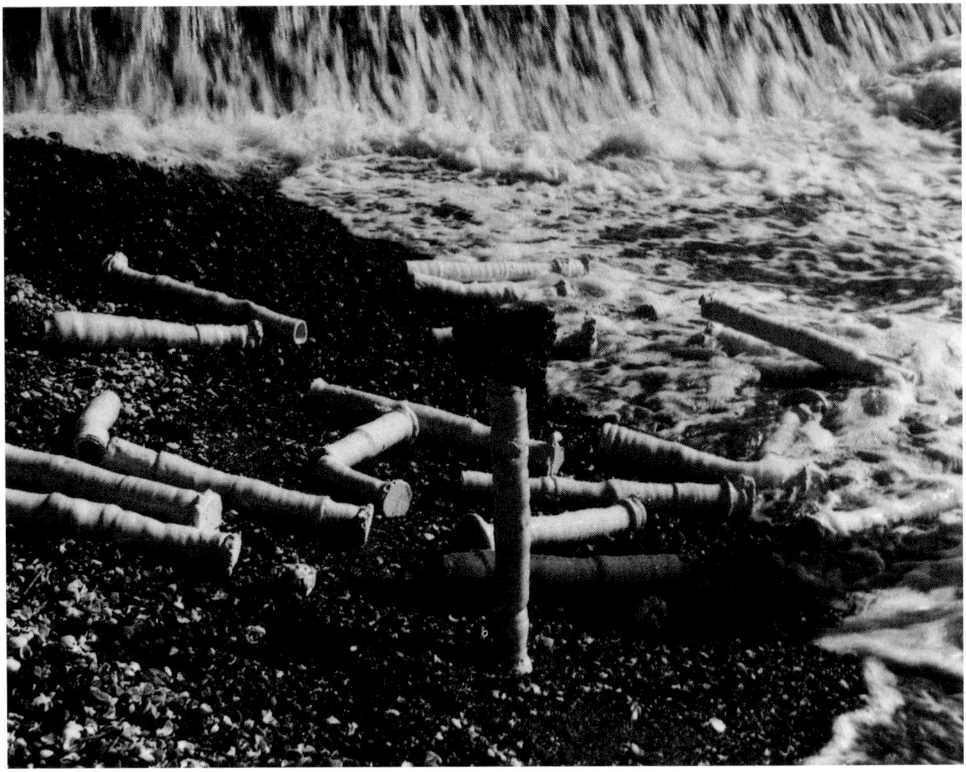

146 **Ryoji Koie**, Installation: white clay with transparent glaze, 1980. The installation *Returning to Earth*, was received with shock. Its theme of recuperating the unmediated materiality of clay was considered insulting in its incompleteness. Koie's aim was to shock, just as his precursors in the Sodeisha movement of the early 1950s had highlighted their passion for earth as both the start and the end of pots and of people.

The bringing of the material into the gallery, of counter-pointing material and artifice, was achieved dramatically by the Japanese potter Ryoji Koie (b. 1938), who made a series of masks out of unfired clay that were shown in different stages of disintegration at the Kyoto National Museum of Modern Art in 1971. Koie also staged a series of happenings, each concerned with how little could be done to define something as 'ceramic'. Some were as simple as video-taping the digging of clay from a river-bank, or blow-torching the ground. At the Earth Festival in 1972 that he organized with Jun Kaneko (b. 1942) in the Japanese industrial ceramics city of Tokoname, they invited the five hundred participants to use clay in whatever way they wanted – to make vessels or sculptures, or even to cover bicycles with clay. The emphasis was on the contingency of meaning of clay: it could be used in multiple ways, and could mean anything. To show this Koie also went back to the Japanese term for pottery, 'yakimono', literally 'fired things', and fired clocks and sewing machines onto slabs of clay. Alongside this he threw porcelain vessels, glazing some of them by firing 'dirt from my backyard' onto them – this throwaway phrase emphasizing the improvisatory attitude to materials. Many of these activities were social, nomadic and unrecorded. Ceramics could be said to connect with some of the elements of play that had been so disparaged in the ceramics of Miró, Picasso and Noguchi.

If the processes of making things from clay were under scrutiny through the anarchic and pointedly non-productive nature of performance, so too were the places in which and for which ceramics were made. In America Charles Simonds (b. 1945) made his own body the site of exhibition: 'I lie down nude on the earth, cover myself with clay, remodel and transform my body into a landscape with clay, and then build a fantasy dwelling-place on my body on the earth.' His archaic ruined constructions made out of thousands of tiny bricks, either on his body or on the edges of steps, window sills, or vacant lots in cities, attempted to make connections between the body and the earth as sacred places:

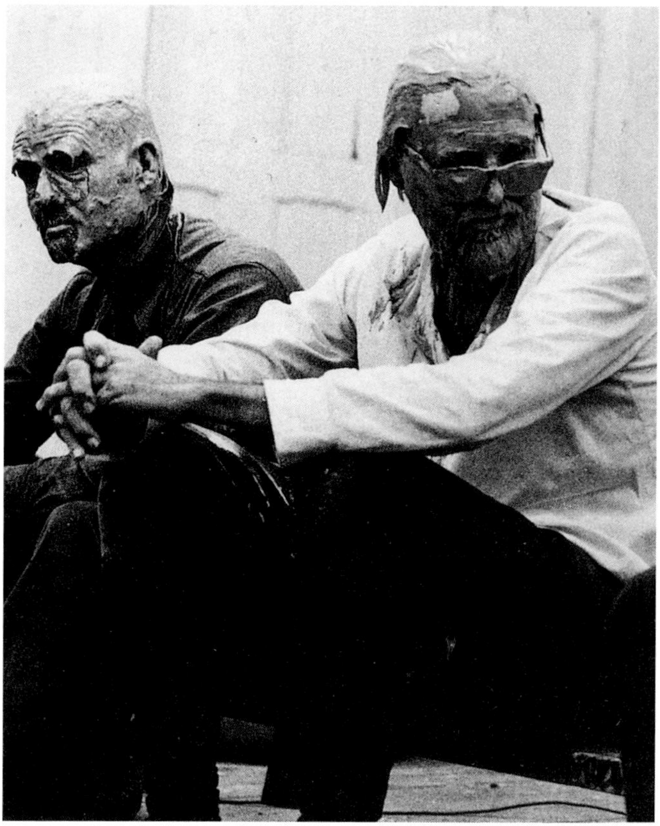

147 **Jim Melchert**, *Changes: a performance with drying slip*, Amsterdam, August 2, 1972. Melchert produced a happening in which people dipped their heads in clay slip and then sat in a room that was cool at one end and hot at the other, while the drying process was filmed.

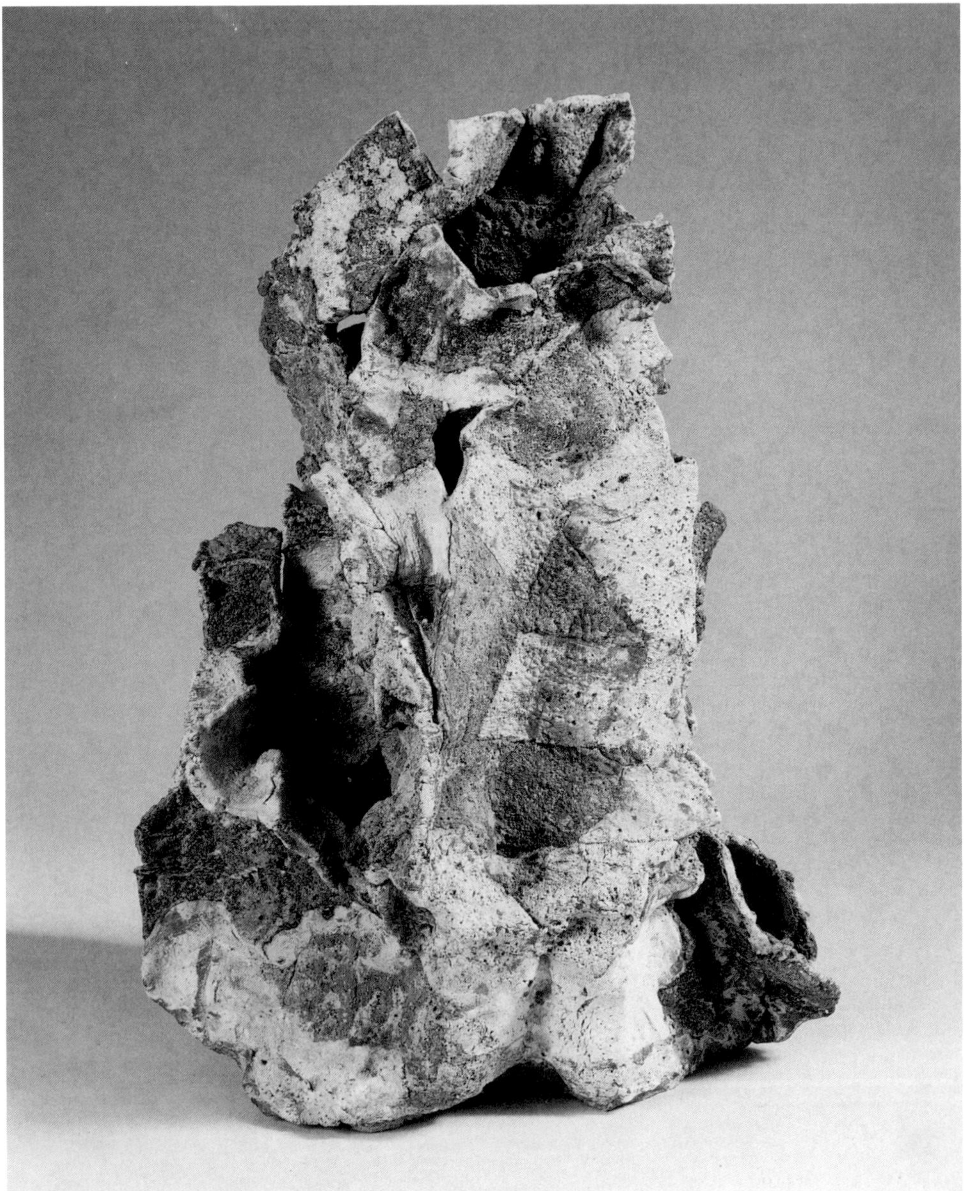

'Landscape-Body-Dwelling is a process of land into body, body into land.' These were temporal and liminal performances and constructions, made in forgotten places. These works were much more interesting out of the gallery environment than the fantasy dwellings for 'the Little People' that Simonds started to make specifically for museum collections. Others made work that used the dialectic of gallery space and landscape, reflecting the increasing perception that, in Robert Morris's words, art now existed in a 'complex and expanded field'. Choosing where to make your work, its site-specificity, could be a way of reflecting on the political nature of ownership. The British potter Elspeth Owen (b. 1938) made pots in 1981 while on a peace walk to an anti-nuclear demonstration outside Greenham Common US air base. She recorded the acts of making, wrapping and unwrapping the pieces, suggesting this as a feminist way of recuperating elemental values that were being threatened by a technocratic society. The exigencies of her materials – pots were fired in leaves or other natural substances – suggested the provisional nature of the enterprise. Her work suggested that how materials were used was a politicized act: it showed that a studio was not essential to art, that political marginality could be reclaimed as creative.

Placing work outside in the landscape happened on significantly different levels. For some it was an act like Miró's placing of glazed boulders outside Artigas's Catalan studio in the 1950s, a way of connecting with a pre-rational and archaic approach to land through totemic objects. These kinds of objects were often specifically tagged as such. The English ceramicist Ewen Henderson (1934–2000) made 'menhirs', large ceramic versions of Neolithic standing stones. The French glass-maker and ceramicist Bernard Dejonghe (b. 1942) made 'stelae', ceramic slabs that recalled prehistoric columns. For both of them the material was a 'field of possibilities': clays provided a base for experimentation and reflection. For both Henderson and Dejonghe, as with Koie, there was an interest with how little has to be done to transform clay. Dejonghe left clay outside until frozen and then fired the boulder, or fired clay until it melted, both 'extreme limits' as he put it.

148 **Ewen Henderson**, *Vessel*, 1987 (laminated stoneware and porcelain clays, h. 61 cm/24 in). Henderson's craggy concretions of different clays laminated together in seemingly random ways to make fissured vessels, dramatized the correspondence between geological morphology and human artefacts. Henderson made a wide range of vessels, from teabowls, little more than a depression in the clay, to more complex volumetric constructions. When placed outside their 'strangeness' seemed to disappear: the ceramic objects fitted into the spectrum of the naturally broken or discarded or fragmentary.

Jun Kaneko, a Japanese-born ceramicist who came to America in 1963 and studied with both Voulkos and Soldner, has also become known for his projects that explicitly deal with how ceramics relate to architecture. Construction and destruction have been central to his work since the early 1970s when he made 'Destruction' pieces that involved the theatrical destruction

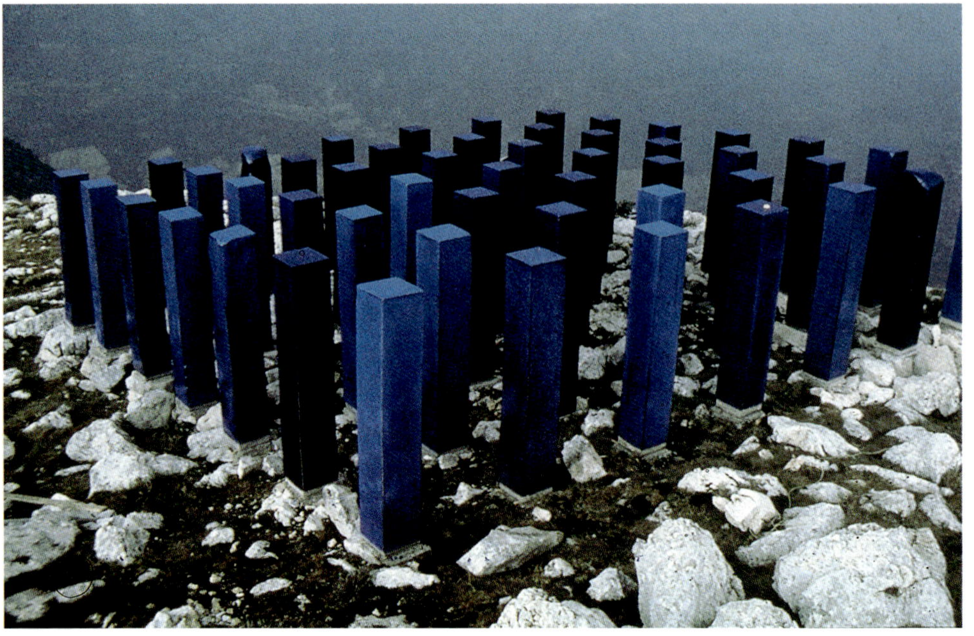

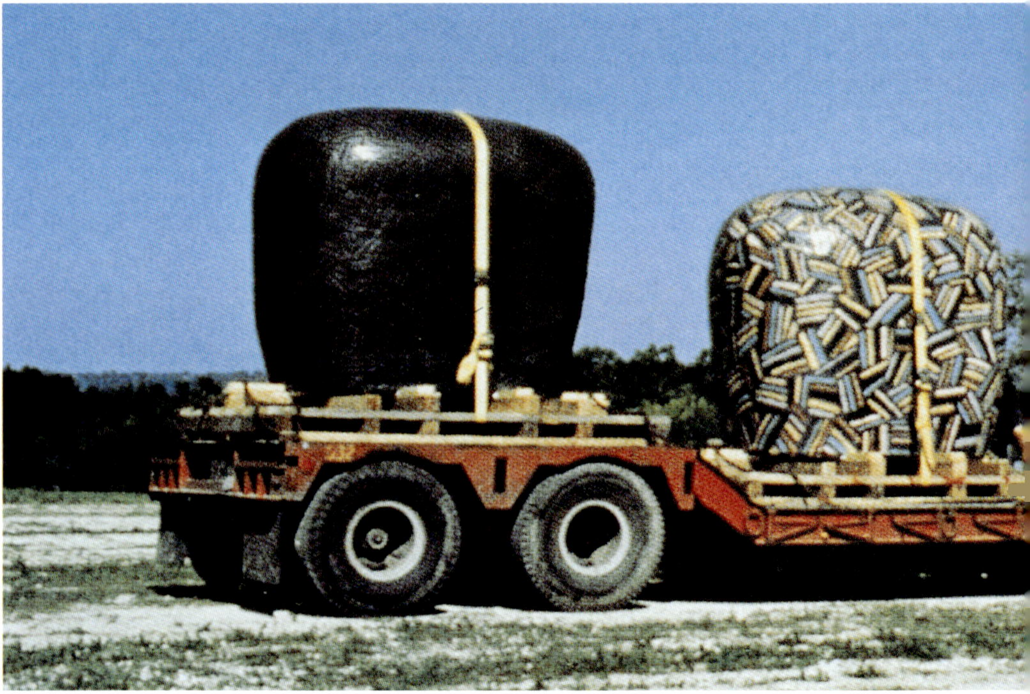

149 **Bernard Dejonghe**, *Bleu Vertical* (Vertical blue), 1986 (enamelled stoneware, 120 × 600 x 600 cm/47 × 236 × 236 in). 'I lined up the blues from east to west, on a high [plateau]. It was an intrusion, a different presence. I wanted to see what kind of dialogue was possible with the stones and the sky.'

150 **Jun Kaneko**, *Omaha Project, Dangos on Truck*, 1984. The monumental presence of the 'dangos' (Japanese for dumpling) was achieved without being in any way archaic – they act as domestic (or domesticated) monoliths, as indicated by their affectionate and diminutive naming.

of large ceramic forms. There is an architectonic element in both his large public commissions for wall reliefs and tiles and in his small scale work where a small structure often holds or protects biomorphic forms. Kaneko's early projects at the Omaha brickworks in Nebraska included making earthworks in the claypit. Then, in 1982, 'I was given the large kiln, I thought, "Should I make 50, 000 cups, or a few big pieces?" ' The resulting 'dangos' (Japanese for a dumpling) weighed 5 tons and were 6 feet tall and 7 feet wide: an achievement on a technical scale as well as aesthetic. Kaneko's placing of them in galleries surrounded by a 'landscape' of polka dots further showed how he differentiated his sense of objects in architectural space from the aura of gravitas surrounding the totems of Mason or Henderson made to be seen in white galleries.

Installation

Although ceramics sometimes followed behind the conceptual shifts and fashions in the art movements of the 1960s and 1970s – particularly in the interest in Performance – much of the 'complex

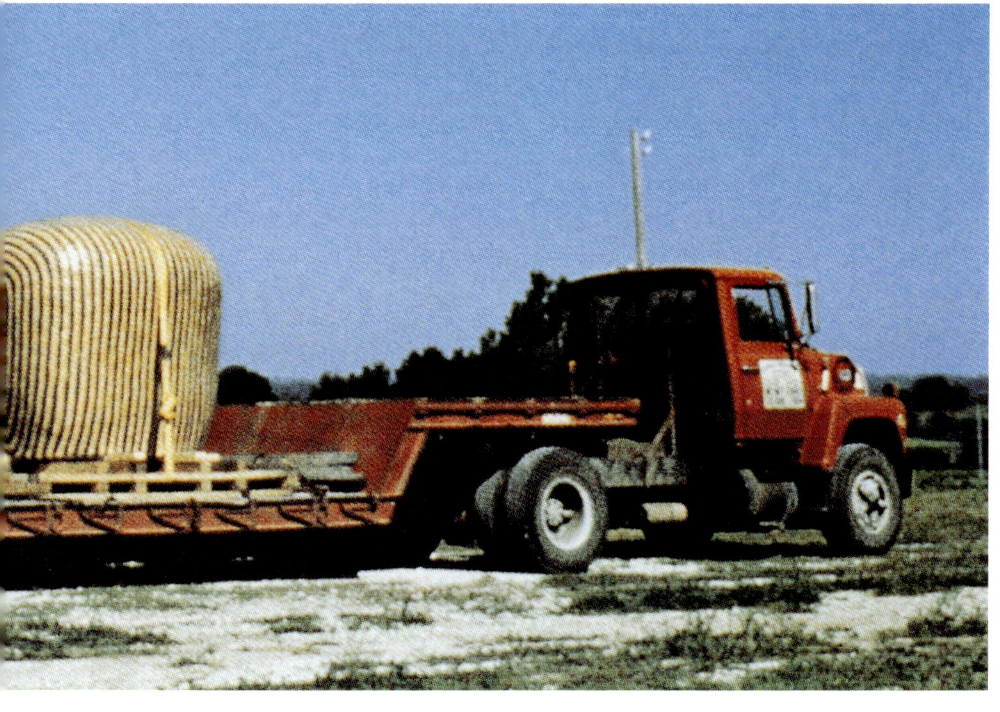

and expanded field' already existed for ceramics but had been neglected. It was as if ceramics needed the critiques and theory around contemporary movements in painting and sculpture to remind it of what was already there. This was particularly true in relation to architecture where the vigour of the relationship between architecture and ceramics and, crucially, the consequent innovative ways of showing work, that had existed in Vienna and in Germany at the Bauhaus, had dissipated. The desire for ceramics to achieve parity with sculpture in 'the white cube' of the modern gallery and museum, the placing of objects on plinths, had led to a less interrogative sense of what was possible – only to find that these sites were being regarded as conventional and outmoded by sculptors and painters. Rosalind Krauss wrote in her seminal essay 'Sculpture in the Expanded Field' (1979) that it was now possible 'to admit into the realm of art two terms that had formerly been prohibited from it: landscape and architecture – terms that could function to define the sculptural… only in their negative or neuter condition.' Both landscape and architecture had provided powerful sites for ceramics and were doing so again. But only a very small section of ceramics was critically validated as ceramic sculpture that could fit into the conceptual mould advocated by Krauss.

151 **Rosaline Delisle**, *Octet 4*, 1996 (earthenware, h. 106.7 cm/ 42 in).
Delisle's stacked geometric earthenware vessels approach human scale. They are inspired, in part, by Oskar Schlemmer's Cubist ballet of the early 1920s, in which dancers wore geometric costumes.

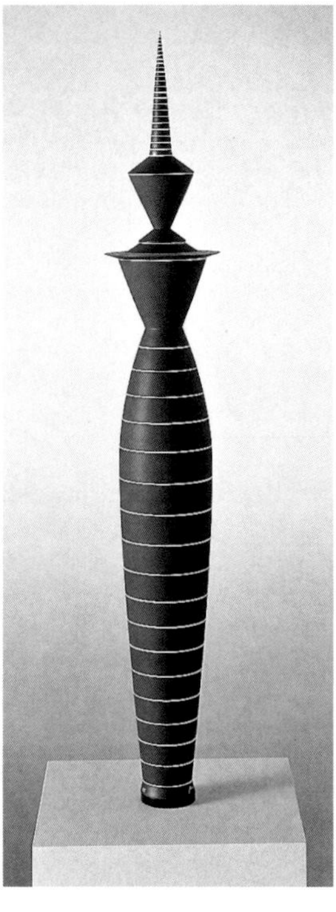

The best example was John Mason's *Hudson River Series* of 1978. Mason had moved from the expressionist surfaces of his walls to using industrial bricks that, with their density and opacity, showed no marks of the hand. Because they were mass-produced they were all identical, and could be used as elements for repetition without emphasis. They moved away from 'the idea of a centre or a focus toward which forms point or build', as Krauss wrote of Carl Andre's contemporaneous sculptures, where no part was more important than any other. In the series Mason made twelve installations for six museums of unmortared firebricks arranged in mathematical sequences, where the composition 'meandered' like the river. Mason's installations fulfilled Greenberg's demand that for artists 'the task of self-criticism [was]… to eliminate from the effects of each art any and every effect that might conceivably be borrowed from or by the medium of any other art.' In ceramics this vision of art as a focus on the eradication of other media's contamination – unlike the eclecticism of Fontana or Miró – found its counterpoint in the work of such ceramicists as Doris Kaiser (b. 1958) in Germany, Rosaline Delisle (b. 1952) in Canada, Martin Bodilsen Kaldahl (b. 1954) in Denmark, Geert Lap (b. 1951) and Wouter

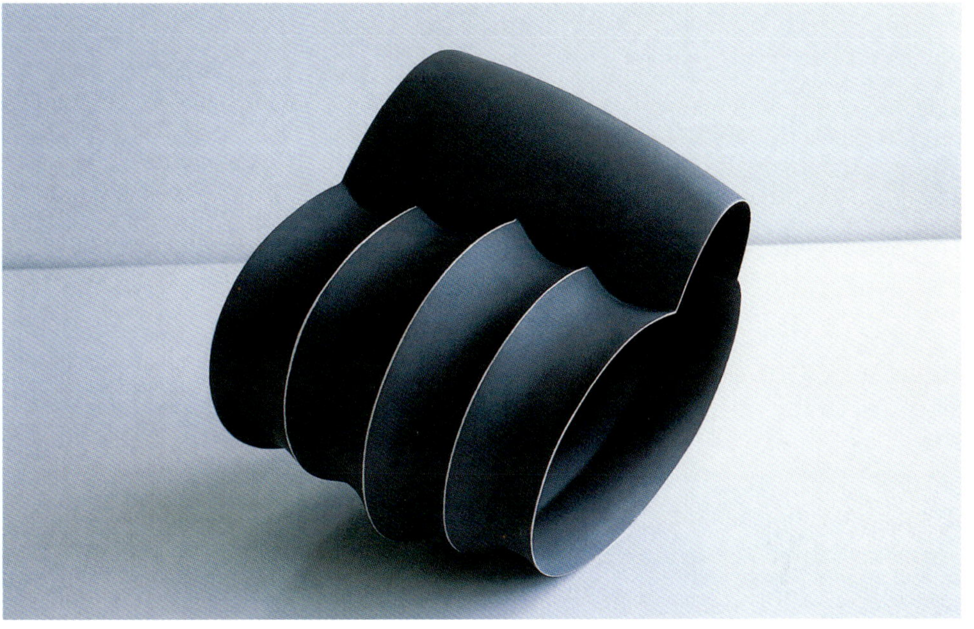

152 **Wouter Dam**, *Blue Shape*, 2000 (stoneware).
Dry monochromatic oxides are rubbed into the surface of Dam's thin walled vessels to make, in his words, 'velvet-like surfaces'. He wants 'a single piece [to] evoke both the coldness of the parts of a machine and at the same time a sensuality reminiscent of the human shape.'

153 **Geert Lap**, *Thrown Form no. 4*, 1998 (stoneware, terra sigillata, h. 15 cm/6 in).
Lap has designed work for the Cor Unum factory in s'Hertogenbosch and is interested in the clarity and precision that are part of industrial process. In choosing to throw he plays with slight variations in surface and profile, evoking tension between the hand made and the industrially made.

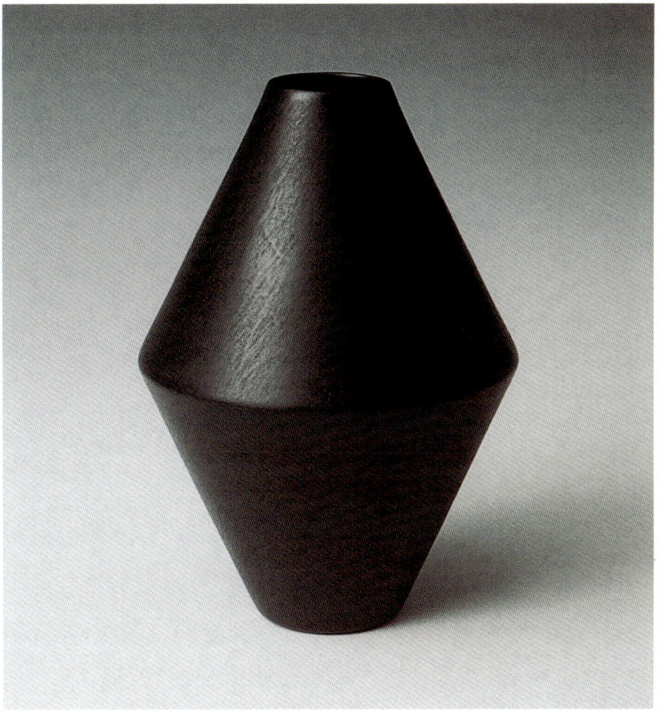

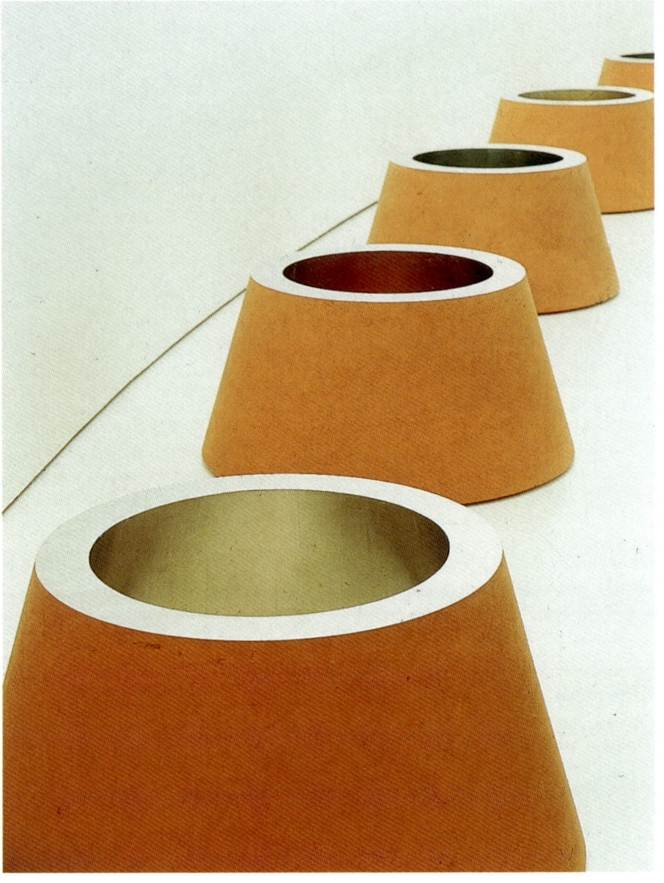

154 **Martin Smith**, *Wavelength*, 2001 (clay, platinum, aluminium, ten-part work, h. 32 cm/12½ in). Smith's installation for a 55-foot curved vitrine in the Tate Gallery at St Ives consisted of ten identical truncated cones made from polished terracotta, each one with interior walls covered with platinum leaf and with a moulded coloured disc 'floating' at the base. Conceived for a white-walled glass vitrine in a museum, *Wavelength* was a homage to the rigour of American Minimalism.

155 **Clare Twomey**, *Consciousness/Conscience*, 2001; installation shot in London, 2002 (slip-cast porcelain). Twomey's floor piece is a made up of hundreds of bone china boxes laid so as to occupy a room. To reach photographs that give information on the piece the viewer must walk on the fragile boxes: Twomey describes this as an 'act of destruction through human curiosity.'

156 **Antony Gormley**, *Host*, 1997 (overall depth 13 cm/5 in). The fine surface, created by flooding a gallery with sea water and mud, counterpoints the formless and the formed, surface and substance.

Dam (b. 1957) in the Netherlands and Martin Smith (b. 1950) in Britain. All these ceramicists make vessels which can be described as minimalist: undemonstrative meditations on proportion and volume achieved through a clarity of profile and tonality that is gained by precise surfaces. The precision of these surfaces is important. Unlike the Orientalist vessel aesthetic, where the variation of texture or tonality in a surface encourages the viewer and handler of the pot to make connections with natural forms or processes, in these 'self-critical' minimalist vessels the connections are most likely to be with industrial process. Indeed the work of Kaiser, Kaldahl, Lap and Smith often explicitly deals with architectonic themes. Smith's *Borromini Cloister Pieces*, for instance, played off images of Mannerist architecture through constructions that used cut and polished terracotta with contrasting planes of colour.

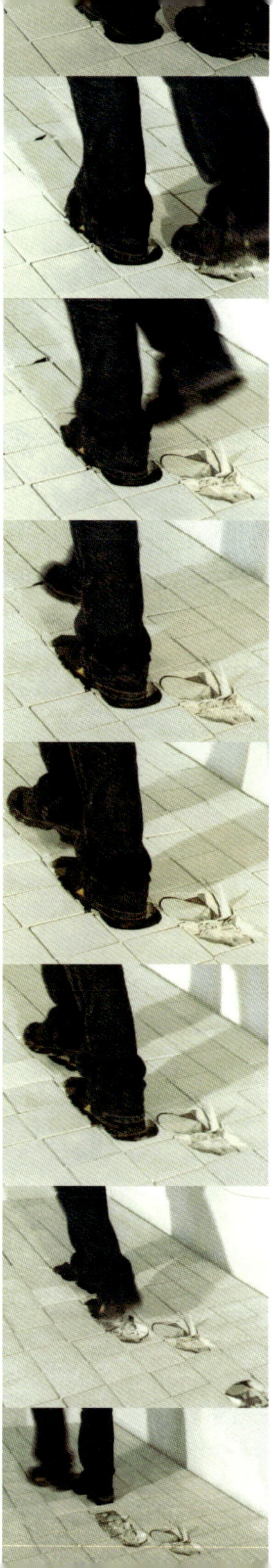

There were different and more exacting strategies to make the experiencing of art more complex. Some were confrontational – the expansion of the work of art to fill the space of the gallery so that the viewer had to realize the formality of the architecture and its impact. This has often been done by emphasizing the 'base materialism' of clay: its colour, messiness and formlessness provides a ready inversion for the whiteness, cleanliness and structure of the gallery. By carpeting the floor of a gallery with a brittle bone china floor the British ceramicist Clare Twomey (b. 1968) made every step of a viewer break her artwork: the consciousness of moving in the space was made contingent on destruction. The Japanese ceramicist Sadashi Inuzuka (b. 1951), who works in Canada, has made a series of installations that also invert the safe anonymity of the gallery. In *Nature of Things* (1995) a pool of unfired white slip 22 feet (6.7 metres) in diameter, ringed with 400 terracotta cones, was placed under the skylight of a Canadian museum. In 1996 the whole floor of an art gallery in British Columbia was covered in clay slip that cracked as it dried.

The British sculptors Richard Long (b. 1945) and Andy Goldsworthy (b. 1956) have both used unfired clay to make installations within museums that bring the specificity of particular places – exemplified by the rawness of Long's muddy handprints of Avon river mud on a white gallery wall – into the internationalism and anonymity of the gallery space. Anthony Gormley (b. 1950), in *European Field* and *Host* (1993), counterpointed the formless and the formed, the specific and the

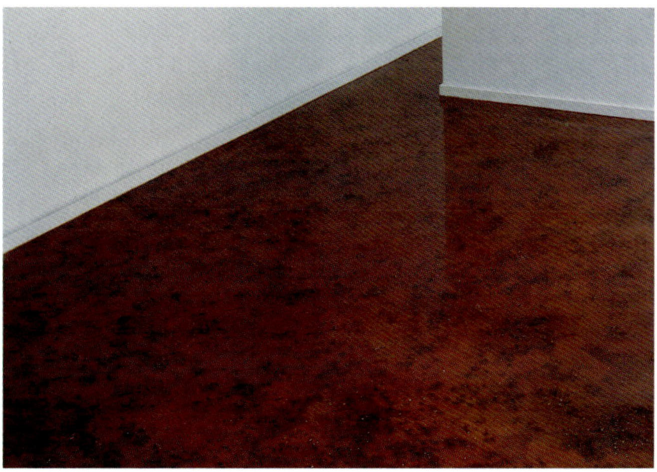

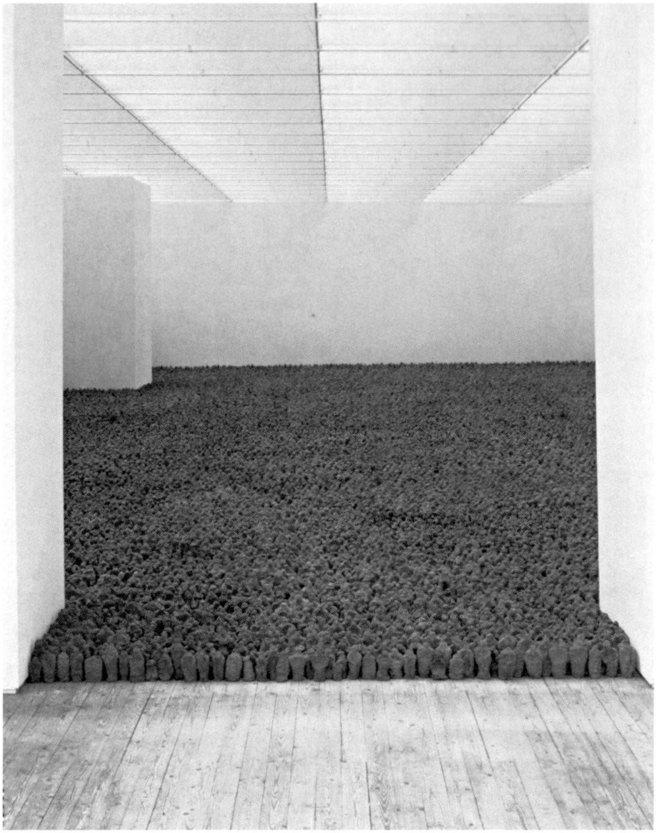

157 **Antony Gormley**, *European Field,* installation at Malmö, Kunsthalle, 1993 (terracotta, h. variable 10–30 cm/4–12 in). Gormley assembled some 35,000 terracotta figures produced by a local community, whom he invited to shape clay figures that could stand up and that had two eyes. Little more than two or three squeezes of clay in the hand, these small figures crowd together to form a mass that is both menacing, or questioning, and absurdly affecting in its vulnerability. The figures' historical resonances (Japanese 'haniwa', Chinese terracotta warriors) are less significant than the impact of the installation itself: the challenge to museological convention is that the artefacts have taken over.

158 **Piet Stockmans**, Installation at Bergkerk, Deventer, 1999 (porcelain)
Stockman's installation for the floor of a Gothic church in Deventer, the Netherlands, played on the Biblical resonances of broken vessels with a grouping of plaster moulds, cast object, glazed object and shards placed where the altar of the church had been, giving the 'life history' of the object. Other vessels were arranged like a congregation, suggesting connections between body and vessel and also acting as a visual and verbal play on the French term for 'still life', nature morte.

general through two parallel installations in the Kunsthalle zu Kiel in Germany. In the contemporary wing, three galleries were flooded with 43 cubic metres (1500 cubic feet) of clay and 15,000 litres (4000 gallons) of sea water to approximately the same height as the terracotta figures in *Field*.

The Flemish ceramicist Piet Stockmans (b. 1940), well known as an industrial designer of ceramics, has developed a way of showing groupings of blue and white slip cast vessels, either in small groups 'framed' in wooden crates that imply arrival or dispatch, or in large groups displayed on the ground.

One of the essential ideas behind such installations is temporality, the relocating of the viewer in the present by disturbing the museum environment or by showing them something that can only be experienced for a short time. This is something that has been explored by ceramicists who make vessels, just as much as by more overtly 'conceptual' sculptors.

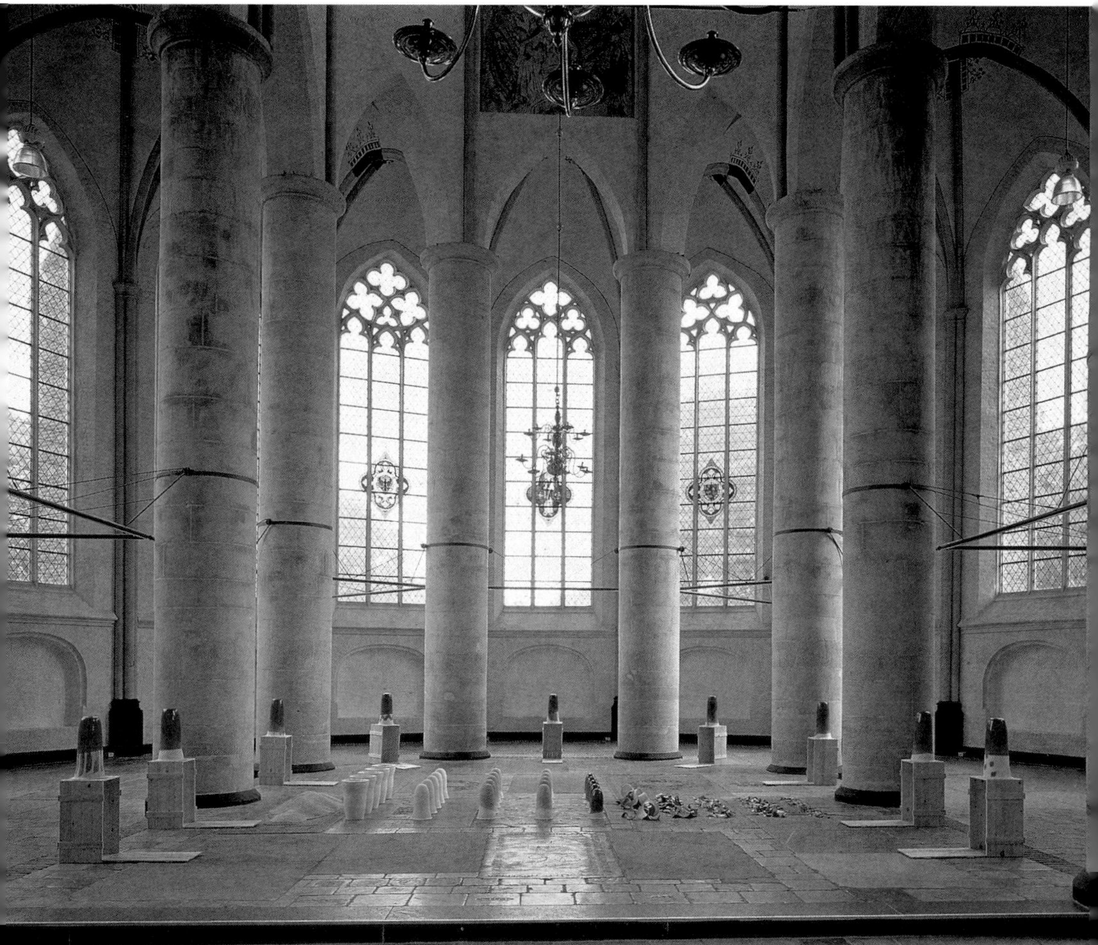

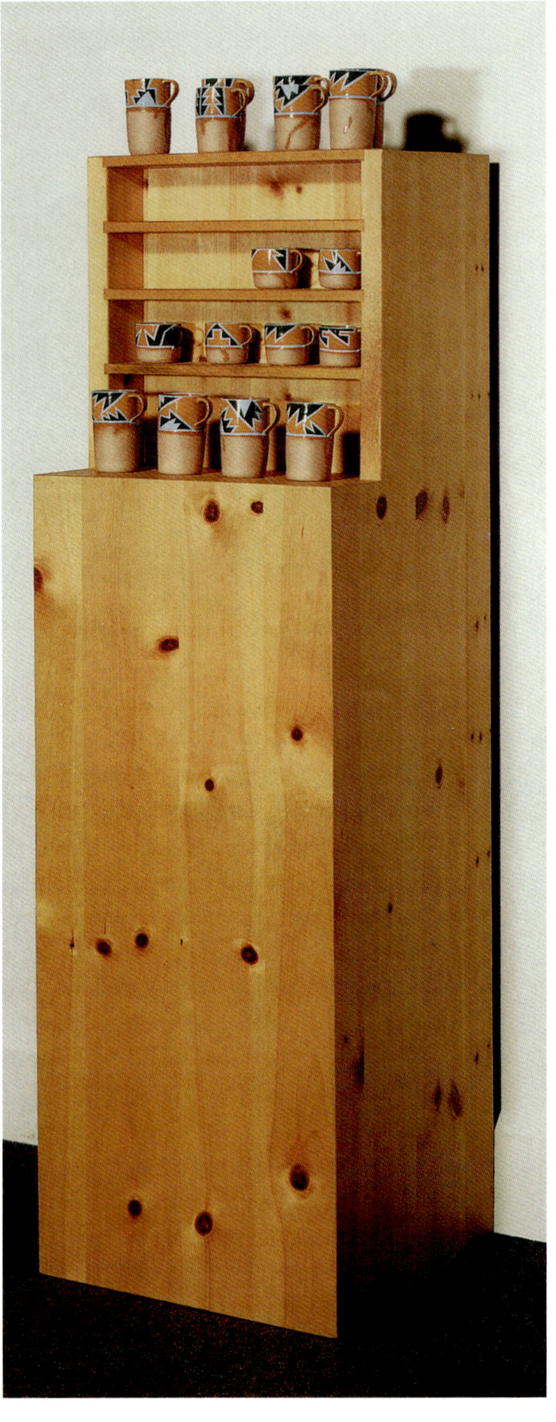

159 **Kenneth Price**, *Happy's Curios, Unit 3*, 1972–77 (cabinet h. 178 cm/70 in, cup h. 6.4 cm/2½ in). Price's installation played complex games with the viewer–buyer–public, centred on taste, ethnicity and trade. His initial intention was to create a complete curio shop – a 'walk-in sculpture made out of pottery' – but he abandoned the plan and fitted these units and shrines into the museum.

'Playing shop' is one way of not being outwitted, of keeping 'the upper hand' with the world of the museum and the gallery. Oldenburg had done this in *The Store* in 1961, with its saleable objects made of brightly coloured plaster objects, and George Segal had segued real-objects and figures in his tableaux. So Price's installation *Ken Price: Happy's Curios*, shown in 1978 at the Los Angeles County Museum of Art, stands within a contemporary context of the framing of objects as commodities. The impact was huge. Price was acting as artist, craftsman, curator, dealer and ethnographer simultaneously: he was offering a critique of the idea of authentic ethnic ceramics and he was 'enshrining' decorative kitsch by installing it so lovingly in his 'units'. Its complexity of ideas and aesthetics made it one of the most compelling postwar exhibitions.

It also brought to the fore the taxonomies of vessels in museum collections. In *Twenty-Eight Pitchers* (1994–96), the German-born artist Cecile Johnson Soliz (b. 1957) created an installation that comments on how the 'still lives' of objects in museum vitrines efface those who made the objects: the pitchers are, according to Soliz, 'portraits of [the] anonymous craftspeople' who made them. Installations were increasingly 'interventions', politicized acts that drew attention to the ways in which objects were put into hierarchies according to material or the status of their maker. In *Fragments* (1977–78), Susan Hiller (b. 1940) installed hundreds of pueblo pottery shards, along with photographs and drawings that documented how they were collected. It reflected the 'anonymous' women who made the pottery, the (female) helper of the archaeologist who collected them, and Hiller herself as the animator of these complex and uneasy relationships between material culture, archaeology and art. The marginalized place of the decorative within these arenas also became a key area for debate.

Much of the current openness to ideas about decoration was due to the feminist art criticism of the 1970s. The knowledge of the inequalities in representation of women artists in art galleries and museums was coupled with a critique of the art theories that lay behind many of the assumptions in the art world. As the American critic Lucy Lippard said, it was the art world itself that had led her towards feminism: 'the seeds of my feminism in my revolt against Clement Greenberg's patronization of artists, against the imposition of the taste of one class on everybody... as well as against the "masterpiece" syndrome, the "three great artists" syndrome, and so forth'. Feminist art critics and historians like Lippard and Linda Nochlin, critiques of ceramic history such as Garth Clark and Margie Hughto's *Century of Ceramics in the United States 1878–1978*, and pioneering work on women in the ceramics industry, all helped to show the powerful – if neglected – presence of women in ceramics. For ceramics, which had an unsteady relationship with the fine arts, and where decoration had been seen as a slightly embarrassing feature best expunged in order to gain critical attention, this recuperation of decoration as a positive element has been of great significance.

One early, robust and politicized outcome was Judy Chicago's (b. 1939) installation *The Dinner Party* (1974–79). In her autobiography *Through the Flower: My Struggle as a Woman Artist*, Chicago, a Californian sculptor and teacher on the first Feminist Art Program at the California School of the Arts in Los Angeles, described her passage out of a strongly anti-decorative Minimalist idiom. Initially working in the Finish Fetish aesthetic where she used power tools and 'hard materials' that allowed her to be assertive, she gradually found that this was at the cost of 'effacing' her gender by achieving what she described as 'the necessary neutrality for the art world'. In embarking on *The Dinner Party*, finally shown at the San Francisco Museum of Modern Art in 1979, Chicago was bringing the personal – and the decorative – into the realm of the monumental. *The Dinner Party* was a huge

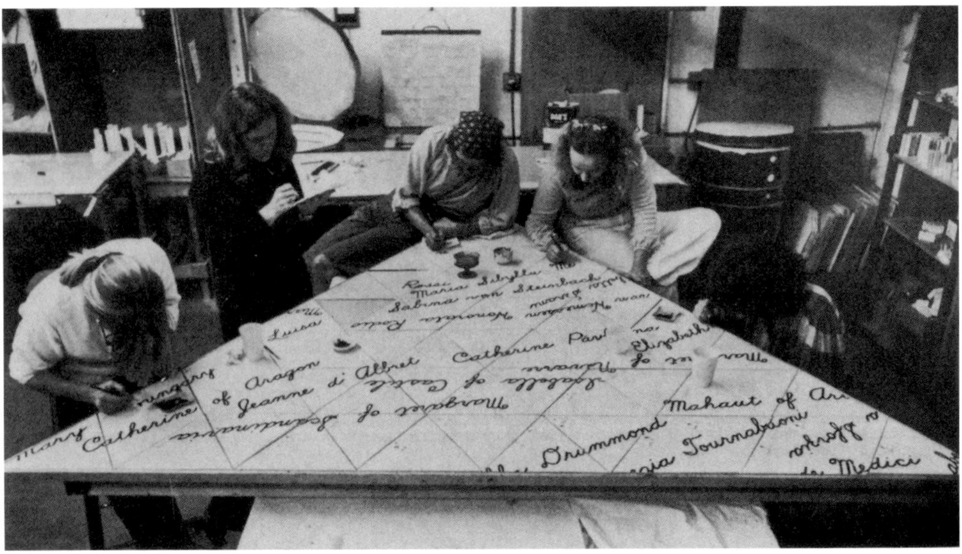

160 Glazing the floor of **Judy Chicago**'s *The Dinner Party*, 1974–79.
Conceived as a party for thirty-nine women from mythology and history seated at a vast, open, equilateral triangular table, another 999 names were inscribed on the floor of ceramic tiles beneath. Chicago spoke of the structure as a community of people participating in the artmaking process, and pointed to the precedents of nuns working in the cloister, of quilting bees, of medieval guild and apprenticeship programs. By using craft skills that were traditionally feminine – and social – such as china-painting and embroidery, Chicago challenged assumptions not only about who possessed skill but where it belonged.

popular success, and it subsequently toured internationally: its robustness and drama have made it an iconic art work. Critics at the time, and subsequently, have been more mixed. Some have suggested that Chicago's use of women 'co-workers' was disingenuous, covering up a Renaissance model of a master's studio. Others have been troubled by the way in which the particularity of cultures from which the women 'guests' came was flattened by being appropriated into her feminist discourse.

Still life

One of the key ways that temporality has been used by ceramicists and sculptors is by using still life, where art looks closely at those things that are usually disregarded, where unassuming pots are defamiliarized and become special objects of contemplation. Still life as a genre takes everyday life as its theme; in the art historian Norman Bryson's words,

The life of the table, of the household interior, the basic creaturely acts of eating and drinking, of the artefacts which surround the subject in her or his domestic space, of the everyday world of routine and repetition, at a level of existence where events are... the small-scale, trivial, forgettable acts of bodily survival and self-maintenance...

By using the framework of still life, referring to the stasis of the picture plane, groupings of vessels whose identity is normally constructed around the 'small-scale, trivial and forgettable' can have what might be called 'sculptural presence'. This is a thematization of the vessel – whether made from clay or not – that has become much used in contemporary sculpture. Still life lies behind Allan Mc Collum's (b. 1944) *Fifty Perfect Vehicles* (1985–89) where huge cement casts, based on the form of a Chinese ginger jar and painted in vibrant colours, are massed together. This installation comments both on the vessel as a 'vehicle', a container of desires, and on uniqueness: which jar is more desirable, which more perfect? Other sculptors have taken an extended view of the vessel, Nicholas Pope making a series of liturgical vessels such as fonts and wash basins .

In his 'Accumulations' series in the 1960s the French sculptor Arman (b. 1928) had collected multiples of the same domestic objects and displayed them in transparent boxes to create collapsed versions of still lives, where all hierarchies of difference had disappeared. In *As in the Sink* (1990) [161], a pile of cups, saucers, plates and teapots are piled together haphazardly: on closer inspection each of these vessels is cut in half, a visual pun

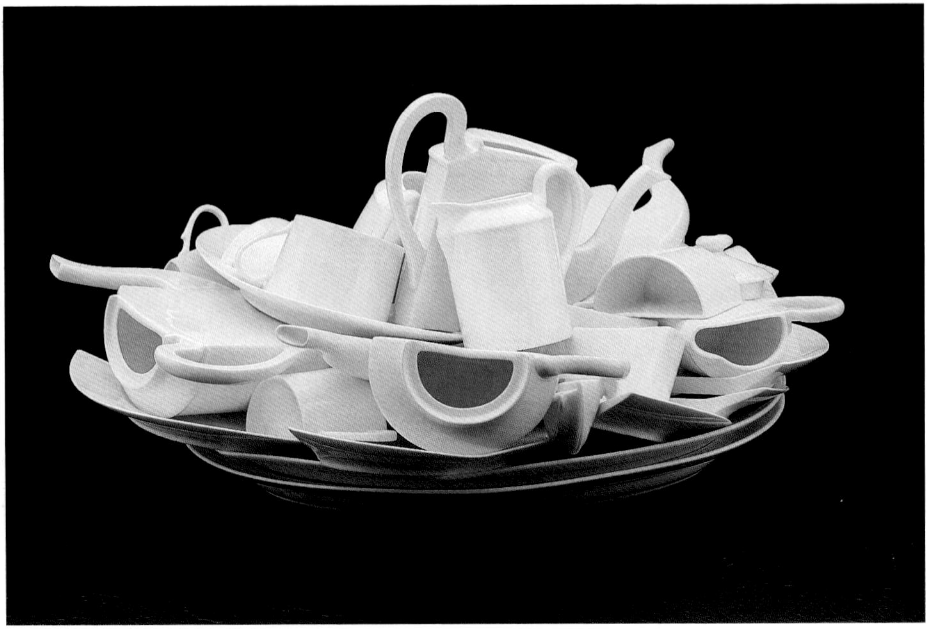

161 **Arman**, *As in the Sink II*, 1990 (porcelain, h. 23 cm/9 in). Arman has used the detritus of everyday life as the building blocks of his sculpture since his Paris exhibition *Le Plein* (Full Up) where a gallery was filled with junk. Here a sink is the imagined frame for the contained objects.

162 **Tony Cragg**, *Shiva*, 1996 (plaster, h. 297 cm/117 in). 'Still life should include all the things we produce', Cragg has said; the sculptor's role is to 'nominate' particular objects for attention. Shiva is the Hindu deity associated with destruction and reproduction.

on the French term for a small cup of coffee, 'demi-tasse', literally 'half-cup'. The sculptor Tony Cragg, known for his catholic use of materials, has worked at the European Ceramic Work Centre in the Netherlands, a pioneering centre established in 1991 'to seek for a new relationship with tradition... in a spirit of permanent enquiry'. This centre has allowed many artists, including Anish Kapoor and Antony Gormley, to make ceramic work by offering them substantial studio space and technical assistance. Cragg's ceramic work engages with the framing of the vessel – but also with the vessel in its most extended and metaphoric form as a container. His work is intuitive: 'What fascinates me is the way in which we look at materials like pen and paper, or a piece of clay... and while we are working with this material it seems to suggest things to us. Leading us to make things we had never envisaged and allowing us to experience emotions and ideas we may not have had by any other method.' *Shiva* (1996), a towering stack of large thrown terracotta-coloured dishes that looks as if it has come from a giant's draining board, enacts the dancing movement suggested by the title: the piece threatens instability and fragmentation. *Laibe* (German for loaf) resembles a butchered still life, solid white stoneware pots sliced through with a cheesewire to produce fragile segments of objects. In both Arman and Cragg's work the still life is made unstable or literally deconstructed.

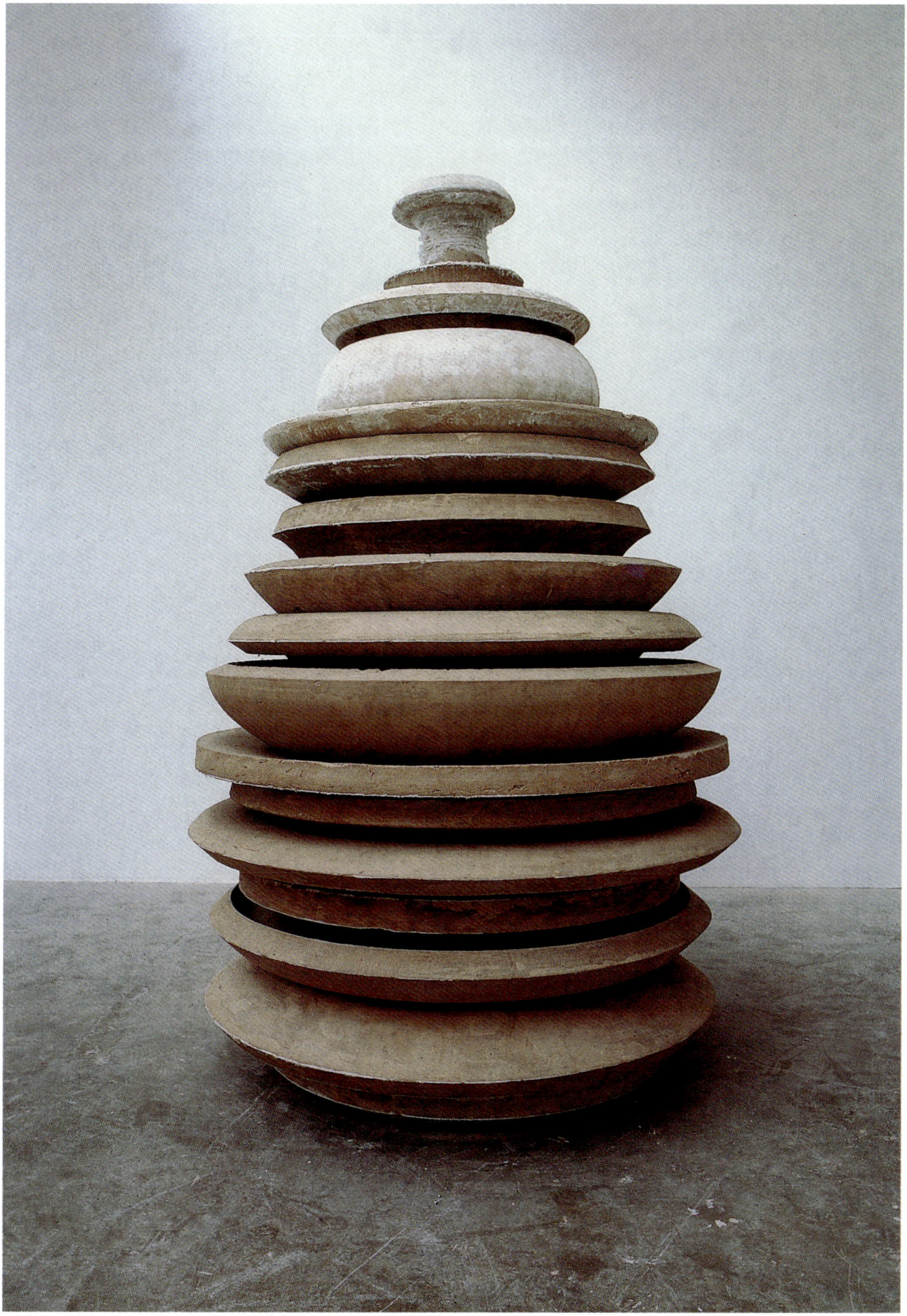

163 **Michael Geertsen**, *Green Wall Object*, 2003 (earthenware, 20 cm/8 in).
Geertsen's work, wheel-thrown, cut and reconstructed, then vividly glazed in synthetic colours, 'reanimates' stacks of crockery.

164 **Andrew Lord**, *Jug Curves*, 1986 (h. 51 cm/20 in).
Lord's ceramics are demotic jugs and cups and vases made from painter's views of objects: he 'retells' these things 'as an object that had been observed in different kinds of light, and different ways of looking and seeing'.

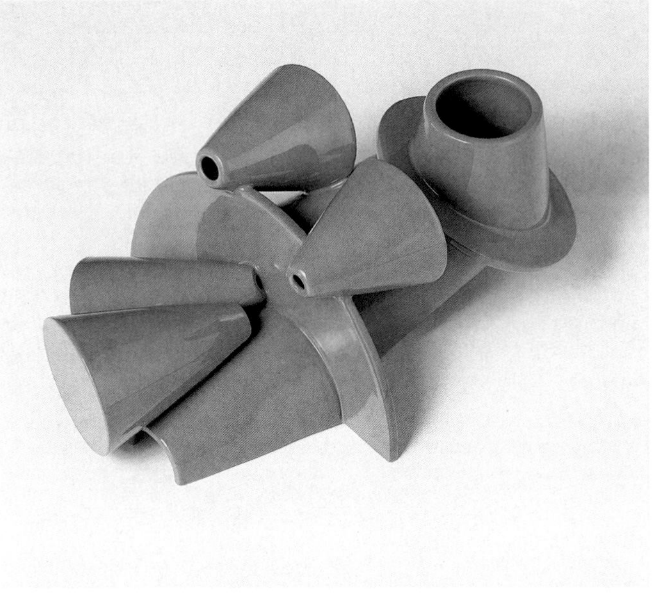

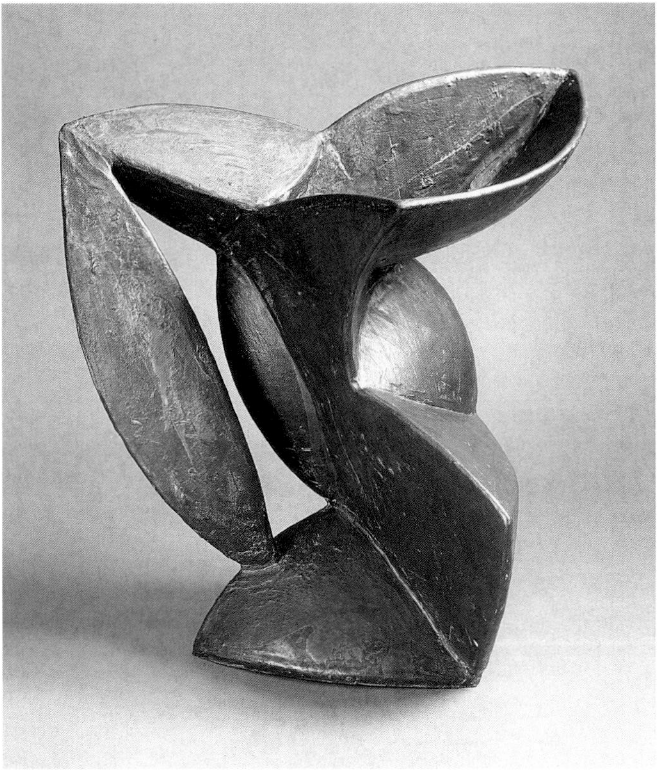

The still life is a delicate area, liable to become precious and mannered if the objects themselves cannot sustain this close reading. Some ceramicists have ritualized the domestic object as a source of disturbance and anxiety, whilst trying to avoid the humour of Funk. Amongst many other kinds of work, Tony Bennett (b. 1942) has made trays of objects that seem like industrial detritus with the whole ensemble covered in a slick of red glaze as if to emphasize a robust non-aestheticism. The Danish ceramicist Michael Geertsen (b. 1966) removes the still life from the tabletop and piles up his accretions of everyday crockery or hangs them on the wall: they play complex games as ceramic versions of Cubist pictures of ceramics. Scale also can disrupt the genre: simply by making her earthenware pitchers and mugs two metres (six feet) high, the Norwegian ceramicist Lisbeth Dæhlin gives her still lives a bodily presence. The American ceramicists Nancy Selvin (b. 1943) and James Makins (b. 1946) and the British potter Julian Stair (b. 1956) have all used the tray, shelf or the stand to provide just this foregrounding. The floor has also been used: in *The Porcelain Carpet* (2002) the Polish-born artist and designer Marek Cecula showed 144 porcelain plates arranged in a grid, each plate printed with part of an elaborate Persian carpet design.

The correspondence between an actual object and its two-dimensional image has also provided part of this renewed thematization of the vessel. There is an almost aggressive and polemical feel to some of this work, a daring of the critics not to take seriously work that appears decorative, or overtly historicist. The celebrity of Andrew Lord (b. 1950), an Englishman working in New York, lay in his ascendancy into the world of Manhattan Fine Art galleries with works that came out of this correspondence.

165 **Gwyn Hanssen Pigott**, *Travellers*, 2000 (porcelain). Hanssen Pigott's porcelain groupings survive their resonance with the paintings of Giorgio Morandi because of their ambiguity. They are carefully contrived of rhythmically repeated beakers and bowls with resonating intervals that created a fine matrix of shadows.

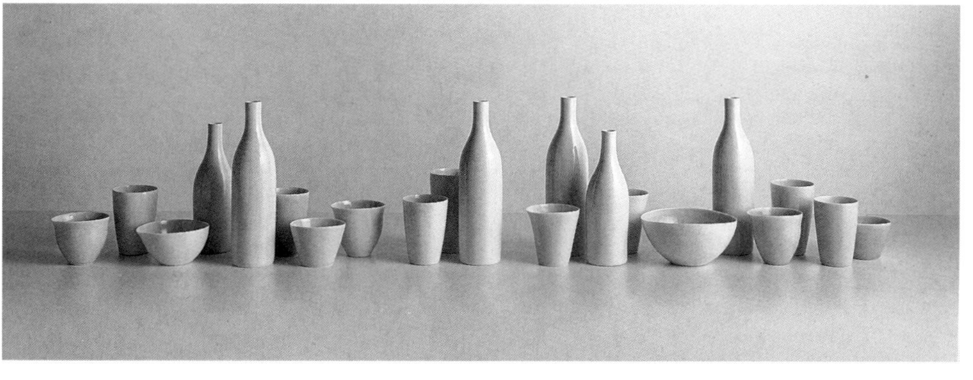

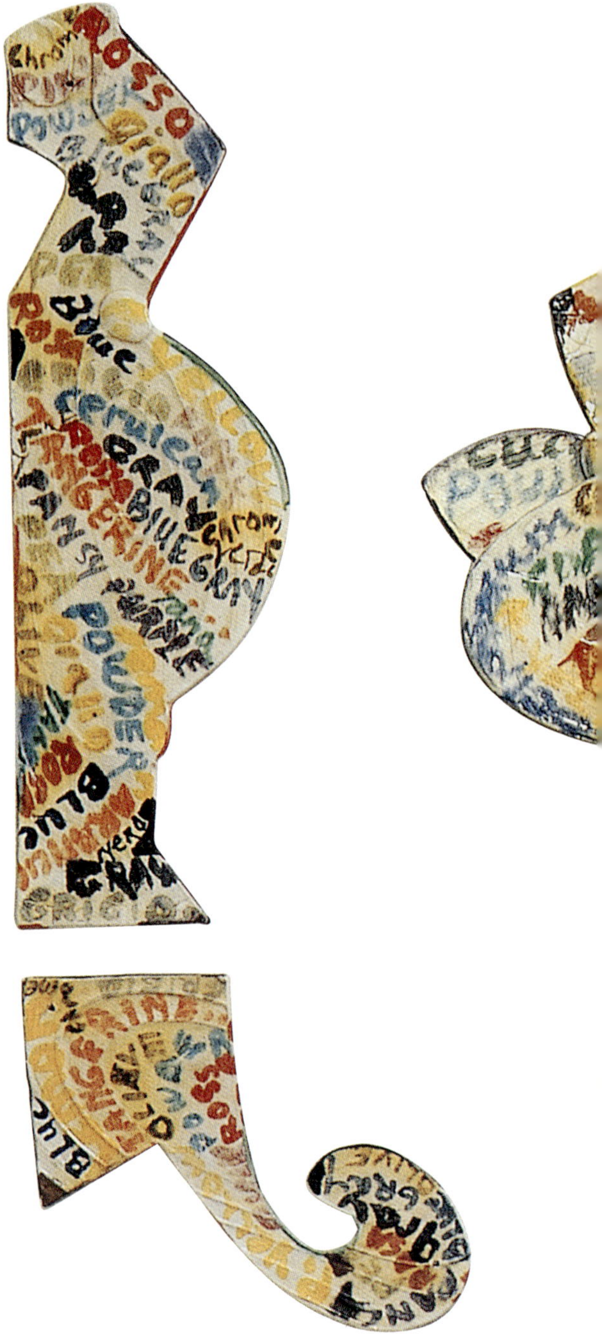

166 **Betty Woodman**, *Balustrade Vase #99-6*, 1999 (earthenware, h. 122 × 152 × 25 cm/48 × 60 × 10 in). Woodman cut and pasted the shadows of her pots into complex assemblages. Using quotations from Minoan, Aztec, Tang Chinese, and Iznik ceramics, the effect is of a vivid indiscreation: they are painted in a wild spectrum of colours, with texts or highly allusive titles. She shows how intertwined is the apprehension of three-dimensional objects and two-dimensional images.

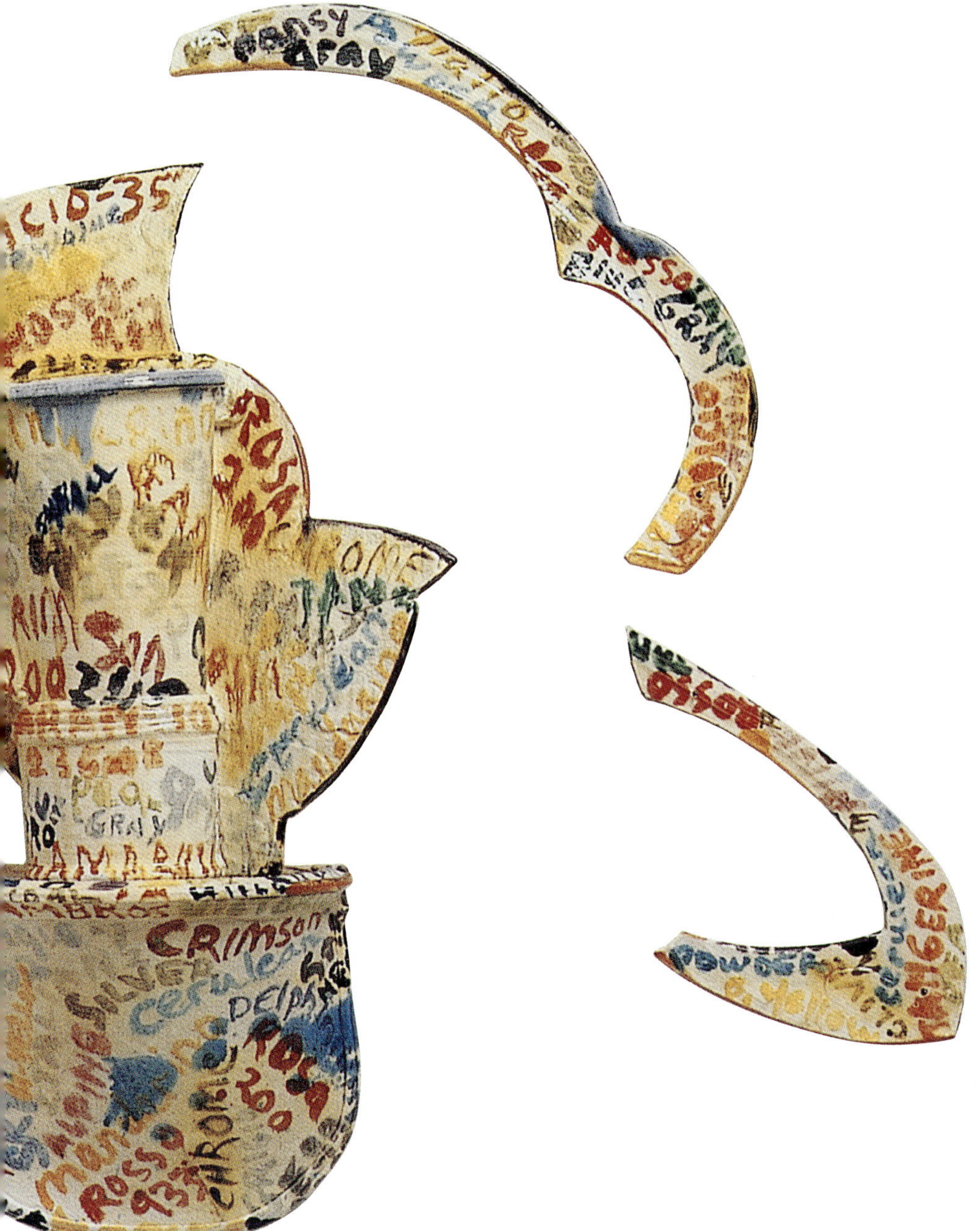
CRIMSON
cerulean
GRAY

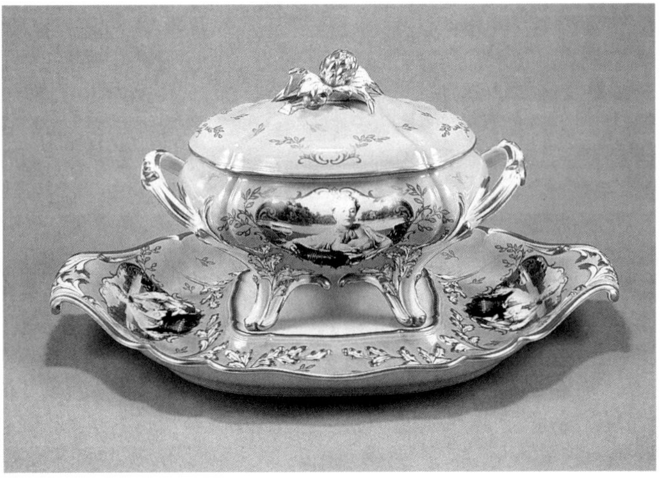

167 **Cindy Sherman**, *Madame de Pompadour (née Poisson)*, 1990 (porcelain, 37 cm/14⅝ in). Sherman's art explores identity through manifold guises taken from film and painting. Here she uses the traditions of court patronage to dramatize yet another persona.

They started in the early 1970s with pieces that recorded the passage of shadows across them, before moving towards his more involved recent pieces where the modulation of objects lies more in happenstance groupings than in formal structures or resolution. Lord's ceramics, with their creased, 'lived-in' surfaces and brash colours, do not attempt so much to be beautiful, as to challenge the viewer to reconsider the place of the decorative in art. Lord, who has studied the work of French Cubist painter Georges Braque, asks: why should an image of a vessel in a Braque painting have so much more value than the vessel itself?

Postmodernism

Postmodernism could be seen as the condition of anxiety about received truths, a self-consciousness about making art and about its reception. In ceramics as in other arts in the 1980s and 90s this led to an extensive use of ironic reference, of pastiche and quotation to unsettle hegemonic notions of cultural identity. Being authentic, being true to a tradition, were unattainable ideas: the ceramicist was a commentator, an ethnographer, a collagist of images, but above all reflexive. At its most bathetic this led to ceramicists breaking their work and reconstructing it or embedding literal fragments or shards. It has, however, led to work that engages with the nature of the history of ceramics: with questions of how national identity is displayed, or how the canon of 'good taste' is created. This has led to the resurrection of certain formal structures concerned with patronage and with display in ceramics, principally the dinner service, the elaborate stand and the garniture, that were not only absent from the repertoire of the studio potter, but anathematized. Indeed, most of the qualities in ceramics that had come to be despised – the excessive use of decoration and gilding, the perfect surfaces, the theatrical display of skill – find refulgent excess in *Michael Jackson with Bubbles* (1988) by Jeff Koons (b. 1955). Part of Koon's 'Banality' series, this life-size statue uses porcelain to create a dead white Jackson cuddling his pet monkey dressed in matching clothing seated on a rose-strewn carpet. It can be seen as a contemporary version of a vanitas portrait, an exploration of image and celebrity. Cindy Sherman's *Madame de Pompadour* service (1990), made at the Limoges porcelain factory for Artes Magnus, an American organization that brings artists and sculptors to work on limited edition works in porcelain, reveals this matrix of commentary. Her dinner service and tureen set copy the forms made at Sèvres in 1756 for Madame de Pompadour with Sherman's image silkscreened onto the porcelain: here the construction of a commodified image of the

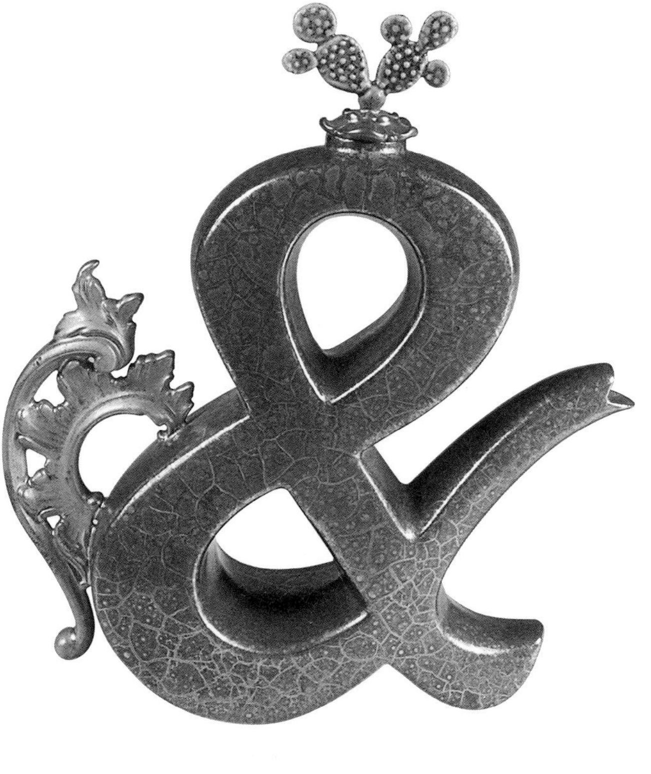

168 **Adrian Saxe**, untitled ewer (Franklin Gothic Italic Ampersand), 1989 (porcelain, h. 26 cm/10¼ in). Saxe's use of the ampersand indicates just how elaborately textual these objects have become; they are objects for close reading and analysis, saturated in textual correspondences.

patron is transposed from the French court to the Manhattan art world. This commentary on luxury was reversed in *Lapsed Quaker Ware* by the American sculptor James Turrell, famous for his light works. Here, a packing case filled with straw conceals Turrell's version of the austere eighteenth-century Quaker ware crockery. Turrell, himself a Quaker, seems to be asking what value there might be in resurrecting old, lapsed forms and skills.

Adrian Saxe (b. 1943) is the postmodern ceramicist par excellence. His work is highly allusive to both ceramic history and to contemporary popular culture; it is verbally dextrous, often acting in conjunction with wordplay in the form of palindromes and anagrams, and knowing about the process of quotation from sources, about the meanings implicit in different making processes and about the process of collecting. His pieces are often highly structured, sometimes through the use of a text (as in his garnitures ELVIS/LIVES) or through the contrast of base and vessel: 'The bases represent their material source, which in turn metaphorically indicates ceramic and aesthetic foundations. The vessel, on the other hand, is a more refined, culturally determined manifestation of the medium.' This can be seen in a work like *Vomituration* (1990). Standing two feet (60 cm) high, the work is a gourd glazed in a dark Ming monochrome 'café-au-lait' glaze, with a surface studded with innumerable gilded buttons, and surmounted by a gilded gothic 'Yo'. A miniature terracotta gourd acts as a stopper, and the whole piece stands on a cream crackle-glazed base that is itself a version of a wooden stand. It is certainly a commentary on taste, a condensed run-through of the periods that Modernism tried to forget – from the Victorian buttons to the 'court taste' of the Chinese references. While some may object to his use of 'deracinated' cultural material, Saxe emphasizes that in the age of mass digital media, such material is constantly decontextualized, that authenticity is impossible to locate amongst the simulcra.

For other ceramicists political commentary is central to their work. This has increasingly been applied through the medium of print on ceramics. Printed ceramics are usually either cheap domestic ware, whose imagery is stock pastoral or Oriental, or commemorative wares. In both cases imagery is susceptible to revocation or parody, to shifts that play on the idea of who or what is being commemorated. It is the conjunction of imagery and object that allows for this, since Pop's accommodation of these demotic objects into the canon is no longer in itself iconoclastic. The British ceramicist Paul Scott took blue and white china –

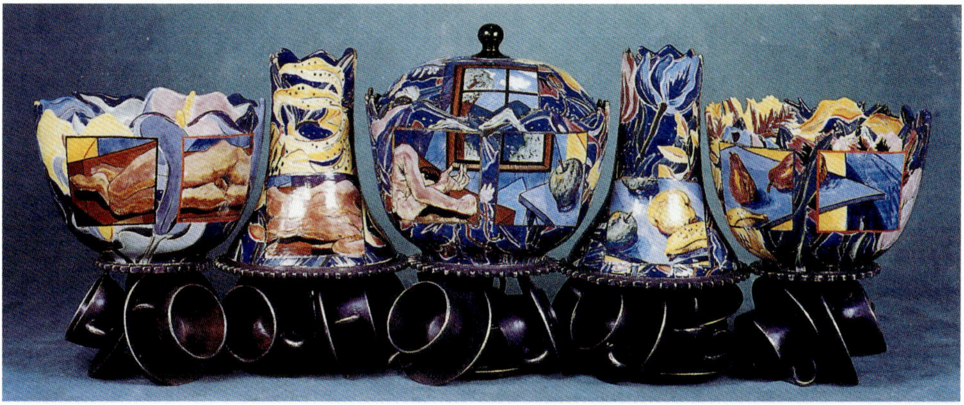

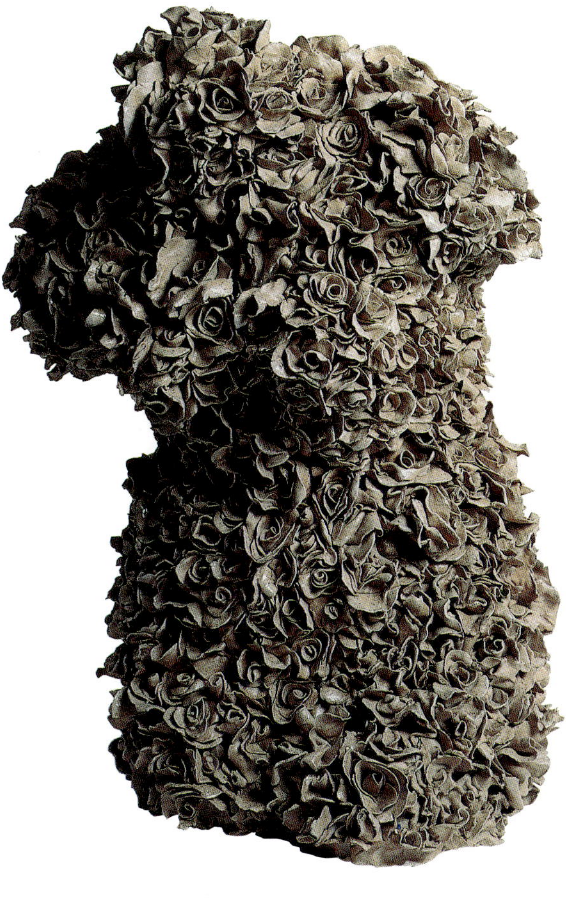

169 **Paul Mathieu**, *Garniture #2 Day (or Night)*, 1993 (porcelain and bronze, l. 150 cm/60 in).
In Mathieu's elaborate tin-glazed and painted garnitures the male body is objectified and made the subject of desire through the intense decorativeness of the surface.

170 **Johan Creten**, *Odore di Femmina Torso 2*, 1997 (stoneware, h. 67.3 cm/26½ in).
Creten's work brings the conventionally sensual images of the female body and roses into contrast with the sharp, brittle surface of the form; it defies touch.

where a pastoral idyll usually resides – and printed a landscape with a nuclear reactor onto it in *The Scott Collection Cumbrian Blue(s)*; Charles Krafft in America has made slipcast pistols and grenades and printed on Delftware patterns.

Decoration has often been seen in a gendered way, as if 'decorativeness' was a secondary, feminine attribute to be contrasted with the masculine primacy of form. In ceramics this idea was powerfully consolidated through the writings of many of the principal writers for whom the areas in which women worked in ceramics (principally china-painting and figuration) were 'invisible' and beneath their notice. Given these essentialist stereotypes, 'decorativeness' has proved a condensed way of exploring issue of gender and sexuality.

Sexuality is also scrutinized in the work of Grayson Perry (b. 1960). Perry's work is deliberately 'evening class'. The form of his pots are chosen to correspond to norms of good decorative china, often vases made in the Arneson hobbyist spirit of 'How to make a big dish'. Their decoration is extreme, with scenes of provincial life mixed up with violence, sex, transvestism and graffiti, in a melange of print, decals and texts. In Perry's ceramics decoration becomes a form of dressing-up: it is as if the 'simple pot' is trying out roles and identities through the multiplicity of images, gilding and text wrapped around it.

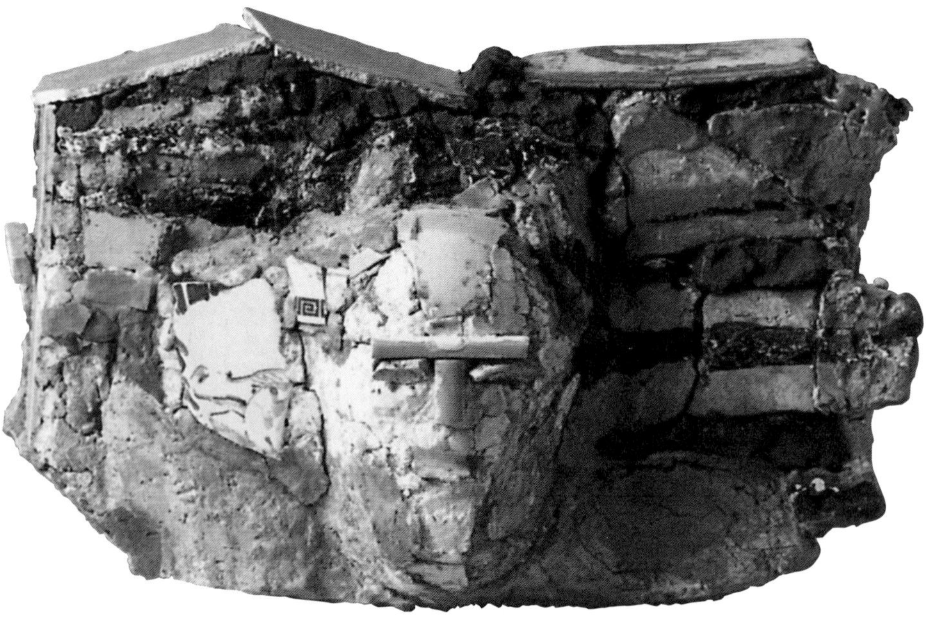

171 **Gertraud Möhwald**, *Head with Striped Hairstyle*, 1999 (h. 26.5 cm/10¼ in). Möhwald collages glazed fragments and broken kiln-elements onto what she has described as 'unexpected and often surprising inner forms with their broken, irregular edges and planes – unrepaired'.

As if to emphasize the distance travelled from the easily handled, smooth, poised and idealized figurines of women made in the 1920s and 30s with their highly glazed surfaces, much contemporary ceramic figuration made by women is either fragmentary, pitted or has intensely layered surface decoration. The German ceramicist Gertraud Möhwald (1929–2002), the British ceramicist Christie Brown (b. 1946), Mary Frank (b. 1933) and Viola Frey (b. 1933) in America all make work that literally cannot be 'grasped' because of its brokenness or its scale. Mythology lay behind much of Frank's unglazed terracotta sculptures. They too break apart, as if connecting with the surrounding landscape. Frey, trained as a painter as well as a ceramicist, has used scale to great effect, making some pieces that are the size of 1930s figurines, and others that are larger than life-size. The depth of colour and surface recall Niki de Saint Phalle's *Nanas* of the 1960s. In *Sky Blue Suit* (1982) a businessman is pictured looking lost, his identity defined by his ill-fitting clothes: monumentality is used to express pathos rather than power.

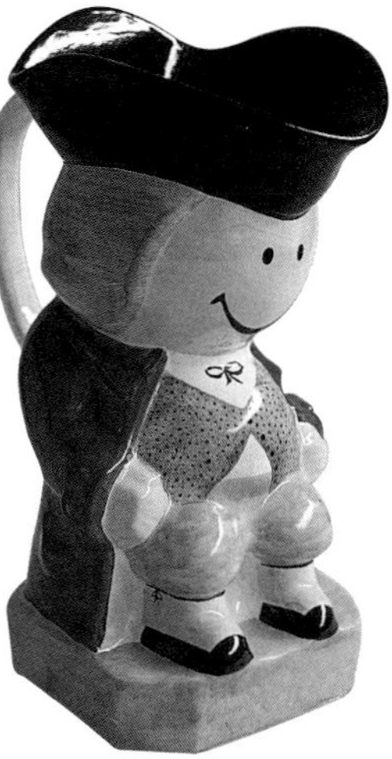

172 **Richard Slee**, *Acid Toby*, 1993 (earthenware, h. 48 cm/19 in). This Toby jug, with its benign aimlessness, refers to the late twentieth-century 'acid' culture of drug-taking and hedonism. *Drunken Toby*, from the same series, questions the tame notion of an Englishman happy in his cups, which becomes rather differently inflected when the violent drunkenness of English youth is the most forceful image of the English abroad.

Nationalism

At the high-water mark of a particularly strongly inflected political nostalgia for a kind of Englishness based on values of continuity, tradition and community in the 1990s, the English potter Richard Slee (b. 1946) embarked on a series of contemporary Toby jugs. Slee had worked in the Pop idiom incorporating parts of popular American culture into his brightly coloured ceramics since the 1970s, a typical example being his *Krazy Kat* teapots. In turning to the Toby jug, a vernacular English decorative tankard of a bluff, pink-cheeked, Henry Fielding country squire with his own tankard of ale in his hands, he was choosing English culture as his focus for the first time. The interest of Slee's work lies not just in his use of the vernacular in a politicized way to explore ideas of ethnicity but in the way that he makes this commentary on his own cultural matrix. As the anthropologist James Clifford has said: '[What] has become irreducibly curious is no longer the other, but cultural description itself.' By taking as his theme the iconic English Toby jug, Slee automatically puts himself into the arena of ethnicity. Slee is his own ethnographer.

This idea of mediating the strongest images of your own ceramic tradition is made more complex when your tradition has become subject to the pressures of tourism. If others – whether tourists or anthropologists – are buying up your pots and labelling some aspects of them as 'authentic', then it is particularly difficult to find a space in your culture in which to work. Contemporary ceramics by American Indian ceramicists show this dilemma. Alongside those who are merely copying the (revived) styles of Maria Martinez, Jody Folwell (b. 1942) and Jean Bad Moccasin (b. 1947) have found ways of commenting in overtly political ways on how their art is seen and consumed. Their pots are beautifully anarchic: angry and ironic pots in place of the contemplative, consolatory ones expected.

A comparison can be made with the work of the Japanese ceramicist Kimpei Nakamura (b. 1935). Nakamura was brought up in Kanazawa, a centre of rarified craft traditions, spent a year in the United States as a Rockefeller Foundation Fellow in 1969–70 and now teaches at Tama University of the Arts in Tokyo. He is a heterodox figure within Japanese ceramics, a maker of ceramic sculpture that acts as a commentary on the foundations of the 'authenticity' of accepted taste; in 1988 he held an exhibition entitled *An Exploration of Japanese Taste*. In *Even Stones have Sap*, a bricolage of disparate man-made industrial and craft objects lies assembled on a gilded rock promontory. It is difficult to read: are these bizarre objects malign growths or benign decorations? From a metallic angle of pipe sprouts a twig;

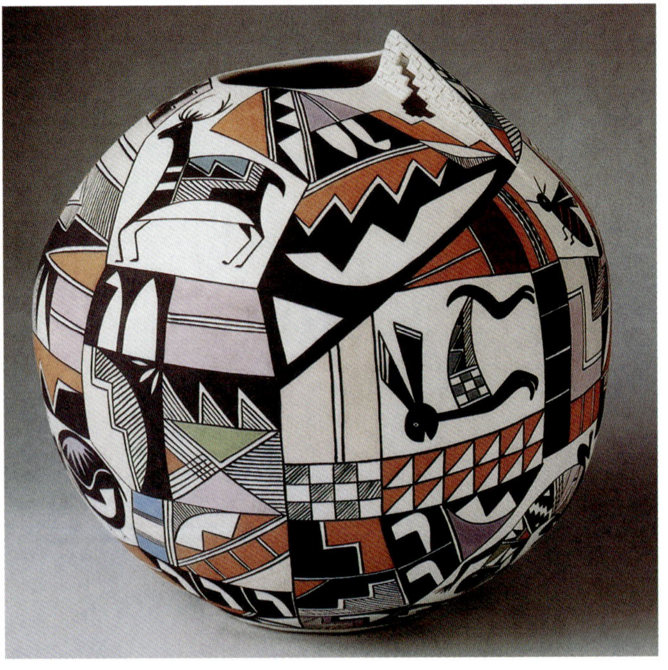

173 **Jean Bad Moccasin**, *Kiva-step Vase*, 1993 (h. 26.7 cm/10½ in). Rather than making pots that fit into a received view of ceramics as the carrier of vital traditions – pots that emphasize continuity – Jean Bad Moccasin's pots show up the disjunction between the original and the contemporary.

174 **Kimpei Nakamura**, *Sumptuousness and Untruth*, 1991 (h. 80 cm/31½ in).
Nakamura seems to be implying, the structures that have allowed the distancing of confused everyday urban living and the objects of fetishized cultural attention, have fragmented. This is the maker as obsessive ethnographer and obsessive collector of data, the maker at large in the modern city.

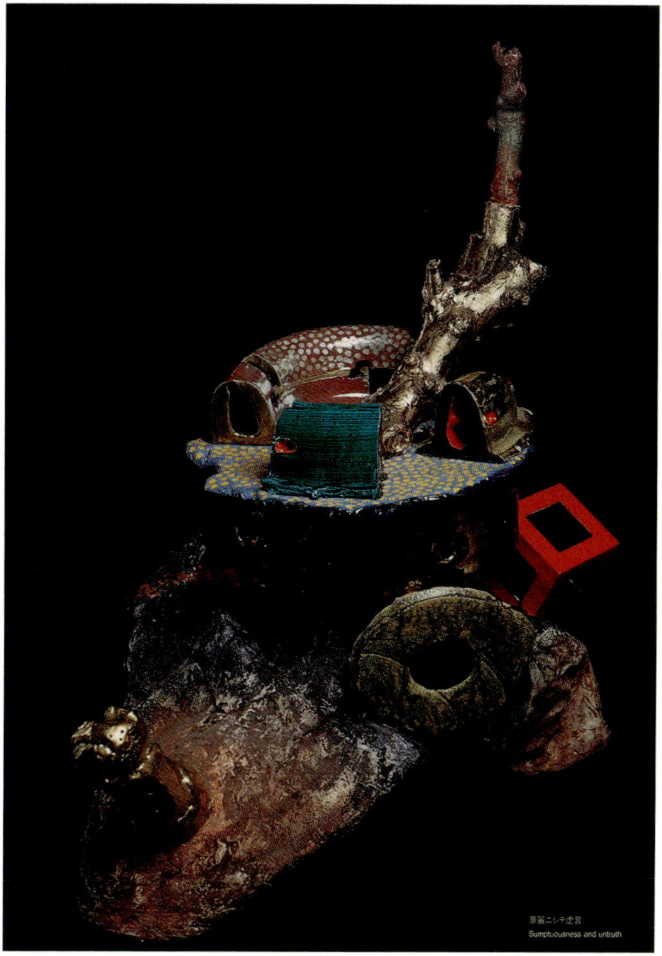

embedded in the rock is an open cube of Shinto scarlet. Nakamura decoded this palimpsest of Japanese cultural motifs by introducing the notion of kitsch: 'the constant reworking of traditional ceramic styles by artists living in an age with different priorities from those obtaining at the time the original works were made, leads to products that cannot fail to degenerate into "mere kitsch replicas".' In his embracing of kitsch as a significant cultural manifestation he makes it as significant as the pursuit of authenticity. The austere aestheticizing of the natural is not so much parodied by its transformation into fired clay cloaked in metallic glazes, as intensified by it. This is not mockery of tradition but a fierce concentration of both the subject and ways of approaching it within the same piece. For here the rock and branch, which should in normative Japanese aesthetics be isolated and cordoned off into the safe places where beauty is allowed to perform its role, have to act within a welter of discursive images of modernity. Nakamura calls his most recent work *Tokyo Ware – Metaceramics*, pointing out that 'The works were fired in an electric kiln in a basement in Aoyama [in Tokyo]'. There could be no greater distance between such a setting and the wood-fired 'old kilns' of Japan. In a further affront to traditional sensibilities, he commented on the floor of this exhibition – strewn with broken sanitary ware and electrical transformers – that 'Like the tea masters, I have uncovered an extraordinary aesthetic in manufactured goods'.

'Cultural description' can be politicized and purgative, as in Slee, Folwell or Nakamura's ceramics, or it can be more formally interrogative, as in the case of Lawson Oyekan (b. 1961). As an African-born ceramicist, his work has been seen in terms of essentialist stereotypes of blackness, the primacy of emotion, and – crucially – the body, as if the African potters were, like Leach's Oriental potters, 'more in touch with their feelings'. Oyekan was born in Nigeria, studied in Great Britain and has worked internationally. His characteristic forms from the *Trials with Light* series are tall terracotta or porcelain monoliths made from small pieces of clay repeatedly smeared together. As there are many small interstices though no central opening, the impression given is not of a vessel but of an architectural structure. They are left unglazed or marked with splashes of white slip, and the surfaces are then gouged or scratched to make indecipherable calligraphic marks. They refuse to be read as 'African' objects. Indeed they refuse to be legible at all: they have an ambivalent sense of objecthood, partly relating to natural structures like termite mounds, partly to urban detritus.

In much the same way in Japan Shugo Takauchi (b. 1937) and Shiro Tsujimura (b. 1947) have made work that comments on how traditions have become broken up into a collage of consumable images. In a culture where ceramic identity is still powerfully regional, they make work that is eclectic – using a particular highly specific glaze over a form from another area, or, in Takauchi's case, transforming a small Oribe bucket into a huge jagged sculptural version. Though he works in Mashiko, the pottery village immortalized through Hamada, Takauchi's work owes little to the folkcraft tradition. Takauchi is eclectic, using glazes and styles from diverse parts of Japanese history in a

175 **Shugo Takauchi**, Vase with handle, 1992 (h. 58.5 cm/23 in). Takauchi's work shows how complex the relationship between Japanese traditions and the American Voulkos traditions of direct working in clay have crossed over.

forceful way. Masamichi Yoshikawa (b. 1946) takes another tradition – that of blue and white decorated porcelain – and constructs architectonic forms on which patterns are defaced and erased by blue scribbled graffiti.

Cultural specificity is particularly amenable to quotation and allusion, something that can be done with great power in contemporary societies where ceramics are a popular art form. In China several contemporary ceramicists use the shard as a

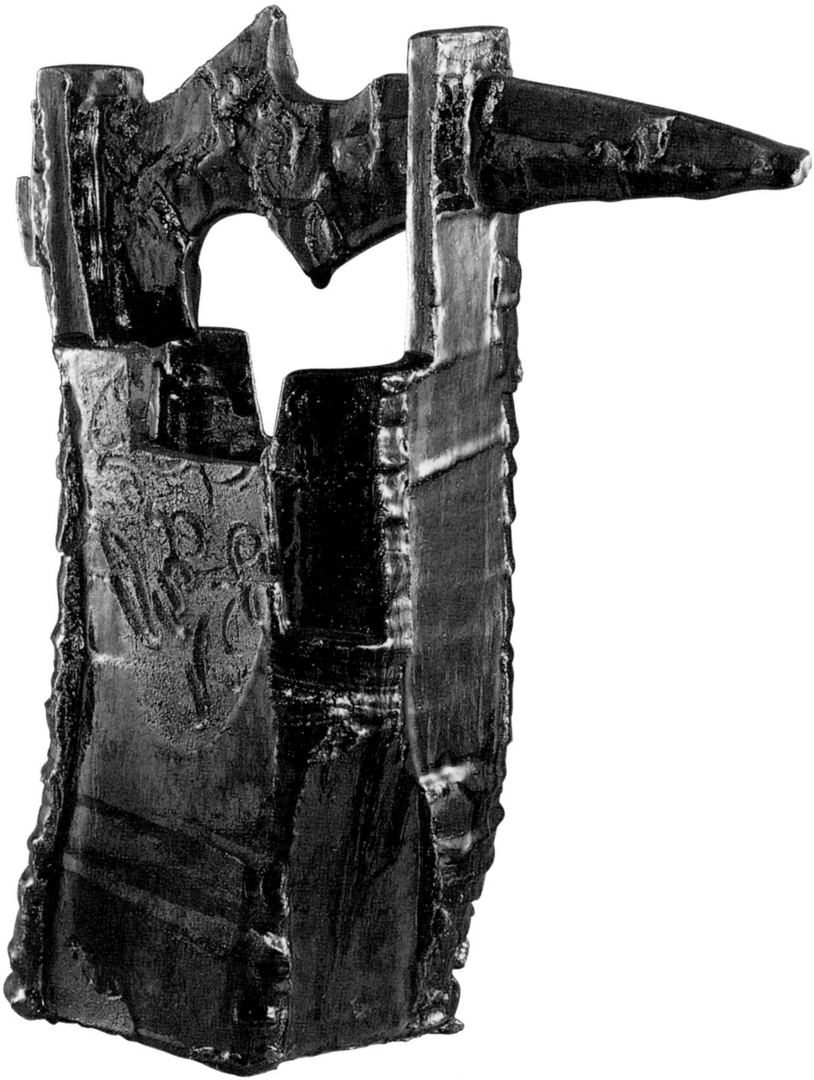

176 **Shin Sang-Ho**, *91 Dream*, 1991 (bunchung ware, h. 56 cm/ 22 in).
Shin's work crosses over from the arena where ceramic history self-consciously becomes the subject of his work, to an expressive eclecticism where particular Korean techniques or images are used alongside references to American action painting.

discrete symbol of cultural upheaval and destruction. In the 'East to West' project of the figurative sculptor Jiansheng Li (b. 1959) shards are decorated and refired 'metaphors for a compressed history', as he puts it. Wenzhi Zhang (b. 1959) embeds shards into her figures to make anxious objects, entitled *SARS Creatures*.

In Korea, ceramics underwent an explosion of interest in the 1970s, with many of the new universities establishing ceramics departments, and the foundation of the first avant-garde groupings of ceramicists. In 1973 at the inaugural exhibition in the newly built National Museum in Seoul, the 'naturalism' of Korean beauty was referred to as 'ultimately based upon national thoughts or sentiments', a 'national art' manifested in two particular traditions, the celadon porcelains and the Punch'ong inlaid slipwares. With traditions so highly inflected in the

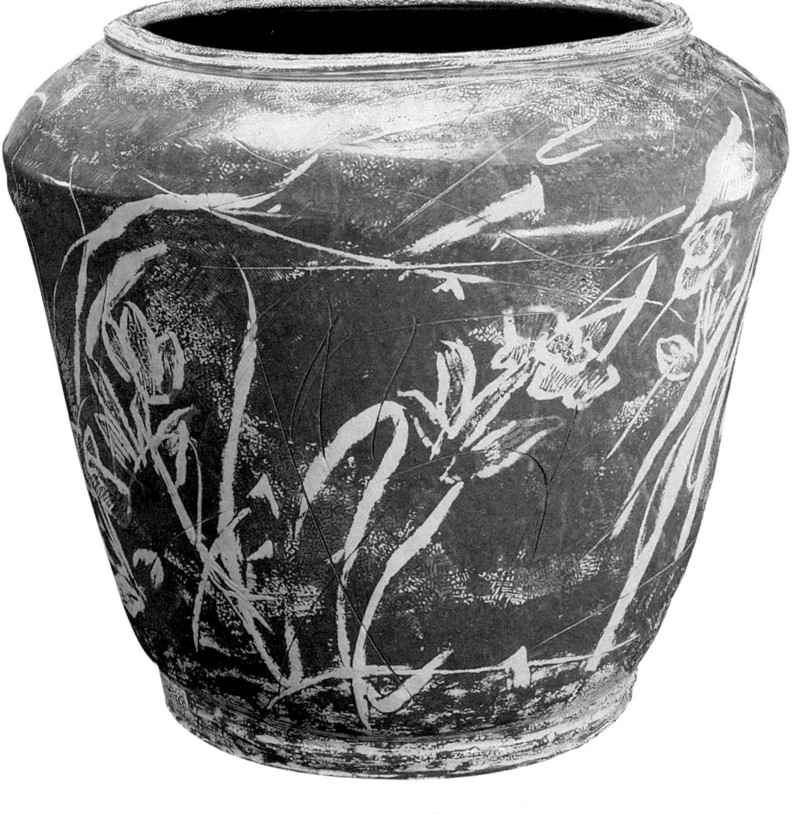

177 **Goro Suzuki**, *Oribe Chair*, 2002 (h. 45.7 cm/18 in). Japanese Oribe wares are known for their complex use of representative pictorialism and wildly gestural glazing. Here Suzuki uses the most clichéd of all Japanese images and collages it into a Western chair.

definitions of nationality it is no surprise that they have proved to be rich areas for a kind of experimentation that, if not postmodern, is highly allusive. Kim Yi-kyung (b. 1935), the first Korean woman to study ceramics abroad, has used porcelain traditions as the basis of her faceted lidded jars. Punch'ong wares, where earthenware is impressed with complex patterns, have been shaken up in the work of Shin Sang-ho (b. 1947) and Yoon Kwang-Cho (b. 1946), where discrete patterning has been exchanged for violent gestural markings.

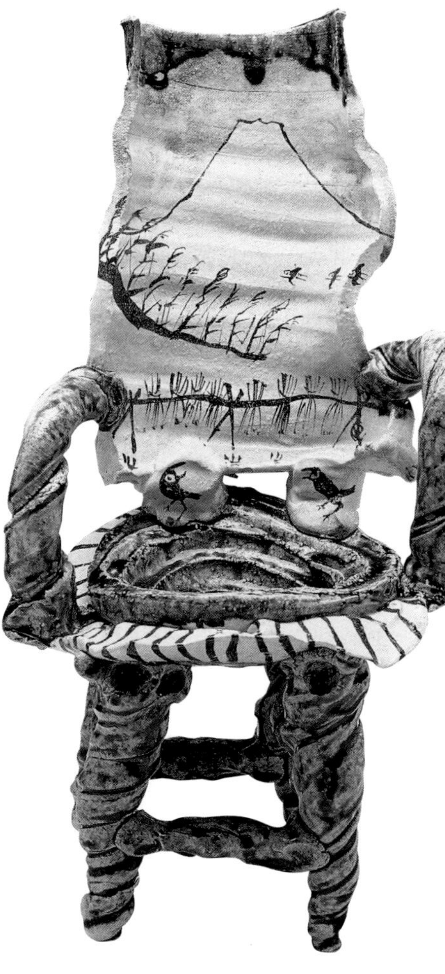

Shin's example is telling because it suggests that the period of sensitivity to national allusion and quotation may be a phase in the history of twentieth century ceramics that is coming to a close. There may be an exhaustion with the idea of postmodern ethnic commentary. With cultural markers that were once specific and highly inflected, like the raku techniques of Japan, now used as expressive tools, and with more 'anagama' kilns in use in America than Japan, the idea of hegemonic traditions has disappeared. With a Sèvres garniture as likely to be appropriated as the basis for a new work by a student in Tokyo as in Los Angeles or Amsterdam, the efficacy of quotation itself, rather than the act of quotation, may serve a more telling purpose.

Conclusion

The search for the experiential in clay, for a pleasure in making that extends beyond the cerebral design of form, is one of the great themes of the ceramics of the twentieth century. It is a phenomenological approach: artists and potters have used clay as an improvisatory and often studiedly non-intellectual mode of expression. George Ohr's vessels made in the earliest years of the century, the wall of clay that the American-Japanese sculptor Isamu Noguchi constructed in his studio in Japan in the 1950s, and the ceramics of the CoBrA group – all point to the embrace of clay as a material for 'direct expression'. As the English sculptor Tony Cragg has said, 'I move, it moves' – a transparency of expression seems possible with his use of clay.

Throughout the century, the non-canonical use of clay has been accorded a particular value. It is this search for beginnings that links the ceramics of the Expressionists at the start of the twentieth century, the Sodeisha movement in postwar Japan and the use of unfired clay in installations at the end of the century. For some, using clay has been the recuperation of 'unmediated' materiality. The powerful sense of clay as earth, as the great formless void, allowed them a kind of expression they could not attain through other materials. 'Returning to earth' carries with it the almost visceral feeling of having been separated, alienated or disconnected from the earth, or land, or culture.

The quest to reconnect with the earth inspires those firing techniques that cannot be completely controlled. Wood-firing and raku, both ancient techniques revived in the current world of ceramics, are now modern pursuits. The French poet Paul Valéry wrote in his essay 'On the Pre-eminent Dignity of the Arts of Fire' that Earth and Mars 'are, after all, nothing but cooled bodies'; for all 'the fire worker's admirable vigilance and all the foresight learned from experience… They can never abolish Chance. Risk remains the dominating and, as it were, the sanctifying element of his great art.' For many ceramicists, it is the symbolic loss of control over the outcome that 'sanctifies' their work. The idea of a reconnection to a natural order through work is strong in the studio pottery world. Indeed, it may be said to be the principal definition of studio pottery, in the absence of a general moral imperative for work such as making pottery for domestic use.

The need to find the roots of ceramic practice lies behind the nationalist animation of particular vernacular forms or styles. Throughout the twentieth century traditions were supported, revivified and reinvented. Whilst some vernacular traditions have disappeared, others have been transformed into carriers of potent meaning and cultural continuity. There are other ceramics whose meaning lies in cultural quotation. This has often led to instances of synergy: the avant-garde flourishing within sites of traditional activity, Yagi relishing the proximity of his more traditional peers, Fontana crashing 'like a Minotaur' through Sèvres.

Conversely, traditional ceramic practice has identified itself in opposition to 'transgressive' new work, gaining sustenance from its sense of the values of continuity. Even in such relatively new sites of activity as Australia and Norway, in whose cultures there are no longstanding traditions of ceramics, there are identifiable groupings of traditional and avant-garde practitioners. Since the 1960s Korean ceramics have been treating their ancient ceramic heritage in ways both 'timeless' and contemporary. It is no coincidence that the leading school of contemporary ceramics in China should be based in Jingdezhen, the centre of traditional Chinese porcelain production. Traditions are not inert: alongside the 'Six Old Kilns of Japan', the centres of Japanese tea-ware ceramics, are avant-garde ceramicists pillaging the same iconic imagery. Kimpei Nakamura, creator of 'Tokyo Ware' and a particularly forceful exponent of cultural allusion, has said, 'Beware of nostalgic ceramics'. However, whether there can be anything shocking about such confrontations is now debatable. While there are cabalistic redoubts where particular entrenched positions are still held, where a technique, a canon of pots or an attitude to making is still considered to be normative, it is more difficult than ever to talk about the field as a single discipline.

Though the domestic pot – the studio pot – is important, ceramics in the twentieth century have been much more than a

178 **Gehry Partners**, LLP,
Ohr–O'Keefe Museum of Art,
final design model, July 2001.

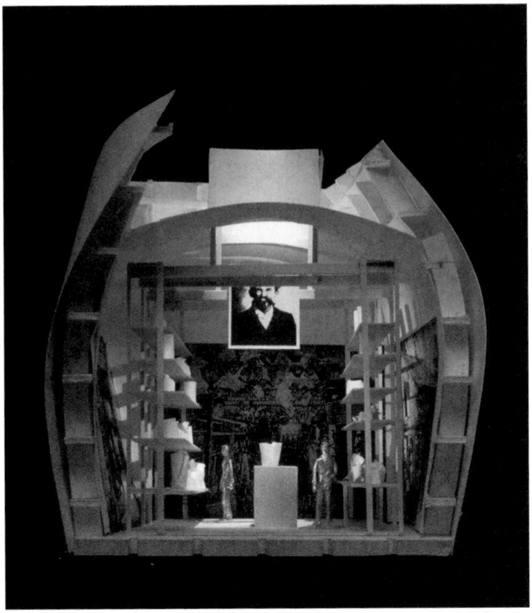

domestic drama. From the grand expositions to the postmodern framing of objects, ceramics have also showed a public, and interrogative, face. The intersection between architecture, ceramics and sculptural installation has been a key area of exploration. There are examples that capture the tension between the isolation of the object and its grouping together. From Lily Reich's exhibition of massed porcelain in Berlin in 1934, at the inception of Nazi control of art, to Ken Price's *Happy's Curios* in 1970s Los Angeles, to Piet Stockmans's installations at the end of the century, there is an alternative history of the formal arrangement of ceramics: ceramics need not be benign. In the words of an anonymous Soviet commentator writing in 1928, 'In this "parade" of objects there are no non-combatants – nor can there be! ...We demand that a plate should fulfill its social function.' This sentiment also seems to describe the efforts of artists of the 1960s and 70s to politicize the ways in which ceramics were made and exhibited.

Although ceramics exist in a complex and expanded field, each generation has to feel the complexity and expansion of the field for themselves, turning away from the past, doubting the previous generation's abilities to renew the art of ceramics. Many of the debates that raged at the turn of the nineteenth into the twentieth century are still heated at the turn of the twenty-first.

The place of technique within the art of ceramics, the status of objects made from clay within contexts defined by the worlds of art, the attraction of clay to sculptors, artists, designers and architects – all are themes that demand attention today.

The architect Frank Gehry is designing a new museum to house the pottery of George Ohr. The 'Mad Potter of Biloxi', rejected by many institutions during his life, is to have his own institution. This does not make his pots any less unsettling, perplexing or beautiful, but it does suggest that objects that failed to fit into previous worlds of ceramics now can have a claim to centrality. Contexts do change. Like the other arts, ceramics have the power to move, placate, anger and inspire, and the ability to redefine the places in which they choose to be.

Select Bibliography

General Histories and Surveys

Berguelt, E. (ed.), *Industry & Design in the Netherlands*, Amsterdam, 1985

Clark, Garth, *The Potter's Art:A Complete History of Pottery in Britain*, Oxford, 1995

——— and Margie Hughto, *A Century of Ceramics in the United States, 1878–1978*, New York, 1979

Deutsche Keramik 1900–2000: Geschichte und Positionen des Jahrhunderts (exh. cat.), Germany 2001

Eidelberg, Martin (ed.), *Design for Delight: alternative aspects of 20th century decorative arts*, Paris, 1997

Fiell, Charlotte and Peter, *Scandinavian Design*, Cologne, 2002

Harrod, Tanya, *The Crafts in Britain in the Twentieth Century*, Yale University Press, 2000

Margetts, Martina, *International Crafts*, London 1991

McFadden, David Revere (ed.), *Scandinavian Modern Design 1880–1980,* Cooper Hewitt Museum, New York. 1983

Opie, Jennifer Hawkins, *Scandinavia: Ceramics and Glass in the Twentieth Century*, London: Victoria & Albert Museum, 1989, new edition 2001

Perry, Barbara, *American Ceramics: the Collection of Everson Museum of Art*, New York, 1989

Préaud, Tamara and Serge Gauthier, *Ceramics of the 20th Century*, New York, 1982

Watson, Oliver, *British Studio Pottery:The Victoria and Albert Collection*, London, 1990

Chapter 1: 1900–20

Orientalism

Franks, A. W., *Japanese Pottery, Being a Native Report*, London 1880

Holme, Charles, 'The Potter's Art – Object Lessons from the Far East', *The Studio*, Vol. XXIV, no. 103, October 1901, pp. 48–57

Mathieu, Caroline, 'Japonisme et pureté', in *Le Japonisme* (exh. cat.), Editions de la Réunion des musées nationaux, 1988

Morse, Edward S., *Catalogue of Japanese Pottery*, Museum of Fine Arts, Cambridge,1901

Watanabe, Toshio, *High Victorian Japonisme*, Peter Lang, 1991

Sato, Tomoko and Toshio Watanabe (eds), *Japan And Britain:An Aesthetic Dialogue 1850–1930*, London, 1991

Art Pottery

Albis, Jean d', *Ernest Chaplet: un céramiste art noveau*, Paris, 1976

Atterbury, Paul, *Ruskin Press:The Pottery of Edward Richard Taylor and William Howson Taylor*, Bloxendale Press, 1993

Binns, Charles F., *The Potter's Craft*, London 1910

———, *The Story of the Potter*, London (no date)

Brunet, Marcelle and Tamara Préaud, *Sèvres des origins a nos jours*, Fribourg, 1978

Doat, Taxile, 'Les Ceramiques de Grand Feu: La Porcelaine dure et le Gres-Cerame', *Art et Decoration*, 1907 pp. 69–80

Eidelberg, Martin, 'The Ceramic Art of William Grueby', *The Connoisseur* 184, no. 739, September 1973, pp. 47–54

A.W. Finch 1854–1930 (exh. cat.), Prins Eugens Waldemarsudde Stockholm, 1981

Freylinghuysen, Alice C. (ed.), *In Pursuit of Beauty:America and the Aesthetic Movement*, , New York, 1986

Haslam, Malcolm, *The Martin Brothers*, Richard Dennis, 1978

Keen, Kirsten Hoving, *American Art Pottery 1875–1930*, Wilmington Delaware Art Museum, 1978

Makus, Horst, *Adrien Dalpayrat: French Ceramics of Art Nouveau*, Arnodische Art Publishers 1998

Sparkes, John C. L., *Potters:Their Arts and Crafts*, London 1896

Thorvald Bindesbøll,A Danish Pioneer, Danish Museum of Decorative Art, 1996

Weiss, Peg (ed.), *Adelaide Alsop Robineau: Glory in Porcelain*, New York, 1981

Expressionism, Gauguin, Ohr

Barron, Stephanie, *German Expressionist Sculpture*, Los Angeles County Museum of Art 1983 – includes translation of P. R. Henning's 'Ton – ein Aufruf' (Clay – A Manifesto)

Bodelson, Merlete, 'Gauguin Studies: Some More Gauguin Ceramics', *Burlington Magazine*, April 1967, pp. 217–21

———, *Gauguin's Ceramics:A Study in the Development of his Art*, London 1964

Clark, Garth, Robert A. Ellison and Eugene Hecht, *The Mad Potter of Biloxi: the art and life of George E. Ohr*, New York, 1989

Miesel, Victor H. (ed.), *Voices of German Expressionism*, London, 1970

Fauves

Espagnet, F., 'André Metthey et les Fauves', *Revue de la céramique et du verre*, no. 19 Nov./Dec. 1984

La Céramique Fauve, André Metthey et les Peintres, with introduction by Dominique Forest, Paris 1996

Sarah Whitfield, *Fauvism*, London 1991, reprinted 1996

Art Nouveau

'Art Nouveau' in *Pottery and Porcelain 1700–1914:The Social History of the Decorative Arts*, London, 1978, pp 319–40

Opie, Jennifer Hawkins, 'The New Ceramics: Engaging with the Spirit', in Paul Greenhalgh (ed.), *Art Nouveau 1890–1914*, London: Victoria & Albert Museum, 2000, pp190–207

Escritt, Stephen, *Art Nouveau*, London, 2000

Europäische Keramik des Jugendstils (exh. cat.), Düsseldorf: Hetjens-Museum, 1974

Omega Workshops

Anscombe, Isabelle, *Omega and After: Bloomsbury and the Decorative Arts*, London, 1981

Fry, Roger, 'The Chinese Exhibition', *The Nation*, 23 July, 1910, pp. 593–94

———, 'The Art of Pottery in England', *Burlington Magazine,* no. CXXXI, Vol XXIV, March 1914

Haslam, Malcolm, 'Some Vorticist Pottery', *The Connoisseur*, October 1975, pp. 98–101

Architects and designers

Campbell, Joan, *The German Werkbund:The Politics of Reform in the Applied Arts*, Princeton University Press, 1978

Pevsner, Nikolaus, *Pioneers of Modern Design: From William Morris to Walter Gropius*, Penguin Books, 1975 (revised edition)

Sembach, Klaus-Jürgen, *Henry van de Velde*, New York, 1989

Van Loo, Anne (ed.), *Henri van der Velde, Récit de ma vie, Anvers, Bruxelles, Paris, Berlin, 1863–1900*, VERSA/Flammarion, 1992

Vienna, Czech Cubism

Fahr-Becker, Gabriele, *Wiener Werkstätte*, 1995

Kallir, Jane, *Viennese Design and the Wiener Werkstätte*, London, 1986

Neuwirth, Walter, *Wiener Werkstätte Keramik*, Vienna 1981

———, *Österreichische Keramik des Jugendstils*, Prestel 1975

Schorske, Carl E., *Fin-de-Siècle Vienna Politics and Culture*, New York, 1981

Schweiger, Werner J. (trans. Alexander Lieven), *Wiener Werkstätte: Design in Vienna 1903–1932*, Abbeville Press, New York, 1984

Wegesack, A. von, *Czech Cubism*, London 1992

Chapter 2: 1920–45

General Histories

Kardon, Janet (ed.), *Craft in the Machine Age – the History of 20th Century American Craft 1920–1945*, American Craft Museum, 1995

Rackham, Bernard, and Herbert Read, *English Pottery: Its Development from Early Times to the End of the Eighteenth Century*, Ernest Benn, 1924

Riddick, Sarah, *Pioneer Studio Pottery:The Milner-White Collection*, Lund Humphries, 1990

Soviet Union

Art into Production: Soviet Textiles, Fashion and Ceramics 1917–1935 (exh. cat.), Museum of Modern Art, Oxford, 1984

Golemstock, Igor, *Totalitarian Art in the Soviet Union, the Third Reich, Fascist Italy and the People's Republic of China*, London, 1990

Lobanov-Rostovsky, Nina, *Revolutionary Ceramics Soviet Porcelain 1917–27*, London, 1990

Lodder, C., *Russian Constructivism*, Yale University Press, London 1984

Scandinavia

Gustavberg 150 ar (exh. cat. with English summary), Stockholm National Museum, 1975

Paulsson, Gregor, *Vackrare vardagsvara*, Stockholm, 1919

Wilhelm Kåge, Gustavsberg exhibition catalogue, Stockholm National Museum, 1953

Germany, Bauhaus

Droste, Magdalene, *Bauhaus*, Berlin, 1993

Keramik in der Weimarer Republik 1919–1933, Germanisches National Museum

Marcks, Gerhard, *Briefe und Werke*, Munich 1988

Naylor, G., *The Bauhaus Reassessed*, London, 1985

Reineking von Boch, Gisele, *Meister der Deutschen Keramik 1900–1950*, Cologne 1978

Weber, Klaus, 'Die keramische Werkstatt' in Peter Hahn (ed.), *Experiment Bauhaus*, Bauhaus Archiv, 1988

Modernism
Aynsley, Jeremy, *Nationalism and Internationalism, Design in the 20th Century*, London, 1993
Machine Art (exh. cat.), Museum of Modern Art, New York, 1934
Marcus, George H., *Functionalist Design: An Ongoing History*, Prestel, 1995
Meikle, Jeffrey L., *Twentieth Century Limited: Industrial Design in America 1925–39*, Philadelphia 1979
Read, Herbert, *Art and Industry:The Principles of Industrial Design*, London, 1932
Troy, N., *Modernism and the Decorative Arts in France:Art Nouveau to Le Corbusier*, London 1991

Futurism and Art Deco
Art Deco (exh. cat.), London: Victoria & Albert Museum, 2003
Buckley, Cheryl, *Potters and Paintresses:Women Designers in the Pottery Industry 1870–1955*, London, 1990
Casey, Andrew, and Ann Eatwell (eds), *Susie Cooper:A Pioneer of Modern Design*, London 2002
Davies, Karen, *At Home in Manhattan: Modern Decorative Arts 1925 to the Depression*, New Haven, 1983
Duncan, Alastair, *American Art Deco*, New York 1986
La Ceramica Futurista da Balla a Tullio D'Albisola, Centro di Firenze, 1982
McCready, Karen, *Art Deco and Modernist Ceramics*, London, 1995

Bernard Leach
Cooper, Emmanuel, *Bernard Leach: Life and Work*, Yale University Press, 2003
de Waal, Edmund, *Bernard Leach*, London, 2001
Bernard Leach, *A Review 1909–14*, Tokyo 1914
———, *A Potter's Outlook*, Handworker's Pamphlet no. 3, New Handworkers' Gallery, 1928
———, *A Potter's Book*, London, 1940
———, *A Potter in Japan 1952–1954*, London, 1960
Yanagi, Soetsu, *The Unknown Craftsman: A Japanese Insight into Beauty*, Kodansha International Ltd, 1972

Shoji Hamada
Leach, Bernard, *Hamada Potter*, Kodansha International Ltd, 1975
Peterson, Susan, *Shoji Hamada:A Potter's Way and Work*, Kodansha International Ltd, 1974
Wilcox, Timothy, *Shoji Hamada: Master Potter*, Lund Humphries, London,1998
The English Arts and Crafts Movement and Hamada Shoji (exh. cat.), Mashiko Ceramic Art Centre, 1998

Kenkichi Tomimoto
Hinton-Braaten, Kathleen, 'Kawai Kanjiro', *Orientations*, 14 no 211, Nov. 1983, pp. 28–41
Mitsuhiko, Hasebe, 'The Ceramic Art of Tomimoto Kenkichi: The Primacy of Pattern', in *Tomimoto Kenkichi* (exh. cat.), Crafts Gallery, The National Museum of Modern Art, Tokyo 1991

UK
Cardew, Michael, *A Pioneer Potter: an Autobiography*, London, 1988
———, *Pioneer Pottery*, London, 1969
Clark, Garth, *Michael Cardew: a Portrait*, London, 1978
Haslam, Malcolm, *William Staite Murray*, London, 1984
Rice, Paul, *Sam Haile: Potter and Painter*, London, 1993
Staite Murray, William, 'Pottery from the Artist's Point of View', *Artwork* vol. 1 no. 4 May–August 1925, pp. 201–5
T. S. Haile Memorial Exhibition, Craft Centre of Great Britain, 1951
Thorpe, W. A., 'English Stoneware Pottery by Miss K. Pleydell-Bouverie and Miss D. K. N. Braden', *Artwork*, VI, 1930, pp. 257–65

USA
Charles Vyse (exh. cat.), Richard Dennis and The Fine Arts Society, London 1974
Cowan, R. Guy, 'The Fine Art of Ceramics as Exemplified in the 1936 Exhibition of Ceramic Art at the Syracuse Museum', *Design* 38, Nov. 1936, pp. 3–7
Hennessey, William J., *Russel Wright, American Designer*, Cambridge MA, 1985
Levin, Elaine, 'Glen Lukens, Pioneer of the Vessel Aesthetic', *American Ceramics*, vol. 1 no. 2, Spring 1982, pp. 40–43
Peterson, Susan, *The Living Tradition of Maria Martinez*, New York 1978
Stubblebine, James, and Martin Eidelberg, 'Viktor Schreckengost and the Cleveland School', *Craft Horizons*, June 1975 vol. xxxv no. 3, pp. 34–35, 52–53
'Vally Wieselthier', *Ceramics Design* 31 November 1929, pp. 101–2
Wright, Mary, *Guide to Easier Living*, New York 1951

Chapter 3: 1945–65

Japan
Kaneko, Kenji, 'Craft Art of the Modern Art Association' in *Forms in Aggression: Formative Uprising of the 1960s* (exh. cat.), National Museum of Modern Art, Tokyo 1987
Kimura, Shigenobu, 'Kazuo Yagi's View of Ceramics' in *Kazuo Yagi* (exh. cat.), Kyoto: National Museum of Modern Art, 1981
Munroe, Alexandra, *Scream against the Sky: Japanese Art after 1945*, New York 1994
Yoshiaki, Inui, et al, *Yagi Kazuo sakuhinshu* (catalogue of Yagi Kazuo works), Tokyo 1980

Isamu Noguchi
Apostolos-Capadona, Diane, and Bruce Altschuler (eds), *Isamu Noguchi: Essays and Conversations*, New York, 1994
Cardozo, Sidney B., and Masaaki Hirano, *Uncommon Clay:The Life and Pottery of Rosanjin*, Kodansha International Ltd, 1987
Cort, Louise Allison, and Bert Winther-Tamaki, *Isamu Noguchi and Modern Japanese Ceramics:A Close Embrace of the Earth*, Washington, 2003
Grove, Nancy, *Isamu Noguchi:A Study of the Sculpture*, Garland, 1985
Isamu Noguchi to Kitaoji Rosanjin, (exh. cat.), Tokyo 1996
Noguchi, Isamu, 'Meanings in Modern Sculpture', *Artnews* 48 (March), pp. 12–15, 55–56
Winther-Tamaki, Bert, *Art in the Encounter of Nations: Japanese and American Artists in the Early Postwar Years*, Hawaii USA, 2001

Axel Salto
Axel Salto's Keramik, Copenhagen 1930
Det braenende nu, Axel Salto (exh. cat.), Copenhagen: Kunstindustrimuset, 1989
Salto, Axel, 'The Sprouting Style' in *Forces of Nature:Axel Salto*, New York, 1999 pp. 3–6

Hans Coper, Lucie Rie
Birks, Tony, *Hans Coper*, London: Sainsbury Centre for Visual Arts, 1983
———, *Lucie Rie*, London, 1987
Coatts, Margot, *Lucie Rie and Hans Coper – Potters in Parallel* (exh. cat.), London, 1997
de Waal, Edmund, 'Modern Things: Lucie Rie and Vienna' in Emmanuel Cooper (ed.), *Lucie Rie*, London 2002, pp. 14–21
Houston, John (ed.), *Lucie Rie*, London, 1981
'Lucie Rie and Hans Coper' in Muriel Rose, *Artist Potters in England*, London 1955, pp. 24–25
Serene Beauty/Lucie Rie (exh. cat.), Shigaraki Ceramic Cultural Park, 2002

Pablo Picasso
Arneson, Robert, 'Picasso the Craftsman', *Craft Horizons*, Nov./Dec. 1967, vol. xxvii no. 6 pp. 28–33
Bemrose, G. J. V., 'Picasso and the Five Towns', *Pottery and Glass*, December 1950, pp. 61–63
Cassou, Jean, 'Les Poteries de Picasso', *Art et Décoration*, vol. 9, 1948, pp. 13–21
Champignuelle, Bernard, 'Picasso poteries nouvelles', *Art et Décoration*, vol. 69, 1958
Golding, John, 'Review of Picasso and ceramics', *Burlington Magazine*, December 1998, pp. 828–29
Harrod, Tanya, 'Picasso's Ceramics', *Apollo* vol. cxxix no. 327, May 1989, pp. 337–41
McCully, Marilyn (ed.), *Picasso, Painter and Sculptor in Clay*, Royal Academy of Arts, London 1998
Ramies, Georges, *Picasso's Ceramics*, Chartwell Books Inc., 1974

Joan Miró, Lucio Fontana, CoBrA
Corredor-Matheos, J., 'Miró-Artigas ceramic in Miró 's oeuvre' in *Miró Ceramista* (exh. cat.), Palacio de la Virreina, Barcelona, 1993, pp. 17–25
Lettere di Lucio Fontana a Tullio d'Albisola (1936–1962), Editrice Liguria, Savona, 1987
McPherson, Anne (ed.), *Miró – Playing with Fire* (exh. cat.), Montreal, 2000
Stokvis, Willemijn, *Alles van waarde is weerloos – everything valuable is defenceless: Ceramic Work by CoBrA Members*, Den Haag, 1993.
Whitfield, Sarah, *Lucio Fontana* (exh. cat.), London: Hayward Gallery, 1999

Postwar Europe and America
Bischofberger, Bruno, *Ettore Sottsass – Ceramics*, Chronicle Books, San Francisco, 1996
Fare, Michel, *Georges Jouve – Céramiste*, Paris, 1965
Heron, Patrick, 'Submerged Rhythm: A Potter's Aesthetic' in *The Changing Forms of Art*, London 1955, pp. 52–65

Jackson, Lesley, *Contemporary:Architecture and Interiors of the 1950s*, London 1994
Leach, Bernard, 'American Impressions', *Craft Horizons* 10, Winter 1950, pp. 18–20
McClaren, Graham, *Ceramics of the 1950s*, London, 1999
Parker-Fairbanks, Dixie, and Helen Abbott (eds), *Essential Passions: Fairbanks–Salmenhaara Letters 1959–1986*, University of Washington Press, 1999
The Ceramic Work of Gertrud and Otto Natzler (exh. cat.), San Francisco: M. H. de Young Memorial Museum, 1971
Schlanger, Jeff, 'Maija Grotell', *Craft Horizons* Nov./Dec. 1969, vol. xxix no. 6, pp. 14–23
Wingfield Digby, George, *The Work of the Modern Potter in England*, London 1952

Marguerite Wildenhain
Marguerite Wildenhain, 'An Open Letter to Bernard Leach from Marguerite Wildenhain', *Craft Horizons* 13, May/June 1953
———, *Pottery: Form and Expression*, American Craftsmen's Council and Rheinhols Corp., New York 1959
———, *Invisible Core:A Potter's Life and Thoughts*, Pacific Books, Palo Alto, 1973

Chapter 4: 1965–2000

USA
Held, Peter (ed.), *A Ceramic Continuum: Fifty Years of the Archie Bray Influence*, Washington, 2001
Lauria, Jo, *Color and Fire: Defining Moments in Studio Ceramics, 1950–2000*, Los Angeles, 2000
MacNaughton, Mary Davis (ed.), *Revolution in Clay,The Marer Collection of Contemporary Ceramics* (exh. cat.), California, 1994
Nordness, Lee, *Objects: USA*, London, 1970

Peter Voulkos, John Mason, Paul Soldner
Frimkess, Michael, 'The Importance of Being Classical', *Craft Horizons* 36, March 1986
Krauss, Rosalind, 'John Mason and Post-Modernist Sculpture: New Experiences, New Words', *Art in America*, May/June 1979, pp. 120–27
John Mason: Sculpture (exh. cat.), with introduction by John Coplans, Los Angeles, 1966
John Mason: Ceramic Sculpture (exh. cat.), with essay by Barbara Haskell, Pasadena, 1974
MacNaughton, Mary Davis and Elaine Levin, *Paul Soldner:A Retrospective*, Washington, 1990
Melchert, Jim, 'Peter Voulkos: A Return to Pottery', *Craft Horizons* 28, Sep./Oct. 1968, pp. 20–21
Peter Voulkos: Sculpture (exh. cat.), Los Angeles, 1965
Pyron, Bernard, 'The Tao and Dada of Recent American Ceramic Art', *Art Forum*, vol. 11 no. 9, March 1964, pp. 41–43
Slivka, Rose, 'The New Ceramic Presence', *Craft Horizons*, vol. XXI, July/August 1961, pp. 31–37
———, *Peter Voulkos:A Dialogue with Clay*, 1978
Coplans, John, *Abstract Expressionist Ceramics*, Irvine, 1966
———, 'Out of Clay: West Coast ceramic sculpture emerges as a strong regional trend', *Art in America*, no. 6, 1963, pp. 40–43.

Soldner, Paul, 'Raku as I Know It', *Ceramic Review*, April 1973

Pop and Funk
Bonansinga, Kate, 'Modern Context: Four Sculptures by Ken Price', *Ceramics Art and Perception* 47, 2002, pp. 44–46
Funk (exh. cat), Berkeley, California: University Art Museum, 1967
Kenneth Price: Happy Curios, with introduction by Maurice Tuchman, Los Angeles County Museum of Art, 1978
Lippard, Lucy, 'Robert Irwin/Kenneth Price', Los Angeles County Museum of Art, 1966
Noah, Barbara, 'Lichenstein's Ceramics', *Artweek* 8 no. 11, March 1977, pp. 5–6
Silberman, Robert, 'Ken Price in Retrospect', *American Craft* 52, August/September 1992, pp. 44–49

Japan
Faulkner, Rupert, *Japanese Studio Crafts:Tradition and the Avant-Garde*, London, 1995
Moeran, Brian, 'A Survey of Modern Japanese Pottery' (in 4 parts), *Ceramics Monthly* vol. 30, no. 8,October 1982, pp. 30–32; vol. 30, no. 9, November 1982, pp. 44–46; vol. 30 no. 10, December 1982, pp. 32–34; vol. 31, no. 1, January 1983, pp. 54–57

Scandinavia
Tarlow Kaplan, Wendy, and Hope Barkan, *From the Kilns of Denmark: Contemporary Danish Ceramics*, Copenhagen, 2002
Zahle, Erik (ed.), *Scandinavian Domestic Design*, London, 1963

UK
Birks, Tony, *The Art of the Modern Potter*, London, 1967
Dormer, Peter, *The New Ceramics*, London, 1986

Australia and New Zealand
Ioannou, Noris, *Ceramics in South Australia 1836–1986: From Folk to Studio Pottery*, Adelaide, 1986
Mansfield, Janet, *Contemporary Ceramics in Australia and New Zealand*, Craftsman House, 1993
———, 'Plurality and Necessity: An Antipodean Case Study' in Paul Greenhalgh (ed.), *The Persistence of Craft*, London 2002

Figuration
Confrontational Clay: the Artist as Social Critic (exh. cat.), Judith S. Schwartz, Exhibits USA, 2000
'Cracks in the Sidewalk: A Chronological Study of the Art and World of Viola Frey' in *Viola Frey Retrospective* (exh. cat.), Sacramento, 1981
de Waal, Edmund, 'Christie Brown: Fragments of Narrative', *Ceramics Art and Perception* 46 2001, pp. 67–71
Flynn, Michael, *Ceramic Figures:A Directory of Artists*, London 2002
Foley, Suzanne, 'Robert Arneson II', in *Robert Arneson* (exh. cat.), Chicago, 1974
Sims, Patterson, 'Viola Frey' in *Viola Frey* (exh. cat.), New York: Whitney Museum of American Art, 1984
The Clay Figure (exh. cat.), New York: American Craft Museum, 1981

Installation
Kastner, Jeffrey and Brian Wallis (eds), *Land and Environmental Art*, London 1998
Putnam, James, *Art and Artefact:The Museum as Medium*, London 2001
Sonfist, Alan (ed.), *Art in the Land:A Critical Anthology*, New York 1983

Postmodernism
Dejonghe, Bernard, *Ceramics Today*, Geneva, 1983
———, *Dialogues Céramiques*, Musée d'Art Contemporain, Dunkerque, 1997
Devore, Richard, 'Ceramics of Betty Woodman', *Craft Horizons* 38, February 1978, pp. 28–31, 66–67
Drexler Lynn, Martha, *The Clay Art of Adrian Saxe*, Los Angeles County Museum of Art, 1993
Geert Lap:The Thrown Form (exh. cat), Rotterdam: Museum Boijmans Van Beuningen, 1988
Guerilla Tactics: Grayson Perry (exh. cat.), essays by Marjan Boot, Louise Buck and Andrew Wilson, Amsterdam: Stedelijk Museum, 2002
Martin Smith: Balance and Space, Ceramics 1976–1996 (exh. cat.), Rotterdam: Museum Boijmans Van Beuningen, 1996
New Tokyo Ceramics: Kimpei Nakamura (exh. cat.), Ishikawa Prefectural Museum, 1993
Peterson, Susan, *Pottery by American Indian Women – The Legacy of Generations*, The National Museum of Women Artists, New York, 1997
———, *Jun Kaneko*, London, 2001
Princethal, Nancy, *Betty Woodman*, New York 2002
Puype, Karel, *Piet Stockmans*, 2002
Rosaline Delisle (exh. cat.), Frank Lloyd Gallery, Santa Monica, California 1999
Ryoji Koie, *Ceramics Today* no. 6, International Academy of Ceramics, Geneva 1984
Shin Sang-ho: Dream of Africa 1996–2002, Seoul, 2002
Smith, Martin, *Wavelength*, Tate St Ives, 2001
Woodman, Betty, 'The Italian Experience', *Studio Potter* 11, June 1983

Contemporary Painters/Sculptors
'Caro and Clay: Retained Innocence' in *Anthony Caro: Ceramic Sculpture*, New York: Garth Clark Gallery, 1999
Gormley, Antony, *Field* (exh. cat.), London: British Museum, 2002
Hughto, Margie, *New Works in Clay by Contemporary Painters and Sculptors*, Syracuse, NY: Everson Museum of Art, 1976
Hans Spinner, (exh. cat.), New York: Garth Clark Gallery, 2002
Koplos, Janet, 'From Picasso to Penck: Playing with Clay' in *The Unexpected:Artists' Ceramics of the 20th Century*, s'Hertogenbosch, 1998

Critical Commentary
Clark, Garth, *Ceramic Art: Comment and Review 1882-1978*, New York 1978
Greenberg, Clement, 'The Status of Clay', in Garth Clark (ed.), *Transactions of the Ceramics Symposium 1979*, Los Angeles 1980

Hepburn, Tony, 'Ceramic and Sculpture' in *To Measure the Unmeasurable World*, International Ceramic Symposium, Ceramic Exposition, Korea, 2001 pp. 138–45
Higby, Wayne, 'The Vessel: Overcoming the Tyranny of Modern Art', NCECA Journal 3, no. 11, 1982, pp. 11–12
Houston, John (ed.), *Craft Classics Since the 1940s*, London 1988
———, *The Abstract Vessel: Ceramics in Studio*, London 1991
Kuchta, Ronald, 'Major Themes in Contemporary Ceramic Art' in Paul Greenhalgh (ed.), *The Persistence of Craft*, A&C Black and Rutgers University Press, 2003
Morgan, Robert C. (ed.), *Clement Greenberg: Late Writings and Interviews*, New York 2003
Nakamura, Kimpei, 'Ceramics: Transcending Fine Art with the Fascination of Compositeness and Ambiguity' in *To Measure the Unmeasurable World*, International Ceramic Symposium, Ceramic Exposition, Korea, 2001 pp. 156–63
Rawson, Philip, *Ceramics – The Appreciation of the Arts*, London, 1971
———, 'Empty Vessels' and Martina Margetts, 'The Potted Word' both in *Fast Forward: New Directions in British Ceramics*, ICA, London 1985
Vincentelli, Moira, *Women and Ceramics: Gendered Vessels*, Manchester 2000

Journals
USA: *American Ceramics*, *Ceramics Monthly*, *American Craft* (formerly *Craft Horizons*)
UK: *Ceramic Review*, *Crafts*, *Journal of Design History*
Germany: *Keramik Magazin*, *Neue Keramik*
Scandinavia: *Kunsthandwerk*, *Scandinavian Journal Of Design History*
France: *Revue de la Céramique et du Verre*
Greece: *Kerameiki techni*
Australia: *Ceramics:Art and Perception*, *Craft Australia*
Korea: *Art & Crafts*

List of Illustrations

Measurements are given in centimetres (inches in brackets); h. = height, d. = diameter. Other measurements are given in the following order: height × width × depth.

1 Yagi Kazuo, *Zamsa no sampo* (The Walk of Samsa), 1954. Stoneware, 27.5 × 27 × 14 (10 ⅞ × 10 ⅝ × 5 ½). National Museum of Modern Art, Kyoto
2 Shoji Hamada, Large Dish, 1962. *Kaki* (persimmon) trailing over tenmoku, d. 53.6 (21 ⅛) Private collection
3 Photograph of cases of Japanese pottery in the Boston Museum, *c.* 1900, Museum of Fine Arts, Boston
4 Léon Rigolet, *Aquatic Double-Gourd Vase*, 1900–11. Porcelain for Sèvres, h. 25.5 (10). Courtesy of Sotheby's, London
5 Photograph of the Ruskin Trade Stand, 1908. *Pottery Gazette*, December 1908
6 Cartoon from Milner White album no. II, *c.* 1936. York City Art Gallery
7 Maurice Biais, *La Maison Moderne*, *c.* 1900. Lithograph, 114 × 78.5 (44 ⅞ × 30 ⅞). Union Centrale des Arts Décoratifs, Paris
8 Taxile Doat, Vase, 1900. Porcelain, h. 20 (8). Danish Museum of Decorative Art, Copenhagen. Photo Ole Woldbye
9 Photograph of Taxile Doat working at the School of Ceramic Art, St. Louis. *c.* 1910. University City Public Library, Missouri
10 Photograph of Adelaide Alsop Robineau at work on the *Scarab vase* at People's University in Saint Louis, 1910. University City Public Library, Missouri
11 Adelaide Alsop Robineau, *Apotheosis of the Toiler (Scarab vase)*, 1910. Porcelain, 42.2 × 15.2 (16 ⅝ × 6). Everson Museum of Art, Syracuse
12 Ernest Chaplet, *Dish*, *c.* 1900. Porcelain copper red glaze. Musée National de Céramique, Sèvres
13 Emile Decoeur, Vase, early 20th century. Stoneware. Musée National de Céramique, Sèvres
14 Drawing of raku teabowl from *Japanese Pottery* edited by A. W. Francks, London 1880
15 Thorvald Bindesbøll, Dish, 1901. Glazed earthenware, made at G. Eifrig's workshop, Valby, d. 44.5 (17 ½). Danish Museum of Decorative Art, Copenhagen
16 Thorvald Bindesbøll, Vase, 1906. Glazed earthenware, made at G. Eifrig's workshop, Valby, 30.8 (12 ⅛). Museum at Koldinghus, Kolding
17 Rozenburg, Vase, 1903. Faience, 32 (12 ⅝). Sammlung Brohan, Berlin
18 Ruth Erikson Grueby, Boston Vase, *c.* 1900. Earthenware, 42.5 (16 ¾). Cooper-Hewitt National Design Museum, Smithsonian Institute, New York
19 Louis Comfort Tiffany, Tiffany Studios Vase, 1904–10. Glazed ceramic, h. 25 (9 ¾). Metropolitan Museum of Art, New York
20 Artus Van Briggle, *Lorelei Vase*, *c.* 1901. Earthenware, 26.7 (10 ½). Everson Museum of Art, Syracuse
21 The Martin brothers, vases, 1897–1914. Photo collection of Martin Dennis
22 Photograph of the Martin brothers, 1912. Southall Public Library, London
23 Photograph of George Ohr from 'High Art at Biloxi, Mass.', *New York Sun*, 22 December, 1898
24 George Ohr, Pitcher, 1895–1900. 12.7(5). Private collection, New York
25 Paul Gauguin, *Double vessel with Breton girl*, 1886–87. Stoneware, h. 13 (5 ⅛). Collection Jacques Ulmann, Paris
26 Ernst Barlach, Double-handled vase, *c.* 1905. 42 (16 ½). Stiftung Schleswig-Holsteinische Landesmuseen, Schloss Gottorf, Schleswig © Ernst und Hans Barlach Lizenzverwaltung Ratxburg
27 Emil Nolde, tile, 1913. Ceramic, cut relief, painted and colourless glazed lead, in a pottery in Flensburg, 29 × 33 (11 ⅜ × 13). Staatliche Galerie Moritzburg Halle, Landeskunstmuseum Sachsen. Photo Ilona Ripke, Berlin © Nolde-Stiftung Seebüll
28 André Metthey, Preparatory sketches, *c.* 1910–11. Cut paper. Collection particulière, Meudon
29 André Metthey, Plate with striped edges, *c.* 1908. Glazed earthenware, d. 21 (8 ¼). Musée du Petit Palais, Ville de Paris
30 Maurice de Vlaminck, *Feuilles Bleues*, *c.* 1907–9. Faience enamel containing tin, 28 (11). Galerie Larock-Granoff, Paris. © ADAGP, Paris and DACS, London 2003
31 André Derain, *Danseuses*, *c.* 1907. Faience enamel containing tin. 19 (7 ½) Galerie Larock-Granoff, Paris. © ADAGP, Paris and DACS, London 2003
32 Roger Fry, Collection of domestic ware, 1914. Buff coloured earthenware, white tin glaze, cream jug 9.5 (3 ¾), cup and saucer 7 (2 ¾), tall sugar pot 9.8 (4 ⅞), tureen and lid 17 (6 ¾). Victoria & Albert Museum, London
33 Cover of Catalogue Iris AB, *c.*1901. Issued by Porvoo Museum, Finland, 1979
34 Alfred W. Finch, dish, d. 34.7 (13 ½) and mug, h. 9.5 (3 ¾), *c.* 1897–1900. Earthenware with incised decoration, coloured slip. Victoria & Albert Museum, London
35 Reginald Wells, bowl, d. 14.9 (5 ¾), and jug, h. 17.5 (6 ¾), *c.* 1909. Given by W. Ridout, Victoria & Albert Museum. London
36 Henry van de Velde, Meissen porcelain, 1903. © Design Museum, Ghent
37 Richard Riemerschmid, tankard, 14 × 15 (5 ½ × 5 ⅞), and jug, 15.1 × 15 (6 × 5 ⅞), 1902. Stoneware, salt-glazed with enamel. Victoria & Albert Museum, London. Richard Riemerschmid © DACS 2003. Peter Behrens, jug, 32.3 × 17.6 (12 ¾ × 6 ⅞), 1903. Stoneware salt-glazed and with enamel. Victoria & Albert Museum, London. Peter Behrens © DACS 2003
38 Josef Hoffmann, design for ceramics in house. © Josef Hoffmann Stiftung
39 Carl Moll, *Breakfast*, *c.* 1903. Oil on canvas, 153.6 × 153.6 (60 ½ × 60 ½). Barry Friedman Limited, New York
40 Jutta Sika, *Mocha Service*, *c.* 1901. Glazed porcelain plate, 3.3. × 24.9 × 24.9 (1 ¼ × 9 ¾ × 9 ¾). Schule Prof. Kolo Moser, Vienna. Gift of Mr and Mrs Roger Labbé
41 Josef Hoffmann, Cabaret Fledermaus: view of foyer and bar, 1907. © Josef Hoffmann Stiftung
42 Michael Powolny, *Autumn and Spring Putti*, 1910. Stoneware made by Wiener Keramik. Photo Gabriele Fahr-Becker

43 Pavel Janák, collection of vases. SUPPOP Archive, Stenc Collection, Prague © Prof. Z. Maratka
44 Vlastislav Hofman, *Ashtray*, 1912. Earthenware, black and white glaze, 4 (1 ⅝). Museum of Decorative Arts, Prague
45 Natalya Y. Danko, *At Work: Self Portrait*, mid-1920s. Russian Museum, St Petersburg
46 Mikhail M. Adamovich, *He who does not work does not eat*, plate, 1921. Porcelain, d. 25 (9 ⅞). The Wolfsonian-Florida International University, Miami
47 Alexandra V. Shchekotikhina-Potoskaya, *The Sailor Takes a Walk*, 1921. Porcelain, d. 34.5 (13 ⅝)
48 Kazimir Malevich, *Suprematist Teapot*, 1923. Earthenware, 16.5 (6 ½). Lomonosov Porcelain Factory
49 Kurt Ekholm, *Sinivalko* (Blue ribbon). Tableware for Arabia. Museum of Art and Design, Helsinki. Photo Timo/Kauppila/Indar
50 Photograph of ceramics from Gustavsberg displayed at the Liljevalchs Art Gallery, Stockholm, 1917, including the *Liljeblå* service by Wilhelm Kåge. Nationalmuseum, Stockholm
51 Wilhem Kåge, *Liljeblå* (Blue Lily), 1917. Dinner service for Gustavsberg. Nationalmuseum, Stockholm. © DACS 2003
52 Ewald Dahlskog, *Vases*, *c.* 1930. Earthenware for Bobergs Fajanfabrik. Christie's Images, London
53 Theodor Bogler, *Combination Teapot with Eccentric Lid*, 1923. 12.7 (5) © Kunstverlag Maria Laach, Germany
54 Theodor Bogler, photo of plaster model of variants of combination teapot, 1923. Bauhaus-Archiv, Berlin. © Kunstverlag Maria Laach, Germany
55 Lucia Moholy, Otto Lindig, Theodor Bogler and Marguerite Friedlander-Wildenhain ceramics, 1923. Photograph, 18.5 × 13.3 (7 ¼ × 5 ¼). Bauhaus-Archiv, Berlin. © DACS 2003
56 Otto Lindig, *Tall Lidded Pot*, 1922. 59 (23 ¼). Kunstsammlungen zu Weimar, Germany. Photo Lepkowski
57 Photograph of Lily Reich's 'Bright Earth, Fired earth' installation at *Deutsches Volk–Deutsche Arbeit* exhibition Berlin, 1934
58 Photograph of capsules used for drying or incinerating chemicals, Coors Porcelain Co. Eimer & Amend. © Museum of Modern Art, New York
59 Josef Hoffmann, design for a coffee-pot, *c.* 1925–28. Österreichisches Museum für Angewandte Kunst, Vienna. © Josef Hoffmann Stiftung
60 Josef Hoffmann, photograph of view of glazed kitchen cupboards, Sonja Knips House, Vienna, 1924–25. Torsten Brohan Collection, Düsseldorf. Photo Angela Brohan, Munich. © Josef Hoffmann Stiftung
61 Photograph of Farfa, Tullio d'Albisola and Marinetti at Galleria Pesaro, Milano, October 1930. © Collezione Esa Mazzotti, Albisola Marina
62 Luigi Colombo (Fillia), *Aerovaso*, 1932. Majolica, 25x 25 (9 ⅞ × 9 ⅞). © Collezione Perseo Vasari, Messina
63 R. A. Bertelli, *Head of Mussolini*, 1933. Imperial War Museum, London
64 Farfa and Tullio d'Albisola, *Vaso Formichiere* (anteater vase), 1931–32. Terracotta, 26 × 21 × 20.5 (10 ¼ × 8 ¼ × 8 ⅛). © Collezione Esa Mazzotti, Albissola Marina
65 Susie Cooper advertisement, 1930s. *Pottery Gazette and Glass Trade Review*
66 Russel Wright, *American Modern Dinnerware*, designed 1937, introduced 1939. Earthenware for Steubenville Pottery Company, pitcher 27 × 6.8 × 20.5 (10 ⅝ × 2 ⅝ × 8 ⅛), teapot with lid 11.7 × 17.2 × 25.4 (4 ⅝ × 6 ¾ × 10), covered casserole 8.2 × 30.5 × 23.5 (3 ¼ × 12 × 9 ¼). Collection William Straus, USA
67 Viktor Schreckengost, *Jazz Bowl*, 1931. Earthenware, 28.8 × 41.5 × 41.5 (11 ⅜ × 16 ⅜ × 16 ⅜). Courtesy of the Cowan Pottery Museum, Rocky River Public Library, Rocky River, Ohio
68 Vally Wieselthier (left), *Wiener Werkstätte Vase*, 1920–25. Glazed earthenware, 39.4(15 ½). Gudrun Baudisch (right), *Wiener Werkstätte Vase* 25.4 (10). Glazed earthenware. Private collection, New York
69 Waylande Gregory, *Woman's Head*, 1933. White glazed ceramic, 61 × 24.7 × 30.5 (24 × 9 ¾ × 12). Everson Museum of Art, Syracuse
70 Gudrun Baudisch, *Head of a Girl*, 1927. Stoneware. Galerie bei der Albertina, Vienna
71 Waylande Gregory, model for *War*, one of six symbolic figures for fountain *Light Dispelling Darkness*, 1937. Terracotta, 78.7 × 122 × 66 (31 × 48 × 26). WPA Project. Roosevelt Park, Edison, New Jersey
72 Viktor Schreckengost, *Apocalypse*, 1942. Earthenware, 40 × 21.7 × 22.5 (15 ⅜ × 20 ⅜ × 8 ⅞). National Museum of American Art, Smithsonian Institution, Washington, D.C. Gift of the Artist
73 Photograph of Vally Wieselthier alongside one of her garden figures, *c.* 1929
74 Photograph *of* treadle wheel with sewing machine base used at the University of Southern California, 1930s/40s. Collection Mrs Boyd O'Dell
75 Denise Wren, drawing of coil pottery produced by students, 1920s
76 Photograph of Bernard Leach, David Leach and Shoji Hamada learning how to pull a handle at Lakes Pottery, Truro, 1923. © David Leach
77 Handbill advertisement for Leach pottery showing large slipware plate, *c.* 1924. Craft Study Centre at the Surrey Institute of Art and Design, Farnham
78 Bernard Leach, *Globular Pot*, 1927. Stoneware, 14.5 × 14.5 (5 ¾ × 5 ¾) Collection of Wingfield-Digbys
79 Bernard Leach, Teapot, 1930. Stoneware, h. 12 (4 ¾). Private collection
80 Norah Braden, Vase, 1932. Stoneware, 16.2 (6 ⅜). Courtesy of Bonham's Auctioneers, London
81 Katherine Pleydell-Bouverie, *Small Bowl*, 1936. Stoneware. Craft Study Centre at the Surrey Institute of Art and Design, Farnham
82 Shoji Hamada, *Bowl*, 1923. Stoneware blue glaze and inlaid floral design in white clay, 12 × 19.5 (4 ¾ × 7 ⅝). University of Wales, Aberystwyth
83 Shoji Hamada, *Bottle*, *c.* 1929. Stoneware tenmoku glaze with trailed slip decoration, 35.5 × 16.5 (14 × 6 ½). The Dartington Hall Trust
84 Tomimoto Kenkichi, *Jar*, 1925. Porcelain, 24.5 × 24.2 (9 ⅝ × 9 ½). Tomimoto Kenkichi Memorial Museum, Japan
85 Michael Cardew, *Bird Dish*, 1932. Earthenware, d. 30.2 (11 ⅞). Courtesy Bonhams Auctioneers, London
86 Photograph of William Staite Murray decorating at Bray, *c.* 1930. Pitshanger Manor Gallery and House, London
87 William Staite Murray, *Persian Garden Jar*, 1931. Stoneware, 56.5 × 30.5 (22 ¼ × 12). York City Art Gallery
88 Sam Haile, *Triumphal Procession*, 1937. Stoneware with black, blue and red brushstrokes, 42 (16 ½). Southampton Art Gallery, Civic Centre, Southampton
89 Hubert Griemert, Vase Prize for Olympic Games Berlin, 1936. Stoneware, 60 (23 ⅝). Staatliche Galerie Moritzburg Halle, Landeskunstmuseum Sachsen-Anhalt
90 Arthur E. Baggs, *Cookie Jar*, 1938. Salt glazed stoneware, 33.3 (13 ⅛) Everson Museum of Art, Syracuse
91 Maria and Julian Martinez, *Cartier Jar*, 1935. Black on black, 38 × 47 (15 × 18 ½). Collection of Lucille and Marsh Miller, Photo Tim Thayer
92 Glen Lukens, *Death Valley Plate*, 1941. Earthenware, 8.1 × 47.7 (3 ¼ ×18 ¾). Everson Museum of Art, Syracuse, Gift of IBM Corporation
93 Yagi Kazuo, *Zamsa no sampo* (The Walk of Samsa), 1954. Stoneware, 27.5 × 27 × 14 (10 ⅞ × 10 ⅝ × 5 ½). National Museum of Modern Art, Kyoto
94 Photograph of Yagi Kazuo, 1969. Courtesy of Akira Yagi
95 Yagi Kazuo, *Portrait (Shozo)*, 1964. Kokuto pottery, 15 × 19 (5 ⅞ × 7 ½). Private collection
96 Junpie Sugie, *Action*, 1965. Clay/coil building, 43 × 70 × 49 (16 ⅞ × 27 ½ × 19 ¼). Collection of the artist
97 Junkichi Kumakura, *Frozen Flames*, 1956. Earthenware, 81.5 × 25 (32 ⅛ × 9 ⅞). Collection of the artist
98 Isamu Noguchi, *Mrs White*, 1952. Shigaraki ceramic on wooden stand, 100.7 × 24.1 × 22.2 (42 ¼ × 9 ½ × 8 ⅞). Published with written permission of The Isamu Noguchi Foundation, Inc., New York. Photo Domon Ken
99 Photograph of Isamu Noguchi earthen wall in studio of Noguchi/Yamaguchi, 1951–52. Published with written permission of The Isamu Noguchi Foundation, Inc., New York
100 Kyllikki Salmenhaara, *Pot*, 1958. Stoneware for Arabia, 43 (16 ⅞). Design Museum Finland, Helsinki. Photo Rauno Tråskelin
101 Axel Salto, *Jar*, 1943. Stoneware with solfatara glaze for Royal Copenhagen. Archiv Torsten, Brohan ©DACS 2003
102 Axel Salto, *Interior Strength*, 1956. Stoneware tenmoku, 127 (50). © DACS 2003. Christie's Images, London
103 Photograph of Hans Coper in his Digswell workshop. Archive of Jane Coper
104 Hans Coper, *Jug with sgraffito design*, 1951. Stoneware, 35 (13 ¾). Crafts Council, London. Photo David Cripps
105 Hans Coper, *Spade Form On Cylindric Base*, 1966–68. Stoneware, 23 × 12.4 (9 × 4 ⅞). Private collection
106 Ettore Sottsass, *Designs for Rocchetti*, 1956–59

107 Gordon Baldwin, *Standing Form*, 1961. Multifired stoneware, 61 (24). Paisley Museum and Art Gallery. Photograph David Cripps
108 Beate Kuhn, *Vertebral Column*, 1973. Stoneware, 46 × 10.3 (18 ⅛ × 4 ⅛). Private collection
109 Ruth Duckworth, *Porcelain Forms*, 1967. Porcelain, 15.2 × 20.3 × 33 (6 × 8 × 13). Private collection
110 Pablo Picasso, *Condor*, 1947. Musée Picasso, Antibes. © Succession Picasso/DACS 2003
111 Photograph of Pablo Picasso and Jules Agard at Madoura, 1947. Archives Musée Picasso, Antibes
112 Pablo Picasso, *Head*, 1948. 30 (11 ¾) © Succession Picasso/DACS 2003
113 Joan Miró and Josep Lloréns Artigas, *Green Plate*, 1956. Stoneware d. 37 (14 ⅝). Collection Mme Sylvie Baltazart-Eon, Paris. © Succession Miró, DACS 2003
114 Josep Lloréns Artigas, *Clair de Lune Pot*, 1927. Stoneware, 25.5 × 2 × 11 (10 × 1 ¾ × 4 ⅜). Museu d'Arte Modern, Barcelona
115 Joan Miró and Josep Lloréns Artigas, *Double figure*, 1956. Earthenware, 44 × 43 × 24 (17 ⅜ × 16 ⅞ × 9 ½). Private collection, Barcelona. © Succession Miró, DACS 2003
116 Corneille, Untitled vase, 1954. 57 × 19.5 (22 ½ × 7 ⅝). Collection Museum Het Kruithuis, s'Hertogenbosch, Netherlands. Photo Peer van der Kruis Heeze, The Netherlands. © ADAGP, Paris and DACS, London 2003
117 Asger Jorn, *Untitled*, 1954. 33 × 31 × 10 (13 × 12 ¼ × 3 ⅞) Collection Otto van de Loo, Munich. © DACS 2003
118 Photograph of Asger Jorn on scooter making ceramic panel, 1959. Asger Jorn modelling his large Aarhus panel at the San Giorgio ceramics factory in Albisola, Italy, 1959. Courtesy Ceramiche San Giorgio, Albisola and Attese: Biennale of Ceramics in Contemporary Art, Milan. More info at www.attese.it
119 Lucio Fontana, *Natura Morta*, 1938. Polychrome ceramic, 17 × 32 × 28 (6 ¾ × 12 ⅝ × 11). © Fondazione Lucio Fontana, Milan
120 Lucio Fontana, *Untitled*, 1968. Porcelain, 16.5 × 43.2 (6 ½ × 17). Garth Clark Gallery, New York. Photo Noel Allum © Fondazione Lucio Fontana, Milan
121 Nicholas Vergette, Ceramic mural for the Moo Cow Bar, late 1950. Photo courtesy of Marcus Vergette
122 Nathalie Krebs and Eva Staehr-Nielsen, *Vase*, 1951. Stoneware made at Saxbo, 15.2 (6). Victoria & Albert Museum, London
123 Gertrud Natzler and Otto Natzler, *Pilgrim Bottle*, 1956. Earthenware with yellow crater glaze, h. 43.2 (17). Los Angeles County Museum of Art, Gift of Howard and Gwen Laurie Smits, photo © 2003 Museum Associates/LACMA
124 Gertrud Vasegaard, *Tea Service*, 1957. Porcelain with white celadon glaze for Bing + Grøndahl Porcelain. © DACS 2003.
125 Lucie Rie and Hans Coper, *7-piece Coffee set*, c. 1955. Stoneware, vertical sgraffito, pots 16–19 cups 8 (pots 7 ½ – 6 ¼; cups 3 ⅛). Private collection
126 Lucie Rie, *Baluster Vase*, c. 1960. Fine stoneware inlaid sgraffito, 26.1 (10 ¼). Christie's Images, London
127 Photograph of Geoffrey Whiting's workshop, 1962. Reproduced courtesy of John Anderson
128 Marguerite Wildenhain, *Tea Set*, 1946. Stoneware, pot 12.5 × 25 (4 ⅞ × 9 ⅞), Sugar bowl 6.25 × 11.25 (2 ½ × 4 ⅜) creamer 7.5 × 13.75 (3 × 5 ⅜). Everson Museum of Art, Syracuse
129 Karen Karnes, *Lidded Jar*, 1973. Saltglaze, 50.7 (20). Private collection
130 Photograph of Shoji Hamada and Peter Voulkos, 1952. Photo courtesy Scripps College, Claremont, California
131 Photograph of Otis Studio with pots by Paul Soldner and Peter Voulkos, 1955–56. Courtesy of Paul Soldner
132 Peter Voulkos, *Tall Covered Jar*, 1956. Stoneware with slip and glaze, gas fired, 64.7 × 45.7 (25 ½ × 18). Everson Museum of Art, Syracuse. Photo © Schopplin Studio. Voulkos & Co. Catalogue Project, www.voulkos.com
133 Peter Voulkos, *Little Big Horn*, 1959. Stoneware,with slip and glaze, gas fired, 157.5 × 101.5 × 101.5 (62 × 40 × 40). Oakland Museum of California. Gift of the Art Guild in memory of Helen Schilling Stelzner. Photo © Schopplein Studio
134 John Mason, *Vase*, 1958. Stoneware, low fired glaze, 61 × 20.3 × 5.2 (24 × 8 × 2). Fred Marer Collection, Scripps College, Claremont, California. Photo Susan Einstein
135 Photograph of *Abstract Expressionist Ceramics* curated by John Coplans, at University of California, Irvine 1966. Los Angeles County Museum of Art photo © 2003 Museum Associates/LACMA
136 Henry Takemoto, *First Kumu*, 1959. Stoneware, 92.1 (36 ¼). Fred Marer Collection, Scripps College, Claremont, California
137 Paul Soldner, *Raku Pot*, 1962. Earthenware, 24.3 × 48.8 × 19.3 (9 ⅝ × 19 ¼ × 7 ⅝). Everson Museum of Art, Syracuse
138 Roy Lichenstein, *Dinnerware*, c. 1967. Earthenware, 30 × 36.8 × 25 (11 ¾ × 14 ½ × 19 ⅞). Everson Museum of Art, Syracuse, Gift of Hui Ka Kwong. © Estate of Roy Lichtenstein/DACS 2003
139 Hui Ka Kwong, *Ceramic Form*, 1968. Stoneware, 55 × 75 × 35 (21 ⅝ × 29 ½ × 13 ¾) Everson Museum of Art, Syracuse
140 Mutsuo Yanagihara, Vase with gold and silver pattern on dark blue base, 1971. Semi-porcelain and lustre, 62 × 31.6 × 29.6 (24 ⅜ × 12 ½ × 11 ⅝). Collection of the artist
141 Kenneth Price, *Snail Cup*, 1968. Ceramic, 7.3 × 13.3 (2 ⅞ × 5 ¼). Los Angeles County Museum of Art, Art Museum Council Fund. Photo © 2003 Museum Associates/LACMA
142 Robert Arneson, *No Deposit, No Return*, 1961. Glazed stoneware, 27.3 × 12.7 × 12.7 (10 ¾ × 5 × 5). Los Angeles County Museum of Art, Smits Ceramics Purchase Fund. Photo © 2003 Museum Associates/LACMA. © Estate of Robert Arneson/VAGA, New York and DACS, London 2003
143 Robert Arneson, *Smorgi-Bob, the Chef*, 1971. Glazed ceramic earth, vinyl tablecloth, wood table, 183 × 152.4 × 152.4 (72 × 60 × 60). San Francisco Museum of Art. © Estate of Robert Arneson/VAGA, New York and DACS, London 2003
144 Michael Frimkess, *Jumpin' at the Moon Lodge*, 1968. Stoneware bisque and china paint, 69.2 × 37.5 × 37.5 (27 ¼ × 14 ¾ × 14 ¾). Fred Marer collection, Scripps College, Claremont , California
145 Victor Cicansky, *Unfired Clay*, 1970. Earthenware, 15 × 12 × 4 (5 ⅞ × 4 ¾ × 1 ⅝). Installation, California
146 Ryoji Koie *Installation*, 1980. White clay fine transparent glaze, 64 × 15 (25 ¼ × 5 ⅞) Installation, Japan
147 Jim Melchert, *Changes*, a performance with drying slip, studio of Hetty Huisman Amsterdam, August 2, 1972. Stedelijk Museum. Photo Mieke H. Hille, video documentation Meatball
148 Ewen Henderson, *Vessel*, 1987. Laminated stoneware and porcelain clays, 61 (24). Photo David Cripps
149 Bernard Dejonghe, *Bleu Vertical*, 1986. Stoneware enamelled, 120 × 600 × 600 (47 ¼ × 236 ¼ × 236 ¼) © Bernard Dejonghe
150 Jun Kaneko, *Omaha Project, Dangos On Truck*, 1984. Glazed ceramics. Courtesy of the artist
151 Rosaline Delisle, *Octet 4*, 1998. Earthenware, 106.7 × 16.5 (42 × 6 ½). Private collection. Frank Lloyd Gallery, Santa Monica, California. Photo Anthony Cuna
152 Wouter Dam, *Blue Shape*, 2000. Stoneware clay. Private collection
153 Geert Lap, *Thrown Form no. 4*, 1998. Stoneware, terra sigillata, 15 × 7 (5 ⅞ × 2 ¾). Private collection © DACS 2003
154 Martin Smith, *Wavelength*, 2001. Clay, platinum, aluminium ten part work, 32 × base 64.5 × top 47.7 (12 ⅝ × 25 ⅜ × 18 ¾). Private collection
155 Clare Twomey, *Consciousness/conscience*, August 2001. Slip cast porcelain, 2.5 × 1500 × 450 (1 × 530 ½ × 177 ⅛)
156 Antony Gormley, *Host*, 1997. Mud and sea water, overall depth 13 (5 ⅛). Courtesy Jay Jopling/White Cube, London. Photo Helmut Kunde. © the artist
157 Antony Gormley, *European Field* Installation Malmö, Kunsthalle, 1993. Terracotta (approximately 35,000 figures dimensions variable, each figure's height 10–30 (3 ⅞ –11 ¾). Courtesy Jay Jopling/White Cube, London © the artist
158 Piet Stockmans, Installation at Bergkerk Deventer, 1999. Porcelain, 1000m (0.62 miles) square. Hannema-de Stuers Fundatie Heino/wijhe. Photo Van Sloun en Romackers © DACS 2003
159 Kenneth Price, *Happy's Curios Unit 3*, 1972–77. Ceramic with wood, cabinet, 177.8 × 53.3 × 54 (70 × 21 × 21 ¼), cups 6.4 × 13.3 (2 ½ × 5 ¼) each. Los Angeles County Museum of Art, gift of Betty M. Asher. Photo © 2003 Museum Associates/LACMA
160 Judy Chicago et al, image of women lustre glazing floor tiles for *The Dinner Party*, 1979. © ARS, New York and DACS, London 2003
161 Armand P. Arman, *As in the Sink (II)*, 1990. Porcelain, 23 × 30.5 × 38 (9 × 12 × 15). Photo Artes Magnus
162 Tony Cragg, *Shiva*, 1996. Plaster, 297 × 184 × 184 (116 ⅞ × 72 ½ × 72 ¼). Courtesy Lisson Gallery, London
163 Michael Geertsen, *Green Wall Object*, 2003. Earthenware, wheel thrown, cut and reconstructed, 20 × 30 × 42 (7 ⅞ × 11 ¾ × 16 ½). Collection of the artist. Photo Serem Nielsen

164 Andrew Lord, *Jug Curves*, 1986. Ceramic, 51 × 51 × 33 (20 ⅛ × 20 ⅛ × 13). Collection of the artist

165 Gwyn Hanssen Pigott, *Travellers*, 2000. 21 pieces woodfired Limoges porcelain. Private collection, Australia. Photo Brian Hand. Courtesy of Galerie Besson, London

166 Betty Woodman, *Balstrade Vase 99-6*, 1999. Earthenware, paint, lacquer, epoxy resin, 122 × 152 × 25 (48 × 60 × 10). Private collection, New York. courtesy of Max Protech Gallery, New York

167 Cindy Sherman, *Madame de Pompadour (née Poisson)*, 1990. Porcelain, 37 × 55.8 × 29.8 (14 5/8 × 22 × 11 3/4). Photo Artes Magnus. © Metro Pictures

168 Adrian Saxe, Untitled Ewer (Franklin Gothic Italic Ampersand), 1989. Porcelain, rhinestones, 26 × 22.9 × 7 (10 ¼ × 9 × 2 ¾). Frank Lloyd Gallery, Santa Monica, California

169 Paul Mathieu, *Garniture #2 Day (or Night)*, 1993. Porcelain and bronze, length 150 (60) courtesy of the artist. © DACS 2003

170 Johan Creten, *Odore di Femmina Torso 2*, 1997. Wood fired stoneware, 67.3 × 48.3 × 38.1 (26 ½ × 19 × 15). Private collection, courtesy of Robert Miler Gallery, New York. Photo Adam Reich © Johan Creten

171 Gertraud Möhwald, *Head with striped Hairstyle*, 1999. Ceramic, 26.5 × 45 (10 ¼ × 17 ¾)

172 Richard Slee, *Acid Toby*, 1993. Earthenware, 48 × 30 (18 ⅞ × 11 ¾). Private collection, USA. Photo ZUL

173 Jean Bad Moccasin, *Kiva-step Vase*, 1993. Polychrome, 26.7 × 28.5 (10 ½ × 11 ¼). Collection of Mr and Mrs William Freeman. Photo Craig Smith

174 Kimpei Nakamura, *Sumptuousness and Untruth*, 1991. Ceramic, 80 × 67 × 46 (31 ½ × 26 ⅜ × 18 ⅛). Collection of the Artist. Photo Etsuhiro Sasaki

175 Shugo Takauchi, Vase with handle, 1992. Ceramic, 58.5 × 46 (23 × 18 ⅛). Private collection, Japan

176 Shin Sang-ho, *91 Dream*, 1991. Bunchungware, 56 × 50 × 50 (22 × 19 ⅝ × 19 ⅝). Private collection, USA

177 Goro Suzuki, *Oribe Chair*, 2002. Ceramic 45.7 × 22.9 × 21.6 (18 × 9 × 8 ½). Frank Lloyd Gallery, Santa Monica, California. Photo Anthony Cunha

178 Gehry Partners, LLP, *Ohr–O'Keefe Museum of Art* Final Design Model, July 2001. Wood, gatorboard, silver paper, 68.6 × 182.8 × 243.8 (27 × 72 × 96). Gehry Partners, LLP. Photo Whit Preston, staff photographer

Index

Page numbers in *italic* refer to illustrations.